Volume 23

Advances in
Librarianship

Volume 23

Advances in
Librarianship

Edited by

Frederick C. Lynden

Rockefeller Library
Brown University
Providence, Rhode Island

Elizabeth A. Chapman

Taylor Institution
University of Oxford
St. Giles, Oxford, United Kingdom

Academic Press
San Diego   London   Boston   New York   Sydney   Tokyo   Toronto

Academic Press
A Harcourt Science and Technology Company
525 B Street, Suite 1900, San Diego, California 92101-4495, USA
http://www.apnet.com

Academic Press
24-28 Oval Road, London NW1 7DX, UK
http://www.hbuk.co.uk/ap/

International Standard Book Number: 0-12-024623-6

PRINTED IN THE UNITED STATES OF AMERICA
99 00 01 02 03 04 MM 9 8 7 6 5 4 3 2 1

Contents

Image and Status
Academic Librarians and the New Professionalism
Michael Gordon Jackson

A Psychological Approach to Creating Stronger Public Libraries
Brian A. Reynolds

Schooling and Skilling Health Librarians for an Evidence-Based Culture
Judith Palmer

Increasing Diversity
Programs and Internships in ARL Libraries
Teri Switzer and William Gentz

What Is Women's Information?
The History and Future of a Longstanding Tradition in Librarianship
Marije Wilmink and Marlise Mensink

Lifelong Learning and the University for Industry
The Challenge for Libraries in the United Kingdom
Andrew McDonald

The Role of Libraries in Providing Curricular Support and Curricular Integration for Distance Learning Courses
Margaret M. Jobe and Deborah S. Grealy

Deconstructing the Indexing Process
Jens-Erik Mai

The United Kingdom Library and Information Commission
Judith Elkin

Contributors

Numbers in parentheses indicate the pages on which the authors' contributions begin.

Richard Biddiscombe (63), Information Services, The University of Birmingham, Edgbaston, Birmingham B15 2TT, United Kingdom

Judith Elkin (299), University of Central England, Birmingham B42 2SU, United Kingdom

William Gentz (169), University of Pittsburgh, Pittsburgh, Pennsylvania 15260

Myke Gluck (1), School of Information Studies and Department of Geography, Florida State University, Tallahassee, Florida 32306

Deborah S. Grealy (239), University Libraries, University of Colorado at Boulder, Boulder, Colorado 80309

Michael Gordon Jackson (93), Reference Department, Brown University, Providence, Rhode Island 02912

Margaret M. Jobe (239), University Libraries, University of Colorado at Boulder, Boulder, Colorado 80309

Jens-Erik Mai (269), Royal School of Library and Information Science, 2300 Copenhagen S, Denmark

Andrew McDonald (207), Chester Road Library, University of Sunderland, Rickleton, Washington NE38 9JG, United Kingdom

Marlise Mensink (189), International Information Centre and Archives for the Women's Movement (IIAV), Amsterdam 1094 RB, The Netherlands

Judith Palmer (145), Health Care Libraries Unit, John Radcliffe Hospital, Oxford OX3 9DU, United Kingdom

Brian A. Reynolds (117), San Luis Obispo City-County Library, San Luis Obispo, California 93403

Gloria Rohmann (39), Electronic and Media Resources, New York University Libraries, New York, New York 10012

Teri Switzer (169), Hillman Library, Colorado State University, Fort Collins, Colorado 80523

Marije Wilmink (189), International Information Centre and Archives for the Women's Movement (IIAV), Amsterdam 1094 RB, The Netherlands

Lixin Yu (1), School of Information Studies and Department of Geography, Florida State University, Tallahassee, Florida 32306

Preface

Volume 23 of *Advances in Librarianship* contains a wide range of articles that discuss matters of importance to the librarian who is dealing with information technology and staffing issues as the 21st century approaches. The 1999 volume begins with two articles on technology and then looks at library staffing issues in the information technology age. These four articles cover staffing in higher education and health sciences and staffing issues important to improving the image of public libraries. The next two articles look at diversity and women in librarianship. The last three articles are concerned with the topics of nontraditional students, indexing, and the role of libraries in the information society.

The first article, by Myke Gluck and Lixin Yu, School of Information Studies, Florida State, is a comprehensive treatise on geographic information systems (GIS). The authors define GIS, discuss software functions and data structure, and then cover applications for GIS. They describe the latest developments and report on standards. Finally, they discuss the "important role that GIS can play in the management of libraries." The purpose of this chapter is to provide "librarians and others with a background in the concepts of GIS and frameworks for the use of GIS in libraries."

The second article, by Gloria Rohman, New York University Libraries, looks at how the academic media center is changed by the new technology. Rohman first discusses the changes occurring in the digital area for providing sound and image media, i.e., music and motion pictures. She then explores how libraries can use the "streaming technologies" and describes how to extend media services via the web, through collaborative relationships across departments, and funding new initiatives. Next, she covers the production of streaming media by the library, covering tools, bandwidth, standards, choice of software, higher priced systems, and bandwidth systems. She also describes various access systems, such as cataloging and indexing systems. Finally, she discusses copyright issues.

Richard Biddiscombe, the University of Birmingham Library, sees signs that professional librarians, who have heretofore not been considered dynamic professionals, are beginning to be seen as serious players in the management of teaching and learning, especially in higher education. He believes that information technology has made this change possible because IT offers information professionals "better opportunities to participate and influence the [learning] process." He recommends that librarians establish learning partnerships with academic staff and provide training for use of information technology. He also argues that "learning support" will become a significant part of librarians' duties in the public library as well.

Michael Jackson, Brown University Library, believes that librarians are undervalued as well. He thinks that librarians must be proactive in defining how they contribute to the educational role of the academic community. He recommends that libarians be "open, flexible, and self-confident about change." Further he suggests that librarians improve their expertise by participating in research, publishing, teaching, and learning about technology. Like Biddiscombe, he believes that librarians need to establish partnerships with faculty and show a genuine interest in scholarship. He also recommends that librarians seek advanced degrees in subject specialities.

Judith Palmer, the Health Care Libraries Unit of Oxford University, looks at how librarians can acquire the schooling and skills necessary to find the evidence needed to treat patients, critically appraise this information, and synthesize this evidence. She reports on the professional development workshops on marketing of library services and technology updates which health sciences librarians in the region of Anglia and Oxford are receiving and then describes a national program in England called the Critical Skills Appraisal Program (CASP). She covers the important elements in such a training program and explains how these techniques can be used in distance learning. This program has "shown librarians *how* to enhance and impove their skills" as well as providing "a cohort of librarians with the same package of experience" and training.

Finally, Brian Reynolds describes how public librarians can use the principles of psychology to market public library services. He believes that librarians must "learn techniques for customer service." He distinguishes between treating the library user as someone with needs and treating the user as a customer shopping for a product. He recommends that staff use "attending and listening skills" and enhance their reference interview skills. He believes it is very important to "treasure repeat customers" and work sensitively with users as "individual clients" by providing local information, giving information that people need to cope with living/dying, and mixing electronic and print media. He sees the importance of public relations in publicizing sevices that users need, doing market research, and attempting to change people's opinions about the library. He emphasizes the importance of emotion in appealing to the users.

From looking at library staff education and training we move on to Switzer and Gentz, who give us a thorough review of the area of diversity in library staff. Recruitment of minorities to library schools is important, especially if we hope to properly serve diverse reader populations. Their contribution focuses on the use of internships by the Association of Research Libraries to increase diversity in libraries in the United States.

Wilmink and Mensink consider women's information from the perspective of the International Information Center and Archives for the Women's Movement in Amsterdam. They provide a fascinating history of both the center in particular and women's information in general, as they embark on exciting new international projects.

McDonald takes us on a tour of schemes to engage nontraditional students in higher education in the UK. He describes the concept of lifelong learning and the new UK University for Industry and puts library services squarely in their new context. Jobe and Grealy continue the theme from a U.S. perspective on distance education. This pair of papers show clearly how library services are responding to new ways of learning, and in particular to lifelong learning.

Our services to readers are crucial and Mai takes a close look at one of our central tasks—that of indexing. He deconstructs the indexing project and shows how little we formally know about the intellectual processes involved in indexing. The whole question of user needs must be weighed with the description of documents that we as librarians provide. Indexing skills must be more, not less, in demand as we are receiving information from so many sources.

This volume is rounded off by Elkin's paper on the evolving UK Library and Information Commission. The commission has invigorated the debate on the place of libraries in the information society and informs our plans for the future.

The next volume in this series will be published in the year 2000, and we plan a group of knowledgeable authors who will be able to take a broad view of past, present, and advances into the future of librarianship.

Elizabeth A. Chapman

Frederick C. Lynden

Geographic Information Systems

Background, Frameworks, and Uses in Libraries

Myke Gluck
School of Information Studies
Florida State University
Tallahassee, Florida 32306-2100

Lixin Yu
School of Information Studies
Florida State University
Tallahassee, Florida 32306-2100

Geographic information system (GIS) is a thriving technology that has been applied in many areas. GIS has begun to diffuse into libraries with pioneers employing GIS technology for library services and library management. Because GIS is a new technology in libraries, it still seems very technical to many library professionals. This chapter presents an overview of GIS technology and a summary of its applications in libraries to date. The first half of the chapter introduces the fundamental knowledge of GIS—the system, data, and the applications. The second half focuses on GIS uses and frameworks for libraries—GIS users in libraries, GIS standards with libraries, geospatial information use in libraries, GIS applications in libraries, and the use of GIS for library management.

I. Geographic Information Systems

A. Introduction—What Is GIS?

Space is one of the most important concepts for humans. When a person is going somewhere, a path must be selected to get there. What advice would one get when purchasing a house? "Location, location, location!" In fact, we make spatially related decisions every day. Computers can help people to manage information resources including geographic information. Inevitably, people seek computer help to solve geographic problems. The solution for geographic problems is a Geographic Information System, the so-called GIS.

What comes to a person's mind when one needs help on spatial informa-tion? Libraries. We can either find spatial data in libraries or seek help from the librarians. Of course, most libraries have maps in their collection. Libraries can help clients locate maps that match, or are close to, the clients' need. However, more and more digital spatial data are available to the public. For example, all the depository libraries in the United States receive CD-ROMs from the Census Bureau that include spatial and spatially referenced informa-tion. However, library patrons have greater demands than simply requesting paper maps in the library. The pressure from both producers and users forces librarians to seek new tools and new methods to provide spatial information reference services.

The developments in GIS are making changes in library services. Not all libraries are using GIS yet because the diffusion of new technology always takes time. It may take years for most libraries to adopt GIS but the trend is clear. Library pioneers have had successful experiences in applying GIS offering better patron services. For example, as early as 1994, a patron walking into the New York State Library with an interest in the distribution of elderly persons in downtown Manhattan could ask the reference librarian to *create* a map with this desired theme using GIS software and digital data (New York State Library, 1994). Because many libraries will eventually implement GIS technology, librarians need to understand the basics and be aware of the latest developments of GIS for libraries.

1. What Is a GIS?

Worboys (1995, p. 125) defined GIS as "a computer-based information system that enables capture, modeling, manipulation, retrieval, analysis and presentation of geographically referenced data."

Most words in this definition can be found in definitions of many other information systems. What makes GIS special is the last three words in the definition—*geographically referenced data*. GIS uses geographic locations as the major link to organize and manipulate information. Therefore, a GIS can be seen as having two major functional components—a database management system, which stores and manipulates the data, and a spatial engine, which performs special topological operations on geographic features.

Data in GIS can also be divided into two categories—spatial data and descriptive data. Spatial data describes the location and shape of geographic features and the spatial relationships or connections among the geographic features. Descriptive data describes the characteristics of the geographic fea-tures. For example, Georgia's location, shape, and the boundaries with other states are spatial data, whereas the population, business, health care, and other information are descriptive information. GIS uses the spatial data to organize the descriptive data and can perform spatial calculations and operations—which is what makes GIS special.

A common misunderstanding of GIS is considering it as merely a computerized map maker. GIS is a powerful analytical tool that is far more sophisticated than a map maker, although it does have powerful output functions and is widely used for generating maps. For example, a GIS-based 911 emergency response system can suggest the fastest path to a destination for an emergency response vehicle. This involves complicated network analysis that few other information systems can accomplish. As Burrough (1990) summarized, a GIS can answer questions like these:

1. Where is 492 E. Allen Street located in Boston?
2. What census tract is the above address located in?
3. How many dentists are within 3 miles from the above address?
4. How many square miles encompass Central Park in Manhattan?
5. The city is planning for a new park. It has a road map, a water system map, and a map showing residential areas and natural forest areas. What are the potential areas that are within half a mile from a road, next to a lake, and in a currently wooded area? This involves integrating the three maps together to make an analysis.
6. An ambulance currently at 159 Main Street is dispatched to an emergency call from 393 Western Avenue. What is the shortest path to get there? With traffic and road condition information at hand, what is the fastest path to get there?
7. A user is facing a map with hotels labeled by icons. What is the hotel located at the intersection of 5th Avenue and 39 Street? What is the rate of that hotel?
8. How many food stamp recipients are within 1 mile from food stores in Milwaukee, Wisconsin? How many are not?
9. When the water level of the Hudson River goes to 15 meters in Troy, what areas will be flooded?
10. What is the spatial distribution of Asian Americans in Chicago by zip code?

These are some typical questions that are fairly difficult for a person but straightforward for a GIS to answer. GIS can perform a series of topological operations and be used on a great variety of problems. Those powerful functions will be introduced in this chapter. We will clarify some basic geographical concepts first to help understanding of the functions.

2. GIS Software Functions

Spatial objects can be classified into three types: point, line, and polygon. A *point* is a spatial feature that has neither area nor length. It represents a location. For example, the position of a car on a street or the top of a mountain are both points. Sometimes, geographic features that have a relatively large area can be treated as a point in an analysis when the scale of the whole area is so large that such a small area can be ignored. A building, for example, has a certain area. It can be treated as a point when an analysis is based on a much larger area at city or street scale. A *line* is an object that is made up of a sequence of points. Lines have no width or area. Lines can be used to represent linear features without width such as contour lines or county or national boundaries. Lines can also be used to represent features that do have width but the width is small at the scale of analysis. For example, a street is often represented by a line on a city map. A *polygon* is an area with an enclosed boundary made of lines, such as a park or a county. Consequently, polygons have areas and parameters. A *layer* or a *theme* is a concept for a *single feature map* in GIS. It is composed of a group of geographic features of the same type. For example, the concept of "all the supermarkets in Boston" is represented by a point layer. The concept of "all the streets in Boston" is represented by a line layer. A census tract map of Boston showing average income level is represented by a polygon layer. All these layers can be integrated together by GIS to make an analysis by overlaying the various layers to build one final image.

GIS also has built-in functions to perform topological operations. First of all, GIS has the capability to build the topology. It can determine which lines are crossing each other and create a node at the cross point. It can detect which lines are connected to make an enclosed polygon. GIS can generate a polygon object that has features of area and parameter. After the topology, or the relationship of points, lines, and polygons, is established, GIS can do sophisticated spatial analysis. The following list contains some typical GIS operations:

1. Calculate the distance between two points.
2. Calculate the shortest distance between a point and a line.
3. Determine whether a point falls in a polygon.
4. Suggest a route between two points, given a network of lines.
5. Build a *buffer* region for analyzing the area surrounding the features. For example, a river (a line) can be buffered to simulate the flooding plain; a food store site (a point) can be buffered to show the area where residents are potential customers. In Fig. 1, a road is buffered 1 mile at each side to show the areas that are at least 1 mile from the road and are not on the wetland. These areas are represented by the white color in Fig. 1.
6. GIS can also merge multiple layers together, a process called *overlay*. Assume that there are two maps printed on transparencies—a map

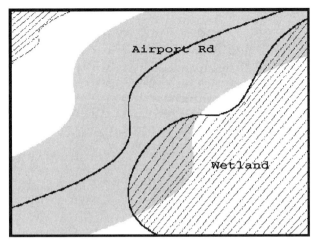

Fig. 1 Buffering. Airport road is buffered to 1 mile at each side (the shaded area).

with all the locations of residential households and a map with all the grocery stores in a city. If both maps are in the same scale and the four corners of the two maps represent the same locations, the two transparencies can be put together to make a new map—with both household and grocery stores overlaid. GIS is a powerful overlay tool. It can overlay different kinds of features (point, line, polygon) and develop new topologies for further analysis. Burrough (1990) lists 44 kinds of overlay analysis capabilities that GIS may do. Figure 2

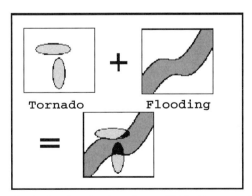

Fig. 2 Overlay. Overlay a layer of high-risk areas of tornado attack with a layer of high-risk areas of flooding. The black areas in the third layer are the areas with high risk of both tornado and flooding.

demonstrates the overlay process. The first map layer shows the areas with a high risk of tornado. The second layer shows the areas with a high risk of flooding. When the two are overlaid, GIS generates a third layer showing the areas of high risk of both tornado and flooding (black-shaded area).

3. GIS Data Structure

Different GIS store and organize geographic data in various ways. One such data structure is called a *raster*. A raster structure is a grid system (Fig. 3). Data are stored in cells in the grid. The cells can be organized in a simple grid like the cells in a spreadsheet. The cells can also be organized in a more complicated hierarchical structure such as the quadtree structure (Star and Estes, 1990). A GIS can produce a map showing the colors of the raster cells; further, other GIS operations such as overlay are also done cell by cell in raster format.

Another data structure often used in GIS is the *vector* structure. In a vector system, data are not recorded by cells; rather, they are described by points with instructions on how points should be connected to form lines. These lines can then be used to form polygons. GIS can form a line internally for spatial analysis purposes or draw a line for output display. The advantage of a vector structure is that high-quality images can be obtained no matter how much a user zooms in. Vectors are very good for representing straight lines, but have the disadvantage that many points are needed to describe

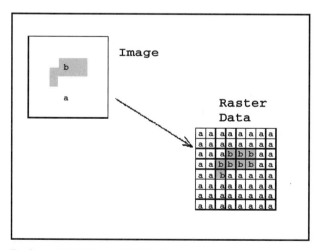

Fig. 3 A map layer in a raster system.

short lines or complicated curves. There are five common varieties of vector formats that are described in detail by Star and Estes (1990). Figure 4 demonstrates one type of vector storage.

Kennedy and Meyers (1977) compared the advantages and disadvantages of raster vs. vector systems in terms of their storage efficiency, retrieval efficiency, data manipulation efficiency, data accuracy, and data display. Their results indicate that there is no clear winner between the raster and vector systems because they both have advantages and disadvantages. In the past, the two types of systems showed a difference in performance for certain GIS operations. Users needed to chose carefully the desired system based on their data, GIS operation, and output. However, with the latest GIS technology, the differences between raster systems and vector systems are getting smaller in terms of efficiencies because both raster and vector GIS have developed new methods and algorithms to strengthen their weak points. The selection of GIS software is now based more on their functions and user interfaces.

4. GIS Hardware

As an information system, GIS is composed of software, hardware, data, and users. GIS hardware include computers and special peripherals. This section focuses on introducing the peripherals specially designed for GIS.

a. Map Scanners—A Data Input Device. Scanners convert an analog data source (a map) into a digital form. They contain a laser light source and

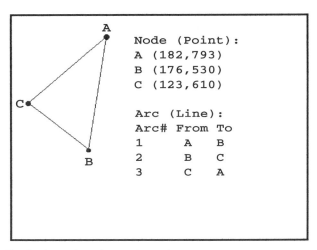

Fig. 4 A map layer in a vector system.

a camera with high resolution lens. Scanners are data input devices. A flat-bed scanner is mounted on rails and can be moved back and forth over a map, similar to the popular image scanners in the market. Most scanners are raster scanners and generate raster images. A raster-to-vector conversion is needed for vector-based GIS.

   b. Digitizers—A Data Input Device.   A digitizer is a data input device consisting of an electronic tablet and a special magnetic mouse. The tablet can detect the position of the mouse and record the coordinates when it is clicked. A window with cross-hairs on the mouse enables the operator to position a point precisely. A map is fixed on the tablet when digitizing. The operator needs to enter the absolute coordinates of the two diagonal corners first. One can then move the mouse across the map and click on points. The tablet can record the position of the mouse and convert the position into coordinates calculated on the absolute coordinates of the two corners. When a line is entered, the operator must click on the starting point of a line, all the turning points to shape the line, and the ending point of a line. The digitizer can be used to input vector data (Fig. 5).

   c. Global Positioning System (GPS)—A Data Collection and Input Device.   The scanners and digitizers convert paper maps into digital format for a GIS to process. Neither of them actually detect and record the positions of objects directly. This more tedious job can now be accomplished with the help of GPS technology. GPS uses satellite technology to capture terrestrial

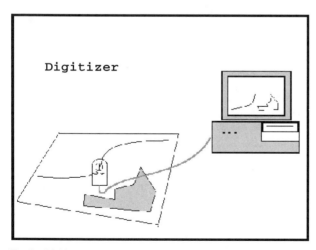

Fig. 5 Digitizer.

positions in real time with position errors no more than 50 ft (Logsdon, 1995). The errors can be reduced to as little as 2 ft with some additional efforts. The data acquired from GPS can also be used directly as input to a GIS for display, modeling, and analysis. Because the data are captured in real time, the input can be used for a great variety of applications including systems that need real-time updates, such as automobile navigation, emergency vehicle management, vehicle monitoring for delivery services, and so on. The United States' GPS system employs 21 satellites positioned in geosynchronous orbits covering the whole surface of the earth.

d. Remote Sensing—A Data Collection Method.   Star and Estes (1990, p. 6) define remote sensing as "the process of deriving information by means of systems that are not in direct contact with the objects or phenomena of interest." This technology captures data using sensors onboard a satellite or airplane. A good example is the satellite weather maps we see daily in the news. A sensor is often a camera that can capture and regenerate images using visible light. The sensor may also be a nonphotographic sensor recording infrared, ultraviolet, or radio frequencies. These data can be presented by a GIS using visible colors to enable a view of data otherwise not visible. The data collected from remote sensing are usually raster data and can be used as input to a GIS. As a result, a raster based GIS can intake the remotely sensed data more easily than a vector based GIS. In either case, objects of study need to be distinguished from the adjacent features or background of the remote sensed region using software. This software process is called extracting. For example, corn fields and roads can be distinguished from each other by a ratio of brightness values. Images captured using infrared rays or other components of the electromagnetic spectrum can even distinguish the composition of soil and rock types.

e. Pen Plotters—An Output Device.   Monitors and printers are common output devices that can be used by GIS to make maps, which are not discussed here. A pen plotter is an automatic drawing machine equipped with one or more pens. The computer gives instructions such as "pick up the red pen; go to position 3492,4129; set pen down; move pen to 3983,4695; raise up the pen; return pen to holder; pick up the blue pen . . ." A plotter can be equipped with a laser beam and can also draw directly on films, including microforms such as microfiche.

B. Data in GIS

As discussed previously, GIS is an information system that processes geographically referenced data. The GIS data can be divided into two categories:

Spatial data, which describes the location and shape of geographic features
    and spatial relationships or connections among the geographic features.
Descriptive data, which describes the characteristics of geographic features.

GIS uses spatial data as the link to organize both types of data. For
example, the shape and coordinates of a park or a road are spatial data. The
park name, annual budget, supervising authority of the park, the road name,
and the street addresses on both sides of the road are all descriptive data.
GIS then builds a relationship or theme among the descriptive data of objects
of the same or different types using location information. As a result, roads
within 30 ft or residents who live within 50 ft of the park can be determined.

Spatial data is the core of GIS data. Users may employ different descriptive data with the same spatial data to analyze different issues in the same
region. Without accurate spatial data, data retrieval and spatial analysis cannot
provide useful results. As discussed in the previous section, data can be acquired using remote sensing technology, GPS technology, and secondhand
data entry devices such as scanners and digitizers. However, if every GIS
application requires practitioners to go to the field and collect the same spatial
data, every project will need a large budget and take a long time to accomplish.
However, descriptive data may be collected repeatedly for the same geographic features at relatively low cost. Therefore, an important issue in GIS
is data sharing, especially the spatial or topological data. Two frequently used
databases that form a basis for data sharing are discussed next.

1. TIGER Files

Topologically Integrated Geographic Encoding and Referencing (TIGER)
is a U.S. digital map database developed by the Census Bureau and U.S.
Geological Survey (USGS). TIGER was created using Geographic Base File/
Dual Independent Map Encoding (GBF/DIME) files and the current
1 : 100,000 USGS maps. Originally designed to support census programs and
surveys, this by-product of the 1990 Census of Population and Housing
provides a single, integrated geographic database for the entire United States.
It has become a major data resource for GIS applications.

The TIGER/Line files contain information describing the points, lines,
and areas on Census Bureau maps. The TIGER/Line files use a vector format
to describe geographic features. In other words, all the associated descriptive
information is tagged with topological line segments. Figure 6 shows a map
derived from a TIGER file. The highlighted street is Main Street, with the
left address range from 456 to 542 and right address range from 471 to 573,
with two shape points in the middle of that street segment.

Often, TIGER files are falsely considered as street maps showing census
data for the whole nation. TIGER is a digital database that can be used to

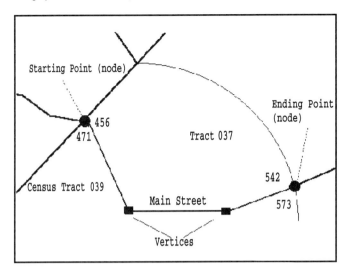

Fig. 6 A map layer derived from TIGER files.

make electronic map layers and link them to other census data products. For each county, there are a series of TIGER files containing different information. TIGER file 1 records each line segment in TIGER as an arc (i.e., a straight line with direction enabling separation of the left or right side of a line). When the lines represent streets, the TIGER file 1 usually stores the coordinates of the beginning and ending points, the address numbers for both sides of the block, the street name, the street class (highway or local road), census tract number on both sides, and other information. TIGER file 2 records give all the coordinates of the turning points of the lines, so if the line is a curve, corresponding records in TIGER file 2 must be used to generate a complete map layer.

In February 1989, the Census Bureau released the *prototype TIGER/ Line* file. TIGER files have been updated frequently for adding features and correcting errors. The latest version is TIGER 1997. The new version reflects an increase in the editing of address ranges and new ZIP+4 codes derived from the latest matching with the Address Control File and the United States Postal Service (USPS) files. TIGER 1997 also shows an improvement in the consistency of highway names and feature identifiers throughout the United States.

2. Zip Code Centroids Files

Another popular spatial data set is the zip code centroids file. Centroids correspond to the coordinates at the center point of a polygon and are used as representative elements for the whole region. In the United States, the most common form of zip codes in addresses is the 5-digit zip code. A 5-digit zip code may encompass an area of any size, from city blocks in an urban area to an entire town or village in rural areas.

The 5-digit zip code area can be subdivided into zip+2 areas, which are also known as zip sectors. A zip+2 area contains smaller groups of streets and blocks than a 5-digit zip code area. Zip+2 areas can be further subdivided into ZIP+4 areas. A ZIP+2 refers to an area that often contains several blocks, whereas a ZIP+4 usually defines a single side of a single city block, or one side of a longer roadway in rural areas. Some ZIP+4 codes refer to a single address, or to a specific floor in a building.

A zip code *centroid* file uses the center point of a 5-digit or 9-digit zip code area. The ZIP+4 centroid is the point corresponding to the address that is closest to the mid-address of the ZIP+4 address range. In other words, the coordinate of the midpoint of one line. GIS projects can use zip code centroids to locate individual addresses, or perform data analysis on the basis of zip code areas. Figure 7 shows a zip code centroid map of the 12208 area in Albany, New York. The map is derived from Mailer's Geocode zip code centroid database. Such data sets are often used for zip code modeling and mass market mailings.

Many vendors are providing zip code products. For example, ZIPFIND from Bridger Systems, Inc. (http://link-usa.com/zipcode/); Pro-Zipcode Deluxe from Professional Computer Consulting, Inc. (http://www.emory.com/progress/US-Zips.htm); Mailer's +4 (http://www.hallogram.com/mailers/mail4/geo.html) are all U.S. zip code–based databases.

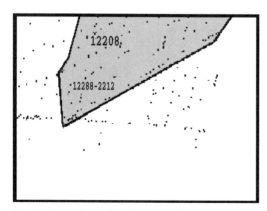

Fig. 7 A map layer showing zip code centroids.

3. Other Ready-To-Use Data

There are other GIS data available at low or no cost discussed in the section "GIS Data and Internet."

C. General GIS Applications

GIS has been widely used in urban planning, land studies, vehicle management, crime control, and many other areas. This section demonstrates the application of GIS to real world settings. The library-related applications of GIS are discussed in detail in Part II of this chapter.

1. GIS for Emergency Response

GPS/GIS can provide fast, accurate data for emergency planning and damage assessment. GIS is used in map creation and maintenance; enhanced 911 mapping; determining addresses in rural areas; dispatching aid (finding nearest available vehicle to dispatch to the site); and many other areas. According to Public Works (GPS/GIS, 1994), Virginia county planners are using a system to produce comprehensive mapping and addressing for an enhanced 911 project. The system automatically provides emergency dispatchers the location of a call. As another example, Musselshell County, Montana, developed a system with 185 map layers covering communications and transportation networks, energy and water systems, and so on.

Emergency planners used a GIS to record 1500 damage sites from an earthquake in a 95-square mile area of Los Angeles County within 3 days. If done manually, the same work would have taken the planners weeks. Florida Power and Light also used a GIS to locate downed power lines and record general damage to the residents' utility system after Hurricane Andrew. As the GPS/GIS article (1994, p. 22) said, GIS technology is very versatile to "answer questions like what is out there and where it is."

2. Database Marketing

Database marketing's roots are in direct marketing. The database is a collection of market research data: collective information about markets, demographics, sales trends, competitive information, and so on (Nash, 1993). More and more companies have changed from "mass marketing" to "accountable advertising." This trend has switched large portions of advertising budgets into promotional and direct mail programs. One of the advantages to database marketing is efficiency. Database marketing may increase the total outlays, but the increase in effectiveness, measured by actual sales, is well worth the added list costs (Nash, 1993).

Suppliers such as Claritas developed the PRIZM system, which matches neighborhoods by similarities based on 73 attributes of the inhabitants (Nash, 1993). They can send mail targeting consumers that are more likely than others, often by a factor of three or four times, to buy particular products. The suppliers base this work on the reasonably accurate assumption that "birds of a feather flock together." It appears that people in similar neighborhoods are likely to spend their income much like their neighbors.

3. Insurance

To set appropriate premiums for homeowner insurance policies, companies often need to answer questions such as: Is it in an area with a high crime rate? What is the population density in that area? How much has the average home value changed in the area last year? Is it close to a nuclear power plant? How far is the nearest fire hydrant? Is the property subject to flooding?

The Geographic Underwriting System was developed by a consortium of Electronic Data Systems (EDS, Dallas, Texas), Insurance Services Office, Inc. (New York), and DataMap Inc. (Eden Prairie, Minnesota). When an underwriter writes a policy, this system can assist the underwriter to evaluate the risks of insuring properties. According to Castle's (1993) description, the underwriter enters the address of a client and can retrieve data such as:

1. Proximity to fire stations or hydrants
2. Auto insurance rate zone for the residence
3. Driving distance from residence to work location
4. Proximity to open bodies of water, and
5. Arson, robbery, and theft statistics of the area.

This information helps the underwriters make quick and accurate price estimate for clients' premiums.

D. Latest Developments in GIS Software and Data Sources

1. Popular GIS Packages

a. ESRI's Products. Founded in 1969, Environment Services Research Institute (ESRI) is one of the largest GIS producers in the United States. Its first commercially successful product, ARC/INFO, was developed in 1981. ARC/INFO was first designed to work on UNIX platform, but now also runs on PC and Windows NT. ARC/INFO is a powerful vector-based GIS. It can import data from TIGER files and build topological relationships for further analysis. As a full-featured GIS, ARC/INFO provides a great variety of GIS operations and is widely used in both the public and private sectors.

Because it is so powerful, it is complicated to learn and use, requiring uses to be trained to understand and effectively employ the system. Because of ARC/INFO's complexity and training requirements, ESRI has also developed ARC/VIEW, an MS Windows– and Macintosh-based GIS viewer system with a more user-friendly graphic user interface but with reduced GIS functions. ARC/VIEW was first introduced in 1991 and replaced ARC/INFO as the major PC-based GIS product from ESRI. Other products from ESRI include MapObject and Spatial Database Engine (SDE), a client-server product for spatial data management.

b. MapInfo. MapInfo was founded in 1986 and soon started to play an important role in the GIS market. MapInfo focuses its products on the PC markets. Its products run on both IBM-compatible PCs and Macintosh Personal Computers. MapInfo may not be as powerful as ARC/INFO, but it does provide an easy to use user interface and powerful routine functions. MapInfo has a series of products from MapInfo Desktop and MapInfo Professional to Map X and Map Maker. MapInfo supports client-server and Internet operations. Its macro programming language, Mapbasic, is easy to understand. MapInfo claims that it has 200,000 users worldwide. MapInfo's website (http://www.mapinfo.com/software/50ways/50ways.html) lists 50 ways to use MapInfo, from locating automatic teller machines to crime analysis.

c. Geographic Resources Analysis Support System (GRASS). GRASS was originally developed by the U.S. Army Corps of Engineers research laboratories as a tool for land management and environmental planning by the military. It is now a public domain GIS and can be downloaded from the Internet. It is a full-featured GIS used for data management, image processing, graphics production, spatial modeling, and visualization of many types of data. Unlike ARC/INFO, it is a raster-based GIS. Traditionally, GRASS runs on a Unix workstation. With the development of the personal computer, GRASS now has a PC version running under Windows 95 or Windows NT—a product called GRASSLAND. GRASS supports data input with many formats, including raster images from satellite and air photos, vector data, DXF, and others.

2. GIS and the Internet

The development of the Internet inevitably stimulated the development of GIS applications on the Web. A recent search using the key word GIS on YAHOO resulted in 6 GIS-related categories and 903 site matches. Many geospatial sites are interactive atlases, some provide network functions to help users in trip planning, others provide zip code information. These sites, most of which are frce, can be categorized as GIS service sites.

Another set of sites aim at sharing data among organizations in both the private and public sectors. Because spatial data are expensive and difficult to acquire, even with the help of modern technology such as GPS and remote sensing, GIS data collection is more cost effective if data collected for one project can also be used by other projects. Some U.S. agencies are promoting the data sharing. On September 2, 1998, the White House took the first step to foster the National Spatial Data Infrastructure (NSDI) (FGDC, 1998a). The NSDI includes policies, standards, and procedures for organizations to cooperatively produce and share geographic data. As the FGDC homepage recorded, Vice President Gore said the administration will expand its support for the use of GIS technologies and encourage increased public access and sharing of geographic data to put "more control, more information, more decision-making power into the hands of families, communities, and regions—to give them all the freedom and flexibility they need to reclaim their own unique place in the world." This section explores several Web sites that demonstrate GIS developments on the Web.

a. Geosystems Global Co. (www.Mapquest.com). This site provides geocoding and network functions. It can display a map with a user's desired location identified if the user enters a street address. The site also provides driving directions, either as door-to-door or city-to-city. Mapquest can provide very detailed instruction such as "stay on Route 10 for 5.6 miles, turn right on MLK Blvd, . . . " Many GIS products, such as ESRI and MapInfo's products, now allow GIS software to run on a server and answer users' requests from the Web in real time. Several copies of the same software can run on the same server, acting as if there were many single computers running the same software.

b. Center for Technology in Government (CTG), New York (http:// www.ctg.albany.edu/gisny.html). The prototype of the NYS Clearinghouse for Geographic Data was developed as part of CTG's New York State GIS Cooperative Project. The Clearinghouse provides geographic data producers a channel to announce available data. Data producers describe their datasets using the Federal Geographic Data Committee Standard for Digital Geospatial Metadata (see Section II B). The site includes such information as who produced the data, the geographic area covered, the dataset category or theme, scale, accuracy information, how to obtain the dataset, and so forth. A search engine helps users to find the datasets of interest. The complete meta data record for each dataset can be viewed permitting the user to determine if the dataset is what they need. Sometimes, a map image of the dataset can be viewed, too. Often the data may be available for immediate download or can be purchased from the producer.

There are other sites similar to CTG's on the web, such as the Illinois Natural Resources Geospatial Data Clearinghouse (http://www.isgs.uiuc.edu/nsdihome/ISGSindex.html). Such sites and the NSDI structure greatly improve the data sharing in the GIS world and are leading to more rapid growth in GIS applications.

In summary, this section has introduced the foundational knowledge for understanding GIS and GIS applications and developments. GIS is an information system that uses spatial information to organize geographically referenced data using two linked databases. GIS is composed of a database management system and a spatial topological processing system. GIS data consists of two categories—spatial data that describe the shape and location of geographic features and descriptive attribute data attached to those features. Both data categories are needed for performing spatial analysis. Data sharing is critical to GIS applications. The most commonly used data are TIGER files and zip code centroids files. The development of Internet services using GIS has facilitated improved spatial data sharing.

Part II of this chapter introduces library-related GIS applications. It covers topics in GIS Technology Standards and Libraries; Research into Geospatial Information Use in Libraries; Applications of GIS in Libraries; and Library Management and GIS.

II. GIS Uses and Frameworks for Libraries

A. Introduction to GIS User and Frameworks for Libraries

As seen in Section I, GIS is an automation tool that has revolutionized geographic and spatial data storage, retrieval, manipulation, analysis, and display. Unfortunately, a revolution never occurs without casualties and costs. For GIS, the casualties and costs are outshone by the benefits. So, with such a useful and effective technology what are the casualties, costs, and benefits to libraries? Part II of this chapter addresses these general questions by (1) discussing standards for geospatial data and metadata, (2) presenting the results of several critical research studies addressing the understanding of user behavior and needs for geospatial information in a library context, (3) describing several library implementations of GIS that illustrate the issues from a library patron perspective, and (4) describing the role of GIS as a management tool for libraries.

B. GIS Technology Standards and Libraries

The advent of GIS as a technology has fostered the development of several information standards. GIS standards significant for libraries include format standards for data representation and storage, standards for data transfer, and standards for description of spatial data (metadata, especially for digital spatial data). These geospatial standards have generally been developed with minimal librarian inputs yet these standards have consequences for the effectiveness of GIS in libraries of all kinds.

1. Standards for Representation

Standards for representation involve both de facto and formal standards for digital spatial data. Historically, a key technical issue centered around the use of raster (a grid or bitmap which quantizes space) versus vector (representing space with continuous magnitude and direction) as the "best" representation standard mechanism (Burrough, 1990). As discussed in Section I, each representation has benefits for system users, but trade-offs differ depending on the purpose for which the format is selected. The choice of format historically affected libraries. A given GIS system would promote raster over vector or vector over raster, complicating or eliminating the use of certain datasets by the library that were not compatible with the chosen GIS. Recent work and commercial systems have minimized this problem for libraries by allowing users to convert between vector and raster as best the mathematics allows. Unfortunately, consequences for quality and accuracy of final map-looking products still impact when choosing between raster or vector data, and users are still required to know a great deal about technical issues to generate information products that effectively address their information needs, wants, and preferences.

2. Standards for Storage

Many GIS vendors maintained and continue to maintain proprietary formats for the storage of data. These storage formats are independent of the raster versus vector issue. Previously, standards for transferring data among GIS programs were nonexistent, with data created in one system often incompatible with other systems. This has been formally addressed by a U.S. federal standard FIP 173 entitled the *Spatial Data Transfer Standard*, or SDTS (Federal Geographic Data Committee, 1994). The standard was designed to serve as a lingua franca for GIS systems and became required of vendors with the U.S. government in 1994. Unfortunately, the standard is complex and few low-cost GIS systems conform to the standard. Rather, de facto standards such as the ESRI file structure and particular public domain standards have reduced (although not eliminated) the problem of intercommunication among the various systems. As particular vendors built market share, their formats have become de facto standards. Other vendors have licensed these formats, reinforcing them as de facto standards (e.g., ESRI) . The ability for data to be used by multiple systems facilitates the use of GIS in libraries and permits expansion of collection development plans and programs to include a larger number of digital geospatial datasets. Storage format issues have not been completely resolved and do constrain development of GIS in traditional library settings, even if the data come from the online world. Some users even choose a GIS simply on the basis of the number of data storage formats the software system can input or output.

3. Metadata Standards

Metadata, sometimes referred to as "data about data," (Weibel and Miller, 1997) plays the role of traditional cataloging in a new guise. The new guise for geospatial metadata involves more intellectual content and authorship/creator fields. Such fields include the software required to operate, storage formats, data collection methods, and accuracy, availability, and specific descriptions of the geography covered by the item. Such fields are highly formalized and more detailed than traditional map- or machine-readable file description fields. Currently, there are three major standards for GIS metadata: Federal Geographic Data Committee content standard (FGDC, 1997), Government Information Locator Service (McClure, Ryan, and Moen, 1994; OMB, 1995), and traditional Machine Readable Cataloging (Crawford, 1989). Each has its supporters and each has advantages for particular users of geospatial data (Gluck, 1997b). Also, two other default geospatial metadata formats are developing as a consequence of the growth of the Internet. First, many Internet users employ the extracts formed by the search engines as metadata for accessing web-based geospatial data; second the use of embedded HTML tags serve as metadata for spatial datasets or pages.

Since 1994, by Presidential Executive Order 12906, the U.S. federal government has required federal agencies to produce metadata that adheres to the *FGDC Content Standards for Digital Geospatial Metadata v. 2.0* (FGDC, 1997). The FGDC standard is highly related to the SDTS standard because FGDC geospatial metadata contains many of the fields of the SDTS, and the field attributes are similar to those in the SDTS. (The SDTS is actually more extensive than FGDC because information in it must include details to permit machines to alter complex data streams.)

The FGDC content standard objectives include providing a common set of terminology and definitions for the documentation of digital geospatial data. The standard establishes the names of data elements and compound elements (groups of data elements) to be used for these purposes, the definitions of these compound elements and data elements, and information about the values that are to be provided for the data elements (FGDC, 1998b). The spatial metadata standard has seven main sections and three supporting sections. The seven main sections cover the following areas:

Section 1: Identification information includes information to reference the dataset, to describe the basic character of the dataset, the dataset's intended use and limitations, and to specify the time period that corresponds to ground "truth." Section 1 also includes status, maintenance, and update information, a description of the area domain covered by the dataset, lists of keywords applicable to the data and the thesaurus used (if any), the contact person for the dataset, description of data security issues, and lists the native software and hardware environment and filenames needed to work with the dataset.

Section 2: Data quality information includes attribute accuracy, logical consistency, completeness, positional accuracy, history of the development of the dataset (called the *lineage*), and the degree of cloud cover for aerial or satellite imagery.

Section 3: Spatial data organization includes indirect reference (names of geographic features), direct reference methods (i.e., vector, raster, or point), and types and numbers of spatial objects, whether vector, point, or raster.

Section 4: Spatial reference information refers to such data as horizontal and vertical coordinates, reference ellipsoid earth model, and cartographic projection.

Section 5: Entity and attribute information includes the description of the content of the dataset, the accuracy of attributes, and the domain from which data attributes may be assigned; that is, a data dictionary.

Section 6: Distributor information describes ordering information.

Section 7: Provides information on the currency of the metadata and the person responsible for maintaining the metadata.

The three supporting sections describe how to encode the citation information, how to describe the time period information, and how to present the contact information. These support sections do not stand alone, but are embedded in the proper sections of the major divisions.

Libraries have rarely used this format, but for expert GIS users such details are critical in determining if a dataset is appropriate for their use. Although the FGDC metadata standard may appear to be overkill from a general or casual user's perspective, it may not be in circumstances such as determining the actual region covered by the dataset. Even with all the information in the FGDC standard, it does not contain information on how to display the data to avoid problems of scale or resolution (Gluck, 1997a). Further chaos exists in the geospatial metadata arena because state and local agencies are not required to meet this FGDC metadata standard. Thus, formal descriptions associated with datasets of local geography that are frequently requested in public or academic libraries (flood plain, hydrology, etc.) lack the details of the FGDC metadata standard and fail to provide a significant portion of patrons with sufficient information for them to make good acquisition or use decisions (Gluck, 1997b).

A locator service may be described as an information resource that identifies other information resources, describes the information available in those resources, and provides assistance in how to obtain the information. The Government Information Locator System, or GILS, is an effort to improve locating, accessing, and acquiring publicly available U.S. Federal government information resources (OMB, 1995). A major impetus to this initiative is the development of the National Information Infrastructure (Clinton and Gore, 1993) and the increasing amount of federal resources in electronic formats. The GILS is a mandatory program for federal agencies driven by A-130, the Records Disposal Act (Title 44 of the United States Code) as well as the Freedom of Information Act (FOIA). GILS uses voluntary standards and is not restricted to spatial or electronic information alone. GILS is 239.50 compliant, and so assists libraries in communicating among disparate automated library systems. Further guidance is outlined for implementing GILS by agencies in the *Paperwork Reduction Act (PRA) of 1995* (PL104-13). For spatial data, GILS includes several elements in common with the SDTS and the FGDC metadata standard. GILS is much less extensive than the FGDC standard but includes an abstract (that FGDC does not) that often proves to be extremely useful for users in evaluating the appropriateness of a dataset for their use (Gluck, 1997b). Some libraries have implemented access to GILS and many federal documents accessible through the Internet or surrogated on the Internet have GILS records associated with them.

The US MARC format has, of course, served libraries well for many years, but some users have had complaints regarding its use for digital geospatial data (Larsgaard, 1996; Goodchild *et al.*, 1994; Gluck, 1997b). The US MARC standard has more information fields than are normally employed and most GIS and expert geospatial data users find MARC too terse to be useful for dataset evaluation and selection (Gluck, 1997b). In many cases, more casual users also find MARC insufficient for addressing the relevance of a retrieved item to their geospatial information needs (Gluck, 1997b). The Alexandria Digital Library Project, discussed later, has suggested and tested significant modifications to USMARC with moderate success with various user groups (Larsgaard, 1996; Hill *et al.*, 1997).

Furthermore, Internet search engines almost always return a terse extract from a site or document for each item in their retrieval sets. These surrogates also act as metadata for many users and can be useful but clearly lack many of the details experts and casual users need to effectively evaluate spatial information for use with GIS (Gluck, 1997b).

C. Research into Geospatial Information Use in Libraries

There is extensive research into the use of maps as information tools both in artificial (laboratory) and more natural (real world) settings (e.g., Kulhavy and Schwartz, 1980; Abel, 1986; Mersey, 1990; Freundschuh, 1991; Monmonier and Gluck, 1994).

Many of the experiments using maps or geospatial information have been guided by human information processing, or HIP, models (Lindsay and Norman, 1977). Such studies only assess the time on task and accuracy of map use (e.g., Lloyd, 1989). In these models, human cognition is represented as analogous to a computer with inputs, processing, and outputs. These models rarely seek the strategies subjects employed during manipulation or the insights subjects perceived during and after the tasks. Also, most studies that do collect users' impressions frequently only do so during a debriefing after an experiment (e.g., Thorndyke and Stasz, 1980; Thorndyke and Hayes-Roth, 1982). Those studies that do formally collect users impressions, deductions, inferences, and understandings often ask what users might do, not what they actually do or have done (e.g., Vanetti and Allen, 1988; Gould and White, 1985).

Spatial information needs and tasks are of several kinds. There have been several simple classifications proposed as well as more detailed schemes. One simple approach states that geospatial information involves only finding responses to two questions: What's there? and Where's that? These questions focus on finding what is present at a particular location and all locations where a particular phenomenon occurs. Muehrcke (1986) suggests another approach to the categorization of geospatial information tasks. He posits that geospatial queries may be matched to the levels of educational objective taxonomies (e.g., Bloom, 1956). Muehrcke describes three levels of sophistication of geospatial queries: reading, analysis, and interpretation. Reading involves extracting facts from a text or map such as the distance between two points, the name of a place, or latitude and longitude of a place. Reading questions generally answer "what" questions, or have "yes or no" responses. Analysis questions involve looking for relationships or seeing patterns in text or maps, such as noting that people living near polluted water supplies have high incidents of intestinal bacterial infections, or establishing a pattern for fossils distributed among rock layers. Analysis questions generally answer "how" and relationship questions. Interpretation questions seek cause and effect, such as noting that cholera is transmitted from individual to individual by water, or that all trees in the region were damaged because of the explosion of Mt. St. Helens. Interpretation questions answer "why" and some "how" questions.

Unfortunately, little observation and analysis of user geospatial information behavior exists in library settings. Research that does exist is rather sparse and incomplete suggesting the need for more investigations. This section describes four experiments that illustrate the kind of research that has been done and describes several forms of research that are beneficial for deeper understanding of geospatial information needs in library settings. These studies further illustrate the sort of user-based results that can result from assuming a rich epistemology and a more realistic ontology of what it is to be human than that represented by the human information processing models. Such deeper understandings of user geospatial information needs and geospatial information–seeking behavior suggest ways to support the resolution of users' needs with GIS.

In one such experiment (Gluck, 1995; 1996a) designed using Dervin's sense-making approach (e.g., Dervin, 1992), four major categories of geospatial information needs were described by 82 subjects who varied in age, education, gender, and race.

1. Educational Geospatial Information Need Situations
   This category included data needed for class assignments, spatial tool training, pilot training, and internship needs. Example: "Needed to find geographic information to make a map of Vermont for an assignment."

2. Professional/Career Geospatial Information Needs Situations
   This category included attendance at conferences, career planning, job interviews and relocation, delivery services wayfinding, field-data collection as part of employment, and seeking businesses and business location analysis as part of employment. Example: "I was driving from Ridgefield, Connecticut, to Hartford, Connecticut (approximately 1 hour) for a job interview."

3. Personal Geospatial Information Needs Situations
   This category included emergency needs (e.g., vehicle breakdowns), moves to a new community, travel and trip planning to visit family or friends or to communicate such information to others, general travel planning and execution, and seeking weather information for planning purposes or midcourse corrections while traveling. This category did not include vacation-, recreation-, or career-related situations; rather, it emphasized connecting with family and friends. Example: "I had to visit my friend at his school, and I had to find my way."

4. Recreational Geospatial Information Need Situations
   This category included vacation, honeymoon, and mixed business/pleasure travel planning and execution, finding a place to go when bored, fantasizing/imagining/daydreaming about other places, travel with children, and weather information for sports activities or to get

out of the elements. Example: "We took a day trip for wine tasting in the Finger Lakes."

Of the 82 situations in this experiment, only 7 (8.5%) of the responses involved the use of libraries. Those that did involve libraries explicitly sought geographic data for class assignments (4) or employment information (3). Others may have used a library but did not say so explicitly and did not find the responses to their questions in a library, indicating that libraries are not the primary source of geospatial information. As a first level of task understanding, Muehrcke's (1986) three-category scheme of reading, analyzing, and interpreting geospatial tasks was used to describe the respondents' questions.

Applying the reading, analysis, or interpretation task category scheme (Muehrcke, 1986) to the 185 questions posed by the respondents was quite straightforward. For example:

Reading questions included:
   Should I continue or return?
   What is it going to cost to get there?
Analysis questions included:
   What kinds of rocks do these fossils hide in?
   How could I ascertain spatial resolution fine enough for this task?
   Where could we find a restaurant?
Interpretation questions included:
   The travel agent is aware of time differences that caused the luggage foul-up. Why can't they prepare for this? [Respondent lost luggage on his honeymoon.]
   Why are there so many dead-end streets in Jersey City? [Respondent was lost in Jersey City and trying to return to Statue of Liberty pier.]
   How could so many hardships be brought upon the Jewish people? [High schooler visiting a museum in Israel.]

Of the 185 questions, 113 (61%) involved reading tasks, 47 (25%) involved analysis tasks, and 25 (14%) involved interpretation tasks. More than one-third of the questions involved more than seeking factual information that could be directly read from a map or geospatial textual description.

Another study (Gluck, 1996b) looked at paper map use in a public library. Specifically asking: What sort of maps do public library patrons request when a wide range of local paper maps are made available? The Leon County Public Library in Tallahassee, Florida, with support from other county agencies including the Geography Department and other offices at Florida State University (FSU) created a Map Resource Center (MRC) in 1994. Volunteer interns from the Department of Geography at FSU staffed the MRC afternoons, evenings, and weekends. The staff of the MRC maintained a log of maps used and some descriptions of their interactions with patrons. The log from this one library points to issues and concerns that may be true for a wide range of public libraries with diverse and multicultural constituencies.

The various types of maps referenced in the logs appear in Table I. The North Central region of Florida had severe flooding and rainwater runoff problems during the period the log was maintained; consequently, most of the uses of the environmentally sensitive areas (ESA) maps, contour maps, and Federal Emergency Management Agency (FEMA) maps related to the natural disaster, such as patrons trying to figure out if they would flood or to verify flood insurance rates. Also, ESA, flood, and FEMA maps frequently would be consulted jointly to conduct an ESA check for a patron. Patrons are also referred to general tourist maps, maps without an explicit reference to roads or street maps. The other geologic, topographic category of Table I included only general reference to geology, elevation, or topography. Also, the explicit use of United States Geological Survey (USGS) quadrangle maps established a separate category. Zoning maps were those that reflected local zoning ordinances. Recreational area map use included seeking information on trails for hiking, biking, or horseback riding; information for fishing sites in recreational or national forest areas; and general information about these areas. Naturally, some patrons were shown more than one product in a visit whereas other patrons returned to look at materials more than once. Many entries in the log confirmed the suggestions that multiple maps are frequently

Table I   MRC Frequency of Use by Category (June 1994 through Feb. 1995)

Paper cartographic products consulted	Local	Florida	U.S.	Other	Total
Appraisal/parcel	21	0	0	0	21
Astronomical charts	3	0	0	0	3
Environmental sensitive area (ESA)/ contours/FEMA	99	1	0	0	100
General tourist	5	6	11	17	39
Historical	3	4	3	5	15
Local comprehensive development plan	2	0	0	0	2
Other geologic, topographic	9	3	4	3	19
Political district boundaries	0	1	0	0	1
Recreational areas	15	1	3	0	19
School district boundaries	10	0	0	0	10
Soils	4	0	0	0	4
Street/road	23	24	20	1	68
USGS quadrangles (7.5 min)	33	7	1	0	41
Zoning	17	0	0	0	17
Totals	244	47	43	26	360

needed to resolve a spatial information need. A scheme was developed to categorize the patrons' explicit purposes for map use: Genealogical Investigation, Mileage Computation, Place Finding, Professional/Career, Radon Check, Real Estate Purchase, School Assignment, and Trip Planning (ground/air).

Significantly, when human assistance with analyses or interpretations was available, patrons sought the assistance. Examples included ESA checks and flooding patterns. Almost one-third of map uses expressed in the logs were for analyses of real property, whereas another large category was map use for school assignments. Reading tasks were rarely explicit in the log; however, the number of street maps sought indicated in Table I imply many reading tasks motivated patrons to seek out geospatial information.

Few of these maps were electronically available through any GIS or GIS data-viewer software packages at the time. The ability to access and use this information in a nonpaper form is rapidly changing, but the need for these types of paper information continues.

A third study describes the geospatial information needs of public library patrons as reported by librarians (Gluck, Danley, and Lahmon, 1996). Forty-seven libraries in 20 U.S. states participated. Although only 2 of the 47 reporting librarians had titles that defined their specialty in geographic information provision (both were map librarians), 7 reported that they had received special training in geography, cartography, GIS, map librarianship, or government documents.

When asked about types of paper geographic products, all libraries reported owning paper maps, atlases, and gazetteers as well as assorted reference books featuring geographic information. Thirty-one libraries (66%) related that they had in their collections government documents that specialized in geospatial information. Only two libraries (4%) reported that they owned globes.

Among the electronic geographic sources owned by libraries in the study, 15 (32%) reported that they had census CD-ROMs and 7 (15%) had TIGER files on CD-ROM. Nine (19%) reported that they owned electronic atlases or geospatial software such as PC Globe, Mac Globe, World Atlas, ArcView, or AutoMap. Three (6%) mentioned that they had encyclopedias with spatial information on CD-ROM (Encarta, Groliers, etc.). Only one library noted that they had locally created geographic databases. Eighteen (38%) libraries reported that they had no electronic geographic or spatial materials. Although they responded that they possessed no electronic geographic sources, 12 of those 18 reported that their libraries were connected to the Internet.

The study further described the situations or what geospatial issues brought the patrons to the library. A five-category inductive content analysis scheme provided a summary and generalization for those issues or situations.

These categories were research, travel, directions, relocation, and government. Each of the categories had several subcategories discussed as follows.

The *research* category represented academic or general research situations that did not explicitly seek travel planning, such as:

Assisted young adult in obtaining geographic/historical information for a school assignment.

A patron (a regular who I think is homeless) wanted to know the area in square miles of Youngstown, Ohio.

The *travel* category represented another category of geospatial reasons for coming to the library; these involved visits to a location for sport, tourism, or business, such as:

Patron wanted information on Disneyland [vacations].

Patron needed to know if he needed a visa to enter Malaysia.

The *directions* category involved geospatial information need situations in which patrons sought directions for wayfinding and navigation, such as:

Patron called the library to find [directions to] a church and cemetery that was located in a rural part of our county.

Patron needed to find location of plant in nearby town, where he was to go for a job interview.

The *relocation* category involved geospatial information need situations regarding job information or moving to a new community, such as:

Patron requested information regarding Pittsburgh, Pennsylvania. Planned to move and wanted to compare Pittsburgh with our area (i.e., housing, cost of living, culture, and arts).

Patron is thinking of moving to Costa Rica and starting a business raising some kind of lumber. Wanted to know about all aspects of living in Costa Rica and what this type of wood was used for.

The *government* category involved geospatial information need situations requesting information concerning relations with governmental bodies or requests for rules or funding, such as:

The patron needed to know where to vote.

Patron wanted information on history of zoning along a particular avenue/commercial corridor versus zoning throughout the city.

Business-related situations were rare and were readily incorporated in other categories of this scheme such as relocation and government relations. Genealogy was not seen as a geospatial category by respondents; however, locating genealogical sites (e.g., cemeteries, churches) were present (although infrequent) and easily accounted for in the categories of the scheme.

The situation categories described present a general overview of what brought patrons to the library for geospatial information. The questions asked by the librarian in supporting the resolution of that need presents a different level of geospatial information needs. The questions represent the librarians' gaps in cognitive processing that required bridging to resolve various aspects of the overall patron geospatial information needs.

Librarians' reading tasks in assisting patrons included reading a distance or name from a map or extracting a number from a table. Specific examples from this study included:

Since we found this bridge on the map, does the patron know of this location?
Was the patron willing to go to the other library or would they prefer to have the book sent here from our other library?
Are the topo maps in order? They are shuffled constantly.
Did the patron need information on the islands as well as a map?

Questions that involve *analysis tasks* require librarians to associate pieces of data within a source or sources. Analysis question tasks in this study included:

How does that zoning pattern compare to the original plans?
How much area would the patron need to see?
How do I explain GIS to this customer?
If I can't find the information here, where else can I find it?

Questions that involve *interpretation tasks* required librarians to resolve cause and effect, frequently answering "Why?" questions. Only two instances of interpretation question tasks appeared in this study:

Why on earth would he want to know the area of Youngstown anyway (supposing that is what he wants)?
Why do different numbers at the top of the chart refer to differences in elevation?

A fourth research project that is still underway evaluates the use of the Alexandria Digital Library (ADL) Project (Goodchild, 1994). The ADL is one of six digital library projects funded by the National Science Foundation (NSF), Defense Advanced Research Project Agency (DARPA), and the National Aeronautical and Space Agency (NASA). It is the only project promoting the construction and use of a spatial digital library. (The following description is an edited version of some aspects of that evaluation based on Hill *et al.*, 1997; Linda Hill, personal communication, October, 1997; Barbara Buttonfield, personal communication, June, 1997; see note 1.)

ADL's collection and services focus on geospatial information and links to web-based geographic locations. Throughout the project, user feedback has been collected through various formal and informal methods, including online surveys, beta-tester registration, ethnographic studies of users and potential users, target user group focus group sessions, and user feedback and videotaping comments while using the ADL built interfaces. The projects' user evaluation activities give a picture of the characteristics of three specific highly sophisticated groups of library users of geospatial information and data.

The three groups were earth scientists, information specialists, and educators. User data indicates the groups have very different task environments and expectations of system functionality and resource contents of such an online library. Earth scientists seek datasets, work in a high-technology environment, have specific search criteria, and want the geospatial information integrated into their working environment. However, information specialists are willing to spend more time learning the broad capabilities of a digital geospatial library and applying them to a variety of user needs. Information specialists are more likely to handle difficult information retrieval tasks and less likely to process the data themselves. Furthermore, educators need to employ digital library functionality in their classroom activities. Educators are interested in the potential for group activities and in content and functionality that support their education goals.

The analysis of these user group activities leads to understanding user expectations, whereas the ethnographic studies focused on users in action. Reference interviews and videotaped interactions indicate that the experience and background knowledge of users affect the way they interact. In the physical workspace, users were able to interact with a reference staff person who facilitated their search process. The data show that all the users, regardless of their task/knowledge proficiency, work well with a facilitated model. In the virtual workspace of ADL there is no human intermediary with whom the user may interact. The users' background and experience are even more important in the virtual world because the users determine how to search the system and select what they perceive as relevant datasets. In both the physical and virtual components of this digital library, users expected to learn from the interaction, be educated about the process, and learn additional strategies for future interactions. In the physical world, this process was implicit in the interaction with the reference staff, whereas in the virtual workspace the learning process was not as completely supported, and users expressed their frustration at various points throughout their interaction. Commonly, users would wonder aloud, or write in their comments, what they were doing "wrong" or what they did not understand, suggesting that they felt the difficulty resided more within themselves than it did within the system. More proficient users tended to identify problems with the system.

These four studies give an overview of the depth of investigation necessary to go beyond the simple counts at the reference desk. They point the way for a role for GIS in libraries and also indicate the general lack of training by librarians in GIS, lack of funding support for GIS in libraries, and the growth of electronic geospatial datasets that librarians will need to use as resources to assist patrons. The next section of this chapter illustrates several success stories of GIS in libraries and how the Internet has made increasing amounts of geospatial information and increasing numbers of GIS datasets available and accessible to library patrons whose libraries are connected to the World Wide Web.

D. Applications of GIS in Libraries

The use of GIS software in libraries is extremely uneven in the sophistication of the technology available, the human support, and the access to digital spatial datasets. GIS software may be categorized as viewer software with limited ability to create, modify, and process datasets or as true GIS software with full features for creation, modification, processing, and translation of data. Most GIS implementations in libraries may be characterized as viewer software environments, although several state libraries and some public libraries are more full-featured installations. The Association of Research Libraries (ARL), in conjunction with the software vendor of ArcInfo and ArcView software, ESRI, and Wessex, a data provider, formed the ARL GIS Literacy Project in 1992 (ARL, 1998). This project promoted the use of GIS in ARL member libraries and provided incentives, including free software to encourage the training of librarians in GIS and to provide GIS support for patrons. This section gives a brief tour of several ARL and other formal and informal GIS implementations in libraries. (Portions of the ARL reports are copyright of the authors; see note 2.)

The St. Louis Public Library, in association with the ARL Literacy Project, encouraged faculty at Southern Illinois University at Edwardsville to develop datasets of local interest (Watts, 1997, 1996). Patrons now access these datasets using ArcView software. The initial thrust of the project was to update the 1970 federally developed Urban Atlas, the electronic atlas of St. Louis City and County. The atlas is mounted on a workstation in the library's public service area. To meet the needs of the general public, ArcView software was customized and the design is capable of handling many questions brought to the library. More complex questions are referred to local data centers in the region that have full GIS installations. Note that the data centers refer some first-time users to the public library. St. Louis Public Library has shown that GIS can be customized for use by virtually anyone, and all users need not be steeped in GIS technology to use the viewer tools effectively. This GIS implementation is frequently used by people who are doing grant applications. The GIS provides maps—for example, of at-risk youth populations in certain areas—that help support the grant applications. Another frequent user group is nursing students doing assignments in public health courses. Continued use and improvement are envisioned, especially when the 2000 U.S. Census data becomes available.

Mentioned earlier was the Leon County Public Library in Tallahassee, Florida. This facility is not part of the ARL Project. Its MRC, now with supported mapping software (ArcView and Landview), blends traditional paper maps and electronic resources for public library patrons. Geography students from FSU assist patrons at scheduled evening and weekend times. The blending of paper and electronic resources with human support has been well received and continues to be an added-value service for the library (Gluck, 1996b).

At North Carolina State University (NCSU) in the spring of 1993, the GIS team developed and taught an introductory class, "ArcView Basics: GIS for the Fun of It," which was offered at NCSU. Subsequently, an instructional team developed a tutorial on the Web, the GIS Tutor Project. NCSU has the goal of more and more of the course-based instruction related to GIS to be conducted online. The GIS Tutor will enable any library user or staff member to move through an introductory tutorial on GIS and begin creating thematic maps. The tutorial includes exercises that utilize North Carolina geographic and census data. In a move to bring more focused GIS and data management expertise into the libraries, the position of Librarian for Spatial and Numeric Data Services was created, with responsibility for the "development and management of GIS and other spatial and numeric data resources and services supporting all areas of the university" and will be required to maintain "a high level of awareness and expertise regarding spatial and numeric data and its evolving applications" (Argentati and Abbott, 1997).

The University of Connecticut (UCONN) has decided to focus on building data collections rather than on GIS or mapmaking services. Building data collections entails an enormous amount of refining of geospatial data for the users, a process similar to the traditional collection development. Thus, a great deal of time is spent selecting from CD-ROM products data that relate to Connecticut and translating the data into formats that are readable by the majority of users. All data are in the public domain. The UCONN project is getting more into contracting and partnering with data than actually building data in-house (McGlamery, 1997).

The University of Minnesota was granted funding for equipment and staff to establish a library facility that serves as a gateway for GIS on the campus. A lab with 10 workstations was set up and equipped with appropriate equipment and connected to the Internet. The University of Minnesota Library handles orientation of users by providing weekly sessions covering basic programs such as ArcView, MapInfo, AtlasGIS, and ERDAS. A staff person is on-site at all times who can help GIS users by coaching but does not make maps for users (Allison, 1997).

The Natural Resource Information System (NRIS), part of the Montana State Library, is one of the most comprehensive and active GIS operations in the country, providing resources both on-site and over the Internet. Of the approximately 25 NRIS staff, 6 are GIS professionals; none of the staff are librarians. NRIS has placed geo-referenced databases on the Internet for several years. Most of the data focuses on natural resources in the state of Montana, but they also provide access to other data. Selectors employ a simple criterion for datasets to support: "How popular is the particular dataset as measured by requests that they have received for access to it?" NRIS fully supports FGDC metadata standards and serves as a node of the national Spatial Data Infrastructure. NRIS provides two levels of GIS service: (1) free access to data, except to private sector clients, and (2) GIS Bureau. Contract services include programming, database design, spatial analysis, cartographic design, and database development. NRIS also has an educational program, providing sessions both on- and off-site in Montana, especially for K–12 teachers. NRIS hopes to shift away from data provision to providing more information services (Gifford, 1997).

The research division of the New York State Library (NYSL) offers GIS-based services by trained generalists with a little help from technical experts. Projects include helping the New York State Police develop maps showing troop boundaries, and assisting the State Racing and Wagering Board in developing a site study. NYSL fully integrates their GIS services into their reference services. It plans to establish a public workstation in the library's reference area to access the library's collection of New York newspapers held on microfilm, with information retrieval search software aiding local historians and genealogists to span political boundaries. This is a system that most users can access without help from library staff. Other anticipated projects include electronic mapping of historical earthquake sites in New York and the provision of point-and-click mapping of parks and boat launching sites around the state (Strasser, 1997).

All libraries with access to the Internet have access to various spatial datasets and to several GIS sites on the web that run software in real time in the background (e.g., NAIS, 1998). Such unmediated access to GIS provides library patrons with access to digital geospatial information and to minor manipulation of the information (Johnson and Gluck, 1997). Such access also creates the need for library staff to be familiar with GIS concepts and processes to aid patrons in the resolution of their spatial information needs.

Many more "case-studies" of GIS in libraries are presented in, for example, the June 1995 issue of *Information Technologies and Libraries* and the July 1995 issue of the *Journal of Academic Librarianship*. Obviously, GIS can be a value-added service for an array of libraries. Costs and benefits must be assessed before implementation but GIS can be done rather inexpensively. However, GIS in a library requires an in-house advocate and management support. Each of the installations described is a unique accounting for the local needs of patrons and talents of the staff. As more digital datasets become accessible to users through the Internet, on CD-ROM, and in other forms, the role of the reference librarian will need to include support for GIS data and analysis of GIS data to greater or lesser degrees. These examples merely suggest how this is already happening.

E. Library Management and GIS

The last section of this chapter discusses the important role that GIS can play in the management of libraries. Independent of the in-house and online reference services, GIS can aid library management in planning library facilities and marketing library services.

Management of the use and delivery of library services is a complex and highly spatial endeavor. Traditional variables for analyzing library use patterns include mainly demographic variables such as age, household income, race, education level, and number of members of a household (Koontz, 1997). Relatively speaking, demographic data are more readily available because of the decennial U.S. Census and other local needs for describing the population. For example, service areas for public library branches are often described by census tracts or blocks (Koontz, 1997). Other variables that have been shown to be important in assessing library use patterns involve life style (Zweizig and Dervin, 1977) and awareness and perception of library services (D'Elia, 1980). The variables of library location and siting that may result in the opening, closing, modifying, moving, or consolidating of library services involve many geologic, topographic, and human spatial components such as soil types, elevation and slope, distance to users, support services for the library, and so forth.

GIS can greatly assist library managers in the analysis of such data to better describe, explain, predict, and prescribe library facilities and services (Thrall et al., 1993). For example, case studies from the work of Koontz (1997) are most illustrative. Koontz demonstrates the use of GIS in Evansville–Vanderburgh County Public Library system, which was facing a decision to close one branch in a decreasing usage area and the opening of a new branch in an expanding population area of the county. She points out the need for knowing which census tracts a branch is currently serving. This permits construction of marketing area maps using GIS that help describe and perhaps explain the current and projected scope of branches' users and services. She goes on to demonstrate the use of GIS to investigate the characteristics of both current and projected market areas to explain and predict usage. Amassing other planning data from city, county, and state sources enhances the understanding of spatial data for library purposes. For example, the addition of a new shopping center or major road renovations influence actions a library's management might pursue regarding facilities siting or marketing. GIS can not only provide various map overlays, but also assist in the creation of data for spatial analysis using correlation, spatial correlation, regression, and other statistical procedures to improve systematic management decision making.

Another example of forward-thinking use of GIS is one that will help increase library and information access for more nontraditional library users such as minorities and immigrants (Koontz and Jue, 1996). GIS can be seen as a tool to better manage public libraries and for better provision of user services. Koontz and Jue treat public library outlets as traditional "traveled-to" type retail facilities (Koontz, 1997) that need better knowledge of where to optimally site library outlets, identify the geographic market area, and analyze the library's demographics. Once these outlets are sited, libraries need complete point-of-sale (POS) data (i.e., data collected at each site on what library users are actually doing, requesting, and using). They point out the overemphasis on using book circulation as painting a complete picture of library usage is akin to a McDonald's restaurant only counting hamburgers sold through the drive-through while ignoring hamburgers consumed in the restaurant (e.g., for libraries, materials used in the library but not checked out, literacy classes, helping users write resumes). In this study of nontraditional library uses, more than 100 public library outlets participated from majority–minority markets identified using GIS. In addition, patron address data were obtained from several of these library outlets so that a determination of the actual library market area for these outlets could be determined using GIS. Bar code scanning technology was also used to collect outlet-specific data (POS data) so that these data could be displayed spatially. As follow-up to this study, they are developing a continuing education course for public librarians using GIS and other technologies to better measure and market public library services in each community (Koontz, Jue, and Gluck, 1998).

F. Conclusion

Developments in GIS technology bode well for libraries and library patrons. Access to spatial information and of the display, analysis, manipulation, storage, and retrieval of spatial data is rapidly becoming more available. Libraries are providing more and more spatial reference services for many user groups from experts in spatial data and GIS in special libraries to casual users in large and medium size public libraries. Developments in standards are an integral part of the increase in understanding and use of spatial data in libraries. In addition, the use of GIS as a library management tool is becoming better understood and employed. This brief overview has attempted to provide librarians and others with a background in the concepts of GIS and frameworks for the use of GIS in libraries.

Notes

1. Copyright permission granted by the American Society of Information Science (ASIS).
2. ARL Copyright Statement:
   Unless otherwise noted, copyright of the material on this [ARL] server is held by its author. Permission is granted to reproduce and distribute copies of the work for nonprofit educational or library purposes, provided that copies are distributed at or below cost, and that the author, source, and copyright notice are included on each copy. This permission is in addition to rights of reproduction granted under Sections 107, 108, and other provisions of the U.S. Copyright Act. These items may be further forwarded and distributed in the network, so long as the statement of copyright remains intact. For further information, contact Patricia Brennan, Communications Program Officer, Association of Research Libraries.

References

Abel, R. (1986). *Instantiating Maps and Text.* Unpublished doctoral dissertation. Arizona State University, Tempe, AZ.

Allison, B. (1997). Professional GIS Degree and State Demographic Atlas Highlight Achievements at the University of Minnesota. In *Transforming Libraries 1: Geographic Information Systems (GIS)* (George J. Soete, ed.). http://www.arl.org/transform/GIS/gistrans.html#P. ARL, Washington, DC.

Anonymous. (1994). *GPS/GIS Applications for Emergency Response.* Public Works, September.

Argentati, C., and Abbott, L. (1997). North Carolina State focuses on data, training, and upgrading staff skills. In *Transforming Libraries 2: Geographic Information Systems (GIS)* (G. J. Soete, ed.). http://www.arl.org/transform/GIS/gistrans.html#P ARL, Washington, DC.

ARL (Association of Research Libraries). (1998). The ARL GIS Literacy Project. Please contact Prue Adler at prue@arl.org or 202-296-2296 for additional information. URL: ftp://www.arl.org/info/GIS/gis.descrip. Washington, DC.

Bloom, B. S. (ed.). (1956). *Taxonomy of Educational Objectives. Handbook I: Cognitive Domain.* David McKay, New York.

Burrough, P. A. (1990). *Principles of Geographical Information Systems for Land Resource Assessment.* Clarendon Press, Oxford, UK.

Castle, G. III, ed. (1993). *Profiting from a geographic information system.* GIS World, Fort Collins, CO.

Clinton, W. J. and Gore, A., Jr. (1993). *Technology for America's Strength: A New Direction to Build Economic Strength.* Government Printing Office, Washington, DC.

Crawford, W. (1989). *MARC for Library Use,* 2nd ed. Hall, Boston, MA.

D'Elia, G. (1980). The Development and Testing of a Conceptual Model of Public Library User Behavior. *Library Quarterly* **50**, 410–430.

Dervin, B. (1992). From the mind's eye of the user: The sense-making qualitative–quantitative methodology. In *Qualitative Research in Information Management* (J. Glazier and R. Powell, eds.), pp. 61–68. Libraries Unlimited, Englewood, CO.

FGDC (Federal Geographic Data Committee). (1994). A prototype SDTS federal profile for geographic vector data with topology. FGDC, Washington, DC. FIPSPUB 173-1, version 1994.

FGDC. (1997). Content Standards for Digital Geospatial Metadata, Version 2.0. FGDC, Washington, DC.

FGDC. (1998a). NSDI. FGDC, Washington, DC. URL:http://www.fgdc.gov/nsdi/nsdi.html.

FGDC. (1998b). Metadata. FGDC, Washington, DC. URL:http://www.fgdc.gov/metadata/metadata.html.

Freundschuh, S. (1991). The effect of spatial pattern of the environment on spatial knowledge acquisition. In *Cognitive and Linguistic Aspects of Geographic Space* (D. Mark and A. Frank, eds.), pp. 167–184. Kluwer Academic Publishers, London, UK.

Gifford, F. (1997). The Montana State Library moves ahead on several fronts. In *Transforming Libraries 2: Geographic Information Systems (GIS)* (G. J. Soete, ed.). http://www.arl.org/transform/GIS/gistrans.html#P. ARL, Washington, DC.

Gluck, M., Danley, E., and Lahmon, J. (1996). Public librarians' views of the public's geospatial information needs. *Library Quarterly*, 66(4), 408–448.

Gluck, M. (1995). Understanding performance in information systems: Blending relevance and competence. *Journal of the American Society for Information Science*, 46(6), 446–460.

Gluck, M. (1996a). The relationship between user satisfaction and relevance in evaluating performance in information systems. *Information Processing & Management*, 32(1), 89–104.

Gluck, M. (1996b). Spatial information needs of the general public: Texts, maps, and users tasks. In *GIS and Libraries: Patrons, Maps, and Spatial Information* (L. Smith and M. Gluck, eds.), pp. 151–172. 32nd Annual Clinic on Library Applications of Data Processing. University of Illinois, Champaign–Urbana, IL.

Gluck, M. (1997a). Standards for electronic access to geographic and spatial information. In *Electronic Publishing: Applications and Implications*. ASIS Monograph Series (E. Logan and M. Gluck, eds.), pp. 27–40. Information Today, Medford, NJ.

Gluck, M. (1997b). A Descriptive Study of the Usability of Geospatial Metadata. Final Technical Report (OCLC Library and Information Science Research Grant). OCLC, Dublin, OH.

Goodchild, M. *et al.* (1994). Towards a Distributed Digital Library with Comprehensive Services for Images and Spatially-Referenced Information (Original Proposal for Digital Library funding from DARPA, NSF, and NASA.). Santa Barbara, CA. URL: http://www.alexandria.ucsb.edu/docs/proposal/index.html.

Gould, P. and White, R. (1985). *Mental Maps* (2nd. ed.). Allen & Unwin, Winchester, MA.

Hill, L. L., *et al.* (1997). User Evaluation: Summary of the Methodologies and Results for the Alexandria Digital Library, University of California at Santa Barbara. Proceedings of the American Society for Information Science (ASIS) Annual Meeting, Washington DC.

Johnson, D. and Gluck, M. (1997). Geographic information retrieval and the World Wide Web: A match made in electronic space. *Cartographic Perspectives* 26, Winter: 13–26.

Kennedy, M. and Meyers, C. R. (1977). *Spatial Information Systems: Introduction*. Urban Studies Center, Louisville, KY.

Koontz, C. (1997). *Library Facility Siting and Location Handbook*. Greenwood Press, Westport, CT.

Koontz, C. and Jue, D. (1996). Market-based adult lifelong learning performance measures for public libraries serving lower income and majority–minority markets. Funded grant sponsored by the U.S. Department of Education (September 1996–February 1999).

Koontz, C., Jue, D., and Gluck, M. (1998). Public sector market research: A continuing education course for public librarians utilizing geographic information systems. Funded grant from the Institute of Museum and Library Services, 1998 National Leadership Grant of Florida State University, Tallahassee, FL.

Kulhavy, R. and Schwartz, N. (1980). Mimeticism and the spatial context of map. *Bulletin of the Psychonomic Society* 15(6), 414–418.

Larsgaard, M. L. (1996). Providing Access to Earth-Sciences Spatial Data: Metadata and the Alexandria Digital Library. In *Expanding Boundaries: Geoscience Information for Earth System Science* (DeFelice, B. J. ed.). Proceedings of the 31st Meeting of the Geoscience Information Society, Denver, CO. October 28–31, pp. 27–30.

Lindsay, P. and Norman, D. (1977). *Human Information Processing: An Introduction to Psychology* (2nd ed.). Harcourt, Brace, Jovanovich, New York.

Lloyd, R. (1989). The estimation of distance and direction from cognitive maps. *American Cartographer* **16**(2), 149–159.

Logsdon, T. (1995). *Understanding the NAVSTAR: GPS, GIS, and IVHS* (2nd. ed.), Van Nostrand Reinhold, New York.

McClure, C., Ryan, J., and Moen, W. (1994). *Identifying and Describing Federal Information Inventory/Locator Systems: Design for Networked-Based Locators* (2 Vols.). National Audio Visual Center, Bethesda, MD.

McGlamery, P. (1997). MAGIC: UConn provides sophisticated GIS services on a shoestring. In *Transforming Libraries 2: Geographic Information Systems (GIS)* (George J. Soete, ed.). http://www.arl.org/transform/GIS/gistrans.html#P. ARL, Washington, DC.

Mersey, J. E. (1990). Colour and thematic map design: The role of colour scheme and map complexity in Choropleth map communication. *Cartographica* **27**(3), 1–150. (Monograph No. 41.)

Monmonier, M. and Gluck, M. (1994). Focus groups for design improvement in dynamic cartography. *Cartography and Geographic Information Systems* **21**(1), 37–47.

Muehrcke, P. (1986). *Map Use: Reading, Analysis, and Interpretation* (2nd ed.). JP Publications, Madison, WI.

NAIS. (1998). NAISMap2:Interactive Mapping Tool. URL: http://atlas.gc.ca/schoolnet/issue-map/.

Nash, E. L. (1993). *Database Marketing: The Ultimate Marketing Tool.* McGraw-Hill, NY.

New York State Library (1994). Geographic information system (GIS) comes to the state library. An Occasional Newsletter for Clients of the New York State Library. January 1994.

OMB (Office of Manpower and Budget). (1995). Establishment of Government Information Locator Service. OMB 95-01. *Federal Register*, December 7, 1994. Vol. 59234, pp. 63075–63077.

Star, J. L., Estes, J. E., and McGwire, K. C. (1997). *Integration of Geographic Information Systems and Remote Sensing.* Cambridge University Press, Cambridge, England.

Star, J., and Estes, J. (1990). *Geographic Information Systems: An Introduction.* Prentice Hall, Englewood Cliffs, NJ.

Strasser, T. (1997). The New York State Library tracks newspapers, earthquakes, and launch sites. In *Transforming Libraries 2: Geographic Information Systems (GIS)* (George J. Soete, ed.). http://www.arl.org/transform/GIS/gistrans.html#P ARL, Washington, DC.

Thorndyke, P. and Hayes-Roth, B. (1982). Differences in spatial knowledge acquired from maps and navigation. *Cognitive Psychology* **14**, 560–589.

Thorndyke, P. and Stasz, C. (1980). Individual differences in procedures for knowledge acquisition from maps. *Cognitive Psychology* **12**, 137–175.

Thrall, G., *et al.* (1993). Using GIS to Visualize Spatial Data (TIN, Voronoi Polygons, Surface Models). *Geo Info Systems* **3**(5), 59–65. URL: http://www.asis.org/annual-97/alexia.htm URL:http://purl.org/metadata/dublin_core.

Vanetti, E. and Allen, G. (1988). Communicating environmental knowledge: The impact of verbal and spatial abilities on the production and comprehension of route directions. *Environment and Behavior* **20**(6), 667–682.

Watts, A. (1996). The St. Louis Public Library's electronic atlas: A successful GIS application in the public library environment. In *Geographic Information Systems and Libraries: Patrons, Maps and Spatial Information* (L. Smith and M. Gluck, eds.), pp. 213–219. University of Illinois, Champaign–Urbana, IL.

Watts, A. (1997). The Saint Louis Public Library brings GIS to the people. In *Transforming Libraries 2: Geographic Information Systems (GIS)* (G. J. Soete, ed.). http://www.arl.org/transform/GIS/gistrans.html#P ARL, Washington, DC.

Weibel, S., and Miller, E. (1997)-11-02. Dublin Core Metadata. OCLC, Dublin, OH.

Worboys, M. F. (1995). *GIS—A Computing Perspective*. Taylor & Francis, London.
Zweizig, D. and Dervin, B. (1977). Public library use, users, and uses: Advances in knowledge of characteristics and needs of adult clientele of American public libraries. In *Advances in Librarianship* (Melvin Volgt and Michael Harris, ed.) Vol. 7, pp. 232–253. Academic Press, New York.

Additional GIS Materials

Understanding GIS

Chrisman, N. R. (1997). *Exploring Geographic Information Systems*. J. Wiley & Sons, New York.
DeMers, M. N. (1997). *Fundamentals of Geographic Information Systems*. J. Wiley & Sons, New York.
Foresman, T. W. (ed.). (1998). *The History of Geographic Information Systems: Perspectives from the Pioneers*. Prentice Hall, Upper Saddle River, NJ.
Kennedy, M. (1996). *The Global Positioning System and GIS*. Ann Arbor Press, Chelsea, MI.
Simon, B. (1997). High-end mapping mania (ESRI ArcView GIS, MapInfo Corp MapInfo Professional). (Includes related article on SPOT MetroView.) *PC Magazine* **16**(10), 62–63.

Applications

Ashley, C. C. (1998). Putting risks on the map. (Use of geographic information systems in property and casualty insurance industry.) *Best's Review—Property–Casualty Insurance Edition* **98**(9), 84.
Baumgartner, M. F., Schultz, G. A., and Johnson, A. I. (1997). *Remote Sensing and Geographic Information Systems for Design and Operation of Water Resources Systems*. Wallingford, Oxfordshire, UK.
Cooney, C. M. (1998). GIS software aids environmental justice, emergency planning. (Geographic Information System.) *Environmental Science & Technology* **32**(9), 211–222.
Goodchild, M. F. (1996). *GIS and Environmental Modeling: Progress and Research Issues*. GIS World Books, Fort Collins, CO.
Lepofsky, M. (1993). Transportation hazard analysis in integrated GIS environment. (Geographic Information Systems.) *Journal of Transportation Engineering* **119**(2), 239–254.
Martin, D. (1996). *Geographic Information Systems: Socioeconmic Applications*, 2nd ed. Routledge, New York.
Pack, T. (1997). Mapping a path to success: Geographic information means business to knowledge manager Cheryl Perkins. *Database*, **20**(4), 31–35.
Soete, G. J. (1997). *Transforming Libraries: Issues and Innovations in Geographic Information Systems*. Washington, DC: Association of Research Libraries, Office of Management Services, Systems and Procedures Exchange Center.

Media on Demand
Approaches to Web-Based Media Services in Libraries

Gloria Rohmann
New York University Libraries
New York, New York 10012

I. Introduction

A. Digital Libraries and Media Services

A brief stroll around the average academic library leaves little doubt that libraries have been transformed by digital information delivery—index tables and reference shelves are often deserted whereas there are long lines to use the online catalog and networked information available via CD-ROM and the World Wide Web. Many of the library's users are not in the library at all, but are sitting in their dorm rooms, living rooms, or offices (which might not even be on campus) searching databases and catalogs, or completing assignments via class Web pages and electronic reserves. These challenges to traditional library service have dominated professional discourse for many years. Yet, how are these challenges affecting the academic media center? Even in a teleconference (Video, 1997) on the future of the "motion media" (video and multimedia CD-ROM) in libraries, the prospect for large-scale Web-based delivery of media services seemed remote. Yet now the rapidly advancing technologies known as the "streaming media" challenge academic media professionals to extend their services to "New Learning Communities" (Rasmussen, 1998) of nonresident students, commuting instructors, and fully employed adult learners as well as to accommodate the expectations of new generations of media-savvy undergraduates enrolled in increasingly multidisciplinary programs. The purpose of this article is to explore ways that academic media centers can use these new real-time and "asynchronous" streaming technologies to improve existing services and extend services to the "New Learning Communities."

39

B. Digital Media: A Brief History

Although the delivery of sound and moving images over the Internet has been possible for some time, there have been many barriers to its large-scale use in education and commerce. To send this type of information over networks, it must first be converted into a "file" containing "information" about the work in binary (1s and 2s) form. Even a few seconds of sound can contain a large amount of such information—moving image files are even bigger. Files containing plain text, such as is found on a typical Web page, are made up of relatively small amounts of information. The rapid growth of the Internet in the early 1990s was possible because the transmission of text (e-mail and character-based information interactive databases such as the OPAC and DIALOG) was efficient even with "slow" dial-up modems using dial-up "plain old telephone service" (POTS).

With the introduction of more advanced desktop computers, higher-speed optical networks, and intelligent switching systems came the birth and explosive development of the World Wide Web. On the Web, text files could be combined with highly compressed image files to provide a user interface that combined the attractiveness of the printed page with the interactivity of an online information system. Although techniques available for digitizing and compressing sound and moving images (such as Apple's QuickTime) were employed successfully in creating multimedia CD-ROMs, results were less satisfactory when transmitted over the Internet. This was a function of file size and transmission speed. The size of one uncompressed digital file containing 1 minute of speech is approximately 5 megabytes (MB). Although the average speed at which information is transmitted from an internal CD-ROM player to a computer's memory is 1.2 megabits per second (Mbps), the average speed of most dial-up Internet connections even today is only 28.8 kilobits per second (Kbps). Even at ideal network conditions, that 5 MB file would take 17 minutes to be received—and the entire file must be received before it can be played.

Imagine if, when you turned on your radio, you had to wait 17 minutes to hear less than 1 minute of news. With this type of functionality, it is unlikely that the radio would ever have developed beyond being a novelty for the hobbyist. Even today, because all the information about a Web page must be received before it can appear on a monitor, many Web users "turn off" their web browser's ability to display images in order to speed up the delivery of textual information over slow networks. Browser software also compensates for "slow" transmission speeds by "caching," or saving, copies of frequently requested Web pages in a temporary file on the computer, rather than requesting them from the remote host each time.

Higher speeds, of course, are possible using internal networks. Pioneers in the delivery of digital music such as the designers of the VARIATIONS

Project at Indiana University's Music Library (Fenske, 1996) chose to avoid the Internet entirely, employing proprietary technology from IBM to deliver high-quality digital sound over closed networks. Such systems are highly efficient at delivering asynchronous (time-shifted) sound to larger numbers of users than could listen to one analog recording delivered in real time. Nevertheless, these systems are probably too expensive to serve as a model for large-scale delivery of media services in many academic libraries. Some libraries and schools, however, are investigating the use of IBM's Global Campus Digital Library system, a brief description of which will be found in Section III.E, "Higher-Priced Systems."

C. Streaming Digital Media: A Low-Cost Solution

In 1995, a company called Progressive Networks (now called RealNetworks) released its proprietary method for encoding compressed digital files to allow a Web user to listen to an audio file almost as soon as the connection had been made. To listen to streaming audio, users must load an additional piece of software called a "player" on their computer, which works together with their Web browser as a "helper application." Using a process called "buffering," the streaming player downloads into the temporary memory of the listener's computer a small portion of the sound before beginning playback. As the audio plays, the player continues to put some of the file in memory. If the file has been correctly encoded for the size of the listener's connection and network traffic does not interrupt the stream, the listener experiences a smooth, "broadcast" quality transmission. Most streaming audio files do not require that special software be loaded on the host Web server. To serve archived audio to more than one listener at a time, or to stream real-time events, specialized server software is required.

Following the usual Web practice, both the encoding software and the players were made available for free. Although the audio quality of the early versions of the software was not high, Web users were enthusiastic about the potential for delivering real-time radio and archived sound with virtually no delay (More, 1995). Early adopters could listen to live and prerecorded news and events from National Public Radio, CBS, and CNN. In early 1996, Progressive Networks announced improved support for FM-quality stereo sound, delivering almost CD-quality sound to Web users with single-channel ISDN (64 Kbps) modems and other high-speed connections. Other products appeared, most notably Xing Technologies' Streamworks, which optimized the existing standards for streaming Motion Picture Experts Group (MPEG) audio for Web delivery. MPEG audio is an internationally recognized standard for digital audio. Files compressed using MPEG are larger than those created using the RealAudio proprietary standard, but because they contain more information, they also provide more acceptable sound quality. It was immediately apparent to music producers and retailers how this technology might be applied. Although record labels set up Web sites offering samples of new recordings, some music executives said that they were already nervous about how high-quality Internet audio might affect their sales (Atwood, 1996). Support for streaming video soon followed that, combined with existing Internet videoconferencing applications like White Pine's CUSeeMe, which began to catch the eye of educational as well as corporate users.

II. Serving Digital Media: The Case for the Academic Media Center

How can academic media centers use these new real-time and "asynchronous" streaming technologies to improve existing services and extend services to the "New Learning Communities?"

In the late 1960s, before technology had transformed the rest of the library world, media librarians were already grappling with proliferating formats for recording and distributing library information. The American Library Association's (ALA) 1988 *Guidelines for Audiovisual Services in Academic Libraries* called on media librarians to take the lead in applying new technology to traditional goals. The guidelines were clear about the importance of new technology. "The reason for embracing new technology, of course, is to extend our capabilities" (ALA, 1988). The previous guidelines were written in 1968, at a time when the existence of media centers in academic libraries needed a strong defense, and had already noted the pedagogical benefits of using media to support learning. Media "offer greater efficiency of presentation, add realism, stimulate interest, clarify communication, speed comprehension" (ALA, 1968). To this, the authors of the 1988 guidelines added, media also "permit repetition and drill, allow students to observe and critique themselves, [and] use large quantities of information." In addition, the 1988 guidelines continued, "support of instruction should not overshadow the growing ability of audiovisual technologies to contribute to academic research" (ALA, 1988).

The 1998, *ACRL Guidelines for Distance Learning Library Services* affirmed the importance of library service in the world of the "New Learning Communities" as well. Noting that "nontraditional study" is becoming more common in higher education, and there is an increase in the number of places where such education is offered, it identifies a greater demand for library services outside the physical location of the main campus. Expanding distance education programs, which are largely technology based, also drive the expectation that library services will be delivered at a distance (ACRL, 1998).

Although the distance learning guidelines do not specifically mention academic media services, the 1998 *Draft Guidelines for Media Resources in Academic Libraries* are very specific. "Media librarians should be advocates for viable new media technologies, and we must expand our knowledge base to include digital delivery systems" (ALA, 1998).

A. Extending Media Services via the Web

What are the "traditional" services offered by library media centers or learning centers and how can they be extended by new technologies? The 1994 *Standards for Community, Junior and Technical College Learning* (Author) identifies a number of services related to media that are available on most campuses. Although not all of them are offered in libraries, they all relate to or can be extended by the new streaming media. More specific technical details are covered in the technical section of this chapter, and important points about funding and collaboration raised by all these guidelines are discussed in the sections on production, funding, and collaborative arrangements (Fig. 1).

B. Collaborative Relationships

The 1998 draft *Guidelines for Media Resources* (ACRL) state that "library staff are uniquely qualified to provide the best access to that collection [the media collection], both physical and bibliographic. The library is also the most qualified to build planned collections responsive to both immediate and anticipated programmatic needs." Yet even academic media centers where most media services are currently performed would be hard pressed to deliver them over the Web without increased funding and collaborative arrangements across many departments in the college or university. As librarians have discovered in other areas of library "automation," new services do not usually replace traditional services, but rather exist alongside them, requiring additional expenditures and skills. Academic media center librarians will be successful if they take a proactive role within the institution as well as the library, working with teaching faculty, computing facilities, telecommunications, and TV and campus cable systems, and avoiding duplication of effort (*Guidelines*, 1998). At the same time, the new learning technologies provide libraries with new opportunities for a greater role in distance education. Universities need a wide range of delivery options, and library media centers may provide not only the content, but also the greatest amount of university-wide staff support for these new ventures (Beagle, 1998).

TRADITIONAL MEDIA SERVICE	WEB-BASED EXTENSIONS
Acquisition, maintenance of collections	Remote media resources are identified, linked to local Web pages; local resources are digitized to preserve obsolete formats.
Access, circulation of collections	Local resources are digitized to extend access; servers, networks, and workstations are configured and maintained to deliver resources.
Audio recording, duplication, and editing	Digital encoding, editing, streaming
Video recording, duplication, and editing	Digital encoding, editing, streaming
Multimedia authoring	Digital capture of existing resources; synchronized multimedia; multimedia production workstations
Satellite uplink and downlink	Used to receive content for webcasting; send content for webcasting by third parties
Radio and television broadcast	Webcasting: Internet radio and TV
Distance learning	Webcasting, serving digital audio, video; creating and serving instructional modules
Reserves services	Digitizing and serving audio and video from existing collections
Learning laboratories	Delivering digital encoding and streaming
Media classrooms	Delivering digital encoding and streaming

Fig. 1   Traditional media service vs web-based extensions.

C. Funding New Initiatives

The 1998 *Guidelines* also recommend several important steps that media center managers should take to make sure that they are using their budgets and staff resources wisely. These recommendations are particularly valuable for centers contemplating major additions or changes to services:

1. Librarians should develop a mission statement for the media resources program based on the mission statement of the library. Although it is important to be advocates for changes in digital delivery services, programs must be carried out with the full cooperation of library administrators and the institutional needs of the educational institution.
2. The responsibilities and functions of the media resources program within the organizational structure of the library should be clearly defined.
3. The library should fund continuing education opportunities for media librarians and professional/administrative staff, and make sure that media support staff have specialized training and skills.

4. The media resources mission statement should be the basis for the program budget and be part of the library planning process. (*Guidelines*, 1998)

Although special funding is often essential to launch new initiatives, media librarians should beware the "soft money" trap. Care should be exercised that new initiatives, which are intended to provide permanent additions to media services, are adequately accounted for by inclusion in library or university budgets. One way to do this is to begin by using low-cost solutions like Web-based streaming media, which can offer the biggest return for the largest number of students. Technology is changing rapidly; media librarians must weigh the trade-offs between jumping into using the streaming media and maybe getting "stuck" supporting obsolete formats, or waiting for higher-quality solutions that may be priced beyond what the institution can afford to support.

Many academic media centers already use some kind of charge-back system for production services. Digital services can be provided to university-wide "clients" on a fee-for-service basis. New York University's (NYU) live webcasting service operates this way, mirroring the fee-for-service model of NYU's TV Production Center, which provides live audio and video coverage of classes and campus events. This model will be familiar to many academic media centers: departments are regularly charged for classroom rental, specialized equipment setups, and teleconferencing services.

The Distance Learning Guidelines call for separate funding of library services for students enrolled in these programs, warning that traditional on-campus libraries cannot be stretched to meet the needs of distance learning students who may never come to campus. This may not always be practical. With careful planning and phased deployment of distance learning applications, media service components to distance learning programs may be integrated into existing services. This author is working on a grant-supported project to produce an entirely asynchronous (time-shifted) version of an existing course in graduate business education, using the instructor's existing Powerpoint slides, RealPresenter from RealNetworks, and Microsoft's NetMeeting. Charge-backs for video, audio, and encoding services associated with the production of the course are minimal, but they have been carefully accounted for. Because the course already exists and the software tools are easy to use, it should be possible to deliver the course online using existing staff. Nevertheless, should these services be in high demand, new staff may have to be added.

There are many services, primarily to individuals, that libraries have always provided free of charge—reserves, interlibrary loan, and many kinds of document delivery operate on this basis. At NYU, the Avery Fisher Center for Music & Media has long provided free duplication of audio cassettes for language learning on deposit in the center under license from the publishers. A program has been launched to extend that service, making entire foreign language tape sets available at all times on the Web, regardless of whether the media center is open. Web delivery of recorded music that is part of the library's permanent collection and has been placed on course reserve will also be made available on this basis. It is easy to see how other high-demand items such as sound effects, dialect tapes for actors, and recordings of Shakespeare (particularly those that are out of print or exist only on phonograph records) would be valuable additions to Web offerings. A detailed discussion of copyright and fair use considerations is in Section VI.

III. Producing Streaming Media

A. Tools

What are some of the tools that are currently available for establishing streaming media services? At NYU, we are using a suite of low-cost content creation tools and moderately priced server software from RealNetworks.

1. Live Webcasting

NYU Libraries also operates campus-wide video and audio production services and broadcast services. In 1997, we started receiving requests to extend these services to include live webcasting of on-campus events. A server was set up in the library's Electronic Resources Center that could be connected to the campus-wide broadband (cable) system. Video and audio coverage of events that were held in areas served by the cable are sent directly to the server, where the free encoder software converts the analog signal to compressed RealAudio and RealVideo and sends it out over the Web. In areas not served by the cable, live audio can be encoded and streamed by connecting a telephone directly to the server. The server software license allows up to 60 users to "tune in" to the webcast at the same time. (Archived video of NYU events, including an all-day conference at the NYU School of Law featuring Bill Clinton, Hillary Clinton, and Prime Minister Tony Blair can be viewed at http://mediatv.bobst.nyu.edu/.) Another solution is to use a "portable" computer that encodes the live analog signal directly from the video or audio recorder and sends it through the campus data network to the server in another location on campus (Ackerman, 1998). Webcasting services can also be purchased from outside companies. Typically, video coverage is provided by the customer; the analog signal is then sent to the webcasting service via high-speed phone lines (ISDN or higher) or via satellite uplink, where the signal is encoded and made available over the Web. Web news sites like CNN and MSNBC use these services to deliver live video.

2. Converting Audio Recording

RealNetworks provides free and low-cost "enhanced versions" of software for encoding existing digital and analog recordings into streaming audio and video. Although it is not absolutely necessary to convert analog audio (on audio cassette and phonograph records) to a digital file before it is encoded, the sound quality of the resulting file is greatly enhanced by doing so. At NYU, we use audio editing software for Macintosh called SoundEdit. To produce RealAudio files for the language lab on the Web, a cassette tape player is attached to the line-level input of the Macintosh. The tapes are played and captured by the software. The uncompressed digital file is then converted to RealAudio, using the free RealEncoder, and sent to the server. Because they are already digital, recordings on compact disk can be encoded directly into RealAudio with little loss of quality. Events such as live lectures could also be encoded "live" and saved as a file rather than webcast. At Monash University Library in Melbourne, Australia, a regular lecture taping service has been replaced by a streaming audio service (Harrison, 1998).

3. Converting Video: RealVideo

To encode video, the free encoding software must be running on a computer with a video card. Although a video card is not standard equipment on most computers, cards that produce excellent results are available for under US $200. Video can be captured and encoded simultaneously. If the high-quality audio reproduction is important (such as in a musical performance), a more expensive video card with dedicated audio input should be used. RealNetworks provides information about a number of different video cards and other third party applications on its Web site, at http://www.real.com.

4. Creating Synchronized Multimedia: RealPresenter

The Realtime Streaming Protocol used by RealNetworks was originally developed so that data streams could be synchronized to contain both a media file (sound and/or video) and instructions to the server to deliver "static" files such as streams of text or a series of separate images. As mentioned previously, NYU Libraries is using the RealPresenter tool to create a distance learning version of an existing course in business education. The instructor records her existing lecture while showing her Powerpoint slides on a computer equipped with Microsoft's Powerpoint 97, the low-cost RealPresenter plug-in, and a microphone. As she speaks, her voice is recorded, encoded in

RealAudio, and synchronized with her slides. The slides are converted to JPEG format (a high-quality compression format supported by all Web browsers). When the resulting RealAudio files and JPEG files are loaded on the server, a student can hear the lecture and view the slides via a Web page. Although the instructor herself is not visible, the slides are clear, and unlike full-motion Web video, the lecture can be "viewed" even by those using low-bandwidth dial-up telephone connections.

5. Recording Templates and File Sizes

RealEncoder tools also allow the user to encode files for optimal delivery at many different network speeds. NYU's foreign language tapes are recorded at 16 Kbps. This is the lowest bit rate (transmission speed) at which files can be encoded, and results in the smallest file size. A typical encoded file of 30 minutes of spoken word is 350 K (kilobytes). For comparison, the unencoded, uncompressed digital version of that same file is 150 MB (megabytes). It is important to remember that at no time does the end-user store that file on any local system: only a few minutes of the file is "buffered" (temporarily stored) in the computer's memory at any one time. When the session ends, this information is lost, and cannot be recovered. This has important implications for copyright and fair use, which are addressed later in the chapter. Propelled by the potential commercial market for delivering music over the Web, the late 1998 version of the RealPlayer G2 is designed to allow a high-quality music experience over low-bandwidth networks. NYU Libraries has found that music encoded at 20 Kbps provides an acceptable, if not quite CD-quality listening experience. A typical file size for 30 minutes of symphonic music for transmission at that speed is 1 MB. Video usually requires both audio and video tracks, resulting in larger file sizes. Based on content, users may choose to devote more bandwidth to visual information (a basketball game, for example) or audio (a "talking heads" presentation) when encoding. Higher transmission speeds, of course, provide smoother video for high-action events like highlights of NYU's 1997 Women's Basketball Championship game (http://mediatv.bobst.nyu.edu/basketball.ram), which was encoded at 70 Kbps. Unfortunately, this bit rate is well beyond the capabilities of 28.8 dial-up modems to receive.

6. Server Software

Although streaming media files can be served from any Web server, there are many advantages to using a server equipped with the specialized streaming software available from the same company whose encoder and players you are using. The most obvious of these advantages is simultaneous use. The server at NYU Libraries has a 60-stream user license installed. This allows up to 60 simultaneous streams of the same media file to be available at any one time. A streaming media file on an ordinary Web server can only be served to one user at a time. This may be sufficient to serve files that may be requested only occasionally, such as oral histories and other items from special collections. Intensive applications like reserve services and distance learning require more flexibility. Another advantage to using server software is for "bandwidth protection." Streaming server software should be able to decrease the data flow in response to changing line conditions. If a server is not being used, line traffic could cause the streaming to simply stop. Most server software also allows a network administrator to control the amount of total network bandwidth to the amount a streaming application is allowed to use, in order to protect other traffic on the network.

To take advantage of another server feature called format scalability, files may be encoded for several different transmission speeds simultaneously. Files will then "sense" the capacity of the end-user's connection, and automatically send the file optimized for that bandwidth. NYU Libraries plan to use this method to provide CD-quality sound over high-speed campus networks and lower quality sound to remote users. Another very important reason to use server software is that live audio and video can only be webcast using such a server. These features put technologies like Apple's Quicktime, which does not provide server software, at a severe disadvantage (Ozer, 1998).

B. Bandwidth Basics

If there is one thing that everybody knows about bandwidth, it is that there is never enough (Miles, 1998). Digital information is delivered over the Internet at many different speeds, depending on the type of connection. There are three main ways that Internet service is delivered to computers: directly over analog telephone lines, via "broadband" (the cable that also delivers TV signals), or via intelligent networks over high-speed leased lines. If students are using America Online (AOL) or an Internet service provider (ISP) in their homes or offices, they may be limited to receiving data at speeds of 28.8 Kbps (*kilobits* per second). Newer dial-up modems are capable of operating at 56 Kbps, but not all service providers can deliver those speeds. Many telephone companies offer Integrated Service Digital Network (ISDN) speeds of up to 120 Kbps, and some are beginning to offer speeds up to 8 Mbps (*megabits* per second), but the student must pay more for these services, and support is not yet widely available from information service providers (ISPs). Cable (broadband) modems are capable of speeds up to 8 Mbps, but are not yet widely available. By late 1998, cable modem service has not yet proved to be as popular as Internet services delivered by the telephone companies (Bannan, 1998). Most corporate and academic Internet users are getting information via high-speed Ethernet connections to a campus or corporate "backbone" that supplies Internet connectivity at speeds of 1.5 Mbps. This type of connection is also known as a "T1" line. Even at these speeds, as many of us know, delivery time can slow to a crawl during certain times of the day, causing the World Wide Web to be dubbed the "World Wide Wait."

C. Standards and Interoperability

Given this broad range of network accessibility, streaming media developers are constantly striving to come up with compression solutions to optimize sound quality and minimize the time it takes to deliver it. However, true interoperability has yet to emerge. RealNetworks uses a proprietary standard, Realtime Streaming Protocol (RTSP), with which it has currently captured a large portion of the Web market because it is designed to work with established protocols like hypertext transfer protocol (HTTP) and internet protocol (IP) multicasting. For a while, Microsoft was working together with RealNetworks toward a common standard. However, Microsoft's free MediaPlayer will not play files encoded with the latest RealNetworks encoders, and RealPlayer will not play any files encoded for Microsoft's Netshow. This is one reason that some academic media centers have chosen to use Streamworks, which is based on the internationally recognized MPEG audio standard (Schneider, 1998). Files compressed using MPEG are larger than RealAudio, but because they contain more information they also provide more acceptable sound quality (Fenske, 1996). The latest Streamworks encoders also allow existing MPEG files to be reencoded at lower bit rates (transmission speed) for smaller file sizes. Streaming technologies based on the MPEG standard have another advantage: support for the MPEG layer 3 (MP3) standard, which provides very high audio quality at variable transmission speeds.

Quicktime Pro, another high-quality, incompatible proprietary streaming format, is being used by some media centers. Apple's Quicktime is the "granddaddy" of interactive multimedia technologies, which is widely used for video in educational, training, and game applications. A serious drawback to using Quicktime for Internet streaming, as mentioned previously, is its lack of support for a server (Ozer, 1998).

D. Choosing the Right Tools

Similar tools to those offered by RealNetworks are currently available free from Microsoft. Microsoft's Netshow produces equally good results, but file formats produced by Microsoft tools are not compatible with RealNetwork's RealPlayer. The same is true for Apple Quicktime Pro encoders and players.

NYU chose RealNetworks tools because they are low-cost, easy to use and support live streaming. RealNetworks formats also currently represent largest installed base of streaming media filetypes on the Web. Media centers will need to consider several factors when choosing the type of tools they will use (Ozer, 1998):

1. *Good delivery at 28.8 Kbps.* Many full-time students and most distance learners will be making connections at low speeds.
2. *Formats supported.* RealNetworks, Netshow, and Quicktime Pro can serve audio, video, and interleaved still images. Real and Netshow can also serve interleaved still images and animations created with Macromedia Flash. RealNetworks and Quicktime can also serve streaming text.
3. *Application support.* The tools chosen should be compatible with tools that may be in use locally for creating Web-based instruction (WBI) modules, such as Asymetrix Toolbook, Macromedia Authorware, Lotus Learning Space, or TopClass.
4. *Ease of use.* Existing media center staff with a minimum of experience with multimedia authoring should be able to use the encoders. TV production routines should mesh with webcasting procedures.
5. *Cost.* NetShow software is currently free, including server software. Most RealNetworks products are free or low cost; however delivering streams to more than 60 users can get pricey. If cost is important, NetShow looks like the answer, but beware the marketing strategies of Microsoft. If RealNetworks wins the current battle to become the de facto standard for low-cost media streaming, NetShow users could be stuck with resources that are not supported and do not readily convert to other formats.
6. *Firewall avoidance.* Institutions that use certain security features to protect their data may have trouble serving and receiving streaming files because of the way they use Internet protocols.
7. *Vendor consulting services.* When NYU Libraries set up its streaming server, technical advice from RealNetworks saved us a great deal of time. Media centers in institutions without much experience in these areas will want to consider this. Quicktime does not offer consulting services, whereas Microsoft does not provide the same level of expertise as RealNetworks (Ozer, 1998).

E. Higher-Priced Systems

Systems capable of delivering high-quality multimedia for marketing, communication, and training across corporate Intranets are available. MPEG-1 video, providing full-screen, full-motion video must be transmitted at 1.5 Mbps.

To deliver this quality signal requires different technologies and much higher costs. Vendors of these products include Starlight/Starcast, Cisco IP/TV, and Streamworks. Some of these applications are being considered for delivering educational material outside the corporate environment. IBM has developed a suite of services especially for higher education known as the IBM Global Campus, which integrates such products as Lotus Notes and IBM Digital Library for managing media assets.

IBM also offers the DB2 Digital Library VideoCharger2 server and player for MPEG video and audio formats. As part of an integrated media management program or used on its own as a server or player, VideoCharger can deliver low bit rate (to dial-up modems), midrange, and high bit rate (MPEG-1 video) streaming. A free player and a "transcoder" are currently offered, which will encode .WAV files (uncompressed digital sound) and .AVI (uncompressed video) into streaming MPEG. Formerly available only for high-end servers, VideoCharger can be mounted on a server running Windows NT.

F. Bandwidth Solutions

High-end systems such as those just discussed are capable of delivering high-quality audio and full-motion video across high-speed internal networks. However, media delivered over the Internet, even if it is destined for use on another high-speed network, is subject to the same bandwidth and traffic limitations as any other data file. Although a streaming server may allow several hundred separate video or audio streams to be served simultaneously, bandwidth and network traffic might prevent their reception. IP Multicasting allows one of those streams to be sent over the Internet and made available to many users at a group address. To use multicasting, special software and hardware must be installed at different points on the Internet. Unfortunately, IP Multicasting is still not widely available to educational or corporate networks (Miles, 1998). In the meantime, some companies are working on technologies called "cache streaming" or "network load balancing" that would allow ISPs like AOL or corporate or educational network administrators to receive frequently accessed media over high-speed lines or via satellite for redistribution at the local level (Vittore, 1998). At some future date, Internet2 may be available to some institutions to enhance delivery of digital media. Internet2 is a consortium of universities working together on ways to use special higher-speed networks that are being made available to researchers. Connections to these networks can be up to 100 times faster than on the regular Internet (also known as the "commodity Internet"). One Internet2 project, the Internet2 Middleware Initiative, will design a set of enhanced network services for delivering digital audio and video. Of particular interest to educators is a part of this project called the Internet2 Digital Video Initiative. Successful implementation of this project may mean that institutions with access to these higher-speed networks could view digital satellite broadcast quality television on desktop computers without any special video-processing hardware (such as a video card; Kiernan, 1998).

IV. Access to the Digital Library

An important consideration for anyone contemplating creating a collection of digital materials is access. Because the "principles of library service that apply to media services also apply to media services," the 1998 *Guidelines for Media Resources in Academic Libraries* stress that "all media resources should be cataloged in accordance with national standards and practices" (*Guidelines*, 1998). However, experienced media librarians know that there are special requirements for access to nonprint media. And access to media in "digital libraries, " many of which may be facsimiles of media also available in more traditional formats, presents special problems.

A. The MARC 856 Field

The 1998 *Guidelines* suggest that "bibliographic and holdings information about media resources be made accessible through the same retrieval mechanisms available for other library materials" (*Guidelines*, 1998). One way to do this is to use the cataloging field 856 in the MARC format to embed links to digital "versions" of existing media types. NYU Libraries has begun adding URLs to existing MARC records for sound recordings that have been digitized for use by authorized NYU users. Because the files reside on a server that is restricted to use by authorized NYU students and cannot be copied, such practices may fall within the definition of fair use. The MARC 856 field can also be used to provide access information to media that exist *only* in digital form. NYU Libraries has begun using this method to provide access to Web sites with significant audio content, such as National Public Radio. The advantage of this is obvious: Many library online public access catalogs (OPACs) are now available via a Web interface. Linking digital records to existing records (or creating new ones based on recognized cataloging standards) provides the same high-quality retrieval method as is available for other library materials, *plus direct access from remote locations.* Similar access to some audio and video items in NYU Libraries' special collections (not cataloged on an item-level basis) is provided via links in finding aids that have been marked up in standard generalized markup language (SGML) and placed on the Bobst Library Web.

B. HTML Database Scripting

There may be many media files for which item-level cataloging does not exist. Audio or video available for use in Web-based instructional packets should logically be organized in some kind of database, which would be searchable on the Web. Scripts can be written to provide access to such a database; "thumbnail" samples of the files can be linked to results to give more information to users. A shopping cart function could be added so that the locations of media files could be delivered to instructors creating course modules. Instructors at Harvard Business School can use "Videotools" (http://www.hbs.ed/it/vidtool.html) to search for video material by subject, preview it, and place a link to it in their personal "briefcase" (a directory on a local server). The file location may then be linked to a course Web page for in-class presentation or as a homework assignment. At no time has another "copy" been made or transferred, an important consideration for fair use.

C. Metafiles

NYU Libraries is using RealMedia metafiles to provide customized access to multipart recordings. Because links to RealMedia files are not made to the actual recording but only to text files that give the *location* of each recording, each track of recording can be encoded and named as a separate digital file. Using metafile syntax, tracks may then be menued to play through or to provide access to only certain clips. In addition, the listener will have a complete "playlist" of every track of a recording, and may pick and choose, just as he would with a CD or a phonograph record. If a recording has been encoded as one large file, start and stop times can be added to metafiles to select only to a specific excerpt of the file for play.

D. Commercial Media Indexing Software

Commercial software packages are available that provide complete database services or just Web-based "front-ends" for an existing database of media resources. IBM provides such a module as part of its Digital Library program. Users of Microsoft NT's IIS Web server may be interested in Microsoft's Index Server and Active Server Pages applications, which come preloaded with the latest version of Windows NT-Server software. NYU Libraries is investigating using the information contained in the RealMedia metafile, because it resides on an NT server, to build such an index.

E. Video Indexing

Library catalogs and Web-based databases will provide access to video at the item level, and descriptors may be added to refine searches. However, there is a wealth of information in even the shortest video that cannot easily be found unless the entire video is viewed and time-indexed by hand. Various indexing systems have been proposed based on indexing the *text* in videos with close captioning. (Most commercial feature films and many documentaries that have been shown on public TV are close-captioned.) A new system, Virage Videologger, uses image-analysis techniques to divide a video into indexable segments based on changes in the visual content, or "key frame." To index a video, a cataloger plays it through the software. The software stops the video at each "key frame" and queries the cataloger to input indexing information. The index can then be used to create HTML or input into existing catalogs or media asset management systems.

V. Copyright and Fair Use

Many of the projects described in this article involve digital encoding—creating a digital copy of a legally acquired copy of an existing work. Should permissions be sought and fees paid to the copyright holders, or does the special nature of the streaming media technology combined with the educational use to which it will be put define such practices as fair use?

The current U.S. copyright law contained in Chapter 17 of the U.S. Code contains four sections that have traditionally been used by librarians and educators to define fair use of copyrighted material in an educational setting. Two have generally been applied to activities in libraries (Sections 107 and 108) and two to classroom displays and distance education [Section 110 (1) and (2) and Section 112].

A. Section 107: The Four Factors

Section 107 states that:

> the fair use of a copyrighted work, including such use by reproduction in copies or phonorecords or by any other means specified by that section, for purposes such as criticism, comment, news reporting, teaching (including multiple copies for classroom use), scholarship, or research, is not an infringement of copyright. In determining whether the use made of a work in any particular case is a fair use the factors to be considered shall include—
> (1) the purpose and character of the use, including whether such use is of a commercial nature or is for nonprofit educational purposes;
> (2) the nature of the copyrighted work;
> (3) the amount and substantiality of the portion used in relation to the copyrighted work as a whole; and
> (4) the effect of the use upon the potential market for or value of the copyrighted work. (http://lcweb.loc.gov/copyright/title17/1-107.html)

Although many institutional copyright policies stress the responsibilities of educators and librarians not to violate copyright laws, others remind them that fair use is a right granted to them by the law. These rights were established expressly to limit the rights of copyright holders in order to further education and the arts. To quote Justice Sandra Day O'Connor:

> The primary objective of copyright is not to reward the labor of authors, but "[t]o promote the Progress of Science and useful Arts." To this end, copyright assures authors the right to their original expression, but encourages others to build freely upon the ideas and information conveyed by a work. This result is neither unfair nor unfortunate. It is the means by which copyright advances the progress of science and art. (quoted in ARL, 1995)

Faculty, librarians and staff should be aware of and exercise their rights in regard to fair use by basing their decisions on whether to seek permissions on these four factors (Indiana, 1997).

B. Fair Use Guidelines

Attempts have been made to provide more specific guidelines for the use of multimedia in education. Representatives attended the Conference on Fair Use (CONFU) from all levels of the educational community, libraries, publishers, and members of the broadcast, recording, and film industries. Their final report was issued in 1997. Although guidelines for fair use in many areas of library and educational activities were proposed, only the Educational Fair Use Guidelines for Multimedia developed by the Consortium of College and University Media Centers (CCUMC) were approved by a sizable number of conference members. The ALA, the ARL, and certain other educational organizations were not signatories to the guidelines, seeing them as inherently limiting Fair Use (ARL, 1997). Educational media organizations have largely supported them, welcoming guidelines that allow them to extend their services into the digital realm with confidence. Although they may seem useful, the guidelines do not have any legal standing and will not necessarily protect anyone from lawsuits.

C. Section 108: Reproduction by Libraries and Archives

This section addresses copying by libraries and has particular relevance for including streaming media in electronic reserves services.

> [I]t is not an infringement of copyright for a library or archives, or any of its employees acting within the scope of their employment, to reproduce no more than one copy or phonorecord of a work, or to distribute such copy or phonorecord, under the conditions specified by this section, if—
> (1) the reproduction or distribution is made without any purpose of direct or indirect commercial advantage;
> (2) the collections of the library or archives are (i) open to the public, or (ii) available not only to researchers affiliated with the library or archives or with the institution of which it is a part, but also to other persons doing research in a specialized field; and
> (3) the reproduction or distribution of the work includes a notice of copyright. (17 USC 108)

Although subsection (h) of this section seems to specifically exclude musical and other audiovisual works from these rights, the ARL contends that:

> without infringing copyright, nonprofit libraries and other Section 108 libraries, on behalf of their clientele, should be able:
> * to use electronic technologies to preserve copyrighted materials in their collections;
> * to provide copyrighted materials as part of electronic reserve room service;
> * to provide copyrighted materials as part of electronic interlibrary loan service; and to avoid liability, after posting appropriate copyright notices, for the unsupervised actions of their users. (ARL, 1996)

But does creating one digital facsimile of material that has been *lawfully acquired by the library and which resides only on a secure library server, and is only "viewed" and not copied or distributed in any other way* constitute a use for which permission should be sought? Or does it constitute fair use? In his description of the VARIATIONS Project at Indiana University's Music Library, Fenske notes:

> our purpose in distributing information is to support the educational mission of Indiana University in the School of Music, on the Bloomington Campus, and on other campuses of Indiana University as well as distance-based education. We do not provide free copies of content to users even in this environment. Only a couple of minutes of sound are in memory at any one time. The VARIATIONS Project never distributes a full copy of a work for use by the end user. (Fenske, 1996)

D. Section 110: Exemption of Certain Performances and Displays

This section of the copyright law is often cited to support the use of media in face-to-face classroom instruction and for using technology to extend library services to students taking part in distance education. According to the ARL, "Users, libraries, and educational institutions have a right to expect that rights of use for nonprofit education apply in face-to-face teaching and in transmittal or broadcast to remote locations where educational institutions of the future must increasingly reach their students" (ARL, 1996). According to this section of the copyright law (110, 1,2):

> the following are not infringements of copyright:
> (A) the performance or display is a regular part of the systematic instructional activities of a governmental body or a nonprofit educational institution; and
> (B) the performance or display is directly related and of material assistance to the teaching content of the transmission; and
> (C) the transmission is made primarily for—
>> (i) reception in classrooms or similar places normally devoted to instruction, or
>> (ii) reception by persons to whom the transmission is directed because their disabilities or other special circumstances prevent their attendance in classrooms or similar places normally devoted to instruction. (17 USC 110, 1,2)

E. Section 112: Ephemeral Copies

This section of the law applies directly to copies that have been made in order to provide the *means by which a musical or audiovisual work can be displayed*, and may not be infringement of copyright if:

> 1) the copy or phonorecord is retained and used solely by the transmitting organization that made it, and no further copies or phonorecords are reproduced from it; and
> 2) the copy or phonorecord is used solely for the transmitting organization's own transmissions within its local service area, or for purposes of archival preservation or security; and
> 3) unless preserved exclusively for archival purposes, the copy or phonorecord is destroyed within six months from the date the transmission program was first transmitted to the public. (17 USC 112)

F. Access Restrictions

The US Consortium for Educational Technology for University Systems (CETUS) provides several "scenarios" that can be helpful in interpreting the rights of libraries and educational institutions in these matters (CETUS, 1995). Of particular interest to streaming media services are the effect of access restriction mechanisms on fair use.

> Access restrictions can have the greatest influence on tipping the factors in favor of fair use. A problem with making text available on any network is that it can be accessible by readers far beyond the intended audience of students registered in the class. Thus, restrictions on access through passwords or other systems can enable the professor to argue that the purpose is solely to benefit the students and not to provide access for others. Restrictions can also limit the potential adverse effect on the market for the original. By limiting the range of users who may find the document, the professor can minimize or eliminate any possibility that someone will retrieve the work from the network instead of purchasing a copy. Some critics of electronic reserves have argued that the educational purpose and the minimal market effects cannot be controlled because the electronic medium allows users to print, download, and transmit copies at little cost or effort and thereby undermine the restricted access. (CETUS, 1995)

G. Copyright Issues: What's Next?

It is possible that some of these copyright questions may soon be resolved, but experience shows that many battles still lie ahead. The Digital Millenium Copyright Act passed by Congress and signed into law in October 1998 mandated further study of distance education issues. The Register of Copyrights was directed to

> provide Congress with its recommendations on how to promote distance education through digital technologies, including interactive digital networks, while maintaining an appropriate balance between the rights of copyright owners and the needs of users of copyrighted works. For the past twenty years, many of the copyright aspects of distance education have been regulated by Section 110(1) and (2) and Section 112. These provisions grant an exemption from copyright liability for in-class performance and displays of certain copyrighted works and the transmissions of those performances to outside locations. However,

these sections were written for a communications medium dominated by face-to-face teaching and one-way, closed-circuit television technology. The emergence and use of digital interactive networks has raised the issue of how to adjust copyright law to two-way, open circuitry. This study will form the factual and legal basis for Congress to organize its review of the law. (Library of Congress, 1998)

Although Guidelines for Electronic Reserves and Distance Learning were proposed as part of the 1997 Conference on Fair Use (CONFU), they failed to win support from any industry groups. Libraries must take care that they do not take any steps to restrict the full exercise of the fair use provisions of the copyright law by their staff or their users. Some recommend that libraries should not rely on guidelines in any case, but instead return to the flexibility of fair use as established by law, not as defined by guidelines (Crews, 1998).

VI. Conclusion

With the arrival of the streaming media technologies, the future looks bright for the extension of academic media services to the Web. Private sector demand for networked media to deliver training and corporate information will speed the development of products and services employing the streaming technologies. The growth of Web-based commerce also ensures that media file format standards will emerge, and low-cost browsers and players will be available to end-users. More Web users means more demand for higher-speed networks. In order to stay competitive, telephone companies, cable companies, and ISPs will have to provide higher-speed solutions. As distance learning becomes a growth industry, many universities and for-profit companies are seizing opportunities to extend their programs to these "New Learning Communities." All of these developments have direct application to programs and services in the academic media center. Although more advanced integrated solutions for producing and managing digital media will emerge, now is the time for academic library media centers to exercise leadership at their institutions. Initiating collaborative projects, forming strategic partnerships with administration, teaching faculty, academic computing centers, broadcasting services, and instructional media departments will help get such projects underway. The current tools are inexpensive and easy to use. Finally, media center professionals should carefully monitor changes in the interpretation of the copyright laws. While observing copyright laws, they should also be careful not to take actions that restrict the fair use rights of their users.

References

Ackerman, D. (1988). Streaming video over the Internet. *Connect: Academic Computing and Networking at NYU.* Fall. http://www.nyu.edu/acf/pubs/connect/fall98/NetsStreamingFall98.html.

ACRL Guidelines for Distance Learning Library Services (1998). The final version, approved July 1998. Prepared by Harvey Grover.

Association of Research Libraries (1997). *Educational Fair Use Guidelines for Multimedia: A Summary of Concerns.* http://arl.cni.org/info/frn/copy/ccumc.html.

Association of Research Libraries (1996). *Fair Use in the Electronic Age: Serving the Public Interest.* http://arl.cni.org/scomm/copyright/uses.html.

Atwood, B. (1996). Higher-quality RealAudio 3.0 debuts. *Billboard.* Sept. 28, 1996, 39.

Bannan, K. (1998). Compaq, Dell take broadband lead. *Interactive Week* **(5)** 48, 32.

Beagle, D. (1998). Asynchronous delivery support for distance learning: A strategic opportunity for libraries. *Journal of Library Services for Distance Education* **(1)**, 2. http://www.westga.edu/library/jlsde/vol1/2/Dbeagle.html.

CETUS (Consortium for Educational Technology for University Systems) (1995). *Fair Use of Copyrighted Works: A Crucial Element in Educating America.* http://www.iupui.edu/it/copyinfo/highered98.html.

CONFU (Conference on Fair Use) *Report and Guidelines.* http://www.uspto.gov/web/offices/dcom/olia/confu.

Crews, K. (1995). *Copyright and Distance Education: Lawful Uses of Protected Works* http://www.ihets.org/distance_ed/ipse/fdhandbook/copyrt.html.

Crews, K. (1993). *Copyright, Fair Use and the Challenge for Universities.* University of Chicago Press, Chicago.

Crews, K. (1998). *Fair Use: Overview and Meaning for Higher Education.* http://www.iupui.edu/it/copyinfo/highered98.html.

Fair Use Guidelines for Educational Multimedia (1996). Nonlegislative Report of the subcommittee of courts and intellectual property committee on the judiciary. U.S. House of Representatives. 1996. http://www.indiana.edu/~ccumc/mmfairuse.html.

Fenske, D. (1996). *The Variations Project at Indiana University's Music Library.* http://www.music.indiana.edu/variations/description_june97.html.

Guidelines for Audiovisual Services in Academic Libraries. (1988). Prepared by the ACRL Audiovisual Committee. http://www.ala.org/acrl/guides/avsrvs.html.

Guidelines for Media Resources in Academic Libraries: A Draft. (1998). Prepared by the ACRL Media Resources Committee. http://www.alal.org/acrl/guides/medresg.html.

Harvard Business School. *Coursetools.* http://www.hbs.edu/it/crstool.html http://www.ala.org./acrl/guides/distlrng.html.

Indiana University Policy on Fair Use of Copyrighted Works for Education and Research (1997). http://www.iupui.edu/it/copyinfo/fupolicy.html.

Kiernan, V. (1998). Project to improve Internet video could make possible webcasts of TV quality. *Chronicle of Higher Education* **45** (11), A36.

Korzeniowski, P. (1998). Streaming media practice blossoms. *Computer Reseller News* **808,** 112. (1998).

Library of Congress. Copyright Office. (1998). Promotion of Distance Education Through Digital Technologies. *U.S. Federal Register.* **(63)** 220, 63749–63750.

Lotus, RealNetworks to integrate software team up in joint licensing, distribution agreement. *Boston Globe.* Oct 12, A-13.

Miles, P. (1998). *Internet World Guide to Webcasting.* Wiley, New York.

More stuff is coming. *Telephony.* July 24, 1995, p. 43.

Nemzow, M. (1998). *Web video complete.* McGraw Hill, New York.

Ozer, J. (1998). Audio, video ready to flow. *Business Communication Review* **(28)** 9, 51–54.

Quinton, B. (1998). Netpodium's mixed metaphor. *Telephony* **(235)** 8, 60.

Rasmussem, G. (1998). *Learning Communities: Getting Started.* Maricopa Community College. http://hakatai.mcli.dist.maricopa.edu/ilc/monograph/index.html.

Schmid, W. T. (1980). *Media Center Management: A Practical Guide.* Hastings House, New York.

Schneider, K. (1998). Multimedia power: UCB's online audio recordings project. *American Libraries* April 1998, 94.

(1994). *Standards for Community, Junior and Technical College Learning Resource Programs.* Final version approved by ACRL, ALA and AECT. http://www.ala.org/guides/jrcoll.html.

(1998). Swimming in the media streams. *Presentations.* **(12)** 10, p. 8.

(1998). Technology (a special report): Pieces of the puzzle—a different course: For many people, college will no longer be a specific place or a specific time. *Wall Street Journal,* November 16, R31.

Video, CD-ROM and the Web: Motion Media and the Library of the Future. (1997). Videorecording. ALA Video/ Library Video Network. Towson, MD.

Vittore, V. (1998). Streaming the bottleneck. *Telephony* (235) **16,** 44.

William and Gayle Cook Music Library. *Listening to Reserve Recordings Online.* http://www. music.indiana.edu/variations/help/tutorial/.

William and Gayle Cook Music Library. *Locating and Listening to Sound Recordings Online.* http://www.music.indiana.edu/variations/help/iucat.

Web References

Apple Computer (http:/www.apple.com)

Association of Research Libraries (http://www.arl.org)

Asymetrix Toolbook (http://www.asymetrix.com/)

Cisco IP/TV (http://www.cisco.com/warp/public/751/advtg/iptv_pa.htm)

Consortium of College and University Media Centers (http://www.indiana.edu/~ccumc)

IBM Digital Library (http://www.software.ibm.com/is/dig-lib)

Indiana University Copyright Management Center (http://www.iupui.edu/it/copyinfo/home.html)

IP Multicast Initiative (http://www.ipmulticast.com)

Lotus Corporation (http://www.lotus.com/)

Macromedia (http://www.macromedia.com)

Microsoft (http://www.microsoft.com)

RealNetworks (http://www.real.com)

Starlight Networks (http://www.starlight.com/starlight/start.htm)

Streaming Media Services at NYU Libraries (http://mediatv.bobst.nyu.edu)

United States Code (http://www.law.cornell.edu/usc/)

United States Copyright Office (http://lcweb.loc.gov/copyright/)

White Pine Software, Inc. (http://www.whitepine.com)

Xing Technology Corporation (http://www.xingtech.com/)

The Changing Role of the Information Professional in Support of Learning and Research

Richard Biddiscombe
The University of Birmingham
Edgbaston, Birmingham, United Kingdom

I. Introduction

The role of the librarian in supporting learning and research has always been an important, although usually understated, one. It is possible to consider the traditional reference desk as an essential part in the learning process whereas more specialized information provision has made many librarians in industry and education into research assistants in all but name. Despite these well-known stereotypes, the image and status of library professionals has not been noticeably enhanced by these efforts. On an individual basis the work may be appreciated, but the sum total of individual user satisfaction over the centuries has not added up to a public perception of a dynamic profession.

Is there now a possibility that this perception is changing and, if so, what are the causes? This article argues that there are signs of change in the way information professionals are being seen in the learning and research process, particularly in higher education. It discusses whether this is a passing phenomenon or likely to be a more permanent feature. The article argues that the changes brought about by information technology will change the traditional view of librarians; it concentrates on the following five aspects:

1. The changing cultural and social structures brought about by information technology (IT).
2. The changed perception of the importance of information provision.
3. The explosion in information provision to the average citizen that presents the paradox of making more information readily available while requiring training in order to retrieve efficiently what is relevant.
4. The developing role of the information professional in the teaching and research process.

5. The growing realization amongst information workers that IT necessitates the cooperation of all those specialists involved in information provision.

As the 1998 president of the Library Association said (Usherwood, 1998):

Recent government announcements and reports on information, education and industry all place some emphasis on the potential role of our services. Moreover, managers in industry, policy makers in government, educators in universities and schools, and all kinds of workers in public and voluntary sector organisations are beginning to discover our value. (p. 258)

Although the effects of IT are changing the role of the information professional the perceptions of what constitutes the formal learning and research process are also evolving. The acquisition of knowledge is less dependent on books and other paper-based information sources and the place in which the formal acquisition of knowledge takes place is becoming less easy to define. Technology is bringing new learning opportunities to both individuals and communities in novel and unexpected ways.

With all these developments, old definitions are becoming blurred, whereas the rapidity of change makes certainty and prediction problematic. In examining the changing role of information professionals in the formal support of learning and research, this article seeks to show how technological developments, administrative changes, and information management structures are being redefined. It also seeks to show that possibilities are opening up in this area that could offer new opportunities and an improved status to those willing to take up the challenge.

II. Scope and Context

The scope of this article inevitably is based on the experience of the author as an academic librarian in the United Kingdom. It also reflects the extent of recent changes in higher education in Britain. References are made to other library sectors and to other countries, particularly the United States, but the bias inevitably is toward his own experience. It is hoped, indeed assumed, that this will have an application elsewhere and that it is not presented in such a narrow way as to limit its usefulness to others who are interested in the subject.

Although the intent of the opening paragraphs is to give some sense of continuity to the role of librarians in the context of learning and research, the purpose of the article is to show how the librarian's role is dramatically changing. The learning and research support that is now offered is no longer a minor part of the profession's *raison d'être*. On the contrary, it can be shown that it is now part of what the commercial world would call our "core business."

Technological changes are at the center of the support issues, and they cannot be ignored even though the weight of the research collections are still measured in tons rather than megabytes. In regard to nomenclature, the noble term "librarian" still implies custodianship, and this remains one important aspect of the work. It must be acknowledged, however, that the breadth of expertise that is necessary to encompass the skills of delivery, access, training, evaluation, and development requires us to talk in broader terms. Therefore, although the term "librarian" is used throughout this article, it should be regarded as coterminus with that of "information professional."

This interdependence is best evidenced in the context of converged services, to which later reference is made. The librarian's training, in the organization of knowledge, the matching of need with solution, and a positive and professional approach to the service ethic, provide essential elements that are important in the era of IT. Such skills, born in a different environment, can now be used to address the demands of the technological age, helping others to solve learning problems by offering dynamic support initiatives. These can best be provided with the help of other information professionals; learning support technicians, IT trainers, computer officers, and television and video engineers all bring essential skills to the provision of effective support for learning and research.

III. Cultural and Societal Changes Brought About by IT

The governments of the developed economies around the world have recognized the need to broaden the base of their educational systems. It is no longer sufficient to educate an elite and hope to compete successfully in international markets. On the one hand, the egalitarian nature of modern society has led to an acceptance of education as a right; on the other hand, the economic prerequisite for a successful nation has become a well-educated workforce. Higher educational standards are essential because economies are increasingly based on technological developments. As the need for manual workers diminishes, the skilled worker is in increasing demand.

The workforce must be reequipped educationally on a continuous basis in order to adapt to the technological and related changes that are taking place. An individual must be reeducated throughout his or her life. In a competitive world, the economic prizes of the twenty-first century will go to those peoples that learn to use and adapt IT in the most successful way. As

Lyotard (1984) pointed out, the information networks of today are the railways of yesterday. He wrote:

> It is widely accepted that knowledge has become the principle force of production over the last few decades; this has already had a noticeable effect on the composition of the workforce of the most highly developed countries and constitutes a major bottleneck for the developing countries . . . knowledge in the form of an informational commodity indispensable to productive power is already, and will continue to be, a major—perhaps the major—stake in the worldwide competition for power. (p. 5)

When it was elected to government in 1997, the British Labour Party made education its first priority, but it has not restricted its sights to the institutions that have traditionally provided it. In the postmodern world, it is no longer possible to confine the education to a formal and definable process. Indeed, it has been argued that the state can no longer be seen as the sole player in the process. Governments and the traditional institutions are now only one of the providers in a more diverse and unstructured global market.

Lyotard (1984, p. 4) suggests that:

> These technological transformations can be expected to have a considerable impact on knowledge. Its two principal functions—research and the transmission of acquired learning—are already feeling the effect, or will in the future. With respect to the first function genetics provides an example that is accessible to the layman; it owes its theoretical paradigm to cybernetics. Many other examples could be cited. As for the second function, it is common knowledge that the miniturization and commercialisation of machines is already changing the way in which learning is acquired, classified, made available and exploited. It is reasonable to suppose that the proliferation of information-processing machines is having and will continue to have, as much of an effect on the circulation of learning as did advancements in human circulation (transportation systems) and later, in the circulation of sounds and visual images (the media).

A. A New Social Hierarchy

The all-pervading changes brought about by IT are affecting all aspects of our social organization in subtle and insidious ways. The structural changes in the workforce and the changing values given to skills are a still-developing aspect of the change brought about by IT.

One view of the social changes that are taking place in what has been described as the knowledge-based economy is put forward by Reich (1993) and quoted by McNair (1997). Reich says that the major economies are developing three classes of worker. The top layer are "symbolic analysts," who are mobile knowledge workers; the second group runs the services that support them; and finally, there are the industrial skilled and unskilled workers, who are in a declining class.

The "symbolic analysts" are, according to Reich, concerned with three areas of skill which are in increasing demand. They solve problems and "put things together in unique ways"; they "help customers understand their needs and how those needs can be met by customised products"; and the "skills required to link problem solvers and problem identifiers."

Reich's new social structure, therefore, has this group at the top. Although it consists of the more traditional professional groups such as doctors, lawyers, engineers, and university professors, it also includes marketing strategists, information scientists, and managers. The second level includes those service professionals who provide supporting services such as restaurant managers, motor mechanics, and computing personnel.

B. A Global Context

The recent fears of global economic collapse have illustrated all too clearly the interdependence that exists between disparate economies. The competition for managers, products, and raw materials is carried out on a global scale. "Global" was once a term used to illustrate the vastness of an enterprise, but it is now possible for quite small companies to be global players through the power of the Internet. The global village becomes more of a reality every day as increasing numbers of individuals link in and log on to electronic mail and the World Wide Web.

Companies now employ global knowledge managers to ensure that their information resources are utilized in the most effective way. Worldwide intranet structures are set up to harness not only the traditional information sources, but also those intangible knowledge assets held by the employees themselves.

Education is also part of this global development, but it will not necessarily be the traditional players who win the spoils in this arena. Major companies are seeing the commercial potential of running courses and feeding the demand for lifelong learning across international boundaries.

C. Toward Lifelong Learning

Technological and economic factors are forcing a change in the culture of learning. In the past, it was possible for individuals to undertake formal learning at the start of their lives and expect such a knowledge base to fit them for a profession or trade for the next 40 years or so. Now the process is likely to be extended over a lifetime. The rate of change in the technology means that many everyday tasks will change and need to be relearned in addition to the learning process at the workplace. Technology also means that even the formal place of learning cannot be defined in the way it used to be. Distance learning is not new, but technology now makes the communication easier and offers a direct link between course provider and student.

Thompson (1997) puts forward three reasons for the development of lifelong learning:

1. In today's environment, new knowledge is being acquired at a greater rate than ever before, so that knowledge gained only a short time ago is useless and obsolete.
2. Advances in technology are accelerating at a rate unimagined 10 years ago, and the workforce is having to change constantly to keep up to date.
3. Jobs are less secure than they were. Gone are the days when a worker could stay in the same job throughout his or her working life. Now, most people will not even stay in the same type of job for very long.

The British Government's Green Paper on lifelong learning entitled *The Learning Age* (Great Britain, Department for Education and Employment, 1998) is a wide-ranging document outlining a number of new initiatives to encourage a learning culture. Among these is the proposal to double the number of adults receiving literacy and numeracy training by 2002, the expansion of higher and further education, and the launch of a University for Industry. This will act, among other things, as an agency to advise individuals on their learning needs. In addition, proposals to test how the basic skill requirements outlined in the Dearing Report (1997), a report into UK higher education, will be translated into practice. It also proposes the setting up of a Qualifications and Curriculum Authority, which will develop a framework for the structure of qualifications nationwide.

Retaining the necessary ability to train others in a continuously changing technological environment is going to be an essential aspect of the information professional's future role. As Laverna Saunders (1998, p. 45) says, "before librarians can train others . . . we must be lifelong learners. We live and work in a dynamic environment where nothing remains static . . . the learning curve is always with us." That there is an urgent need to reflect this in the structure of present courses in library and information science is referred to later.

Roddie Shepherd (1998, p. 252) suggests, among others, three opportunities for librarians in this new climate. They are as follows:

1. Inclusive learning: The focus here is on improving learning opportunities and access for people with special learning difficulties.
2. Information and learning technology/communications technology: We need to develop the fullest possible understanding of how technology can facilitate and deliver learning.
3. Professional skills and competences: Lifelong learning has profound implications for our professional education and development. We

need to work out our skills, competences and qualifications and fit in with those of other professions involved in the development and delivery of lifelong learning.

The emphasis on lifelong learning and its further encouragement creates new demands for distance learning courses and brings additional challenges to institutions and information professionals. Although the concept is not new, the information and communication technology (ICT) provides the opportunity to develop novel approaches to the experience and offers information professionals, like others, new ways to develop their learning and research support skills.

In a survey of distance learning students at the University of Birmingham, United Kingdom, Tracy Mulvaney and Elaine Lewis (1998) give the results of a student questionnaire. They found that distance learners felt themselves at a disadvantage compared with campus-based students in areas such as the provision of the following:

local book borrowing
basic training in information skills
basic knowledge of the electronic sources to which they were entitled
printed information sources
easy access to general information and enquiry services

In reminding us that distance learning is nothing new, Blaise Cronin (1998) points out that although there are presently more than three million Americans enrolled in DETC-approved courses, it is estimated that more than 100 million Americans have taken distance learning courses since the end of the nineteenth century.

It is the use of IT in the learning process that is new in this area and offers information professionals better opportunities to participate and influence the process. Some of the problems that students highlighted in the University of Birmingham survey may be easier to alleviate through the use of technology. An innovative approach to ICT by information professionals is possible so long as institutions provide the resource base and acknowledge the undoubted ability of their staff.

IV. Changing Status Patterns and the Information Professional

The sweeping changes that affect the whole of the world of work and communication have not left untouched the world of librarianship. Obvious examples such as the use of the World Wide Web in providing new information sources are often cited. The fact that the global knowledge manager for Price Waterhouse Coopers is a trained librarian shows what potential opportunities there are for information professionals if they choose to pursue them.

What is arguably more significant even than this is the subtle change in the role of the librarian, or information professional, in the quality of support they provide. Although still intermediaries in the information process, they are moving away from being the traditional facilitator in the library context but applying the same enabling skills on a broader canvas. They are using these enabling skills in novel ways to bring enquirer and information together. They are also being better recognized for these skills as the value of them becomes more evident to others. In higher education and business management, in the offices of accountants and lawyers, and in school classrooms the skills of information professionals are beginning to be valued in a new way. The acknowledgment of their dynamic role is thereby reinforcing the concept that information professionals are among those "symbolic analysts" that Reich (1993) refers to in his analysis of the new social order. Although librarianship is one of a number of the traditional professions to adopt such a role, it may well be the one that is set to most dramatically improve its social and cultural status as a consequence.

It is in this spirit that governments appear to be seeing the value of information professionals in their plans to improve the quality of their citizens' education. The traditional library and information skills were rarely acknowledged because of their unimportance economically, but now they have been transformed by IT, their value is more evident. Consequently, the stereotypical image of dowdy librarians should be set to improve.

Government initiatives are certainly repositioning public libraries in the educational process by encouraging their use in the lifelong learning process. In the United States, since the 1993 Clinton–Gore initiative, public libraries have been linking up to the Internet through a program called the National Information Infrastructure (NII). In 1996, the European Libraries Programme was established to encourage the creation of information resource centers in public libraries. In Singapore, where the Library 2000 project has been established since 1992, the aims have been better defined. Libraries are seen as a major focus of a policy designed to produce a society that utilizes IT in every aspect of daily life.

Singapore has become the model for action in other parts of the world. In the United Kingdom, after years of inaction, the incoming Blair government acknowledged the role that public libraries can make in the international race to create an IT-literate society. The policy paper entitled *New Library: The People's Network* (Great Britain, Department for Culture, Media and Sport, 1997) was followed, as mentioned earlier, by the Green Paper called *The Learning Age* (1998). These have become central pillars for current developments in the sector, with the government affirming through the Green Paper and elsewhere that it sees public libraries as an essential part of the education process.

In an interview, British Culture Secretary Chris Smith told Don Watson (1998, p. 142):

> We very much want to see public libraries as a crucial element in the National Grid for Learning. We are aiming to establish new broad-band communication linking schools, colleges, universities and public libraries in a network, so people will have the best possible access to the best educational material.

The British government has promised GBP70 million for the project: GBP20 million will be dedicated to the training of public librarians while the rest will be spent on the digitization of education and learning materials. Tony Blair even made the first official visit of a prime minister to a public library when he visited Croydon Public Library south of London. Here he sought to demonstrate the importance of public libraries' service to the government's plans for learning in the community. The promise of investment in the public library service is being fulfilled through a number of funding initiatives.

The British Government has also realized that any lifelong educational initiative must start at the school level. In today's terms, this means making school children IT literate at the earliest possible time. To achieve this, there are programs to link schools to the Internet and provide enough basic computing equipment within them. Achieving this would make no sense without investment in training teachers to use the technology.

To establish an IT-literate teaching profession, the British Government has set up the Initial Teacher Training (ITT) initiative. All teachers in the United Kingdom will be trained and expected to have IT skills by 2003. Such a goal not only requires investment in classroom teachers, but also in the reeducation of school librarians. A separate element of this vast educational program has been created to ensure that those responsible for school libraries will have special training. This should certainly concentrate on the way electronic information can be used to develop and enhance the learning support process. The fact that the training of school librarians is thus acknowledged as an essential element in the initiative is an encouraging acknowledgment of the importance now attached to the special skills of librarians in schools.

That the important role of information professionals is being so publicly acknowledged in the highest levels of government can do nothing but good for their status. The contribution that librarians can make to the development of their communities and the organization of work is beginning, however slowly, to change the way they are viewed by society in general and their clientele base in particular. There is considerable evidence in commercial and higher education sectors that major status changes are under way. In the public library sector they have yet to manifest themselves, but this reflects the relatively low level of technological investment in that area to date. This points up the obvious fact that any status change for information professionals is IT led.

V. Information Professionals and the Changing World of Higher Education

In higher education, the investment already made in the introduction of IT to the teaching, learning, and research process has resulted in a changed role for information professionals. Librarians are an increasingly essential part of the development process, and their input into decision making at the highest levels of institutional government is proof of this. At other levels too, the changes are significant. Many universities, for example, are seeing the need for converging libraries and computer services, and this brings information professionals together from different professional disciplines. Their combined skills provide a sound basis for moving forward with an integrated infrastructure and can underpin the sort of initiatives that are essential to the development of both traditional and distance learning. These hybrid professionals are pioneering a new approach to the management of information provision and are increasingly active participants in learning and research support. As a consequence, they are becoming an integral part of the academic process in a way that would never have been possible before the introduction of IT.

A. Technological Change on Campus

To address the technological changes brought about by ICT and the social revolution that is a consequence of them, higher education is having to consider its position in an increasingly global market. As Blaise Cronin (1998, p. 243) points out:

> With the rapidly changing work environment, the non-traditional population is expected to grow at an even more rapid rate. Indeed, there are projections that the workforce alone will add 20 million FTE students by the year 2000. Demand for the traditional campus experience, where education is bundled with socialisation, cultural exploration, athletics and a sense of history, will persist, though competition will intensify amongst generic providers.

Higher education (HE) is coming to terms with this new scenario. Its future suitability for which requires at its base people with an understanding of information and how to present it in the educational context. HE has begun to acknowledge the role that information professionals can play in this new environment. As suggested earlier, these individuals are becoming clearly identifiable as real partners in the educational process. This should not be seen as surprising, given the changing pace of information provision and the need for universities to adapt to the new environment.

The traditional purpose of an undergraduate degree was to give a basic grounding in a particular subject. This is no longer the case. With the rapidly changing economic and social structure, current students will benefit more from a set of useful skills that can be applied in various circumstances throughout their lives. HE can no longer consider itself as merely purveying predigested factual information, the absorption of which provides the basis for a once-for-all assessment. As Breivik (1998, p. 2) states:

> To address the definition of an educated graduate, higher education must step boldly and acknowledge the fact that the traditional literacies accepted in the past as sufficient for supporting a liberal education—those in writing, speaking and mathematical reasoning—are now insufficient. In fact, information literacy must be added to the other literacies because students must be information literate to stay up-to-date with any subject in the Information Age.

B. The Information Professional and Generic Skills

Information, its value, and the need to educate students in its use has always been advocated by librarians in higher education. This, however, has not usually been greatly valued by the academic teaching staff. Although lip service has been given to claims of equality in the past, the partnership between academic staff ("faculty" in U.S. terms) and library staff cannot be said to have been an equal one. Although librarians had always tried to convince their academic colleagues that their role in the learning process was essential, they rarely succeeded. Although librarians were convinced that teaching students how to use the library, its catalogs, and information resources was a vital part of the educational process, only a minority of academic staff appeared to be supportive.

In 1989, the American Library Association released a report from their Presidential Committee on Information Literacy. This called for more attention to be drawn to this aspect of learning. Under the heading "Opportunities to develop information literacy," the report stated:

> To any thoughtful person, it must be clear that teaching facts is a poor substitute for teaching people how to learn, i.e., giving them the skills to be able to locate, evaluate and effectively use information for any given need. What is called for is not a new information studies curriculum but, rather, a restructuring of the learning process based on the information resources available for learning and problem solving throughout people's lifetimes—to learning experiences that build a lifelong habit of library use. Such a learning process would actively involve students in the process of
>
> * knowing when they have a need for information
> * identifying information needed to address a given problem or issue
> * finding needed information and evaluating the information

- organizing information
- using the information effectively to address the problem or issue at hand

Such a restructuring of the learning process will not only enhance the critical thinking skills of students but will also empower them for lifelong learning and the effective performance of professional and civic responsibility. (American Library Association, 1987)

The need to identify the key skills with which students should be equipped by the time they have finished their full-time education is now becoming an acceptable part of the educational agenda; it was certainly an important part of the Dearing Report.

Inevitably, there are some traditionalists who worry that all these discussions are about the essential "dumbing down" of a university education and, consequently, defining these essential skills has been a controversial process. However, five skills have now been identified by the majority of educationalists as necessary elements in a modern undergraduate program. The exact terminology sometimes differs, but the Open University produced a study pack (Open University, 1998) in which the skills are outlined. They are described as follows:

- Communication: communicate clearly and concisely—write essays and give talks
- Numeracy: understand numbers and use them to convey information—make charts and graphs, work out costings, analyze statistics
- Working with others: participate in team activities
- Improving your own learning and performance: plan and organize your study, monitor and assess your own progress
- Information technology: use IT effectively—word process reports, present reports

The development of the key skills concept has caused controversy because it inevitably includes areas that traditionalists do not regard as purely academic.

Resistance to the increasing emphasis on these skills and the group work that often goes with them is outlined by Brown and Scase (1997, p. 92), who state:

Ability and performance, like the concept of meritocracy, is assumed to be judged on an individual basis. Group assessment, which could be introduced as a way of encouraging teamwork in a formal educational context, is also rejected given that it is difficult to evaluate when individual grades need to be assigned. Equally, a greater emphasis is also unlikely to gain widespread support, especially from elite schools colleges and universities. This is because the credibility attached to academic credentials remains based on the "objective" assessment of "knowledge" epitomized by the "unseen" examination paper.

Therefore, as the market for graduate labour has become flooded through the expansion of higher education, employers will increasingly target the elite "old universities" on the grounds that they have the best intellectual talent due to the assumption that because access is extremely competitive, only the best will get in.

Although these views have merit, they can overestimate the values that have been attained from the existing system. There is a danger that it is an elitist rather than a rational argument. In the United Kingdom, the Dearing Report (1997), in making recommendations for the future development of higher education, illustrated the need to accept a changed approach to learning and teaching. By default, his proposals strengthened the role of the information professional, for who else on campus can offer expertise in some of these vital areas?

Practical experience has shown that even the "elite universities" cannot totally ignore the need to identify and enhance the skills base of their students. Some mechanism for teasing out the skills embedded in existing courses is necessary so that students can identify, particularly at the job interview stage, the skills they have acquired during their university career. The Personal Academic Development for Students in Higher Education (PADSHE) scheme, in which students are encouraged to keep a personal development file of their academic progress, may well point to a future option here.

Whatever the approach by an individual university, information professionals can provide the necessary support and training in a number of the generic skills areas that have been identified. The approach can be either through an integral part of the educational process or as "bolt-on" options, although the former approach is much preferred. If integration is chosen, then students realize that some academic importance is attached to the process because the skills must be assessed. In such circumstances, there is obviously an increasingly central academic role for information professionals. This is necessary not only in developing new approaches to course content, but also in planning for hardware and software provision and material support. All of these are essential to the successful course provision and assessment process.

As the concept of core skills in the curriculum is pursued, the participation of information professionals becomes ever more embedded in the learning process. This enhanced role can only be regarded as central to the whole process and significant changes to the status and focus of the information professional in higher education should follow.

C. Training the Teacher

The need for information and related skills does not cease once the undergraduate career is over, as we have seen in the concept of lifelong learning. The input of information professionals should not, therefore, be seen as being confined to the student body. Academic staff will require regular updates about IT and information resources in their areas. Although this is often done on an *ad hoc* basis already, it is not usually seen as important by the majority of them and is rarely part of any compulsory personal development process. Nevertheless, it should be regarded as essential. Academic teaching staff must keep themselves aware of new developments in their field, especially, for example, in the area of database provision.

Whereas ensuring that existing academic teaching staff are retrained is still a problem that must be solved, the training of new teachers in HE is being addressed in the United Kingdom. Following the recommendation made in the Dearing Report (1997), a new Institute of Learning and Teaching (ILT) in HE is to be established in the academic year 1999–2000. Its function will be to accredit professional achievement in the management of learning and teaching, commissioning research and development work into learning and teaching practices, and stimulating and co-ordinating the development of innovative learning materials. It is also intended that the ILT will take a leading role in assisting institutions to exploit the potential of communications and information technology for learning and teaching to ensure that academic teachers have some teaching qualification.

Under Clive Booth (1998), a committee was set up by the Committee of Vice Chancellors and Principles to consult on the matter and a report was produced that set out the terms of reference of this new body. The courses that new entrants will undertake, and it will not be retrospective at the outset, will inevitably include various aspects of IT. Information professionals are already involved in course development exercises and the presentation of relevant modules in preparation for the new qualification. As Richard Downing (1998, p. 311) said:

> Whatever the impact of Dearing may be in terms of government support for the implementa-
> tion of its recommendations there remains at least an authoritative recognition of the role
> that librarians have in promotion of teaching and learning and a recognition to formalise
> and develop the role.

In playing a more visible role, the information professional should have a more firmly acknowledged place in the educational process. Obtaining a formal qualification as a teacher in HE under the new arrangements would help this to happen. At present, because of the way the outcomes will have to be achieved, it will not be possible for information professionals to gain the certificate. The "authoritative recognition" referred to by Downing has yet to become anything more. Although information professionals will have an input to courses run in individual universities, and despite the fact that this may also entail the assessment of academic staff, they will not as yet to able to achieve the qualification themselves. The active involvement of information professionals in the learning process, so effectively demonstrated here, should be cited as a reason for trying to ensure that this view does not continue to prevail. Although an associate status may be awarded, Clive Booth's (1998) expressed view that "all staff in the learning and teaching process" can be regarded as teachers should be taken as the real basis for progress.

Such a short-sighted decision by the ILT would not reflect the general trend. The participation of information professionals is a fact, and it is bound to continue in the future. As Breivik (1998, p. 92) states:

> Information literacy is a goal for all people and resource-based learning is a people-orientated process. For the goal to be effectively addressed, students, faculty and librarians, along with other information specialists, must come together in a dynamic partnering.

D. Faculty Acceptance of the Learning Support Role

In an age where competition has become a part of the educational world, it is essential for all groups to work together. The reliance on strong and reliable learning and research support has become more necessary than ever. Although at the micro level academic staff are having to come to terms with closer cooperation with learning support personnel, at a macro level universities have had to become aware of the possibility of nontraditional players involving themselves in educational provision. A number of possible players have been identified as already waiting to move into the educational market: the BBC, telephone companies, and international multimedia corporations are all possible candidates. These organizations are increasingly interested in using their extensive visual library materials and their experience of IT in selling distance learning courses in the marketplace.

It is in the context of such developments that universities need to see their IT provision. Their concern must not only be for the quality and extensiveness of hardware provision for students, it must concern itself also with the ways in which this equipment can deliver a better learning interface so that students can obtain a higher quality of education. This begs a number of questions about the quality of teaching in the context of IT use. It also questions the importance attached by an institution to the quality of their teaching rather than just their research.

As information technology has become an integral part of the academic process, the need to incorporate IT skills and adapt IT to the learning process has become as irresistible as it has become inevitable. It is now a dynamic process involving more than just information professionals. The pressures on all academic staff to improve their research performance at a time of increasing numbers of students and reduced levels of resource makes further reliance on information professionals inevitable. In this climate, librarians and other related professionals should be better able to demonstrate that the support they can offer and the expertise they have can help provide a better learning experience for students and staff. The changes should, therefore, create a more equal partnership in the sector between academic staff and information professionals. This will lead to their involvement in areas of curriculum development and student assessment in a way not seen to any great extent before.

Although computing staff are usually better able to cope with the technology than the average academic, they are not often good communicators. Librarians, however, usually have reasonable communication skills and are able to understand how the technology can be used to further the learning experience. Librarians and computer officers together have begun to impress many of their academic colleagues with the possibilities being offered. They have also, in many cases, begun to realize that the support role offered by these professionals can release them for improving their teaching and raising their research profile.

From those academics who have been less impressed, the cry that used to go up of "Anyone can run a library" has changed to "Librarians are taking over the world!" However, their ability to explain the changing dynamics of information provision, present information in an accessible way, and willingly broaden IT access has enhanced the reputation of information professionals in HE.

McNair (1997, p. 30) applies Reich's (1993) theory about the "symbolic analyst" approach to the traditional notions of universities, and says it has "clear implications for higher education." He goes on to say:

> Some of the knowledge which the consultant sells is academic in the traditional sense— proportional knowledge of how to analyse situations and contexts and skills of questioning, listening, interpreting, and a body of experimental knowledge developed over time in many contexts. This knowledge is no less real than the academic, and is as subject to debate and theorising. It is made, however, outside the academy, and starts not from academic theory, but from problem solving. (p. 30)

It is this intermediary problem-solving role that is becoming the crucial element in the position and status of information professionals in the HE sector. It has been in the converged services where computing and library services formally come together that such roles are particularly significant and, perhaps, where most progress has been made in effective learning support. It is here also that the very qualities demanded of information professionals in the context of the academic community are no less needed in the relationships between the differently qualified professionals in a hybrid team. The open problem-solving approach is equally necessary for effective teamwork in the learning support environment.

In essence then, it can be said that it is no longer possible to regard the skills of the information professional as peripheral in the educational process.

They are no longer optional, but key elements in the process of lifelong learning.

The important thing to note here is not that librarians are being recognized as central players in the learning process because they have suddenly been welcomed in by traditionalists like long-lost prodigal sons. It is, rather, because the learning and teaching axis is changing that the new relationship has developed. As Mendrinos (1994, p. 12) says:

> Resource-based facilities including information technology provide alternative learning environments to the classroom. The teacher and the instructional librarian are the guides and facilitators, but the student is in charge of the learning, making use of available resources to solve the problem. The resource-based learning environment can also provide co-operative learning experiences, generating feedback from peers and developing social knowledge along with logical knowledge. Co-operative learning among two or three students has been shown to increase self-worth, self-esteem and self-actualization.
>
> Resource-based learning and high technology foster a non-directive teaching style in which the student controls learning within the framework of the curriculum. The student chooses the colour from the palette that reflects the multitude of resources available, thinking, creating, and often exceeding the confining expectations of the teacher.

VI. The Role of the Information Professional in Learning and Research Support in Higher Education

Having outlined the changes that are taking place in the HE sector, it is now possible to identify the changing support areas in which the information professional should have an increasingly important role to play. Just as the technology has changed traditional techniques elsewhere in the workplace, so it is with librarianship. Technology has released the individual professional from the chores that were previously part of the work profile. In the area of collection management, cataloging and classification have become clerical operations. In reader services, the production of current awareness services is done automatically by computers, whereas enquiry and reference services are carried out by para-professional staff (Biddiscombe, 1996).

So, although the traditional education process has always had librarians as an essential element, the growth of IT has liberated them from basic tasks and now offers new opportunities to use their skills in more challenging ways. Through the process of IT, the value of information has increased in direct relationship to its availability and accessibility. As a commodity in the educational process, information is no longer confined to the printed page or the need to undertake laborious searches of abstracts and indexes. Less polluted by the dust of books, librarians have been liberated to offer a new intermediary role in the global village.

In terms of learning and research support, their function is therefore a vital economic necessity for all progressive economies. Helping to unlock the doors of knowledge and facilitate access to user communities is an increasingly recognized role for the librarian of the late twentieth century. The inclusion of information managers into Reich's premier group of the new social structure shows the significance of the development. Their role is to do the following:

> . . . solve, identify, and broker problems by manipulating symbols. They simplify realist into abstract images that can be rearranged, juggled, experimented with, communicated to other specialists and then, eventually, transformed back into reality. The manipulations are done with analytic tools sharpened by experience. (Reich 1993, p. 178)

In practical ways, this changed role is best seen in the integration of selected information professionals into decisive new positions in the educational structures even of relatively conservative institutions. Some converged services have separated their traditional provision from academic support areas and produced information managers who have a significant part to play in the academic process. In doing so, it can be said that a new breed of information professional has been emerging. They have a newer focus for development centered on supporting learning and research in a more proactive and focused way, usually centered on the use of IT. These services are increasingly sought after, bringing as they do added value elements to information provision in all its aspects.

A. Learning Support

There are four areas in which information professionals have increasingly vital parts to play.

1. Course Management

Although this is certainly an area in which academic staff will maintain their dominant role, they should be more willing to acknowledge the specialist skills of the information professionals with whom they work. If skill modules are to be embedded in courses, the support staff delivering them should logically be involved in the intellectual development of such a course. So often, this is not the case. It was Dearing's (1997) view that lecturers should become course managers rather than just teachers. If this were to be better accepted among academic teaching staff, then a more fruitful partnership could develop.

Developing a course of study, deciding on research programs, or allocating undergraduate projects are all areas that need to remain at the center of the academic teaching staffs' responsibilities. However, it should now be less of an exclusive element because information professionals have a constructive part to play in these aspects of the educational process. In fact, for the exploitation of the databases and web interfaces that are now so often an essential aspect of course and research development, the involvement of information professionals is essential if a sound approach is to be made in these areas. This is ever more so given the emergence of the independent learner who is taught through project work and encouraged to develop individual researching skills.

The integration of information skills courses into the formal curriculum is increasingly becoming an accepted practice, although there is still some way to go before it becomes commonplace. Adalian *et al.* (1997) report on interesting developments in the California State Polytechnic at San Luis Obispo, where simple information skills courses are being broadened into information modules developed around a subject core. An "Information Competence Class Syllabus" runs for a semester.

It is reported that, although some changes in the organization of the course were now planned, in the light of the experience gained so far:

> the course content will remain the same, focused on teaching students skills that form the basis of an information literate person. Course outcomes will continue to include the ability of students to understand the research process; be aware of the ethical and social issues related to information technology, and be able to communicate this information using tools that visually enhance verbal presentations. (Adalian *et al.*, 1997, p. 21)

The development of distance learning options will underline the need to call on the skills of the information professional. Their early involvement, therefore, in important academic decisions is becoming ever more essential for the success of the curriculum. Without the effective integration of information skills, students will experience unsatisfactory learning experiences, for they will come to see these as basic aspects of the learning process. This can be expensive for a university, both in terms of its academic reputation and consequently its recruitment and financial success.

2. Quality Assessment

In the United Kingdom HE sector, the emphasis on maintaining and improving the quality of the educational process has been evident since the late 1980s or so. Driven by the policies of central government, a number of successive schemes have been developed. For librarians, these schemes, in which academic courses on particular subjects in each university are scrutinized by independent assessors, have been an important element in raising their profile within the academic community. They have not only helped to underline the information professional's role among their academic colleagues in the learning process, they have also helped to ensure that there is an improvement in the quality of the learning resource provision itself.

The element of quality inspection covering learning resources has remained in the formal assessment process despite fears that it would be subsumed or diluted; the most recent version of this process still maintains the link. The new Quality Assurance Agency (QAA) in the United Kingdom will undertake assessments of the quality of learning support given by the library and computing centers as part of the general process of expanding quality in teaching. It will seek proof that there is a constructive relationship between these services and the academic departments. The independently appointed assessors will continue to be able to award points and make recommendations for improvements in the learning support process.

These assessment visitations have been in place for some years, with all subject areas being assessed in rotation. Before each visit by assessors, the appropriate academic teaching staff work closely with the subject-based information professionals to ensure that their learning support activities are presented in the best light possible. The relationship between a subject, its information resources, and the integration of information skills into course modules are all considered as the deadline of the visitation approaches. Such consultation processes are essential in the preparation of learning support materials and programs prior to an assessment visitation, the final outcome of which gives a seal of approval or otherwise to the role of a subject department in the academic institution. The compulsory status given to learning support has therefore ensured that consultation between academic teaching staff and information professionals takes place. They are seen as equal partners in the process. Although the gains in practical learning support for the students may not always be maintained after the visitation, the gains for information professionals are cumulative. At the departmental level, new bonds of respect do emerge, whereas at an institutional level, where the preparation for quality inspections are now an established part of the scene, cooperation with information professionals is essential.

3. IT Support Planning

The practical resource issues for learning support are becoming ever more complex. In the broadest sense, these include providing library materials, ensuring access to information databases, establishing adequate numbers of computer workplaces, and providing appropriate software support.

To ensure that there is adequate provision of library materials for particular courses, it is essential for academic staff to consult the relevant subject librarians at the course approval stage. This will only be possible in practice if the university has enforceable rules to make sure this happens. Sound academic decisions on the establishment of a new course can only be made after there have been assurances that it is to be academically viable in learning support terms. Although this is still something of a novel approach to the management of learning resources, the rationale is hard to deny. The advice of information professionals can be essential, either in suggesting approval or in making recommendations on which areas of the collections need to be improved.

In many converged services, the traditional role of the librarian has been extended to include responsibility for the provision and management of campus IT. Equally in such services it may be the computer personnel who take the management responsibility over librarians. Where these management structures are in place, the information professional's role in the support of both learning and research can be considerable. As a consequence, many ill-informed decisions can be avoided because of the coordination of learning resources of all kinds in the hands of one team. Such integration helps to formally reinforce the need for active consideration to be given to the planning for, and interoperability of, such resources. Consequentially, in such circumstances there is a greater involvement by information professionals in the decision-making process of the academic institution at every level.

4. IT Skill Provision and Enhancement

An acknowledged part of the learning support activity in HE institutions has been what used to be termed "user-education." This often only amounted to a brief introduction to library services, or guidance on the use of the catalog at the start of a student's academic career. The value of such sessions was often questionable and not usually taken as a real enhancement of the learning process by either students or academic staff. This is no reflection on the dedication or sincerity of the librarians concerned, but rather illustrates the problem that existed in convincing students that it was important to search abstracts and indexes manually for those vital references that they needed. Accessing databases and the World Wide Web has made the process of literature searching more productive and interesting, while the numbers of students needing to undertake such work has increased through the development of project-based curricula activities.

The need to master the use of IT as part of a core skills activity on which students may well be assessed has helped to focus the minds of students and academic staff on the importance of these skills. Breivik (1998) describes a number of examples in the United States where "moving beyond the concept of traditional library/bibliographic instruction to integrating information resources and technology into the curriculum" is taking place. She also goes on to give international examples from countries such as Australia, South Africa, and China.

The outcome for all the examples she gives is to help each participant to become an information-literate person, one who "engages in independent, self-directed learning" according to the program developed by Griffith University in Queensland, Australia. Breivik also reproduces a draft of Standards for Students Learning (1996), a work produced by the American Association of School Librarians and the Association for Educational Communications and Technology.

It is surely necessary for all information professionals in this area to consider the standards that they wish to achieve and produce verifiable outcomes as part of the educational process. If the role of the information professional in the formal learning structures of an institution is to be taken seriously—and not overtaken by others less qualified in these areas—some written supporting evidence should be created.

B. Research Support

Learning is the gathering and assimilation of information and, as we have seen, a legitimate province for the skills of information professionals. Research can be described as the analysis and reworking of information into a new understanding, and librarians have a clear role here. There are thousands of theses and learned monographs in which researchers have acknowledged the invaluable help and advice of librarians. In addition, of course, the collections for which librarians are the custodians have played a vital role in the research process. From Alexandria onwards, the keeping of the books has been a vital part of the research process. Such work, both personal and institutional, is rarely acknowledged in any high profile way, but perhaps this is changing, for to this age-old role, four additional roles have been added:

1. Research training.

Research training covers the active input that librarians now have in the training of researchers in identifying, using, and evaluating the resources most important to them. This refers inevitably, but not exclusively, to the training in IT that has been discussed elsewhere. The proper understanding of IT and information skills at an early stage of an undergraduate career allows students to develop good research skills. Used for project work in the first instance they can, with further help, be applied to the formal research process.

This further help is now being offered at the start of a student's PhD program when a formal qualification on research methodology in a subject may well be awarded. This has been part of the American HE process for some time, but in the United Kingdom it is relatively new.

From the outset, librarians in the United Kingdom have provided in many institutions the basic elements in these new Master of Research courses.

By concentrating on the specialist subject elements, it is possible to provide insights and guidance on the best way to search the literature.

2. Research assessment exercises.

Just as there is an exercise in teaching quality assessment in the British higher educational system there is also an equivalent process in the research area. The need for academic research staff to quote their publications from refereed journals over a period of years often means that library staff are involved in the process of advising, helping, and collating references. Benefiting from their skills and advice, faculty members are often able to provide a better assessment, especially when citation counts are involved.

3. Identifying research collections.

Improved technology allows there to be a better dissemination of information about research collections. IT can help in providing better information about the collections in particular libraries and also enable researchers at a distance to become aware of what is located where. Indeed, there is something of an obligation on the part of librarians to provide as much information as possible on their local research collections for the benefit of everyone. The defining of a research collection and the devising of equitable ways in which libraries can be compensated for providing access to researchers from outside the institution is the subject of a research project now under way in the United Kingdom.

4. Accessibility of research collections.

The use of union catalogs, especially in a national context, and Z39.50 technology to locate collections is developing fast. Providing access to digitized material on the Web is being undertaken in a number of areas. The details of individual libraries' opening hours through Web sites is also an aid for researchers, but the availability of a large, subject-based Web index has yet to be created; its value would be considerable.

The creation of effective data in which the quality of research collections can be identified is now possible through applying metadata protocols such as the Dublin Core. Any progress depends, however, on identifying locally what can be regarded as a research collection. The academic libraries in Scotland have worked on their Conspectus projects over a number of years so that it is now possible for researchers to identify appropriate collections for their needs. The Research Libraries Group has also drawn up useful working criteria for assessing the quality and depth of collections.

C. The Web and Learning and Research Support

There can be no doubting the importance of the Web, particularly in the potential it offers for real innovation in the learning process. Although many academic staff have seen the advantages for themselves and begun to develop sites for their own interaction with their students, most academics have not. The opportunities here for information professionals are considerable, and many libraries and converged services are leading the way on their campuses.

There are four main areas in which the Web can be used to enhance learning and research support.

1. Information Gateways

Since the early 1990s, a number of important Web gateways have been set up. In the United Kingdom, some of the most important ones were created under the Elib (electronic libraries) project. These include EVIL for engineering information and SOSIG, for social sciences. Many others exist nationally, internationally, and on a local basis. New ones are being encouraged to set up in the United Kingdom through central competitive funding initiatives.

Subject gateways help to organize the Web and make it easier for users to find their way around. Many of them use the skills of local librarians to ensure that they are kept up to date, so they provide excellent examples of cooperative learning support sites used on a global basis.

2. Webmasters

Webmasters in general are those people "tasked with making the web work and with staying on top of the fast-paced changes in what it can do" (Pardue, 1998, p. 10). Exactly what responsibilities a webmaster has depends on the particular university. In smaller institutions one person may be responsible for an institution's official web site, but usually a more federal approach is taken. Specialist individuals, responsible for different discrete areas of individual sites, reflect the way that most sites are now run. There is, however, usually one webmaster who coordinates and edits the work of the many other contributors, rather like heading up the editorial board of a printed publication. This webmaster may be ultimately responsible for the appearance, organization, and editing of a site. He or she probably has ultimate responsibility for policy on email response and monitors the use made of the site, ensuring that it remains dynamic, up to date, and true to its mission.

Information professionals often act as webmasters for parts of an academic web site. They may well provide help and training for those academic staff that wish to maintain and run their own sites. Their expertise can help ensure that any related databases are properly managed and defined structures allow the user to navigate effectively around the site.

3. Information Resources Pages

The setting up of in-house resource pages to support information skills programs has become a normal part of the librarian's armory of learning support devices. The sites are not designed to duplicate what is already available in the growing number of information gateways. What they do is augment these with sites of particular relevance to local courses. Such sites can provide good examples of active cooperation between librarians and academic staff. They can be used in the information skills sessions run by information professionals and, hopefully, can be integrated into the module structure of university courses.

Instruction sessions on teaching how to use the Web effectively should also instruct students how to use it critically.

> When teaching the Web to students, I include a section on evaluation. I pattern my Web evaluation lecture like a librarian who evaluates print items for inclusion into a library collection. I base web evaluation on five criteria that I use for print evaluation: accuracy, authority, objectivity, currency and coverage. To develop the model I had to first acknowledge that most students today tend to conduct research with speed rather than accuracy and rarely evaluate resources. So the criteria I present must be digestible and almost transparent to the student. In other words the student must be trained to evaluate a web document like second nature. (Kapoun, 1998, p. 522)

D. Learning Support Partnerships

This concept is being developed at the University of Birmingham. Information professionals set up a partnership with academic staff in identifiable subject areas, such as an academic school or department, and work jointly on learning support projects. Essentially, these are intended to develop the use of IT applications. In identifying possible projects, it is intended to kick-start the process so that academic staff can then carry the project forward themselves.

Essential to such arrangements is a formal agreement with the head of school so that there is an official understanding that academic resources can be allocated to the partnership. In this way, it is intended to use a growing number of projects as examples to encourage other, less venturesome academics to pursue their own projects.

These partnerships illustrate the advantages that can accrue from a converged service environment. For example, while the computer staff set up and administer the Web server, the learning support specialists design the Web site and may also train the individual academic staff in the use of appropriate packages. Through such training the academic staff member is empowered to further develop his or her project, while the librarian in the team helps to train the lecturer's students on the use of the Web and maintains the Web pages that provide a subject gateway for their learning.

E. Study Skills

Study skills should be seen as an essential aspect of learning support in the modern university environment. Information professionals are, of course, not the only people who have a contribution to make to the process. They are, however, by default often the ones who can best organize an electronic structure for providing help and information, guidance, and practical examples. This is most notably evident in managing effective Web sites and the use of discussion lists.

Using their skills it is possible for information professionals to adapt print-based publications for the Web, or load commercial packages and make them available to the student body. Creating such an interface can offer student skills guidance on a 24-hour-a-day basis and can be made available to distance learning students.

Information professionals also have useful advice and guidance to offer students on improving their learning, organization, and writing skills. Among the topics that can be covered are the citing of references, information on copyright and plagiarism, bibliographical management skills, literature searching, and the use of referencing techniques. In addition, such a Web site is a good place to link library publications and any support materials from information skills sessions so that they can be readily available for consultation. Many of these aspects of study skills have been offered on an individual basis by information professionals over the years, but often not with any view of coordinating them on a grander scale. Study skills can therefore be regarded as another area on which information professionals can fairly claim to be actively supporting the learning process.

VII. The Learning Support Approach in the Public Library Sector

Although this article has been concerned with learning support in the HE sector for the most part, it is in the public library sector that the most interesting and exciting developments are likely to take place in the beginning of the twenty-first century. Long ignored by governments, the public library sector has been seen in some parts of the world (notably the United Kingdom) as, at best, an irrelevance, and at worst, a drain on public funds. In the United Kingdom, the inability of public librarians, with notable exceptions, to clearly identify their mission has not helped this situation. A lack of clear direction led to a near moribund and decaying service. The impact of IT in public libraries has been slow to be felt in the United Kingdom because the necessary investment has not been forthcoming.

As we have already seen, there is now an economic need for governments to retrain their peoples and encourage citizens to reach their full educational potential. Since the early 1990s, a number of countries have highlighted public libraries as channels to help bring about this transformation. They have found that there is no other public agency that can undertake such a task. The trust that has been built up in the service over the years helps to ensure that citizens see public libraries as nonthreatening and user-friendly.

Information is, of course, the core business for public and other libraries, and the process of linking up this sector to IT networks will help to unlock their real potential. The networking of the individual libraries is one part of the equation; training of the library staff and convincing them of the importance of the project is another.

Once the investment in these two aspects is achieved, the training and support of the community can begin. Learning support will become an increasingly central part of the librarian's role in public libraries, just as it has been elsewhere. There will be a research role also, for many important special collections will become more widely available as the technology is used increasingly effectively.

The lessons learned over the years by their academic counterparts and the services offered by them to their clients in support of this approach can be copied for the benefit of the community at large. It should mean that the educational purpose for which the public library movement was founded in the middle of the nineteenth century will be revived through the PC and the Network.

VIII. Questions for the Information Profession

The changing nature of the work of the information professional has been indicated throughout this brief outline of current changes. The effects have already been quite profound in some areas—for instance, where the convergence of libraries and computer services has seen new approaches to the management of information.

The pace of change has revolutionized the information profession, transforming the approach to traditional services but opening up new possibilities for professional development while adding value to new services. It is among these opportunities that the growing importance of the information professional's role in learning and research support can be found.

In such a changing environment, there is something reassuring for the information professional in seeing the need for learning support stretching into the future. The training that is proving essential in every user community seems set to continue on a number of levels well into the next millennium. The information professional has a role to play in this, both in the formal and informal sense.

As suggested earlier, if this role is to be adopted seriously, then information professionals must have continuous training; lifelong learning will become more essential to them than to many others. Courses presently run by library schools rarely provide the "toolkit" necessary for librarians to adapt easily when called upon to do so. Penney Garrod (1998, p. 199) says,

> Library Schools may also have to consider offering short courses aimed at updating professional skills. This would ensure that the vital "information" aspect is not neglected as is often the case with in-house courses provided by computer services. Training and skills need to be planted in the information framework.

There is a diversity of knowledge and skills that cannot be restricted to a "library school" approach, and some broader arrangement will need to be developed. "The schools need, above all to accelerate their ability to grasp change, and in particular to release the innovative talents and energy of their staff to develop new programmes rapidly and regularly" (Johnson, 1998, p. 158).

It is necessary to consider the way that the present professional bodies are organized. Bob Usherwood (1998, p. 258), in discussing the possible merger in the United Kingdom of the Library Association with the Institute for Information Scientists, said, "All this points to the need for a strong professional coalition that promotes the values of accuracy, honesty, openness, and ethics in the communication of information and ideas." It is also necessary to add that the promotion of effective technical expertise is also a vital ingredient. What has to be considered in the medium term is the creation of a unified professional organization that will represent and promote the work of the diverse and overlapping group of individuals called "information professionals." Although it would not be easy to represent all the strands of such a disparate group, some federal coming together under an overarching body could be the first step to recognizing the common interests that are drawing previously separate skills together. Existing bodies will find themselves failing an increasing percentage of their potential constituency if these issues are not faced in the medium term.

Again, the process begs the question about how the information professional can be defined and organized. It also comes full circle in raising the problem of the education of the information professional in a formal sense.

IX. Summary

Computer officers, librarians, and others are beginning to acknowledge that they are part of the same process and are exploring hybrid management and structures, collectively calling themselves "information professionals." It is evident, I believe, that others outside this skilled group are beginning to recognize this too, although there is still a need to press the case in a forceful and united manner.

In HE, for example, the battle has still to be completely won.

> Library and university administrators, teaching faculty and librarians should recognise the impact of an information-based society and assume a greater leadership role in encouraging librarians to teach library skills, research strategies, and methodologies (information literacy) for lifelong learning. Librarians should form partnerships with classroom faculty and be encouraged to teach both subject content courses and research methodology courses. Learning how to identify, locate, access, and evaluate information using the latest technology and critical thinking is crucial to scholarly enquiry. Librarians are experts in this role and must ensure it is taught and fully integrated into every academic course. Librarians should be encouraged to take such work in all settings and libraries and librarians should be reimbursed and rewarded for this increasingly important responsibility. (Winner, 1998, p. 28)

As Adalian and others (1997, p. 21) put it:

> From the first library Internet course taught in the 23-campus California State University system in 1991, the Cal Poly Library has come a long way. Yet, our educational and instructional outreach mission has remained unchanged—to assist computer literate students to become information competent users of information in a global marketplace with an ethnically and economically diverse workforce; to meet the needs of the workplace that requires students to have information technology and evaluation skills; and to solidify the library as a campus leader in creative teaching and multimedia curriculum development.

The Chief Executive of the Library Association has echoed that statement. In reviewing the present position of the profession, he said (Shimmon, 1998, p. 25):

> We have argued that librarians are "can-do" people, forging alliances with others to provide innovative and effective services in periods of severe financial restraint. Here is our opportunity to take advantage of the higher political profile of libraries nationally to ensure that they also move centre stage on local agendas.

The changing information scene brings both promise and threat to the profession, and there will be a fight to gain the right to be the principle provider of such an approach. The battle will be hard, and will need continuous ingenuity and tireless energy to ensure that information professionals continue to develop the role for which they are so well fitted. What seems to be true at the present time is that the information profession has at least won the right to be considered a serious player in the process.

References

Adalian, T., *et al.* (1997). The student-centred electronic teaching library: A new model for learning. *Reference Services Review*. Fall/Winter, 11–22.

American Library Association. (1987). Presidential Committee on Information Literacy. *Final report*. American Library Association, Chicago.

Biddiscombe, R. (1996). The changing role of the reference librarian. In *The End-User Revolution: CD-ROM, the Internet and the Changing Role of the Information Professional* (R. Biddiscombe, ed.), pp. 79–95. Library Association Publishing, London.

Booth, C. (Chair). (1998). Accreditation and teaching in higher education: A consultation paper. CVCP, London. (http://www.cvcp.ac.uk/consult.html).

Breivik, P. S. (1998). *Student Learning in the Information Age.* Oryx Press, Phoenix, Arizona.

Brown, P., and Scase, R. (1997). Universities and employers: Rhetoric and reality. In: *The Postmodern University?: Contested Visions of Higher Education in Society* (A. Smith and F. Webster, eds.). Society for Research into Higher Education and Open University Press, Buckingham.

Cronin, B. (1998). The electronic academy revisited. *Aslib Proceedings* **50**(9), 241–254.

Dearing, Sir R. (Chair). (1997). *Higher Education in the Learning Society.* National Committee of Inquiry into Higher Education. HMSO, London.

Downing, R. (1998). Capturing the curriculum. *Library Association Record* **100**(6), 310–311.

Garrod, P. (1998). Skills to keep pace in the IT age. *Library Association Record* **100**(4), 199.

Great Britain. Department for Culture, Media and Sport. *"New Library: The People's Network" The Government's Response* (1997). Stationery Office, London. (Cm 3887)

Great Britain. Department for Education and Employment. *The Learning Age: A Renaissance for a New Britain.* (1998). Stationery Office, London. (Cm 3790)

Johnson, I. M. (1998). Challenges in developing professionals for the 'information society.' *Library Review* **47**(3), 152–159.

Kapoun, J. (1998). Teaching undergrads Web evaluation: A guide for library instruction. *College & Research Library News,* July/August, 522–523.

Lyotard, J.-F. (1984). *The Postmodern Condition: A Report on Knowledge.* Manchester University Press, Manchester. (Theory and History of Literature, Volume 10.)

McNair, S. (1997). Is there a crisis? Does it matter? In *The End of Knowledge in Higher Education* (R. Barnett and A. Griffin, eds.), pp. 27–38. Cassell, London.

Mendrinos, R. (1994). *Building Information Literacy Using High Technology: A Guide for Schools and Libraries.* Libraries Unlimited, Englewood, Colorado.

Mulvaney, T., and Lewis, E. (1998). Analysis of library services for distance learning students at the University of Birmingham. *Education Libraries Journal* **41**(1), 29–34.

Open University and University of Nottingham. (1998). *Key Skills: Making a Difference.* Open University, Milton Keynes.

Pardue, J. (1998). So, what's a "Webmaster," anyway? *Internet Reference Service Quarterly* **3**(1), 7–14.

Reich, R. B. (1993). *The Work of Nations: A Blueprint for the Future.* Simon & Schuster, London.

Saunders, L. (1998). Lifelong learners and risk-takers: Today's librarians. *Computers in Libraries,* January, **45.**

Shepherd, R. (1998). A renaissance for the profession? *Library Association Record* **100**(5), 251–252.

Shimmon, R. (1998). Libraries move to centre stage. *Bookseller,* 8 May, 24–25.

Thompson, G. (1997). Changing universities: From evolution to revolution. In *Facing up to Changes in Universities and Colleges* (S. Armstrong, G. Thompson and S. Brown, eds.), pp. 1–8. Kogan Page, London.

Usherwood, B. (1998). From unity comes strength. *Library Association Record* **100**(5), 258.

Watson, D. (1998). Man of the people's universities: Chris Smith interview with Don Watson. *Library Association Record* **100**(3), 141–143.

Winner, M. C. (1998). Librarians as partners in the classroom: An increasing imperative. *Reference Services Review,* Spring, 25–30.

Image and Status
Academic Librarians and the New Professionalism

Michael Gordon Jackson
Brown University
Providence, Rhode Island 02912-9101

I. Introduction

Academic librarians always seem to be complaining that they just do not get the respect or status they deserve from the university or college community. Library budgets are generally inadequate, with the dramatic gains of the library expansion of the 1960s changing by the 1990s into a disturbing reality of resource cutbacks, branch closings, and declines in staffing and services (Ferguson, 1994, pp. 78–79). Faculty often perceive librarians not as "equals" or full "colleagues," but as service providers, not "educators" like themselves (Haynes, 1996, pp. 192–198). According to a survey conducted by *Library Journal* in 1994, librarians in general feel "underappreciated" and "undervalued" (St. Lifer, 1994, pp. 44–45). Moreover, their complaints are expressed within a higher education environment of tremendous uncertainty about funding, mission, the impact of new technologies on teaching and learning, and what the face of universities will look like in the 21st century. Libraries and their professional staff are not immune to these external forces and constraints.

However, useless handwringing or wishful thinking on the part of academic librarians will only worsen the problem. Although Jerry Campbell's dire warnings about the need for library staff to acquire more electronic/technical expertise and be open to major organizational restructuring can be over-the-top at times, his points about complacency and fatalism are on target—librarians must stop being so reactive: "our ability to survive depends upon our ability to change" (Campbell, 1993, p. 562). Librarians must play "active" roles in creating their destinies—be "drivers," not "passengers" (Campbell, 1991, p. 151).

Susan Martin also has pinpointed accurately the nature of the problem. University and college administrators exhort librarians to downsize and "do more with less." If librarians do not assert their worth, importance and need for institutional support, the "best qualified" and "strongest" may burn out

(Martin, 1998, p. 318). If academic librarians do not define their profession and mission, others—university administrators, politicians, public interest groups—most assuredly will do the work for us.

A rigorous and proactive philosophy, which results in a new definition of academic librarian professionalism, and a concrete action plan is required. The goal should be to deepen academic librarians "professionalism" and "collegiality," sharpen their sense of how they contribute to the educational role of the academic community, and *value* and promote what they do. This new professionalism would include gaining real institutional support for research/publishing activities, earning advanced subject degrees, and becoming professionally involved in the academic activities of their subject disciplines. They must be true "librarian educators," seeking real partnerships with faculty and administrators. Academic librarians must also become more effective and persistent publicists, and be willing to market their skills and specialities to the university community, especially to the faculty. Outreach is critically important in making the "invisible" (i.e., what we do as professionals and colleagues) "visible" and respected by the university and college community.

Analysis of this problem requires a multifaceted approach. It is also generally presented from the perspective of the "public service" academic librarian, or those who have the most direct and ongoing contact with students and faculty. The question and debate about academic librarians' desire for status and respect can be explored within the context of the following issue areas: (1) image, self-perception, and self-promotion; (2) faculty status; (3) librarian education, research skills, and scholarship; and (4) advanced second degrees and subject expertise. In conclusion, an outline of "new" professionalism for academic librarians—in thinking and action—is presented.

II. Image, Self-Perception, and Self-Promotion

Although some may downplay the significance of the connection between how others see us and the development of our own self-image, the fact is that "the importance of image lies not so much in its truth as in its consequences" (Grimes, 1994, p. 3). Like it or not, the image of "Marian the Librarian"— bookish, shy, orderly, willing to please, and a bit eccentric—lives with our profession. She/he is the ultimate service provider, intelligent, not interested in material gain or prestige. To the public, there is little distinction between the missions of academic, public, and special librarians. In their eyes, librarians are all cut from the same cloth as Marian.

In 1992, O'Brien and Raish compiled a "filmography" of the image of librarians in commerical motion pictures. Although there were one or two portrayals of librarians as energetic information professionals, the majority of films presented librarians engaged in "shelving, stamping, shushing" activities (O'Brien and Raish, 1993, pp. 62–63). This traditional image can have consequences. It can result in library underfunding and low use of the library (Schuman, 1990). It also does not follow that because librarians consider themselves to be in the cutting edge of developing and applying new information technologies that the old image has automatically changed. In 1995, Rugge and Glassbrenner published a handbook for "information brokers." They explicitly urged technically skilled librarians to avoid the "librarian label" if they hoped to enter this field. Although they stressed that there is nothing "wrong" with being a librarian, the reality was that most high-powered information clients would be deterred from seeking their services because of their traditional librarian image (Firebaugh, 1996, p. 3).

Not surprisingly, this image contributes to librarians having a "chronically low profile," as even members of the information/education professions do not understand the depth and breadth of academic librarian skills and expertise (Beaubien, 1992, p. 97). Indeed, prominent commentators within the profession itself have noted with frustration the unwillingness of many librarians to go beyond this self-deprecating image and develop and present a new picture of themselves. One exlibrarian administrator asks, "Why are librarians so modest? No one else is!" (Watson-Boone, 1986, p. 495). Herbert White is perplexed by the reluctance of librarians to specify what professional librarians actually do versus nonlibrarians (White, 1991, p. 68).

One especially difficult problem involves the blurring of roles among library staff and image. A study of faculty perceptions of librarians at Albion College confirmed what most librarians know: that they have great problems making distinctions between support staff and librarians and that they (librarians) are characterized as "passive gatekeepers" and guardians of books. "A clearer image of who they are and what it is they do" is needed to be put forth by librarians (Oberg *et al.*, 1989, p. 225). If faculty and other members of the university community see academic librarians performing clerical work, regardless of the fact that "in the absence of enough clerks, professionals will do clerical work simply because it must be done," they will presume that "all library work is clerical" (White, 1998, p. 117).

Being a clerk is not a pejorative term, or a bad thing; but, the lack of distinctions results in a diminution of professional image. Clients or customers never mistake legal assistants or medical assistants for lawyers or doctors. What does a librarian do that a clerk, or student assistant, does not? The public usually does not know (Wallace, 1994, pp. 6–7).

In another interesting study, letters and opinions published in the *Chronicle of Higher Education* were analyzed to find what metaphors faculty, administrators, and librarians used to describe libraries. In general, faculty took a more myopic view of the library as a location, a storehouse collecting and preserving information and providing access to information for their own research. And what about librarians? They were really not visible (Nitecki, 1993, pp. 272–273).

This invisibility can result in negative outcomes. For example, in 1996, the University of California offered library professional staff only half the pay increase given to faculty members while shrinking its librarian pool by 20% over a period of 5 years in spite of growing student admissions. One UC Berkeley librarian noted that many of her colleagues believed that the university viewed them as "expendable. They don't know anything about us. They don't have a high regard for us" (Flagg, 1996, pp. 17–18).

The fuzzy, if not negative, perceptions of librarianship and their influence on image are not phenemona confined to the United States. In 1991, a survey was conducted by the International Federation of Library Associations and Institutions Round Table for the Management of Library Associations regarding image and status of librarians around the world. Asked to react to the statement, "The status of the library profession is low," an overwhelming majority (82%) were convinced that the profession has low status. Respondents also ranked some of the most important reasons for their poor status—invisibility, low salary, marginal roles, lack of funding, female image, social responsibility, and so on. The study also concluded that librarians focus too much on "techniques, skills, processing," lack communicative abilities, and are "close-minded" (Prins and Gier, 1992, pp. 111, 115–116).

The evidence does suggest that librarians suffer from an image problem and confusion about what they do and its importance. The public often can slight and distort what librarianship can offer. For example, a report issued by the U.S. Department of Commerce's Office of Technology Policy in 1997 deplored the shortage of information workers in the United States—computer scientists, engineers, systems analysts, and similar positions. There was no mention of librarians or technical support staff as "information technology workers" (Kniffel, 1997, p. 28). This is quite an omission. Are librarians doomed to be an "accidental profession" then, lacking the status to attract members who are moving into librarianship from a previous second or third career choice (Martin, 1995, p. 198)?

Definite steps can be taken to reinvigorate and strengthen the image and self-esteem of librarians as it particularly relates to academic librarians and their relations with faculty, administrators, and students. What is not needed are empty exercises like changing the name of "library schools" to "information schools" or the like. It fools no one, and is rightly seen by some as a step to improve image within the academic community (Crowley, 1996, p. 48), but with no real substance behind it.

A French librarian expressed his opinion about the status of librarians as "honourable but without prestige" (Freeman, 1996, p. 180). As shown in this chapter, steps can be taken to change this unflattering perception.

III. Faculty Status

If there is one solution that has been regularly advanced over the years, it is the goal of academic librarians achieving faculty status. It has been hotly debated and argued. As Slattery (1994, p. 193) describes it, "a significant question of the 20th century within academic librarianship is whether the rights and obligations that come with faculty rank, title, and status are applicable to librarians." For many, faculty status became a reality in the 1960s and 1970s. Library literature is filled with studies and surveys about the subject and its importance to academic librarians (Huling, 1973; Werrell, 1987; DeBoer, 1987; Krompart, 1992; Lowry, 1993). Although the bulk of the literature supports the movement to faculty status, strong dissent also has been expressed. Dougherty wonders if the struggle is still worth it (1993, p. 67). Shapiro (1993, pp. 562–563) challenges the idea that faculty status is appropriate for librarians at all, let alone beneficial in terms of increased salary and influence. Indeed, Kingma (1995) criticizes the "opportunity costs" associated with this model—it detracts from other pressing library duties. Also, Applegate (1993) "deconstructs" the assumption that faculty status actually confers benefits.

The problem with this debate is that it is like beating a dead horse. Although there are abundant weaknesses associated with the model of faculty status, the fact is that in 1992, Association of College and Research Libraries (pp. 317–318) strongly endorsed the goal with its "Standards for Faculty Status for College and University Librarians." It emphasized that librarians are "partners" with teaching faculty in the academic community. Indeed, one of the participants drawing up the standards argued that, "being faculty was the most valuable mode of participation in campus life." Because campus society is not "egalitarian," she would "rather serve at the bottom of the faculty hierarchy than in some 'other' status" (St. Clair, 1993, pp. 7–9). Werrell (1987, p. 96) noted that most academic librarians (almost 79%) had acquired some form of faculty status. Lowry (1993, p. 163) puts the figure closer to 67% by the early 1990s.

Nor is there a serious movement, at least among academic librarians, to reverse the gains in attaining faculty status. Although sceptical of the drive for faculty status, Biggs (1995, p. 46) still would not give it up, "Once you've got it, you can't afford to lose it." Moreover, the model is appealing considering that many faculty, as suggested later in the chapter, are dubious about the credentials and research abilities of librarians.

The fact is that faculty status can only advance the profession to a certain point. Yes, academic librarians will gain more respect and status from the university community when they buy into the model of research/publication, teaching, peer review/tenure, collegiality, and university governance. It is also not unimportant that key studies show a link between faculty status and higher job satisfaction on the part of librarians (Benedict, 1991; Horenstein, 1993; Koenig, 1996). However, as White (1996, pp. 39–40) perceptively states, "It's simplistic for librarians to believe that faculty status or faculty equivalence also earns automatic collegial respect." Librarians must *earn* the respect of the academic community, through individual efforts and, as proposed later in this chapter, institutional support, and a new and vigorous definition of professionalism and subject expertise. It cannot be done by empty desires about parity—be it salary or status—with faculty. This is unrealistic. Although faculty status can be positive, it is crucial that academic librarians realize that they have their own discipline, body of knowledge, literature, ethics, and uniqueness. In short, as Hill (1994, pp. 71–76) notes, we must be comfortable "wearing our own clothes" when we function as faculty.

This issue is strongly related to the next area of context, namely the nature of library education, the acquiring of research skills, and academic scholarship.

IV. Librarian Education, Research Skills, and Scholarship

Is there a connection between what is taught (or not taught) in library schools today and the current debate about image, status, and professionalism? With the closing of great library schools such as the University of Chicago and Columbia, and increasing efforts to exorcise the descriptive term "library" from the masthead of library graduate education and replace it with "information science" or folding library programs within "Schools of Communication" or "Schools of Education," there is a perception that something is amiss and lacking in the curriculum. Librarians are being left with the unsettling feeling and question that if library schools disappeared tomorrow, would anyone notice or care?

Most library schools are not ignoring the problem. Kempe (1997, p. 85) rightly points out that "Library education is beginning a period of profound curricular reform." In preparing new library students to be the "knowledge navigators" of the future, library schools such as the University of Illinois/Urbana–Champaign, Florida State University, the University of Michigan, and Drexel University are strongly emphasizing competencies in technological/computer information systems (Marcum, 1997, p. 35). Interdisciplinary relationships with other disciplines such as computer science, engineering, and education are being incorporated into more library school curriculums (Kempe, p. 85). Library school programs emphasize how to use the new technologies, design software, evaluate databases and platforms, systems analysis, critical thinking, and user-centered approaches (Sinclair, 1998, pp. 42–43).

Indeed, the latest *Library Journal* Annual Placements and Salaries Survey of library school graduates suggests that library school curriculums are in fact preparing new librarians to be technology experts. A plurality of respondents stated that "technological or computer skills" were the most useful skills they acquired in library school, with many employers wanting "HTML skills" from their new employees (Gregory and McCook, 1998, pp. 32–38). According to Bertram and Olson (1996, pp. 36–37), in the battle between the "soft-edged" service culture philosophy of librarianship and the "entrepreneurial infotech culture," library schools are increasingly adopting the "infotech" approach.

Yet, especially in regard to the problem of strengthening the image of librarians in academia, and building partnerships based on real respect with university administrators, faculty, and students, it is not clear that primary reliance on the "infotech" model is sufficient. In analyzing recruitment of new library school students, Penniman (1995, p. 89) cautions that "it is essential that they (library students) are not led to think that library education is mainly technique. Some technique must be kept, but it should not occupy so large a place, as it has to date."

Although there is nothing wrong with library schools going beyond the traditional "canon" of library science courses—subject bibliography, reference, cataloging, administration, preservation—it is shortsighted to simply increase the number of courses students take in computer and information systems. The solution is not for librarians to become more and more indistinguishable from computer science specialists. Broderick (1997, pp. 42–43) puts it well: "turning library into a dirty word" in library education will ensure the demise of the profession." There is a "body of knowledge called librarianship, that it has value and coherence, and that it can be passed from one generation of librarians to the next" (Gorman, 1990, p. 463).

A more productive line of questioning, especially for the academic librarians, is to ask whether library school education prepares our students to be researchers and scholars, not just trade school practitioners of a highly skilled nature. That other members of the academic community undervalue librarian's participation in research and theory building can be illustrated by the comments of one prominent scholar. Jacques Barzun once described librarians and journalists as "intellectual middlemen" who confuse "the assembling of items found here and found there" with real research (Crowley, 1996, p. 116).

Does this mean that library professional literature is by definition superficial or third rate? The answer is no. Even a cursory examination of *Library*

Literature Index reveals a rich and varied selection of topics—instruction techniques, learning theory, user studies, collection management, and statistical analysis. However, as Hernon (1996, p. 1) points out, there is a tendency for librarians to describe the research process in "wash and wear" context, action-based, descriptive, and frequently "devoid of any theoretical context." Library researchers should also be prepared to "look beyond disciplinary boundaries" (Hernon, 1996, p. 98).

Furthermore, library education programs, although teaching new students about information systems and basic statistics/research methods, are not focusing on *that type of research that faculty engage in and respect.* Taking one course in statistical methods is insufficient. If one accepts the argument that it is desirable for academic librarians to be respected and work as "partners" with the faculty, "and if they (librarians) are to join in the community of scholars, then the education of academic librarians should at least approximate that of their colleagues" (Budd, 1984, p. 16).

A major problem is the nature of the "acculturation process" new graduate students face in library schools. Mitchell and Morton (1992, pp. 380–382), in a major study about the socialization of library students, cited Shulman's 1979 academic model that most new scholars in other disciplines follow: (1) research is the primary focus of the university; (2) academic work requires peer judgment; (3) scholarship is a vocation in its own right; and (4) the academic profession serves important social goals. These four points comprise the "state of mind" of a true academic. They also describe Clark's "sources of integration," which unite academics as a "true community of scholars"—academic freedom, scientific norms, scientific methodology, and ethics of scholarship (Mitchell and Morton, 1992, p. 381).

According to Mitchell and Morton (1992), library school education does not socialize its students to believe in the previously mentioned canons. For most nonlibrary students, graduate education, teaching, and research are stressed. This is not the case with library education. Students apprentice in the library, not teaching in the classroom. Nor in most programs is a research thesis or dissertation required. "The role of research and scholarship is not so central to the duties of academic librarians as it is to instructional faculty" (p. 384). Library students are taught to think "passively" about information—organizing and retrieving it (p. 382). Library education conditions students to be "myopic," to think in terms of indexes or bibliographies, not ideas or knowledge as being dynamic and nonlinear, even random in nature (p. 385).

Another study investigated whether academic librarians felt that library school education prepared them for understanding the academic community, or whether they were fundamentally different from faculty. In regards to the question about adequate graduate school education, there was an "overwhelming no" regarding the MLS graduate degree. In fact, most respondents felt very distant from the faculty "frame of mind." One noted that, "Being faculty is a twenty-four hour a day vocation. It is not just a job. *Being a librarian is just a job*" (italics mine; Bushing, 1995, pp. 37, 39).

The result? Faculty and administrators perceive librarians to be service providers, not scholars, let alone "true" colleagues, and usually out of the faculty research loop. In fact, "there is little evidence that librarians, well-trained or poorly trained, have ever been much a part of the 'scholarly research process'" or that scholars rely on them except for the most basic assistance (Jones, 1991, p. 585).

According to Anne Lipow, the "misguided" perception that many faculty have of librarian research skills "doesn't come out of the blue." She argues that librarians often "reinforce" it. If, in fact, the only interaction faculty have with a librarian is at the reference desk, answering "quickie questions," they often come to the conclusion that they (librarians) are not real subject specialists who are experts in research methods (Lipow, 1992, p. 10).

Nor is it entirely suprising that library schools may be viewed by some university administrators negatively if they are convinced that "library and information sciences are short on scholarly substance" and that those library programs do not "enhance the university's scholarly image." Some library school educators were not able "to justify the existence of their programs (library)" and that they were "isolated from their academic peers . . . perceived as out of touch and out of date" (Slattery, 1994, pp. 193–199).

What is interesting about this shortcoming is how few academic librarians feel cheated by this. In fact, many argue that higher status is not linked to deficiencies in research graduate preparation. In a draft report of the ACRL Institutional Priorities and Faculty Rewards Task Force in 1996, the Task Force observed that many academic librarians objected to faculty status because they believed that they should not have to do the same kind of research that faculty do, that it detracts from librarians' normal responsibilities, and that trying to compare the research that librarians do with faculty, is like trying "to force square pegs into round holes" (ACRL, 1997, p. 414). They see a deep conflict between service to users and commitment to conducting research. Librarians, in contrast to faculty, work a 40-hour week, 12 months a year, instead of a typical 9-month term. Release time for research is a luxury. If librarians have to be concerned about publication and tenure, and maintain their usually overwhelming "routine" duties, the quality of library services could drastically decline.

As Black and Leysen note, "Viewing librarianship as an eight-to-five job that requires constant job presence severely limits the librarian's ability to meet promotion and tenure expectations" (Black and Leysen, 1994, pp. 230, 233). Strauch decries the lack of the "power of positive thinking" among librarians when thinking about conducting research—library literature is not as significant as the faculty, it detracts from their real jobs, they are not paid enough, or that it is "tedious" and "boring" (Strauch, 1992, p. 100). Another study, examining the question as to why librarians are reluctant to participate in research, reported that besides lack of time, funding, background, there was just a "lack of interest" (Stephenson, 1990, p. 51). The nonresearch bent of many academic librarians seems to match the perception of faculty that librarians are not scholars and do not engage in serious research.

Nor do the concerns of academic librarians about lack of release time or institutional support lack a foundation of truth. A survey conducted in 1990 showed that "research time for librarians at the present is generally limited and is rarely considered an ongoing, integral part of the job." Also, illustrating the reluctance of librarians to commit to scholarly activity, one respondent complained, citing reference desk duties, collection development online, bibliographic instruction, "I'm too exhausted to do anything else! I guess basically the reason we're given no time for research is that we're too understaffed and too overworked to do research. . . . It's very frustrating!" (Arlen and Santizo, 1990, pp. 210–211).

As for those academic librarians who do publish, what are their attitudes and motivations? In a study conducted by Floyd and Phillips in 1997, librarians who publish indicated that they do so for a variety of reasons. Nearly 80% said they did so for promotion and tenure reasons. Interestingly enough, however, "the majority were motivated internally by a desire to establish a professional reputation." "Peer pressure" from colleagues is another factor. As with other surveys, they reported little tangible support for their efforts from their home institutions (Floyd and Phillips, 1997, pp. 81–93).

It is clear, then, that if increased status and respect is needed for academic librarians, and that receiving that respect and collegiality from faculty and administrators is desired, there is a problem with the curriculum of most library education schools. For those librarians who want to have careers in academic libraries and provide "high-value" expertise to the academic community, they must be more than just "technology experts."

V. Advanced Second Degrees and Subject Expertise

If there is controversy among academic librarians about how their image and status depend on their library education, research skills, faculty status, and publications, one area that is carefully dealt with is the question of earning advanced subject degrees in their fields. Indeed, if librarians already feel they are exhausted and overwhelmed by the demands of their job, engaging in the rigors of an MA or PhD program might seem to be an impossible burden with little benefit. Yet, if academic librarians accept the argument that faculty and administrators do not see them as "intellectual" equals and that their graduate training makes them "different" from other educators, obtaining a graduate degree might go a long way to alleviating the problem.

Herubel points out that many in the profession see little value in pursuing additional "paper" qualifications or degrees. They miss a fundamental point. To really begin to work with the faculty as partners, academic librarians need advanced subject degrees in order to make themselves "credible" to the scholarly community. Nor is this added respect and status the only benefit: by successfully completing a subject degree program, the librarian learns about that discipline's modes of research, theory, methodologies, and mission, thereby being better able to provide services to the faculty and students as real subject specialists (Herubel, 1991, p. 437).

Herubel does not believe this approach is without risk, however. For example, although the PhD is a "formidable symbol of intellectual strength, persistence, and dedication," it is also imperative that the librarian understand that a bifurcation of his role as PhD specialist and librarian is *not* possible; he should not be "practitioner" in the subject field as well (Herubel, 1990, pp. 626–627).

Jones argues that academic librarians who have earned second advanced degrees would help contribute to positive outcomes on campus. These would include adjunct/joint appointments in teaching departments, membership on dissertation committees, participation in research seminars, and teaching of courses on bibliography (Jones, 1991, pp. 585–586). Increased contact, visibility, and credibility for the librarian would most likely result.

Also, in an extensive survey conducted by Grosch and Weech, 49% of academic librarians believed that their salaries were higher because of their advanced subject degree. In comparison to 31% of public librarians, 38% of special librarians, and 47% of school library media specialists, 62% responded that their subject master's degree had been important to advancing their career. They report that most librarians would choose to earn their subject master's degree again (Grosch and Weech, 1991, pp. 190, 196).

VI. New Professionalism—An Outline of Thinking and Action

Given the constraints imposed by external factors (lack of funds, low respect from the academic community, technology-driven library school curriculums) and internal barriers (resistance to learning and conducting research and earning advanced second degrees, passivity, confusion about mission, lack of self-confidence) what should academic librarians do in the future to increase their skills, knowledge, status, and image? Is a 'new' definition of professional-ism needed now? As Abbott notes, ". . . Professional work changes all the time and in many directions" (Abbott, 1998, p. 432). Below is an interrelated set of proposals to use in defining the characteristics, role, education, of the new professional, and required institutional support systems to allow them to be effective librarian educators.

A. Academic Librarians Must Be Open, Flexible, and Self-Confident about Change

It is tempting to downplay the significance of this section and describe it as an exercise in "consciousness raising" with little importance to the question of how to improve the professional status of academic librarians. Yet, the ability to rethink one's roles and duties, challenge stereotypes and not be rigid, and be able to transform them is critical. Indeed, as Peter Young suggests, librarians may be helping students and faculty of the "postmodern" information world not by focusing on fixed, permanent collections, standard services, or hierarchical library systems, but by expertly navigating within a scholastic environment that has "fluid and transient multimedia resources . . . flexible virtual information spaces . . . tailored services to collaborative teams . . . personalized consulting . . . participative and collegial relation-ships" and other dimensions (Young, 1996, pp. 114–115).

The new professional must be creative and flexible. As Lee points out, students of "Generation X" (those born between 1961 and 1981) have certain unique needs—they crave stimulation and variety; need personal contact from educators; want concrete, speedy, accurate information; and want to learn "leading-edge technology" (Lee, 1996, pp. 56–57). And, as Cooper and Cooper point out, more and more new MLS students reflect the orientation of this generation—technical savvy, and having the ability to synthesize diverse sources of information in creative and integrated ways (Cooper and Cooper, 1998, p. 20).

Very importantly, they must be *self-confident* about their educational mis-sion and future. Academic librarians will not begin to be taken seriously by faculty, administrators, and students unless they assert their specialness and importance to the academic community. The new professionals must define themselves—what they do and who they are.

B. A Strictly "Service" Approach Is Not Enough

One problem when discussing this subject is the prevalence of the "fallacy of the false alternative"—namely that if one course is chosen, the other must be chosen too or abandoned. For instance, if academic librarians become educators, by logic they can no longer be good service providers. Hisle asserts that among all the values being discussed now and challenged, "One of the more important is an altruistic sense of service" (Hisle, 1997, p. 764). In fact, the idea of "service" to patrons has a long and noble tradition in all aspects of librarianship. Drake is quite correct to point out that an important reason for joining the profession can be described in one word: "altruism," a desire to help and serve (Drake, 1993, p. 922). Many job satisfaction surveys indicate that when asked what part of the profession they like the most, "the most popular answer typically revolves around the value of their service" (Lanier, Carson, and Carson, 1997, p. 193). Librarians do want to help people; this is a motivation that should not be downplayed.

However, this should not preclude the option of adopting an educator model and frame of thinking. When new professionals are involved in research, publishing, teaching, and understanding information systems, this expertise will lead to improved service for patrons. Dispensing with the clerical elements of our work will not lead to the end of librarian's role as service providers. Service provider can coexist with the educator model.

C. Continuing Education and In-Service Training, as Traditionally Done, Is Not Sufficient

There is little controversy over the fact that academic librarians are in the thick of the information revolution on campuses. Technological change in libraries is now a constant. Competencies among academic librarians include proficiencies with presentation software; Web products and networks; SGML; HTML standards; and technical knowledge of DOS, Windows, networks, multimedia, and basic computer and information science concepts. They need the skills and knowledge in order to critically evaluate information sources and help students and faculty with this task. Indeed, many LIS programs are producing graduates who are technologically adept (Woodsworth, 1997, p. 46), in keeping with earlier descriptions of the characteristics of Generation X. It is proper that not only in library school but on the job, new professionals should expect to gain more than just passing competencies in information technologies, computer systems, and networks via in-service training and continuing education.

Yet, the new professional must do more to be an librarian educator. As Norman Cousins points out, if one does not move beyond mere professional learning, the practice of a profession becomes impaired—professionals must grow beyond total immersion in their work. "Aesthetic" and "intellectual" development depends on librarians cultivating interests and developments in nonlibrary issues (Collins, 1990, p. 30). Technical competency is not enough; there are other computer services experts on campus who can usually program and setup networks much better than librarians can ever hope to do. Academic librarians presently excel in evaluating these new systems. And, as shown later in the chapter, to be a librarian educator and respected by the campus community, academic librarians must develop *real* subject expertise, respect and practice the canons of scholarship, and develop a much deeper understanding of the scholarly subject matter being accessed.

D. Academic Librarians Must Become Comfortable with Research, Theory Building, and Scholarly Publishing—That Is, Become True "Librarian Educators" and Partners with Faculty and Administrators

This is of fundamental importance for the new professional. To truly begin the process of earning real respect and higher status from faculty, administrators, and students, academic librarians must demonstrate that they are comfortable with the role of conducting research, teaching, and publishing and peer review.

Starting in library school, graduate education must also attract students who possess the "academic frame of mind"—love of learning; intellectual inquiry; a desire to publish and conduct research; and rethink ideas, systems, and theories. Library schools in turn must provide a relevant curriculum and more rigorous requirements (research thesis, methods, canons of scholarship). Librarianship cannot just be a job and vocation; an educator is *on* all the time.

Is this pollyannaish and unworkable in the real world of low librarian status? Certainly, as noted earlier, the obstacles can be formidable. For instance, beyond the fact that many librarians are not prepared in library schools to conduct research that faculty would respect, or simply lack the interest, in a study conducted in 1987, both librarians and faculty expressed similar complaints about the rigors of the publishing process—not enough time, too busy for writing, service comes first (librarians to patrons; faculty to teaching), no blocks of time available for writing, only original thoughts merit publication, fear of failure and rejection from harsh editors, and laziness. "Scholarship was tantamount to personal indulgence" (Boice *et al.*, 1987, p. 501). Thus, librarians and faculty may share some of the same impediments against doing research and publishing. In fact, "librarians can better understand their own struggles with faculty status by looking at the struggle of traditional faculty" (p. 510).

Another big obstacle is subtle, but crucial. It relates to the differing socialization processes of library school students and most graduates from other disciplines, and the impact it has in faculty–librarian interaction. Hardesty's article about the existence of "faculty culture" and resistance to cooperation with librarians, especially bibliographic instruction (BI), is provocative. Hardesty concludes that most faculty believe in research, mastery of knowledge/content, and specialization; unlike librarians, they are not interested in the "process" of teaching or discussing pedagogical techniques; and they are fiercely autonomous and devoted to academic freedom and resistant to offers of help from librarians. They often mistakenly interpret these offers as interference. They also do not view librarians as "peers" for all the reasons given earlier (Hardesty, 1995, pp. 339–367).

This seems an almost insurmountable problem. Librarians think in terms of hierarchy and teamwork/participation, whereas faculty think in terms of decentralization and autonomy. As Carpenter observes, there is a "librarian–scholar enmity" between librarians and faculty. Librarians resent the idea that they are not recognized as "experts," and faculty reciprocate by wanting to keep the title (scholar) for themselves (Carpenter, 1997, pp. 398–401).

Yet, unless librarians start actively thinking about how to establish real faculty partnerships, their status and ability to provide good service to the university community will suffer. With perserverence, imagination, patience, and "marketing" (discussed later), academic librarians have been able to work with faculty and convince them that librarians have something to offer. Haynes' survey article about librarian–faculty partnerships and library instruction suggests that there are more success stories than imagined. To Haynes it is clear that "the library is the principal unit of the college that supports all academic programs." Librarians are "educators" and have a special mission; they can make themselves "indispensable to faculty and students as the principal information provider" (Haynes, 1996, pp. 218–219). However, strong librarian–faculty partnerships must be more than just helping faculty build web sites or be viewed as only "technology experts"—they must also be perceived as researchers and subject specialists.

Major seconds this argument. She describes "mature librarians" and how they are accepted as colleagues by faculty. Their positive attitude was fundamental in creating an environment wherein faculty respected them. Half of the respondents "indicated that interests in students, teaching, and the learning environment were commonalities that enhanced the collegial atmosphere between librarians and other faculty." They shared experiences; both placed value on "research." Librarians were confident of their skills and knowledge. They considered themselves "equals," experts on information systems and subject disciplines. Timidity was not an option: "too many librarians are timid souls; they wring their hands and want people to recognize them." Librarians respected themselves; they believed in what they were doing for the scholarly world. They gained collegial respect, not just professional respect for their technology skills, from their faculty partners (Major, 1993, pp. 467–468).

Thus, the new professional, after developing a much deeper background in research, teaching, and publishing, must be willing to combine the best of the profession's services to faculty, with a demonstrated interest in the canons of scholarship and a willingness to work at establishing collegial relations with faculty. Will it require hard work? Absolutely. As Newman argues, "academic librarians should publish more and complain less." He is right that conducting scholarship is an "obligation" and a "pleasure." "By establishing ourselves as scholars, librarians can more honestly claim full membership in the academic community with corresponding access and influence" (Newman, 1998, p. 19).

E. To Improve Their Work and Expertise, Librarians Must Seek Advanced Second Degrees in Subject Specialities

This is a very important goal for the new professional. Although it would not be a popular course of action for most librarians, earning an advanced second degree—MA, MS, PhD, or other degrees—would be time-consuming, expensive, and difficult.

Yet, there would be a considerable payoff for librarians who are searching for higher status/respect from the academic community. With a second subject degree, the librarian has gone a long way to establishing a closer and collegial partnership with faculty and administrators. It would help demonstrate that they have the rigor to master a discipline's body of knowledge, theories, and methodologies, and have the capability and temperament to conduct research and engage in tough-minded intellectual inquiry.

The advantage of an advanced degree is not just improvements in faculty relationships or more status/respect. It *directly* improves the service librarians provide to their patrons, particularly students. Speaking from experience, a PhD or Masters degree, for example, allows the librarian to understand the theoretical concerns of patrons' questions, methodologies, and issues. Instead of just pointing out what databases are available, the librarian can discuss with the patron the appropriateness of sources, research design and strategies, writing tips, and interpretation. An advanced degree would help begin the transition from traditional bibliographic assistance to something more: a true educator or, as you will, "educational consultant." Patrons quickly sense your subject expertise and seek you out—you become *their* consultant. The new professional would be offering "high-value" assistance in a way students and faculty would appreciate and respect.

F. Librarians Must Be Prepared to Constantly Promote and Market Themselves and the Library Profession to the Academic Community—Complacency Is Not Acceptable

New professionals definitely must be willing to "sell" themselves more to the campus community. Traditional passivity in the face of library budget cuts, ignorance about what academic librarians do, and low image/status must be assertively and strategically dealt with. As Butcher rightly argues, "Neither librarians nor anyone else in higher education has done a successful job of explaining and marketing their services. . . . We have assumed that those in charge value us as much as we value ourselves" (Butcher, 1993, p. 292). Anne Lipow also supports outreach to faculty—these efforts help "redefine" ourselves in the eyes of the academic community. Indeed, "if we don't adopt some clear strategies for new forms of outreach to faculty, librarianship is in trouble" (Lipow, 1992, p. 12).

There are a myriad number of ways academic librarians can market themselves—newsletters, advertising, consultations, holding events, attending faculty talks and meetings (seminars, lectures) going to departments and meeting key faculty, focus groups, and more. It is beyond the scope of this article to list them in detail. Librarians must listen to faculty and their concerns while at the same time inform faculty about the many skills and resources that they can help provide. The key is to establish relationships with faculty and administrators by being accessible, reaching out to them, not being reactive.

Dilmore studied the question of librarian/faculty interaction at nine New England colleges in 1996. One key finding was that greater interaction between faculty and library/librarians resulted in more favorable perceptions of librarians and greater use of the library (Dilmore, 1996, p. 280). Academic librarians should approach faculty with confidence about what librarians have to offer them. Ideally, along with colleagues, librarians should develop an intelligent marketing plan, with timetables, criteria for success and evaluation, feedback. The effort has to be continuous.

Even something as small as your "title" can be part of the outreach effort. As Low asks, what is it about the profession that encourages professional librarians to not even print MLS on their business cards? By not putting and advertising those "three little letters" after our names, "we are validating the public's misconception that anyone can be a librarian regardless of what education or skills they may possess." To Low, individual efforts to publicize your education can help in the effort to gain more respect for the profession (Low, 1994, p. 882).

G. Academic Librarians and Administrators Must Be Willing to "Think Out of the Box" and Rearrange Their Work Schedules and Job Duties/Responsibilities

This is perhaps the toughest task for the new professional. No profession or workplace likes to change the ways things are done. However, this model is predicated on doing new things. For example, one could reasonably argue that what is being proposed is totally unrealistic, there is no time, no clerical support, there are lots of detailed library tasks to be done, there is no need to demonstrate expertise beyond our technical competence about information systems, and after all, "the reference desk *must* be staffed."

Professionals must begin to imaginatively address the problem. Something must give—the librarian educator cannot handle all of the profession's traditional duties as well as the new ones being proposed in this article.

Solutions can be achieved. For instance, the move in some academic libraries to adopt "tiered" reference service (the Brandeis and Johns Hopkins models) and the decision whether to staff the reference desk with nonprofessionals, eliminate it altogether, change the configuration of professional and staff at the desk, or have the librarian meet with faculty and students by appointment is a promising one. It would free up time that normally would be spent on the reference desk (Massey-Burzio, 1992; Ferguson, 1994, pp. 88–90).

Indeed, the essence of making appointments is to allow the librarian to exhibit their subject expertise in a less hectic and less anxious environment than the reference desk. New, smarter positioning of service points in the library must also be considered. Locations and allocation of staff cannot become static; it cannot become unthinkable to place staff in new work configurations.

Many of the traditional duties associated with librarians may have to be switched to others. Alan Veaner argues that "one key to the improvement of librarian's academic status may be further off-loading of their production work onto support staff. For librarians to reach genuine parity with faculty, it is necessary to get librarians completely out of the 'manufacturing' business" (Black and Leyson, 1994, p. 234). Although one could expect some resistance from support staff, much resistance could be expected to be received from professionals themselves. In other words, only *they* have the expertise and experience to complete the myriad number of bibliographic tasks that need to be done. Attitudes must be more flexible, and the new professional must work with administration to find ways to get away from the clerical image (valuable and indispensable as library assistants are to fulfilling the mission of the library) associated with librarians, improve their status, and be able to work and be perceived as true librarian educators.

Library workers can have distinctions in rank and responsibilities and still work cooperatively together. Massey-Burzio, in writing about what users really want from academic libraries, states this point succinctly: "Librarians should be clearly differentiated from other staff, however much that offends democratic sensibilities." Patrons need to know who the research and subject specialists are (Massey-Burzio, 1998, p. 214).

H. Home Institutions Must Be Far More Willing to Create the Infrastructure and Support Network to Allow Academic Librarians to Be Librarian Educators

Along with changing ways of thinking and attitude, this last proposal can be a real challenge, especially in a higher-education climate of declining budgets and squabbling among factions about which service or department should be fully funded. For the new professionalism to work, a myriad number of support mechanisms, changes in administrative thinking, and concrete action(s) need to be in place. Some examples include release time for research and publishing; adequate equipment, supplies, and clerical help; research sabbaticals; flexible time, not only receiving blessings to get a second masters degree or PhD from administration, but time off with pay and tuition assistance; funding for attending professional conferences in your subject fields; job flexibility; grants assistance; and much more. In 1989, 555 librarians responded to a questionnaire about their research activities with the University of California and California State University library systems; on the positive side, 59% said they had engaged in research as defined in the study. However, 81% of the respondents reported that they had conducted, on at least one occasion, research with no funding or time off (Selth and Hutchinson, 1989, p. 487). In a 1991 survey of 185 academic librarians, it was confirmed that a "supportive organizational climate" had a very positive impact on academic librarians' professional activities, including research output (Havener and Stolt, 1994, pp. 34–35).

Library administrators and university officers must do more to support the research efforts of their librarians. Although individual librarians will continue to buck the odds and publish on their own time, so much more could be accomplished with generous and intelligent support and the existence of an infrastructure that would positively further the research efforts of librarian educators.

VII. Conclusion

It is proposed that to deal with the problem of low status and image, a new professionalism, both in thinking and action, is required. Such a change would not be easy. However, academic librarianship cannot remain an "accidental profession," a second career choice, or a refuge for the timid. It is currently a field with great excitement and potential for its members—expertise in new information systems, teaching and research, publishing, exposure to cutting-edge technologies and methods, and the opportunity to help users with the mass of information and scholarship that is available and assist them in evaluating and making sense of it.

Is this model for everyone? Perhaps, as Susan Martin advocates, a "two-track" system of academic librarianship should be offered for those who want to be "Occupational Librarians" and evaluated on their 9-to-5 status, and a track for the new professional (or "Professional Librarian") who would contribute much more via professional growth, publishing, and engaging in research. These Professional Librarians would have high expectations for themselves and certainly engage in the type of "risky" thinking and behavior needed to reinvigorate the profession (Martin, 1993, p. 24). The payoff would be higher status, more respect from the academic community, and the beginning of the creation of a galvanized, new professional class of academic librarians.

References

Abbott, A. D. (1998). Professionalism and the future of librarianship. *Library Trends* **46**(3), 430–443.

ACRL Institutional Priorities and Faculty Rewards Task Force (1997). The Redefining Scholarship Project: A draft report. *College & Research Libraries News* **6**, 414–418.

ALA Standards Committee (1992). Standards for faculty status for college and university librarians. *College & Research Libraries News* **5**, 317–318.

Applegate, R. (1993). Deconstructing faculty status: Research and assumptions. *Journal of Academic Librarianship* **19**, 158–164.

Beaubien, A. K. (1992). Image counts. *College & Research Libraries*, **53**, 97.

Benedict, M. A. (1991). Librarians satisfaction with faculty status. *College & Research Libraries* **52**, 538–548.

Bertram, S., and Olson, H. (1996). Culture clash. *Library Journal* **121**, 36–37.

Biggs, M. (1995). Librarians as educators: Assessing our self-image. *Public & Access Services Quarterly* **1**(1), 41–50.

Black, W. K., and Leysen, J. M. (1994). Scholarship and the academic librarian. *College & Research Libraries* **55**, 229–241.

Boice, R., Scepanski, J. M., and Wilson, W. V. (1987). Librarians and faculty members: Coping with pressures to publish. *College & Research Libraries* **48**, 494–503.

Broderick, D. M. (1997). Turning library into a dirty word: A rant. *Library Journal* **122**, 42–43.

Budd, J. (1984). The education of academic librarians. *College & Research Libraries* **45**(1), 15–24.

Bushing, M. C. (1995). Academic librarians: Perceptions of the acculturation process. *Library Acquisitions* **19**, 33–41.

Butcher, K. S. (1993). Political networking. *College & Research Libraries* **54**, 291–292.

Campbell, J. D. (1991). It's a tough job looking ahead when you've seen what's dragging behind. *Journal of Academic Librarianship* **17**(3), 148–151.

Campbell, J. D. (1993). Choosing to have a future: We can transform ourselves and the profession, or be swept away by a technological torrent. *American Libraries* **24**, 560–566.

Carpenter, K. E. (1997). The librarian–scholar. *Journal of Academic Librarianship* **23**(5), 398–401.

Collins, M. E. (1990). Continuing education for ARL librarians in multi-faceted public service positions. In *Continuing Education of Reference Librarians* (W. Katz, ed.), pp. 17–34. Haworth Press, New York.

Cooper, J. F., and Cooper, E. A. (1998). Generational dynamics and librarianship: Managing Generation X. *Illinois Libraries* **80**(1), 18–21.

Crowley, B. (1996). Redefining the status of the librarian in higher education. *College & Research Libraries* **57**, 113–121.

DeBoer, K. and Culotta, W. (1987). The academic librarian and faculty status in the 1980s: A survey of the literature. *College & Research Libraries* **48**, 215–223.

Dilmore, D. H. (1996). Librarian/faculty interaction at nine New England colleges. *College & Research Libraries* **57**, 274–284.

Dougherty, R. M. (1993). Faculty status: Playing on a tilted field. *Journal of Academic Librarianship* **19**, 67.

Drake, D. (1993). The "A" factor: Altruism and career satisfaction. *American Libraries* **24**, 922–924.

Ferguson, C. (1994). Reshaping academic library reference service: A review of issues, trends, and possibilities. In *Advances in Librarianship* (I. Godden, ed.), Vol. 18, Academic Press, San Diego.

Firebaugh, J. (1996). *From Old Maids to Young Professionals: Depictions of the Image of Librarians in the Twentieth Century.* MS degree, Library School of Information and Library Science, University of North Carolina at Chapel Hill.

Flagg, G. (1996). Univ. of Calif. seeks to slash librarians' pay scale. *American Libraries* **27**, 17+.

Floyd, B. L., and Phillips, J. C. (1997). A question of quality: How authors and editors perceive library literature. *College & Research Libraries* **58**, 81–93.

Freeman, M. (1996). *The International Information & Library Review* **28**, 177–180.

Gorman, M. (1990). A bogus and dismal science: Or, the eggplant that ate library schools. *American Libraries* **21**, 462–463.

Gregory, V. L., and McCook, K. P. (1998). Breaking the $30K barrier—Placements & salaries 97. *Library Journal* **123**, 32–38.

Grimes, D. J. (1994). Marian the librarian, the truth behind the image. In *Discovering Librarians: Profiles of a Profession* (M. J. Scherdin, ed.), Association of College and Research Libraries, Chicago.

Grosch, M., and Weech, T. L. (1991). Perceived value of advanced subject degrees by librarians who hold such degrees. *Library and Information Science Research* **13**, 173–199.

Havener, W. M., and Stolt, W. A. (1994). The professional development activities of academic librarians: Does institutional support make a difference? *College & Research Libraries* **55**, 25–36.

Haynes, E. B. (1996). Librarian–faculty partnerships in instruction. In *Advances in Librarianship* (I. Godden, ed.), Vol. 20, Academic Press, San Diego.

Hernon, P., and Schwartz, C. (1996). Editorial: Interdisciplinary and scholarly research. *Library and Information Science Research* **18**, 97–98.

Hernon, P., and Schwartz, C. (1996). Editorial: "Wash and wear" research: Unrealistic expectations. *Library and Information Science Research* **18**, 1–2.

Herubel, J. P. V. M. (1991). To "degree" or not to "degree": Academic librarians and subject expertise. *Indiana Libraries* **10**(2), 90–94.

Herubel, J. P. V. M. (1990). The Ph.D. librarian: A personal perspective. *College & Research Libraries News* **7**, 626–628.

Hill, J. S. (1994). Wearing our own clothes: Librarians as faculty. *Journal of Academic Librarianship* **20**, 71–76.

Hisle, W. L. (1997). Values for the electronic information age: Facing the new millenium. *College & Research Libraries News* **11**, 764–765.

Horenstein, B. (1993). Job satisfaction of academic librarians: An examination of the relationships between satisfaction, faculty status, and participation (survey of 638 academic librarians). *College & Research Libraries* **54**, 255–269.

Huling, N. (1973). Faculty status: A comprehensive bibliography. *College & Research Libraries* **34**, 440–462.

Jones, W. G. (1991). The education of academic librarians: How many degrees are enough? *College & Research Libraries News* **9**, 584–586.

Kempe, J. (1997). New trends in library education: The attitudes of students and recent graduates towards library school curricula. *Mississippi Libraries* **61**, 82–86.

Kingma, B. R., and McCombs, G. M. (1995). The opportunity costs of faculty status for academic librarians. *College & Research Libraries* **56**, 258–264.

Kniffel, L. (1997). The deficit is in the data. *American Libraries* **28**, 28.

Koenig, M., Morrison, R., and Roberts, L. (1996). Faculty status for library professionals: Its effect on job turnover and job satisfaction among university research library directors. *College & Research Libraries* **57**, 295–300.

Krompart, J. (1992). Researching faculty status: A selective annotated bibliography. *College & Research Libraries* **53**, 439–449.

Lanier, P., Carson, P. P., and Carson, K. D. (1997). What keeps academic librarians in the books? *Journal of Academic Librarianship* **23**, 191–197.

Lee, C. A. (1996). Teaching Generation X. *Research Strategies* **14**(1), 56–59.

Lipow, A. G. (1992). Outreach to faculty: Why and how. In *Working with Faculty in the Electronic Library: Papers and Session Materials Presented at the 19th National LOEX Library Instruction Conference Held at Eastern Michigan University 10–11 May 1991.* (L. Shirato, ed.), Pierian Press, Ann Arbor.

Low, K. (1994). Confessions of an M.L.S. librarian. *American Libraries* **25**, 882.

Lowry, C. B. (1993). The status of faculty status for academic librarians: A twenty-year perspective (1990 survey of 459 academic librarians). *College & Research Libraries* **54**, 163–172.

Major, J. A. (1993). Mature librarians and the university faculty: Factors contributing to librarians acceptance as colleagues. *College & Research Libraries* **54**, 463–469.

Marcum, D. B. (1997). Transforming the curriculum: Transforming the profession. *American Libraries* **28**, 35–36+.

Martin, S. K. (1995). The accidental profession: Seeking the best and the brightest. *Journal of Academic Librarianship* **21**, 198–199.

Martin, S. K. (1993). Visions: Raising our professional expectations with a two-track approach to librarianship. *Journal of Academic Librarianship* **19**, 24.

Massey-Burzio, V. (1998). From the other side of the reference desk: A focus group study. *Journal of Academic Librarianship* **24**, 208–215.

Massey-Burzio, V. (1992). Reference encounters of a different kind: A symposium. *Journal of Academic Librarianship* **18**, 276–286.

Mitchell, W. B., and Morton, B. (1992). On becoming faculty librarians: Acculturation problems and remedies. *College & Research Libraries* **53**, 379–392.

Newman, J. (1998). Academic librarians as scholars. *College & Research Libraries News* **1**, 19–20.

Nitecki, D. A. (1993). Conceptual models of libraries held by faculty, administrators, and librarians: An exploration of communications in the Chronicle of Higher Education. *Journal of Documentation* **49**(3), 255–277.

Oberg, L. R., Schleiter, M. K., and Van Houten, M. (1989). Faculty perceptions of librarians at Albion College: Status, role, contribution, and contacts. *College & Research Libraries* **50**, 215–230.

O'Brien, A., and Raish, M. (1993). The image of the librarian in commercial motion pictures: An annotated filmography. *Collection Management* **17**(3), 61–84.

Penniman, W. D. (1995). Preparing librarians for the twenty-first century—assuring that they will measure up. In *Mapping Curricular Reform in Library/Information Studies Education: The American Mosaic* (V. L. P. Blake, ed.). Haworth Press, New York.

Prins, H., and Gier, W. D. (1992). Image, status, and reputation of librarianship and information work (survey conducted by the IFLA Round Table for the Management of Library Associations). *IFLA Journal* **18**(2), 108–118.

St. Clair, G. (1993). Elysian thoughts on librarians as faculty. *College & Research Libraries* **54,** 7–9.

St. Lifer, E. (1994). Librarians have a different perception of their jobs than outsiders do. *Library Journal* **119**(18), 44–45.

Selth, J. P., and Hutchinson, H. L. (1989). Research report from California (comparison of research activity in the University of California and California State University systems). *College & Research Libraries News* **6,** 487–489.

Shapiro, B. J. (1993). The myths surrounding faculty status for librarians. *College & Libraries News* **10,** 562–563.

Sinclair, G. E. (1998). Ways that library school education has changed to meet the challenge of new or emerging technologies. *Sci-Tech News* **52**(3), 42–43.

Slattery, C. E. (1994). Faculty status: Another 100 years of dialogue? Lessons from the library school closings. *Journal of Academic Librarianship* **20**(4), 193–199.

Stephenson, M. S. (1990). Teaching research methods in library and information studies programs. *Journal of Education for Library and Information Science* **31**(1), 49–65.

Strauch, K. P. (1992). On my mind: The power of positive thinking (librarians' psychological road blocks to doing research). *Journal of Academic Librarianship* **18,** 100–101.

Wallace, D. P., and Van Fleet, C. J. (1994). The invisible librarian. *RQ* **34,** 6–9.

Watson-Boone, R. (1986). Beliefs and realities: Libraries and librarians from a non-library administrator's point of view. *College & Research Libraries News* **8,** 492–493+.

Werrell, E. L., and Sullivan, L. A. (1987). Faculty status for academic librarians: A review of the literature. *College & Research Libraries* **48,** 95–103.

White, H. S. (1998). What is a professional in our field? (librarians or clerks). *Library Journal* **123,** 117–118.

White, H. S. (1996). Faculty status for academic librarians: The search for the holy grail. *Library Journal* **121,** 39–40.

White, H. S. (1991). Librarianship—accept the status quo or leave it? *Library Journal* **116,** 68–69.

Woodsworth, A. (1997). New library competencies. *Library Journal* **122,** 46.

Young, P. R. (1996). Librarianship: A changing profession. *Daedalus* **125**(4), 103–125.

A Psychological Approach to Creating Stronger Public Libraries

Brian A. Reynolds
San Luis Obispo City–County Library
San Luis Obispo, California 93403-8107

I. Introduction

People strive to reach their highest potential. They get closer to or further from this goal based on a variety of factors such as good or bad luck, good or bad decisions, and so forth. Efforts toward this goal are governed by a set of largely verifiable psychological principles.

Similarly, people—either working on their own or with others—strive to raise their neighborhoods and communities to their highest potential. Community building of this type happens in largely verifiable and predictable ways, responding to characteristics and priorities unique to that geographic area and in an environment characterized by constant, rapid, and fundamental change.

Public libraries can and must be an integral part of this process. Public libraries should use marketing techniques based on psychological principles to provide services and public relations that are more pertinent, convenient, and valued by users and nonusers alike. This process will happen both one-on-one and community wide.

Social and environmental factors combined with psychological principles create a matrix of threats to and opportunities for the survival of public libraries. These social and environmental issues include fiscal support, demographic changes, competition for people's time and attention, electronic technology, information overload, plus changing attitudes and skills of current/potential library customers. Psychological principles are survival needs, the search for meaning, the importance of emotion over intellect, and people's need for relationships and a sense of community.

Recommendations are provided for marketing public library services and public relations based on these issues and principles. We explore marketing and information-gathering activities; improving buildings, collections, and public services; the special role of electronic technology in public libraries;

public relations ideas; and a brief discussion of a pilot consumer health project currently underway that puts many of these ideas into practice.

II. Dramatic Changes/Challenges Face Public Libraries

A. Fiscal Support Is Insufficient/Unstable

Tax-supported public libraries in the United States date from approximately the middle of the nineteenth century. Throughout this time, it is probably safe to say that none of them have been well funded relative to other governmental agencies or to their supposedly vital relationship to democratic values and lifelong learning. Since the late 1970s or so, public libraries nationwide—large and small, rural and urban—have suffered serious fiscal problems.

The problems seem to relate not just to overall shortfalls in revenues available to government. In many instances, public priorities are shifting away from proactive, preventive services such as public schools and libraries to reactive, punitive services such as law enforcement and prisons. California, where the so-called nationwide tax revolt began in 1978, has often been described as a precursor for trends elsewhere in the United States. On a per-capita basis, California ranks among the 50 states: thirteenth in personal income; ninth in total state/local expenditures for all purposes; and third in combined state/local spending for corrections. However, California ranks thirty-sixth for higher education and forty-ninth for public libraries and branches per 10,000 population ("How Does California Rank . . . ?" 1998). It is painfully obvious that relatively high levels of personal and governmental wealth do not necessarily guarantee similar or adequate levels of public library funding. This is a not only a huge problem, but also defies logic. Public librarians and library supporters nationwide must all "put on their thinking caps" and address this issue carefully, scientifically, and persistently over time.

Public libraries have an admirable history in our nation. They are among the most popular and well-used of all governmental services. The public library is the *only* library whose constituency is the entire community. Nonetheless, the public's support for their libraries appears to be both shallow and vulnerable. Funding elections sometimes fail for reasons as peripheral as proposed building locations and Internet policies. Similar "red herring" issues can also damage a library's programs and reputation. These problems are not just limited to California. A Pennsylvania study "concludes that public libraries have several positive impacts on their communities but that their funding levels are generally inadequate to sustain the benefits over time" ("Pennsylvania's Public Libraries . . . ," 1998). The positive impacts of public libraries have produced "minimal rewards for such efforts" ("Pennsylvania's Public Libraries . . . ," 1998).

Public libraries are very popular yet woefully underfunded. Understanding and solving this mystery requires that some of the most basic assumptions about our profession be questioned. For example, one of the most popular mantras in librarianship has been "Information is power." If this assumption were correct, it might follow that those who bestow information—teachers and librarians, for example—would be powerful too. Unfortunately, the evidence for this is lacking. Clifford Stoll observes that "Information isn't power. Who has the most information in my neighborhood? Librarians, and they are famous for having no power" (King, 1998).

There are verifiable reasons why strong public libraries are undervalued. Many of these reasons relate to the fact that for too long, public librarians have focused on the wrong issues. Specifically, they have not marketed their services to users and the public at large based on proved *psychological principles.* It is necessary to first consider several societal trends that have a significant impact on public libraries, people, and their psyches.

B. Demographic Changes Alter Public Library Customer Base

At a meeting in May 1997, hosted by the California State Library in Sacramento, political columnist Dan Walters was a featured speaker. He discussed the dramatic changes affecting California—fiscal, political, and demographic. He shocked everyone by trivializing public libraries and urging librarians to "prove" (to him and to all Californians) that public libraries were worth his time and taxes. The audience was dismayed for two reasons: First, they expected that a respected political journalist would place a high value on public libraries without question; second, if Dan Walters wants proof, then public librarians and library supporters have a gargantuan challenge of marketing and selling public libraries to the more than 32 million people of the Golden State.

Public libraries' traditional customer base (white, middle class, and largely female) was assumed to be a constant. Use patterns by this clientele were relatively predictable, as was the political, fiscal, and technological environment in which public libraries operated.

As the twentieth century dawned, urban public libraries served immigrants who eagerly used library resources, but did so to become literate in English and assimilated into American life. As the twenty-first century turns, the customer base has changed. For example, the Queens Borough Public Library tries to serve their customers in more than 40 languages, including newspapers in Hindi, mystery novels in Chinese, and potboilers in Urdu

(Toy, 1998). Now, even rural public libraries own collections in languages other than English. Many of these new public library users show little interest in traditional services aimed at a white, English-speaking clientele.

Not only do we see a change in ethnicity and language, but in many areas of the United States, population centers have also changed. They have shifted from urban or even suburban centers to broadly scattered communities whose boundaries are not consistent with traditional tax-based jurisdictions. Thus, the relatively stable nexus between where tax revenues for a particular library jurisdiction are spent, and where those taxes are actually collected is distorted.

Furthermore, in California, as elsewhere, the bell curve of age distribution shows increasing growth at both ends of the scale—senior citizens and young children, with corresponding drops in the middle of the curve, especially in the number of young couples with children. Besides women, families with children have been the historical bulwark of public library users and supporters. These demographics portend dramatic changes for public library services—from materials collections and staff skills/training to historic levels and methods of tax support.

C. Public Libraries Face Increased Competition for People's Time and Attention

Historically, public libraries served some people very well and many others not at all. Major barriers to better service included inadequate buildings, book and materials collections, and open-hour schedules. Traditional public library services have not been that convenient or productive for too many customers. Occasional and potential users often complain that a trip to the public library just is not worth the trouble; their local branch library either is not open at the right times or the books and materials they need are not there when they make the effort to go. Now, however, traditional barriers to good service for users and perceived value among potential users are further exacerbated by competition from other sources. Libraries must compete for people's time. Families with two working parents struggle to keep their jobs, raise their families, and enjoy scarce leisure time. One has to ask, "How many soccer moms (and dads) make time to take themselves *and* their kids to the public library?" Renting a video or using the Internet for homework seem to take a lot less time and provide more immediate payoffs.

Until recently, public librarians have not sufficiently valued the importance of time and convenience to the library's survival. That is changing. Library school professor Nancy Van House believes that public library users have an economic and sociological value to their time. This time "cost" affects how and when people use a public library (Reynolds, 1986, p. 23).

Political commentator Alan Ehrenhalt (1998) observed that there is "a preoccupation with time, both the scarcity of it for ordinary purposes and the common perception that events are somehow speeding up out of control." Ellen Altman and Peter Hernon (1998, p. 54) observe that "Time and attention are . . . two of the most valuable assets that individuals have. Those who choose to spend these assets in the library or in using library resources should be recognized and treasured as valued customers, especially those who are frequent ones."

D. Electronic Technology Challenges Public Libraries

It is difficult to overestimate the changes being created by the use of electronic technology in public libraries and in society at large. Electronic technology is altering public libraries in important and often misunderstood ways. Bad decisions and assumptions about the proper use of electronic technology in libraries are rampant. These decisions are too often based on media hype and shoddy or nonexistent research. Properly used, computer resources are tools that will help people solve problems. Machines cannot and should not supplant interactions between and among people.

In just a few years, public libraries' use of technology has moved from the automation of internal processes and materials catalogs to the use of on- and off-site databases and the Internet. Although the internal processes and public services of public libraries have been adapting to these technologically driven changes, many people in and outside of the profession have wondered if public libraries will even survive these changes. That is, will ubiquitous and convenient consumer access to electronic information make public libraries obsolete? The long-term implications of these technological changes for public libraries are unknown.

Predictions about these issues; mundate libraries, but empirical research and data are scant and we need a lot more. We need less study about electronic gadgets and more about how people do/do not use them successfully. Librarians should be leading, not following, in this effort. Computer scientist Phil Agre believes that research on how people do and do not use information successfully should not focus on better designed computers. Rather, he urges that research should be conducted by social scientists, psychologists, and librarians—to study people instead of machines—so that one gains "a better understanding of how to organize and present information, and how people use that information once they have it" (Chapman, 1995).

Even without further research, some basic conclusions about the proper use of electronic technology in public libraries are clear. Computers can intimidate people in a variety of ways, ranging from the barrier of not knowing how (or being physically able) to type on a keyboard to not being able to separate "treasure from trash." Library Dean Patricia Breivik observes that "We are putting a great investment into technology, thinking it will solve problems. . . . But technology has never solved our educational or social problems" (Valenza, 1998). College librarian John Swan (1993, pp. 42–44) discusses the almost hysterical pressure for librarians to adopt technology, discard the "print prison," and "change or die." He suggests: "That the technological consensus, while true, is a seriously insufficient response to the electronic challenge. Vital concerns about the relationship of information to the people who use it are simply missing. . . . We must resist the unexamined, widely repeated claims that all answers are electronic."

Some specific challenges of the use/misuse of electronic technology in public libraries include the following:

Increased workload for staff (to explain and troubleshoot the hard- and software)

Increased workload for customers (who may receive too much, too little, and unreliable information)

Barriers to learning and an increased sense of isolation and depression

Reduced interactions among people in public libraries

E. Information Overload: A Different Kind of Challenge for Public Libraries

The hallmark of the Information Age for many people is information overload. People are bombarded with stimuli on a daily basis, much of it tragic, depressing, and confusing. Can public librarians help people cope with information overload?

At the end of the nineteenth century, the role of public librarians was to gather scarce information in one place and hope their customers could get to the library on foot, horseback, or some other conveyance. At the turn of the millennium, public library customers (who now commute to the library physically and virtually) find that information on most topics is no longer scarce, but overabundant.

Furthermore, electronic communications create an overwhelming flood of information, where "office workers send and receive an average of 190 messages a day, and most get interrupted by such communications at least three times an hour" ("Workers Swim in a Sea of Information," 1998). According to urban cultural anthropologist Jennifer James (1996, pp. 29–30), people's short-term memory neurons are receiving data at four hundred times the rate of people living in the Renaissance Era. James suggests that a direct result of this information overload is forgetfulness—not remembering how to spell a familiar word, or the name of a person one knows well. Novelist Robert Stone (1998, p. 354) views information overload a bit differently, when he has a character say, "It's like nobody ponders information anymore. There's more information available than there is stuff to know about, if you know what I mean."

F. People's Attitudes/Skills Are Changing and Challenging the Traditional Public Library

The stresses of modern life are changing the way people think, feel, and function in daily life. These changes—many of them negative—have an impact on public libraries' customer base. According to psychiatrist Erol Giray (personal communication, 1998), some of the ramifications of rapid change (e.g., the overwhelming emphasis on instant gratification, information as 2-minute sound bytes) are having dramatic and deleterious effects on people's mental health. Some effects of this phenomenon include a pervading emphasis on simple and superficial information (including simplistic solutions to complex problems) and a loss of skills for sustained reading of texts. To the extent that this scenario is accurate, public libraries could lose current/potential customers due to intellectual "laziness," reluctance to research issues in depth, or even an inability to read material pertinent to information needs.

Furthermore, current and potential public library customers—society at large, in other words—are characterized by anxiety, disillusionment, and cynicism. Rapid change and the uncertainty it creates are pervasive. Not only are fundamental and historical values and traditions being drastically modified, but the pace at which these changes are taking place seems to accelerate daily. Unlike the 1960s, people are not tuned in or turned on, but they *have* dropped out. These phenomena challenge public libraries in several ways. In dangerous neighborhoods, some people are afraid to leave their homes. Others do not use public library services to improve themselves, because "Why bother?" People do not join public library support groups or vote favorably in public library funding elections because of a deep, unswerving cynicism about the local governments that operate most public libraries.

Most people are avid consumers of media, and especially television. Certainly, the world has often been a grim, frightening place. Today, however, the media bring worldwide tragedy into our living rooms constantly. According to television news commentator Eric Sevareid (1998), "The biggest big business in America is not steel, automobiles, or television. It is the manufacture, refinement, and distribution of anxiety." Even though life is relatively "good" at home, media content would have us believe otherwise. A National Issues Forum study concluded that, "Despite peace and prosperity, people continue to feel alienated and disaffected" (Broder, 1998). The study recommends seeking ways to enable people to become active participants in civic life—to become players, not spectators. Only in this way is a "genuine sense of empowerment and trust likely to be rekindled" (Broder, 1998).

Urban cultural anthropologist Jennifer James (1996, pp. 16, 20) claims that the stress of modern life is a fundamental threat to people's sanity:

> We are all confused and ambivalent, trying to get our bearings in an age of such rapid change. We are experiencing an epic shift in the way we think and feel about ourselves and our jobs, about the way we live, and about the future itself. . . . Never before in history have we had an economic shift of this magnitude. We moved very slowly from hunter–gatherer (ten million years) to agriculture (eight thousand years) to urban industry (two hundred years). But now, in what seems an instant, we are in a global service world speeding toward a bioeconomy that combines gene manipulation with electronics. Vast numbers of people will not make it over this economic abyss. . . . There is an absolute connection between the speed of this change in work, economic status, and mental health and violence. . . . We must find ways to build new careers and new communities [as in the past] but we must do it faster and with greater sophistication.

James (1996, p. 28) goes on to say that "a clear perspective is the linchpin in any process of change [and] losing perspective can make us crazy." Public libraries offer this perspective, providing valued-added access to the wisdom of philosophers and average people—through the centuries and throughout the world.

III. Three Psychological Principles Affecting Public Library Services/Public Relations

Three psychological principles critical to public library service design include (1) the primacy of basic needs over all others, plus the search for meaning and personal identity; (2) the primacy of emotion in human behavior; and (3) people's need for relationships with other people and the places they live.

A. Human Survival and the Search for Meaning

Psychologist Abraham Maslow (1994) developed a hierarchy of needs to help explain many aspects of human behavior. At the top of this hierarchy were the human imperatives of safety, food, and shelter. Intellectual pursuits such as art and education were seen by Maslow as likely priorities only after these basic human needs were met.

Another aspect of human nature is that, even when involved in a life-and-death struggle, people try to figure out "what it all means." Psychotherapist Viktor Frankl (1992) discovered that even amid the horrors of the World War II Nazi concentration camps (where there was no safety, and precious little food and shelter), the inmates were concerned with trying to make some sense out of senselessness.

Psychologist Tom Sabo (personal communication, 1998) confirms this drive to discern meaning. He believes that "a major human activity involves creating coherence out of chaos, finding meaning in life, and constructing a reality that makes sense to us. And, as Frankl found, this can take place even when our very physical survival is threatened." Psychiatrist Erol Giray (personal communication, 1998) claims that people have a "cognitive imperative" that compels people to make sense and create meaning.

Research on how people use libraries to seek meaning has been conducted by communication specialist Brenda Dervin of Ohio State University. In a study conducted for the California State Library (1985), she discovered that most people visiting a public library are engaged in what she calls "sense-making." In simple terms, many people use a public library and its resources (people, books, buildings, etc.) to make "sense" out of a daily reality that is all too often less than sensible. Significantly, a person's sense-making strategies vary continuously, depending on circumstances of the moment. Some of Dervin's (1983) premises are as follows:

Reality is neither complete nor constant, but rather filled with fundamental and pervasive discontinuities or gaps.

Information is not a thing that exists independent of and external to human beings, but rather is a product of human observing.

All information is subjective and limited by human physiology and time–space constraints of past, present, and future.

Information seeking and use are posited as "constructing" activities—as personal creating of sense.

Daily survival (physical as well as mental) appears to be driven by people's desire to convert an often incoherent reality into a coherent, personal story. Brenda Dervin's research (1983) confirms that people's sense-making is responsive to and mandated by changing situational conditions, and in studying sense-making, the research must adhere consistently to actor-perspectives. That is, people's need for meaning and sense is unique to that person's situation in space/time or, as Dervin (1985) describes it, the "micro-moment." The micro-moment probably corresponds to a brief but important passage or interval in a person's daily storyline. According to Dervin, "It is the needs of a person's micro-moment which typically characterize their visit to a public library."

Many of the problems from which people suffer today are seen in a mind/body continuum. Apparently, mind/body health is strongly affected by people's sense of being "in control" of events in their daily life. As Jon Kabat-Zinn (1990, p. 201) writes:

One thought pattern that appears to be extremely powerful for improving health status is what is called *self-efficacy*. Self-efficacy is a belief in your ability to exercise control over specific events in your life. It reflects confidence in your ability to actually do things, a belief in your ability to make things happen, even when you might have to face new, unpredictable, and stressful occurrences.

Public libraries can help people can gain better control of their lives and the environment around them.

B. Emotions Are at the Heart of Sense-Making

Brenda Dervin's (1985) California State Library study found that the overriding reason her research subjects came to the public library was not so much to "get ideas and understanding," as might be expected, but to "get support and emotional control." Her research suggests that a person's search for meaning and "sense" is primarily driven by emotion, not intellect.

Thus, information seeking is driven by a sense-making approach. Paramount in this process is the role of emotion. Researcher Daniel Goleman (1995) developed the concept of "emotional intelligence," and asserts that "the mystique of a high IQ has led us largely to ignore emotional savvy, which can be every bit as vital in determining the course of our lives." The intellect is less important in making decisions than emotions.

Emotional opinions often have little basis in objective fact. Advertisers recognize that a scantily clad blond will attract more initial attention to a new automobile than will a gasoline-mileage chart. Library directors seeking support for their budgets understand that use-statistics are less potent than a well-publicized child's plea for more open hours. People's psychic history, emotions, and needs of the moment drive their information-seeking behaviors and decisions to use or not use public libraries.

People's emotions are the bedrock of behavior. Cognitive psychologists have long recognized that human beings filter sensory stimuli through a psychic net or profile of beliefs, biases, and assumptions. Events in the outside world are accepted, modified, or rejected, based on the level of assonance or dissonance between a person's emotional "net" and the environment. Librarian Wayne Wiegand (1998, p. 57) described his mother's quest for a new car—and the decisions she made—as being determined by her "personal information economy." Quoting Barbara Herrnstein Smith, Wiegand describes a "set of values that determines an individual's needs, interests, and resources . . . that the values themselves are 'radically' contingent on a variety of factors unique to each person's life."

C. The Role of Relationships and a Sense of Community

Most people, most of the time, seek the company of other people—human beings are, by nature, gregarious. The context of a person's situation at any given micro-moment usually involves interactions with other people—loved ones, friends, neighbors, and colleagues. A personal context also involves a sense of community and place.

Many people remember "the good old days" when neighbors knew neighbors and relationships were based on common need and interest. The sense of community was alive and vibrant. These good memories of the past are obscured by the anonymity and isolation of the present. Television and computer use—often exclusively solitary activities—tend to increase a sense of isolation. Modern society seems to discourage connections among people and with the places they live. Modern media especially parlay programming that is designed with a generic market in mind. Modern media communication is typically a monolog, not a dialog such as would take place among real people. In addition, much of media content is focused on tragedy and crime, which tends to increase the level of fear among people who already feel anonymous and isolated. Well-designed public library services can be a potent antidote for these modern "poisons."

Clinical psychologist Tom Sabo (personal communication, 1998) suggests that the success of people's quest for information and meaning hinges on relationships with other people—friends helping friends. Psychiatrist Erol Giray (personal communication, 1998) agrees with Sabo that information seeking and sense-making are maximized by personal relationships nourished over time by sustained interactions with other people.

Support for the importance of personal relationships also comes from the world of evolutionary psychology. Modern media would have people believe that people can and should always "look out for number 1." Evolutionary psychologists paint a picture of humanity quite different from common assumptions and media portrayals. Late in the nineteenth century, Charles Darwin noted that both Englishmen and Tierra del Fuegians possessed common social instincts, chief among them being sympathy for their fellow man (Wright, 1994, p. 184). Evolutionary psychologist George Williams wrote that, "Simply stated, an individual who maximizes his friendships and minimizes his antagonisms will have an evolutionary advantage, and selection should favor those characters that promote the optimization of personal relationships" (Wright, 1994, p. 190).

The same kind of conclusion is being drawn by modern social theorists. In trying to understand key elements in the success or failure of social movements, Lizbeth Schorr (1997, pp. 10–11) found that "Successful programs operate in settings that encourage practitioners to build strong relationships based upon mutual trust and respect."

Relationships among people are the building blocks for strong communities. It appears that community context, defined as a "sense of place," is another powerful concept that is now being rediscovered by researchers. People want to be connected to their communities and to the people who live there. Daniel Kemmis (1990, p. 6) claims that "the demise of public life has to be understood in terms of space (or place) as well as time. Putting it more positively, public life can only be reclaimed by understanding, and then practicing, its connection to real, identifiable places." National Endowment for the Humanities Chair William Ferris says that if he could be remembered for one thing as NEH Chair, it would be to "be remembered for helping Americans rediscover America and have a deeper sense of place. . . . We need to embrace the places where we live, whether they be neighborhoods in large cities or rural communities. Those in many ways are the key to who we are and the library is anchored in these places in ways that are really unique" ("Our most American institution: The new NEH chair on libraries," 1998, p. 47).

In the 1980s a nonprofit organization called Partners for Livable Places planned and implemented a variety of economic development projects across the United States. Its unique method involved identifying and enhancing the "cultural signature" of a community by carefully sculpting cultural ameni- ties—such as museums, parks, the arts, and libraries (Reynolds, 1994, pp. 172–173). By creating a set of circumstances that attracted local people to local affairs, the organization also attracted tourists and entrepreneurs. In fact, the Partners group claimed that no other method has as certain a track record for promoting economic development. The key vision of the Partners group was that by identifying and "polishing" a community's cultural identity, a set of circumstances was created that was compelling and attractive to residents, tourists, and business interests. A strong sense of place reflects a bond between people and a particular location. This has probably been an attribute of human nature from time immemorial.

IV. Strategies for Integrating Public Library Services/Public Relations into People's Priorities

Using psychological principles to create stronger public libraries is an impor- tant but complex task. On one level, the issue is simple: People have needs and librarians should address them as best they can, crafting a better fit between public library services and the community. Library users and non- users will become better people and public libraries more vigorous in a win–win situation. On another level, this seemingly simple goal is blocked by several barriers: Psychology as the "science" of human nature is, at best, imprecise. Furthermore, how can public library staff, already overburdened with too many responsibilities and inadequate resources, take on *more* respon- sibilities, especially ones that may more properly belong with trained clinicians? Finally, how can these principles be used with people who cannot or will not visit public libraries and interact with trained staff?

One way to implement these ideas successfully is to consider a marketing loop or circle, which begins and ends with customer input—first as a way to gather clues about customer preferences and finally to evaluate progress towards meeting those preferences. The essential goal of public library *services* should be to create a perfect match between customer needs and available resources in the shortest time period possible. In this way, public librarians can help people maximize sense and meaning in their lives, reduce stress and anxiety, and get closer to their optimum potential as human beings. The goal of *public relations* is similar, but must also address the psychological needs of people who cannot or will not visit public libraries and interact with library staff.

A. Information Gathering in the Marketplace—Within and Without Public Libraries

Most organizations, public and private, have historically used an inside-out approach to product and service development. That is, the organization has pondered what it does best and striven to "sell" that product or service to current and potential customers. On occasion, and more so in recent years, organizations have tried an outside-in or marketing approach. That is, before designing a product or service internally, the organization carefully looks at external issues and priorities among current and potential customers.

As public institutions, public libraries have been firmly planted on the "selling" side almost since the beginning for a variety of legitimate reasons: both the customer base and knowledge base were slow to change; social change in general was slow; as entities of local government demands for fiscal improvement and increased accountability were low; change in the internal and external use of technology was measured in decades, and not months; and competition from other sources (e.g., electronic media) was minimal.

The public library profession suffered from two defects in this regard: (1) the demand for sophisticated market research was low; and (2) the techniques of conducting market research were undervalued and poorly understood by public library leaders and managers. Library literature is as replete with "feel good surveys" about library service as it is with bored, ho-hum reactions to these same surveys. Public libraries seem to enjoy widespread approval. Yet this perception conflicts with extremely tenuous support both in terms of market penetration and success at the ballot box. A new approach to market research and public opinion is needed.

Much of the "scientific" approach to promoting public libraries over the past few years relates to studying internal processes—costs and outputs.

Management guru Peter Drucker (1998, pp. 168, 170, 174–176) says this is dead wrong. Drucker says that if an organization hopes to survive, several perceptions need to change: (1) management needs more information about what is happening *outside* the organization; (2) technologies likely to have the largest impact on a company and its entire industry will usually be found outside of its own field; (3) customer values (not technology or end-use) should drive management policy; and (4) whereas customer *wants* are unique, the *means* to satisfy them are varied.

A traditional *weakness* of public libraries is that, in trying to be all things to all people, the net effect was amorphous and of marginal impact on many members of the community. With carefully designed market research— especially to key niches such as active voters, families with children, ethnic minorities, and the business community—this defect can be converted into *strength*. In a sense, public libraries can act like a chameleon—adapting priorities, services, and public relations efforts to achieve a better blend with changing community needs, environmental conditions, and so on.

These ideas should be studied carefully by public librarians across the nation. Public libraries, like almost all organizations, serve less than a total market share of the customer base. Most public library opinion surveys and research focused on users. Drucker says that noncustomers are as important (if not more important) than customers. It is with the noncustomers that important changes always begin. Furthermore, "All our experience tells us that the customer never buys what the supplier sells. Value to the customer is always something fundamentally different from what is value or quality to the supplier. This applies as much to a business as it applies to a university or a hospital" (Drucker, 1998, p. 169).

Drucker (1998, p. 176) emphasizes that, to date, no one has discovered how to get meaningful outside data in any systematic form. These data are still largely at the anecdotal level. Discussing knowledge workers and the information technology industry, Drucker believes that "It can be predicted that the main challenge to information technology in the next 30 years will be to organize the systematic supply of meaningful outside information." If history is a guide, public librarians are poorly equipped to conduct this kind of necessary research. However, there are positive signs of change, including the latest Public Library Association Planning for Results process that approaches service design from the customer's vantage point.

At the San Luis Obispo City–County Library, staff have taken some tentative steps in the direction of customer-centered market research. In Summer 1997, the library worked with an outside consultant and Friends of the Library groups to plan and implement 15 focus groups countywide. Attempts were made to attract groups of 10 to 15 people, evenly mixing library users and nonusers. The main purpose of the focus groups was to identify issues that would be featured in a public opinion survey mailed to registered voters about a year later. Each group had a facilitator, recorder, and a third person whose job it was to "watch" participants' body language, eye contact, and other cues to attitudes such as tone of voice. All three focus group staff later compared their impressions of the events, based on their recollections and using both tape-recorded and "butcher paper" notes of the session. As far as possible, questions were designed to elicit people's feelings "from the heart" and avoid an institutional, inside-out approach.

Then, the public opinion survey was mailed to approximately 5000 registered voters countywide in June 1998, receiving almost a 25% response rate with a less than 2% error margin. Survey questions, whenever possible, were structured to discover people's daily *priorities* for information and knowledge and their *understandings* of local conditions. Some very interesting results were received. The library is about to embark on a new series of focus groups aimed at a largely Spanish-speaking audience in an area currently served only by a Bookmobile. Focus group structure and question design will emphasize participants' hopes and dreams, worries and fears, rather than how they see the library helping them. Whenever possible, focus group and survey activities are "niche-marketed" at population groups (e.g., senior citizens, teenagers, Latinos) and geographic regions within the county.

Public library marketing techniques will involve a balance of focus group and survey activities. Public librarians should also consider, however, an "environmental scanning" activity currently becoming popular in long-range planning efforts. Environmental scanning involves scrutinizing social trends, news and media content, and paying special attention to innovations and/or threats from competitors. This activity is easily accomplished if planned well and delegated properly. Library staff, Friends of the Library groups, and other library supporters can perform these tasks more or less effortlessly and continuously by acting as "listening posts" or "scouts" and feeding key information back to "headquarters."

B. Prioritizing Library Services and Public Relations

Prioritizing library services and public relations requires an understanding of the issues discussed in the two earlier sections of this paper: environmental challenges and psychological principles. In both of these arenas, public library staff can and should do at least two things: (1) adapt services to be more meaningful and convenient for individuals, and (2) publicize public libraries to users and nonusers in ways that address psychological priorities of a given community. Four areas of concern are addressed in the final section of this essay: buildings, collections, services, and public relations. A brief example of putting these ideas into practice through a library consumer health grant is also discussed.

1. Library Buildings and Facilities

There is no question that library buildings and facilities must be designed to match people's psychological priorities. When planning buildings, librarians balance their needs and ideas with competing groups (e.g., architects, interior design consultants) and with competing conditions (e.g., finite funds, building codes, energy regulations). It is likely that none of these "players" in building design know nearly enough about the psychological needs of current/potential library users. Retail outlets such as grocery and department stores have paid much more attention to location, layout, and internal amenities such as lighting, noise, and air circulation. Aaron and Elaine Cohen (1979, p. 3) believe that "it is the behavioral elements that are little regarded and even less understood by those involved in the [library] space planning process. . . . This viewpoint is a relatively new school of thought—behavioral architecture/ interior design."

Designing library buildings (as well as kiosks in malls, bookmobiles, etc.) must take into account psychological aspects of individuals and communities. In a macro sense, locating buildings with an eye to meeting the needs of people who drive *and* walk to the library is essential. In a micro sense, there are many people who cannot or will not take advantage of a library staffer; a different approach is needed. Subject-oriented pathfinders, building maps, and other pamphlet-type material should be prominently displayed at or near library entrances or—at the very least—near the adult and juvenile nonfiction and reference collections. Signage should be improved. Building-specific, computer-generated maps guiding the customer to his/her resources should be available. Private spaces for confidential research should be maintained, balanced with issues of library and customer security. Private spaces might also be used for reference interviews on such personal topics as health, divorce, and legal research.

2. Library Collections

Over the years, the author has had a couple of personal barriers to using marketing techniques to improve collections. First, public libraries do not generally produce the items that people want to use. That is, libraries are not publishers of books, magazines, or any other medium. Second, limits of money and space mean that the collection available in any particular library building is finite and inadequate for many people's needs. Later, the author began to realize that he had been looking too closely at the "trees" and not enough at the "forest." Public libraries are well equipped to prioritize and publicize *aspects* of the collection based on identified community needs. Examples include genre publishing (e.g., romance and mystery novels) as well as content-oriented collections of interest to the community (e.g., local history, genealogy, consumer health, business services). The author strongly believes that one of the keys to success for public library collections is to give each customer something tangible to take away from each library visit. With traditional collections and attitudes, this has not happened a significant percentage of the time. With new technologies available and new attitudes in place, there are great opportunities for improving services and expanding market penetration.

Some library research provides solid background for this point of view. A nationwide study ("Gallup Poll: Two of Three Adults . . . ," 1998) "found that sixty-six percent of Americans used a public library at least once in the last year, in person, by telephone, or online. Sixty-five percent consulted a librarian. The vast majority, sixty-four percent, still visit the library in person, thirteen percent more than in 1978 . . . eighty-one percent checked out a book." However, another survey in Iowa ("How the Library Serves its Patrons," 1998) concluded that title availability was only 54%, down from earlier surveys in 1990 and 1995.

The key aspect of this research is that, although many people use the public library at least occasionally, when searching for a particular item to borrow, success was only achieved about half the time. A 2-year study of reference service in California public libraries (Childers, 1997, p. 2) revealed some interesting facts about information-seeking behaviors:

70% of users claimed they had found just what they wanted
81% of users claimed to be satisfied
the majority of requests were about a subject—as opposed to requests for short answers
yet the user's question (not the user) was referred elsewhere . . . only [for] 2.5% of the total questions analyzed

The implications of this analysis are that most people most of the time found something useful at the library. For those who did not or needed more information, only a tiny percentage (less than 3%) seem willing to wait for other resources to be located and delivered. When considering the other numbers noted previously about "market share," these data imply that for a typical 100 people in a public library's service community:

44 potential library users do not use the library at all
20 actual library users did not find what they wanted
19 of the 20 users who could not find what they wanted did not pursue their information need further, at least within the library

If these numbers can be trusted, in a typical public library service community of actual/potential users, 63% do not use the library at all, do not find what they need, and do not use public library resources beyond the first, unsuccessful visit. The market share potential for improved public library services is large. Public library leaders, managers, and staff have huge opportunities to promote meaningful public library services to their communities.

3. Staff Services

After conducting outside-in marketing research, and as a precursor to service and public relations design, a public library should reconsider its role in serving various niches in the community. A public library's community typically is defined by the entire population living in a certain governmental jurisdiction. However, we can divide that population into three distinct groups: library visitors who use the buildings/collections in a self-service manner, with no staff intervention; those who interact with public service staff; and a huge percentage of the community that uses the public library seldom or not at all. Each of these population subsets requires a different approach.

In my opinion, one of the potentially misleading—and potentially dangerous—theories in public libraries is that staff should create a setting in which most users are as self-sufficient as possible. An ideal condition much discussed in the literature describes a user who comes anonymously to the library with an information need, finds the materials, and leaves with their needs met. This might have been true before the age of automation, it might be correct in a grocery store, but not in public libraries today. The premise that the goal of public library service is "disintermediation" is misleading for a variety of reasons. The role of public librarians should be to carefully consult with their clients and select just the right resources in a timely manner from a plethora of confusing and conflicting possibilities. Library staff must help people sift information "wheat" from "chaff." In the Internet age, this role will probably become even more fundamental. Accomplishing this, however, is no simple task.

Many people have not used public libraries as their first (or even last) choice for information gathering. We have served a few people very well, some marginally well, and most not at all. Part of the problem lies in the nature of public libraries themselves. As repositories for the collective product of human intellect, organized by complex codes, they intimidate many people. It would be interesting to know how many opportunities for service are "lost" over time because people either never visited a public library, or if they did, got part way into the process and quit because they did not want to appear "stupid" in the presence of the "smart" librarian.

As electronic technology becomes more widespread, even greater threats are posed to the survival of public libraries. For most people, most of the time, quality public library service is built on customized delivery brokered by personal relationships. If the only interface a person has with a public library is a machine (whether on-site or from a remote location), the service will be incomplete and, perhaps, inaccurate. The best thing that can happen in a visit to the public library is for a human user to interact (even for a brief moment) with a human staff member to begin to build relationships, fine-tune information needs of the micro-moment, and leave the building with a customized package of information products.

For public library service to succeed in this regard, public service staff must learn techniques for customer service. In some cases, these techniques will involve strengthening the traditional qualities that are the hallmark of a librarian: intellectual curiosity, broad knowledge, a desire to help, and the skills to work with people *without* intimidating. In other instances, these techniques will have to be learned from professionals from outside librarianship. A few suggestions for service improvement follow.

4. Staff Interactions with Library Users and Supporters

Staff should "begin with a change in attitude, mind set, orientation, and approach. The focus should be on understanding and treating the public as clients with needs who are seeking direction and guidance from helping professionals. There is a fundamental difference between this and treating them like customers shopping for a product. . . . The key to making it work is communicating a sincere desire that you want to understand and to help" (Tom Sabo, personal communication, 1998).

Staff should use attending and listening skills, especially verbal and nonverbal messages they are receiving from their clients. Special attention should be paid to content, feelings, meaning, and intercultural and intergenerational cues. "These [skills] are not difficult to learn and can be mastered by lay people with a minimal amount of time and effort" (Tom Sabo, personal communication, 1998). Other listening techniques include setting aside one's own opinions for a moment, using nonverbal communication to show that you are listening, mentally summarizing the speaker's main points as he/she is talking, restating or paraphrasing the speaker's main message, and—above all else—making time to listen (Kelley, 1998). An extremely important communication technique, and currently somewhat of a "lost art," is following up an interaction with a written note—whether a thank you or a clarification. Because a written note is rare, it has all the more impact in promoting people's positive feelings (Bauman, 1998).

Active attending and listening techniques should alert staff to critical aspects of the context of a user's need of the moment. Issues such as deadlines or language are obvious. More important matters relate to cognitive clues of assonance and dissonance. People's psychological biases are developed

in childhood and are usually insurmountable (Maggie Cox, personal communication, 1998). Careful attention to verbal and nonverbal clues about
these biases should enable the staff to know what they need to be sensitive
to (Tom Sabo, personal communication, 1998).

Many aspects of traditional public libraries can intimidate current and potential users (Maggie Cox, personal communication, 1998). Library services
and collections are complex and organized by codes many people do not
understand or use easily. Computer resources of all kinds, especially, can
be daunting. Even when an "answer" is found, it may or may not meet
the user's need, but many people are unwilling to admit ignorance or
failure and do not approach a staffer for help. Some potential users
may lump public libraries into the general government mode, which
characterizes governmental services as difficult to use, expensive, and so
on. People from other countries where a strong public library does not
exist may not even be aware of the breadth and depth of services available.
To counter these issues inside the library, reference and other public
service staff should "wander" the building and be alert for people who
might need assistance. For people outside the library, carefully structured
public relations efforts are required.

Surviving and crafting meaning in daily life are inhibited by anxiety, disillusionment, and cynicism. Public libraries can help reduce people's negative
emotions and promote positive ones in a variety of ways. For example,
reading a library book as opposed to watching television promotes imagin-
ing, reduces stress, and encourages interactivity. "Bibliotherapy" is for
everyone. Another example is public library sponsorship of book discussion groups, whose popularity seem eternal. Jon Kabat-Zinn and many
others believe that mind/body health relates directly to a person's sense
of self-efficacy. Public librarians can help people promote self-efficacy
by providing resources that solve everyday problems unique to each
person's needs and priorities. In this fashion, public libraries also become
a more integrated, valuable resource in more people's lives.

Reference interview skills need to be enhanced in new ways. In an interview
for *American Libraries*, Kathleen de la Peña McCook (1998, p. 161) noted
that "We try to look at the reference interview as we always have, but
with a keen focus on the individuals and their context." A library in the
Chicago suburbs "offers personalized service to patrons. In a three-step
process called a learning journey, guides . . . work with patrons in order
to identify interests and learn new skills" ("Arlington Heights Memorial
Library, . . ." 1998).

Paraphrasing Emerson, Brenda Dervin (personal communication, 1998) suggests that, above all else, public library staff should:

TREAT PEOPLE WELL, treat them as if they are real . . . in short, stop constructing people as if they are made to fit some preconceived mold and respond to them, to their needs, and on their terms. Learn to build responsive iterative systems. Learn to build dialogic systems. . . . LIS systems as now defined are based on domain characteristics of the world—as reified by those in power at a given time. . . . Learn how to put a human overlay on top which addresses human dimensions.

Dervin strongly believes that library and information systems (LIS) need to move beyond "factizing" to sense-making and to helping people narrow the gaps in reality that occur hundreds of times each day.

Ellen Altman and Peter Hernon (1998, p. 54), as noted earlier, believe that we should treasure repeat customers, who "tend to be loyal . . . have proven their interest in reading and seeking information . . . recommend library services and collections to their friends and colleagues, and tend to be forgiving when the system errs." Furthermore, public libraries must design services and increase public relations that demonstrate that we can actually help people *save* time, not *spend* time.

Psychiatrist Erol Giray (personal communication, 1998) puts it very succinctly: "Libraries must educate customers to the possibilities without being condescending." Furthermore, Giray believes that mental health professionals can and should train librarians in these skills. This training should be linked with schools so that successful library experiences can begin as early as possible in a child's life.

The staff response to requests for service should carefully match the context of an individual client at a specific point in time. For example, a common practice in academic library bibliographic instruction programs is to discard generic curricula in favor of course-driven needs. Simply put, the students remember the course material better if it was customized to fit a real-life research need. This applies also to public library users.

Public relations expert Maggie Cox (personal communication, 1998) suggests services be designed and prioritized based on segmentation of the broad market of users. Services should emphasize, when possible, the largest market segment(s) and always answer the library user's question: "What's in it for *me*?" A typical example would be the promotion of children's programs, which reach a very broad segment of nuclear/extended families and the social infrastructure that supports them.

Clinical psychologist Tom Sabo (personal communication, 1998) confirms Maslow's hierarchy of needs and suggests that public library services adapt accordingly. "For that matter, health and life/death issues can strongly motivate our information-seeking behavior. . . . Libraries that readily make available resources that help people cope with these 'problems in living,' and staff that are sensitive to their client's needs for assistance with these dilemmas will certainly reach a wide audience."

Sabo further asserts that "The focus [of services] should be on understanding and treating the public as clients with needs, who are seeking directions and guidance from helping professionals. There is a fundamental difference between this and treating them like customers shopping for a product."

Public libraries can become more important to current/potential customers in at least two ways: (1) emphasizing services that help people reach their top priorities (e.g., safety, shelter, health); and (2) providing services that treat people with kindness, attention, sensitivity, and respect.

Taking a cue from the Partners for Livable Places group, public libraries can help people articulate and polish the identity of their community. Public libraries can serve as a catalyst for this process to begin, as well as providing resources and guidance for ongoing information needs. This goal is especially important because much local information (e.g., history, social and economic data) is not easily researched. By working toward this goal, public libraries not only provide valuable services but enhance their reputation as a vital local institution.

C. The Proper Role of Electronic Technology in Public Libraries

The pervasive influence of electronic technology in public libraries deserves special emphasis. Generally speaking, people seek information and solve problems most successfully when they work together—not in isolation, and not by simply using a machine. The wrong emphasis on computer machinery can actually hinder, not help, this effort.

For example, it is easy to imagine two people (a library staffer and a client) discussing how to approach the solution to information needs. It is difficult to picture the same interchange being a success when of the two participants one is human and one machine. Some reasons for this phenomenon are listed as follows:

85% or more of client communication of meaning is nonverbal (e.g., eye contact patterns, body language, vocal qualities; Ivey, 1994). MIT Media Lab Director Nicholas Negroponte (1995, p. 92) says virtually the same thing when he asserts that a computer will probably never be as interactive as one's dog—which reacts instantly to his/her master's presence, moods, and so on.

Acquiring information from the printed page in a room full of books, people, and furniture and acquiring the same information from a computer screen are distinct psychic phenomena. Physical objects such as books provide a wealth of clues about completeness, integrity, and structure of information. Electronic information, generally, does not (Roszak, 1992).

The Internet's emphasis on hypertext

> [R]epresents the forefront of a technological wave in education that is driven more by enthusiasm for the computer than by reliable knowledge of the human user. . . . It is generally assumed (and rarely demonstrated) by advocates of hypertext that humans are constrained by the (supposedly) inherent linear qualities of paper. . . . In the world of hypertext, that is seen as a bad thing. . . . Research has shown that reading from screens is frequently slower, less accurate, and more fatiguing. (Dillon, 1997, p. 2)

It is not just learning that suffers, but people's moods as well. A *New York Times* article reports that "Internet users who spend even a few hours a week online at home experience higher levels of depression and loneliness than if they had used the computer network less frequently" ("Report: Internet can make you lonely, depressed," 1998).

If the average library customer is seeking meaning rather than information per se, then a mix of electronic and print media is best: "the library's *information* services will be supported best by electronic technology and . . . its *knowledge* services will be supported best by physical collections supplemented by electronic resources" (Crawford and Gorman, 1995, p. 180).

Electronic technology must be used very carefully in the quest to help people gain meaning and sense in their lives. If public librarians depend too much, or unwisely, on technology, service excellence will deteriorate and the viability of public libraries be diminished. The key to improve public library service is about relationships among people.

D. Public Relations

A well-known technique in library collection development is to create a loop of activities that begins and ends with customer opinions. Focus groups, surveys, book reviews, and many other informal activities tell us, in the beginning, what the public's priorities are for books and materials. Other parts of the "loop" involve deciding who will be responsible for various activities, what will be accomplished when, costs, and so forth. Unfortunately, most public libraries have not adapted these techniques for public relations. Typically, there is no one even on the staff who is assigned these duties or has the requisite skills. A few tips include the following:

Publicize services that address Maslow's hierarchy of needs. In other words, emphasize services that address deep-seated emotional needs, as identified in public relations research.

When possible, use whimsy, humor, and "image-busting" techniques. The traditional image of public librarians as boring and tame (at best) and stifling and rigid (at worst) can work to our advantage. One of my own favorite ideas (as yet untried) is to design a highway billboard that would say, in large letters "Get Even at the Library!" That is, use library resources to divorce the grumpy spouse, disinherit the ungrateful heirs, evict the difficult tenant, and confound one's enemies!

Every public relations person with whom I have spoken has emphasized the following key concepts about public relations: conduct carefully designed market research, look for compelling benefit, develop a distinctive message, and repeat the message. Even doing all of this, Maggie Cox (personal communication, 1998) warns us that although the long-term benefits of advertising are useful and productive, these benefits are notoriously hard to track. Cox further asserts that public librarians must be constantly alert to consumer "price sensitivity" as it relates to a person's willingness to choose library services over other competing activities with a lower price.

If a public librarian wants to persuade a person to change their opinions, attitudes, or behavior, he/she will be most successful if "The message appeals to emotions, particularly to fear or anxiety" (Coon, 1997, p. 631). This concept is equally important to increasing the user base or to convincing users and nonusers to vote favorably in public library funding elections. Traditional public library services and public relations have been designed to appeal to the intellect, not the emotions. As much as possible, these activities need to be marketed to people's emotions, biases, and prejudices—not to rational, intellectual characteristics.

E. A Pilot Project in Promoting Community
Health Resources

Several years ago, the author became interested in conducting a project to promote the San Luis Obispo City–County Library based on some of the principles discussed in this essay. The Library knew that consumer health information was a popular service. Good health is certainly at or near the top of Abraham Maslow's hierarchy of needs. Focus groups and a mailed public opinion survey confirmed that access to better health information was a high priority, especially among senior citizens living along the coast in our county.

In December 1997, we applied for and received a California Endowment grant in the amount of $147,000. Grant activities were centered in Morro Bay and had two primary purposes: (1) to better position the Morro Bay Branch Library as a provider of consumer health information, and (2) to conduct an asset mapping and community building process based on the principles of John McKnight and John Kretzmann of Northwestern University. The project also had two primary goals: (1) to make the Morro Bay Branch Library more pertinent, convenient, and valuable to local residents;

and (2) to invigorate the community through asset mapping and community building.

Some of the activities conducted so far include hiring consultants, training staff, purchasing consumer health materials in various formats, designing a database, forming and training a community collaborative, establishing partnerships with community groups and agencies, attracting other sources of funding (in-kind help, equipment, and cash), and planning for year two of the grant process. A "time dollar bank" is being established to track and reimburse people who donate time or services with discounts on other health-related services.

Library staff feels that this grant activity is significant and innovative. If handled well, it could provide great benefits to the library and the community of Morro Bay. It addresses very high community priorities and involves senior citizens who are active voters and heavily involved in community affairs. The Community Collaborative is helping prioritize and fine-tune activity areas. It provides community ownership of the health project, which is essential. Collaborative members will gather surveys of assets of individuals and organizations in Morro Bay for input into the database. They will also help publicize and market the database to the community. Members are especially interested in establishing intergenerational links between seniors and teenagers as well as reaching out to the Latino residents of Morro Bay. If successful in the year two grant application, they will also publicize and train potential collaboratives in other areas of the county. If this particular consumer health effort is a success in Morro Bay, the staff hopes to expand it to other communities. It is even possible that a countywide database of individual and organizational assets might be designed and maintained by the library and other partners, and thus promote community building for a countywide community of more than 200,000 people. That is my dream.

V. Conclusion

Public libraries need to provide services and public relations in new ways. These new activities are actually based on old-fashioned ideas of marketing goods and services to people through psychological principles. Advertisers and retailers have used social and psychological principles to conduct their businesses for a long time.

Public librarians need to learn from experts outside their own field and apply what they learn to make their libraries stronger. Social and environmental trends are relatively easy to identify and respond to. Psychological principles are more complex, imprecise, and varied. Environmental and psychological issues present to public librarians a mixed bag of both threats and opportunities. These ideas require deeper and broader scrutiny, yet hold much potential for public libraries nationwide.

Public libraries are places where people help people get a little closer to their potential. This is perhaps the most human of endeavors, and librarians should be proud of the roles they play. There is an exciting future for the library profession.

References

Abraham Maslow (1994). *The New Encyclopedia Britannica.* 7, 911, Britannica Press, Chicago, IL.

Altman, E., and Hernon, P. (1998). Service quality and customer satisfaction do matter. *American Libraries* **29**(7), 53–54.

Arlington Heights Memorial Library, IL, offers personalized service to patrons. (1998). *Library Hotline* **27**(11), 3.

Bauman, R. (1998). The best words come on paper. *The Rotarian* **173**(4), 12.

Broder, D. (1998). Cynicism prevails in apathetic nation. *San Luis Obispo County Telegram–Tribune* (June 27), B-10, San Luis Obispo, CA.

Chapman, G. (1995). Search tool of the future? Librarians. *Los Angeles Times* (August 17), D-1.

Childers, T. A. (1997). *Reference Performance in California Public Libraries, 1996–1997.* College of Info. Science and Technology, Drexel University, Philadelphia, PA.

Cohen, A. , and Cohen, E. (1979). *Designing and Space Planning for Libraries: a Behavioral Guide.* R.R. Bowker, New York, NY.

Coon, D. (1997). *Essentials of Psychology: Exploration and Application.* 7th ed. West Publishing Company, St. Paul/Minneapolis, MN.

Crawford, W., and Gorman, M. (1995). *Future Libraries: Dreams, Madness, and Reality.* American Library Assn., Chicago, IL.

de la Peña McCook, K. (1998). Keeping the library in library education. *American Libraries* **29**(3), 59–63.

Dervin, B., and Fraser, B. (1985). *How Libraries Help.* University of the Pacific, Dept. of Communication, Stockton, CA.

Dervin, B. (1983). An overview of sense-making research: concepts, methods, and results. Paper presented at International Communication Assn. Annual Meeting, Dallas, TX, May 1983.

Dillon, A. (1997). Myths, misconceptions, and an alternative perspective. (October 3), School of Library and Information Science, Indiana University. Available at http://www.slis.indiana.edu/adillon/adillon-myths.html.

Drucker, P. F. (1998). Management's new paradigms. *Forbes* **162**(7), 152–176.

Ehrenhalt, A. (1998). Politics and the goulash of everyday life. *Governing* **11**(11), 7.

Frankl, V. (1992). *Man's Search for Meaning: an Introduction to Logotherapy.* Beacon Press, Boston, MA.

Gallup poll: two of three adults are library users. (1998). *ALA Cognotes* (July), 10.

Goleman, D. (1995). The new thinking on smarts. *USA Weekend* (October 8–10), 4–5.

How does California rank among the 50 states? (1998). *California Libraries* **8**(6), 6.

How the library serves its patrons (1998). *Library Administrator's Digest* **32**(3), 20.

Ivey, A. E. (1994). *Intentional Interviewing and counseling: facilitating client development in a multicultural society.* Brooks Cole, Pacific Grove, CA.

James, J. (1996). *Thinking in the Future Tense.* Simon & Schuster, New York, NY.

Kabat-Zinn, J. (1990). *Full Catastrophe Living: Using the Wisdom of Your Body and Mind to Face Stress, Pain, and Illness.* Delacorte Press, New York, NY.

Kelley, M. N. (1998). Are you listening? *The Rotarian* **173**(3), 6.

Kemmis, D. (1990). *Community and the Politics of Place*. Univ. of Oklahoma Press, Norman, OK.

King, P. H. (1998). The enfeebling effect of the Internet. *San Luis Obispo County Telegram–Tribune* (April 28), B-5, San Luis Obispo, CA.

Negroponte, N. (1995). *Being Digital*. Alfred A. Knopf, New York.

Our most American institution: the new NEH chair on libraries. (1998). *American Libraries* **29**(8), 44–47.

Pennsylvania's public libraries, public good, limited resources. (1998). *Library Hotline* **27**(28), 4.

Report: Internet can make you lonely, depressed. (1998). (August 30), Available at: http://customnews.cnn.com/cnews.

Reynolds, B. A. (1994). Public library funding: issues, trends, and resources. In *Advances in Librarianship* (Irene P. Godden, ed.), **18**, pp. 159–188. Academic Press, San Diego, CA.

Reynolds, B. A. (1986). Proactive management in public libraries in California and in the nation. In *Advances in Library Administration and Organization* (Gerard McCabe and Bernard Kreissman, eds.), pp. 1–78. JAI Press, Greenwich, CT.

Roszak, T. (1992). Environment of Mind: Selecting the Content of our Mental Habitat. A program presented at the California Library Assn. Annual Conference, Long Beach, CA, November, 1992.

Schorr, L. B. (1997). *Common Purpose: Strengthening Families and Neighborhoods to Rebuild America*. Anchor Books/Doubleday, New York, NY.

Sevareid, E. (1998). Thought for Today. *San Luis Obispo County Telegram–Tribune* (May 8), B-4, San Luis Obispo, CA.

Stone, R. (1998). *Damascus Gate*. Houghton, Mifflin Company, Boston.

Swan, J. (1993). The electronic straitjacket. *Library Journal* **118**(17), 41–44.

Toy, V. S. (1998). Nation's busiest library speaks in many tongues. *New York Times* (May 31), Real Estate Section, Front Page.

Valenza, J. K. (1998). Information literacy is more than computer literacy. (May 11), Philadelphia Online's School Crossings Available at: http://crossings-phillynews.com/archive/k12/infolit4_16.htm.

Wiegand, W. (1998). Mom and me: A difference in information values. *American Libraries* **29**(7), 56–58.

Workers swim in a sea of information. (1998). *San Luis Obispo County Telegram–Tribune* (May 23), E-2 23 pp., San Luis Obispo, CA.

Wright, R. (1994). *The Moral Animal: Evolutionary Psychology and Everyday Life*. Pantheon Books, New York, NY.

Schooling and Skilling Health Librarians for an Evidence-Based Culture

Judith Palmer
University of Oxford
John Radcliffe Hospital
Oxford OX3 9DU, United Kingdom

I. Introduction

The world of information is a world of turbulence. For library and information professionals the scale and rate of change since the late 1980s has been unprecedented. Major social, political, and organizational trends have been reflected in the workplace. We have seen a shift from hierarchical structures to flatter and networked cultures with increased emphases on team working and the needs of customers. This shift has been accompanied by a greater concern for quality assurance and value for money (Marshall, 1997). Many organizations and professions, recognizing that these changes require new attitudes and changed practices on the part of their employees and members, have built programs of continuing professional development and lifelong learning into their corporate strategies. New ways of learning and new approaches to the provision of learning materials have been enabled by the developments that have taken place in information technology, networking, and telecommunications. With easier access to networked information sources and services has come an increased expectancy for desktop delivery, 24-hour access, personalized services, and easy-to-use systems. For many people, some degree of competence in information skills has become an essential part of their working life. For organizations has come the realization that their success rests on the effective management of their knowledge base and the need to support the continuing education and professional development of their employees.

These trends have affected libraries and librarians at all levels—organizational, professional, and personal—and have provided many new opportunities for librarians and information professionals to move beyond the boundaries of their workplace, take on new responsibilities, and operate in a more dynamic mode within the work environments of those who require access to the information services they manage. To do this has required a shift in perspective and a willingness to remold the way in which we traditionally think of libraries and librarians.

Core competencies in the traditional skills of the management and organization of text, data, and information must be augmented by a continuous development and extension of expertise, a broader range of professional and technical skills, a higher level of interpersonal and communication abilities, more sophisticated application of management tools, and enhanced understanding of organization and culture (Corrall, 1996; Corrall and Lester, 1996). The librarian of the future will be a change agent, a facilitator with a broad vision able to challenge the status quo, operate flexibly within rapidly changing environments, and take the lead in knowledge management.

There is evidence that this view is becoming more widespread. Few journals or conferences resist the temptation to include papers on the changing role of the librarian and professional bodies, such as the Library Association and the Institute of Information Scientists in the United Kingdom and the Special Library Association and Medical Library Association in the United States, have all reviewed the position of librarians and specified what skills and competencies are necessary and desirable for the next millennium. In the higher education sector in the United Kingdom there has been major investment in helping to effect a change in professional working in an electronic environment. Several projects within the Electronic Libraries (eLib) Programme (http://ukoln.bath.ac.uk/elib) have focused on the skills and competencies that are now necessary in order to practice as an effective information professional.

Nowhere have the opportunities for librarians been greater than in the field of health care, where concurrent changes since the late 1970s have disrupted traditional views of the place of information in patient care.

II. Changing Paradigms in Health Care

In 1978, dissatisfied with existing assumptions of clinical practice and recognizing the unruly nature of the biomedical journal literature, a group of physicians at McMaster University in Hamilton, Ontario, began developing a method to teach students and colleagues how to read a clinical paper critically. The exponential rise in the volume of the literature was not a new phenomenon (Price, 1963). What was different at McMaster was the systematic way in which the problem of information overload was approached, and the value and applicability of the clinical evidence questioned.

The process they adopted was given the name *critical appraisal.* This formed the core of what was then called *clinical epidemiology,* subsequently named *evidence-based medicine* (Guyatt, 1991), and now known more generally as *evidence-based health care*. "For the clinician, evidence-based medicine requires skills of literature retrieval, critical appraisal and information synthesis. It also requires judgement of the applicability of evidence to the patient at hand and systematic approach to make decisions when direct evidence is not available" (Guyatt, 1991, p. A-16). This approach deemphasized intuition and unsystematic clinical experience and stressed the examination of evidence from clinical research and the use of the medical literature to guide more effective medical practice. It was hailed as a new paradigm for medical practice (Evidence-Based Medicine Working Group, 1992). The foundations of the paradigm shift were said to lie in the gradual adoption since the late 1960s of a more methodological approach to clinical research, an increased emphasis on biostatistical approaches, and a recognition of the value and importance of randomized controlled trials and meta-analyses.

In Britain, in an influential book, *Effectiveness and Efficiency*, published in 1972, Archie Cochrane drew attention to the value of randomized control trials in guiding decisions about health care and lamented the lack of ready access to the results of such research. In the 1980s, collaborative work resulted in the preparation of many systematic reviews of randomized control trials (Peto, 1987). Much of the work was done in Oxford, where there was a particular constellation of people and influences. Also, links over a number of years between the Oxford Region of the National Health Service, Oxford University, and McMaster University meant that many of the ideas and philosophies of the Oxford researchers and the Evidence-Based Medicine Working Group in McMaster were shared.

III. The Research and Development Strategy and Health Care Reforms in the United Kingdom

A series of reorganizations and reformations in the UK National Health Service (NHS) began in 1979 and continues to the present day, with the publication of *The New NHS* early in 1998. In 1991, the first comprehensive research and development (R&D) strategy for the UK National Health Service, *Research for Health*, was published that had the following three broad aims: (1) to promote knowledge-based decision making; (2) to encourage the NHS to look to research as a way of tackling service problems; and (3) to encourage the rapid dissemination of research data to inform clinicians, managers, and policy makers (Langlands, 1994).

The NHS reforms and the evidence-based movement in the United Kingdom are inextricably linked. Without the NHS reforms, clinical epidemiology and a recognition of the importance of evidence-based medicine might never have spread further than Oxford, or might have taken much longer to spread and, without the stimulus of the ideas that emanated from McMaster and from Archie Cochrane, the NHS R&D strategy might have taken a different form.

The aims of the R&D strategy placed information firmly at the center of the agenda and reflected the NHS plans, some of which were already in motion and some nearly complete, to set up and support an evidence-based approach to healthcare. The UK Cochrane Centre was established in 1992. In January 1993, the task of compiling a register of NHS research was begun, and in December 1993, the Centre for Reviews and Dissemination was set up in York. In Oxford in 1995, the Centre for Evidence-Based Medicine was opened under the leadership of David Sackett. Important information sources have been developed through government support.

The UK Cochrane Centre provided the impetus for the establishment of the International Cochrane Collaboration, a collaboration of groups throughout the world that carry out systematic reviews of randomized control trials. There are now 15 Cochrane Centres that facilitate the work of the Collaborative Review Groups, Methods Working Groups, and share the responsibility for helping to coordinate and support members of the collaboration in areas such as training. They also promote the objectives and work of the collaboration at a national level. The systematic reviews constitute the Cochrane Database of Systematic Reviews (CDSR), a part of the Cochrane Library with the Database of Reviews of Effectiveness (DARE) produced by the Centre for Reviews and Dissemination and the Cochrane Controlled Trials Register (CCTR), an essential information source for evidence-based health care. The Centre for Evidence-Based Medicine has played a key role in the development of the new journal *Evidence-Based Medicine*, modeled on the *ACP Journal Club*. Similar journals for nursing and health management and policy have followed.

These developments mirrored similar trends in medicine in the United States, Canada, and Australia, where pockets of support for an evidence-based approach sprung up in university medical faculties, in particular hospitals or in other institutions. However, in Britain, this trend was underwritten, supported, and promoted by government policy. Subsequent government white and green papers have reinforced and emphasized the centrality of evidence-based practice in achieving greater clinical effectiveness and an increased national health gain.

IV. Health Libraries in an Evidence-Based Culture

In 1991, several groups of health librarians were tackling the problems precipitated by the NHS reforms in different ways. The King's Fund Library in London and the NHS Regional Librarians Group both carried out reviews of health information services. These reviews found that libraries were becoming increasingly marginalized, that librarians were facing competition from other information providers, and that there were no recognizable national strategies for the management and provision of health information. Furthermore, there was massive duplication, fragmentation, and information hoarding, and worst of all, little research was being done to investigate the contribution that libraries and information services might make to improving the quality of patient care.

As a result of these shortcomings, the British Library established a Medical Review Panel in 1992. The first and major achievement of this panel was to sponsor a national seminar (British Library, 1992). Because Baroness Cumberlege, then Parliamentary Under Secretary of State in the Department of Health in the Thatcher Government, gave her active support to this venture, the seminar and its successor a year later came to be known as the Cumberlege seminars (Haines, 1995). These provided a common platform for health professionals from every sector—managers, clinicians, the professions allied to medicine, researchers, technicians, and librarians—to discuss information issues that straddled discipline boundaries and the value of developing a national health information strategy. At a second seminar (British Library, 1993) a year later, the following strategic objectives were identified:

To improve the quality of the knowledge base and its coordination
To ensure that the knowledge base is disseminated widely using the technology that is becoming available
To identify, promote, and disseminate good local practice
To improve the local organization and transmission of the knowledge base
To use critical appraisal as a means to filter the literature for all health professionals, including librarians

Following on from the second seminar, Cumberlege 2, the NHS recognized the role that libraries must play in the collection, organization, and dissemination of information and in providing access to the knowledge base by establishing the post of NHS Library Adviser, whose task it was to take forward the Cumberlege objectives.

However, health care librarians had to cope with changes other than the NHS reforms. Developments in computing, networking, and almost every aspect of information management required constant monitoring. Although the Internet had been in existence for more than 20 years, commercial providers began to appear in the United Kingdom in the early 1990s, and it became possible for the first time for individuals who were not part of the academic or research sectors to gain access to global networks. In the NHS, with no tradition of wide area networking, libraries had been unable to communicate with each other except by mail, telephone, and fax. The emergence of new Internet service providers (ISPs) anxious to woo individual customers and drive down the cost of connection to the Internet, promised new opportunities for communication, the exchange of knowledge, and sharing resources.

Thus, changes in health care, information technology, and knowledge and information management were combining to force the pace of change in health care libraries. No pressure was more significant than the pressure for libraries and librarians to support evidence-based health care.

V. The Role of Information in Evidence-Based Practice

There are many definitions of evidence-based health care, but all are based on five essential steps:

1. Formulate a question
2. Search the literature
3. Critically appraise the results
4. Incorporate into practice
5. Evaluate the results

These five steps are similar to the stages in any basic problem-solving model. For example, Gordon proposed the following steps (Gordon, 1974):

1. Identify the problem
2. Generate alternative solutions
3. Evaluate alternatives
4. Choose a solution
5. Implement the solution
6. Evaluate the results

It is not difficult to see that problem-solving and evidence-based practice both require some expertise in information handling. There are many listings, both formal and informal, of what can be regarded as information skills; for example, the UK Institute of Information Scientists publish their Criteria for Information Science, Barry (1997) cites Marland's nine sequential stages, and there are other listings. Most suggest that information skills include the ability to frame questions, devise appropriate strategies, locate information, interrogate sources, judge relevance, understand bias, record and organize information, interpret and analyze, reorganize/reorder information, and present evidence to others—skills commonly possessed by library and information professionals, but not necessarily by other health professionals.

The extent to which librarians might therefore occupy a pivotal position in the delivery of evidence-based health care became apparent. Early in the 1990s, important studies at McMaster, at Rochester General Hospital (New York) (Marshall, 1992), at the Children's Hospital of Michigan (Detroit) (Klein *et al.*, 1994), and elsewhere in the United States demonstrated the value and impact of library and information services on patient care. In the United Kingdom, the British Library sponsored similar research on the effectiveness of NHS library and information services and their impact on clinical decision making (Urquhart and Hepworth, 1995ab).

To what extent the effectiveness of health care library and information services *depends* on the skills, knowledge, and expertise of health care librarians has become an increased focus for attention. Bradley (1996) recognized early that it was important to redefine and communicate how changes in health information and health care delivery would affect health science librarians. The need for graduate programs of professional development were investigated in an interesting project that involved interdisciplinary multi-institutional alliances to develop graduate educational programs for health science librarians (Smith, 1996). Both the Medical Library Association and the National Library of Medicine in the United States have initiated efforts to effect change in order to better recruit, educate, and retain health sciences librarians. *Platform for Change* (MLA, 1991) set out a new program for professional development. Since 1995, the National Library of Medicine has awarded grants to encourage and challenge the health sciences community to plan for continuing professional development. Planning is focussed in four areas: (1) the evolving role of healthcare librarians, (2) professional education, (3) continuing education and lifelong learning, and (4) recruitment (Johnson, 1998). Much of this work reflects similar interests throughout the profession on the changing role of the librarian and the importance of traditional and new skills in effective professional practice. However, in health care there have been few coordinated programs of professional development specifically designed to equip health service librarians to play an active role in evidence-based health care.

In Oxford, we recognized that the spread of an evidence-based culture would have a direct impact on libraries and librarians, requiring new attitudes, new services, and new skills. We believed that if these changes were to be accepted, a process of education and development was necessary in order to enable people to feel comfortable with the new concepts and structures.

VI. Librarian of the 21st Century

In the United Kingdom, health care is administered regionally. Since 1991, there have been two national reorganizations in which regions have merged and boundaries altered. The most recent was in 1998. In the first reorganization, in 1994, the Anglia and Oxford Region was established, one of seven other regions in England. In the Anglia and Oxford NHS Region, there was a strong tradition of human networking among health care libraries and coordination and cooperation had long been orchestrated by a regional library unit, based in the University of Oxford and currently called the Health Care Libraries Unit (HCLU). The work of this unit is both strategic and intensely practical (http://www.lib.jr2.ox.ac.uk). It acts as a focus of support for all the librarians in the Health Libraries and Information Network (HeLIN) and also provides advice to a wide range of health care organizations and departments within the region on all issues related to library and information services. One of the most important areas of the work of HCLU has always been to provide a program of continuing professional development for librarians to ensure best practice throughout the region.

In 1994, with the support of the Regional R&D Director, Dr. Muir Gray, a program of professional development for the librarians in the region was planned called the *Librarian of the 21st Century*. This was implemented in the west of the region in 1995 (Palmer, 1997; Palmer and Streatfield, 1995) and repeated, with revisions, in the east of the region in 1996.

An independent consultant was invited to work with the HCLU to organize a program of training events. The aims of this program were to enable health care librarians in the region to consider how their roles as information workers were likely to change over the next few years and to begin to develop some of the specific skills required for their new roles.

More specifically, the objectives of the program were to enable program participants to do the following:

Consider the changing health care scene and envisage how library and information services should develop in relation to those changes
Assess the likely effects of these changes on their work roles as librarians
Examine some aspects of critical appraisal of health care information and work on some practical elements of critical appraisal
Look at how adults learn and assess their roles in supporting adult learning in relation to information searching, analysis, and presentation

Diagnose their own strengths and weaknesses in information retrieval and appraisal and engage in practical activities to enhance their skills in these areas

Review their progress through this program and consider further development of their roles in managing information

The program included five events over a period of 6 months. All library managers in the west of the region, of which there were 25, were urged to attend. The result of establishing a cohort of trained practice managers who would be able to support and encourage each other once the program was completed was anticipated as being one of the benefits of the program. We also expected that library managers would pass on their learning and awareness to more junior staff.

A. New Horizons, New Skills, and New Opportunities

The program began with a workshop that reviewed trends that affect libraries and librarianship and introduced the program. This event, held in January 1995, was led by Joanne Marshall, then Associate Professor in the Faculty of Information Studies at the University of Toronto. She gave a *tour de force* review of the trends that affect the information world in general and libraries in particular, covering "megatrends," "Workforce 2000" trends, workplace trends, the changing library environment, and library trends. She emphasized throughout how the work of health librarians will change from judgment to evidence-based practice for both themselves and their clients.

B. Critical Appraisal of Information Sources for Librarians

The introduction workshop was followed a month later by a workshop on critical appraisal for librarians. The event was led by a public health consultant and was based on the series of workshops aimed at public health physicians, NHS purchasers, and other health care professionals and had been developed in the old Oxford Region under the Critical Appraisal Skills Programme (CASP). By the end of the workshop, participants were expected to be able to define the phrase "clinical effectiveness"; understand the terms "systematic reviews" and "meta-analysis"; be able to explain why these are so important for health care librarians; and also to have critically appraised a published review article.

C. Teaching and Training

In March, two workshops were held to equip librarians with some appreciation of the teaching and training skills needed to work more flexibly with a wider range of information seekers. The aim of these events was to enhance the ability of participants to plan and provide effective sessions with information users and the objectives were to ensure that by the end of this workshop, participants had done the following:

Explored some of the components of effective adult learning and related them to their own teaching priorities as librarians

Looked at some theories of learning and related teaching strategies

Prepared a learning activity and practised some relevant teaching skills in relation to that activity

Assessed some of the problems of applying learning theories and strategies in working with individuals and groups

In preparation for the next pair of events, a self-assessment questionnaire was distributed to potential participants. The main needs identified by the questionnaires were for sessions on the Internet, working with databases, and on the implications of critical appraisal for librarians. Considerable interest was also expressed in locating and using "gray literature" (i.e., semipublished reports and other material), but it was felt that this theme could more easily be addressed as part of the normal regional training program.

D. New Sources of Information and Information Retrieval and Handling Skills for Librarians

The next pair of 2-day seminars, held in June, was based largely on the results of this survey under the title. The first pair of events began with a 1-day workshop on "Demystifying the Internet" that consisted of a brief introduction to the Internet; a guide to getting started; an outline and practical exercises on the World Wide Web; coverage of e-mail, news, and lists; and an introduction to and practical exercises using other search tools then commonly available such as Gopher, Veronica, and WAIS. This event was followed by a "Superhighways and Byways" day, the aim of which was to introduce participants to new evidence-based information sources such as the Cochrane Library and also to new techniques in searching for high-quality information.

E. Managing Information

In the final half-day workshop an attempt was made to "find out what this really means for the Librarian of the 21st Century." Here, the objectives of this session were to do the following:

Review the Librarian of the 21st Century project as a whole and consider what changes should be considered if the program is repeated

Identify elements in the program that should become part of the regular
    repertoire of professional development for the region

Consider how best to build on the knowledge and experience gained through
    the program and to practice any skills acquired

Identify any other areas where staff development would be useful in equipping
    participants to be more effective Librarians of the 21st Century.

VII. Participants' Evaluation of the Events

Events were evaluated individually using feedback sheets, and the final event
was intended to provide an evaluation of the entire program.

1. New Horizons, New Skills, and New Opportunities
   This workshop was very well received, and the 30 participants said
   that they would have welcomed more time for questioning, possibly
   at the expense of the group planning activity that followed.

2. Critical Appraisal of Information Sources for Librarians
   The CASP team administered their own evaluation instrument that
   showed that overall the event was pronounced "good" to "excellent"
   by all 32 participants and was unusually enjoyed "quite a lot" or "very
   much." One person commented, "I would like to have seen more
   discussion about the boundaries of what libraries are expected to do.
   I am not sure I am equipped to help our readers in a constructive way
   yet." The question of the part librarians play in doing and teaching
   critical appraisal remains an issue for discussion.

3. Teaching and Training Skills
   These events were again, well received, although some participants
   felt that it would have been better to confine the second afternoon
   to interaction with groups rather than trying to address one-to-one
   interaction at the same event. The balance in the sessions on individual
   and group-working with clients was altered as a result of the first
   event and the improvement here was reflected in the feedback.

4. New Sources of Information and Information Retrieval and Handling
   Skills and Demystifying the Internet
   These two workshops were generally seen as enjoyable, felt to address
   people's needs, and encouraged 10 of 11 current users to use the
   Internet more and 6 other people to consider doing so. The presentations were deemed very good by all but 1 respondent, and the practical
   sessions were judged "good" to "very good."

5. Superhighways and Byways
   This workshop and seminar received mixed reviews. Most respondents

at both events found the session on on-line searching and new data-bases of about the right length and complexity. Several participants at both events suggested that a whole day would have been preferred to a half-day event.

The final event was designed, in part, as an evaluation event. The 21 participants were split into four groups and asked to consider the following:

1. What were two of the high points in the program for you?
2. What changes should be made to the program order, shape, or content if this program is to be repeated? Why should these changes be made?
3. What elements in the program should become part of the regular repertoire of professional development for the region?

There was a strong consensus that the high points of the program were the teaching skills workshops (picked by all four groups) and Internet workshops (three groups), with the critical appraisal workshop, database search sessions, and the introductory day all mentioned. There were varying opinions as to the content and sequence of events.

Some concern was expressed about the exclusiveness of the program and it was agreed that library assistants and junior professionals should have received copies of all the course documents, although it is doubtful whether such documents supplied out of context would be of much use.

Participants were also invited to discuss the way forward. They were asked:

1. What further staff development would you welcome? Please identify the skills, knowledge, and expertise required.
2. How should this further staff development be addressed? Should the emphasis be on regional training events? Is there scope for visits, work shadowing, paired mentoring, or longer courses?
3. How much time should be committed to further staff development and over what period?
4. In what order should these issues be tackled?

VIII. The Way Forward

All four groups identified "marketing of library services" as one of their development priorities. This was envisaged as a "one-off two-day event" ("including homework"), possibly as a residential weekend. Two groups identified "technology updates" ("particularly the Internet") as their other priority area. Another group called for a training needs assessment and program for library assistants, envisaging an "Assistants of the 21st Century" course. They also felt the need for further training through a mix of regional and local events, work shadowing, and monitoring. Other missing elements identified were training in facilitation skills and presentation skills.

Overall, the "Librarian of the 21st Century" program was deemed to be successful. In 1995, a similar program was held in the east of the region that incorporated elements missing from the original program.

Following on from the program in the west, the Regional Professional Development Group assessed the program and drew up a strategic plan for a comprehensive program of professional development. The Regional Strategic Plan recognizes the need to do the following:

Provide training for new librarians in our network
Continually update and enhance existing competencies and skills
Evaluate the training
Assess how evidence-based our practice is

IX. Concurrent Library Developments

Soon after the Librarian of the 21st Century Project was underway, we recognized that concurrent developments in networking and health care should be integrated into our plans for personal and service development. The development of the World Wide Web, the growing importance of the Internet (especially in the continuing absence of the NHS Net), and the move toward a primary-care led health care system in the NHS suggested that we should extend our horizons beyond a simple program of professional development. We obtained additional resources to build on what had already started and develop a wider program—the Libraries and Librarian Development Programme. It was clear that a major initiative of this sort was necessary if we were to do the following:

Educate librarians about the philosophy and concepts of the new culture
Provide them with the skills both to do it themselves and be more proactive and competent in training their users
Provide them with access to the new information sources in the United Kingdom and on the Internet
Provide them with access to the Internet
Educate libraries about the explosion of new sources and old sources from new places
Find a way to encourage and support information services to those who worked in primary care and who might be remote from hospital libraries

The broad aims of this programme were to ensure that all libraries and librarians in the Anglia and Oxford Region had the knowledge, skills, and facilities to provide health care professionals with access to the knowledge base of health care and thus to ensure that all decisions in health care were based on the best available evidence.

The Libraries and Librarian Development Programme covered three areas—Networking and the Internet, Continuing Professional Development, and Primary Health Care. It is important to point out that resources for this broader program of development would not have been secured without the success of the Librarian of the 21st Century Project, which subsequently became a model for other NHS regional library networks in the United Kingdom who have implemented similar programs of professional development based on the Librarian of the 21st Century Project in Anglia and Oxford.

X. Benefits of the Librarian of the 21st Century Programme

Within the Anglia and Oxford Region the existence of a 25-year long active tradition of human networking and resource sharing enabled the benefits of the program to be realized much more quickly than might otherwise have been the case. The greatest benefits have been in raising awareness and confidence amongst the librarians. This has enabled them to take on roles beyond the management of the library within the organizations that employ them and meant that both the participants in the program as well as those who use their services have benefited.

Apart from gaining confidence, librarians have also recognized that they have unique and valuable skills within an evidence-based culture, most notably as trainers and instructors. Thus, librarians in Anglia and Oxford have been involved in running the annual Search Clinics at the International EBM Workshops run by Dave Sackett's Centre for Evidence Based Medicine in Oxford and are also involved in a new University of Oxford's Masters Programme in Evidence-Based Health Care—an important module of which is concerned with information skills. However, the most fruitful developments have occurred in the relationship that has developed between the Health Care Libraries Unit, the Health Libraries and Information Network, and the Critical Appraisal Skills Programme team. It is worth examining how the teaching role for librarians has developed in this region in the light of the Librarian of the 21st Century Project, the Libraries and Librarian Development Programme, and the Critical Appraisal Skills Programme.

XI. Librarians as Educators

Beginning in 1992, a series of workshops based on the experience at McMaster (Milne and Chambers, 1993) was held in Oxford to introduce public health physicians and those working closely with them to the techniques of critical appraisal and the special importance of systematic reviews and meta-analysis as a means to sift and synthesize the evidence. Their success encouraged the organizers to believe that the program could be developed to cover other target groups, and in 1994 a new series of workshops—Critical Appraisal Skills for Purchasers (CASP) was launched.

The aim of CASP is to help all health care professionals develop the skills they need to make sense of evidence about clinical effectiveness. The three essential elements of evidence-based decision making—finding the evidence, appraising the evidence, and acting on the evidence—formed the slogan: "Find, Appraise, Act" for CASP.

Since January 1994, approximately 3000 people from all professional groups have attended CASP events throughout the United Kingdom and eight events are being held every month. Plans are being made to run these workshops in other languages and in other countries. All have been well received. Participants have included all the health professions—physiotherapists, occupational therapists, public health physicians, researchers, managers, librarians, general practitioners, hospital consultants, clinical auditors, purchasing managers, pharmacists, and dentists. These workshops demonstrated that critical appraisal can be taught to nonclinicians, that workshops for mixed audiences were fun and popular, and that critical appraisal of reviews does not require a knowledge of research methodology.

Quite early on a number of participants at the CASP appraisal workshops expressed an interest in learning more about "finding the evidence." As a result, in May 1994, the CASP team and HeLIN began planning a workshop on "Finding the Evidence" (Palmer, 1996). The coincidence of this timing with the ongoing Librarian of the 21st Century Project was not entirely fortuitous. Public health personnel, who knew of the Librarian of the 21st Century Project currently underway, believed that librarians were not only aware of the impact of evidence-based health care on their own profession, but that they were also willing and even eager to take on new roles.

In November 1994, a pilot workshop was held, and as a result of the feedback from this event, a revised version was designed. This process has continued and few workshops follow a rigid pattern. The aims and objectives have, however, remained constant. The aim is to help participants improve their ability to find evidence systematically about clinical effectiveness, especially in reviews and other summaries. The objectives are as follows:

1. To be aware of the range and quality of available sources of evidence about effectiveness, irrespective of format
2. To be aware of how searching techniques and search strategies may affect outcome and to be aware of the problems associated with searching different sources

3. To be aware of the options available to obtain and organize journal articles and other documents

4. To share and learn from the experience of other participants

XII. Finding the Evidence Workshop Program

It is interesting to look at the development of the workshop program in some detail as it reflects the way in which ideas and practice changed as a result of feedback from participants and illustrates a willingness to adapt and change on the part of the librarian–trainers. The early workshops were based on the premise that learning would be most effective if participants completed a preworkshop exercise. Thus, before the day of the workshop, participants were asked to find information either on a given topic or on a topic of their own choosing, complete a preworkshop worksheet and to send the worksheet to the workshop organizer ahead of the workshop. Trainers believed that this would allow the small-group facilitators and workshop organizers to get some feel of the kinds of problems that participants might need help with at the workshop. In practice, participants were generally tardy and reluctant to complete the preworkshop task. Consequently, this element was abandoned.

At the workshop, after a brief Introduction to CASP and the origins of the workshop, participants were split up into small groups (no more than eight) with a facilitator to discuss the problems they encountered when searching for information. Groups are asked to identify a reporter who would provide feedback to the whole group. Workshop organizers could decide whether they wished groups to structure their discussion under certain headings, or leave the discussion unstructured. Groups were asked to report back in a number of ways. It was considered to be of paramount importance that each member of each group be given the opportunity to share their experience and for groups to report back to the whole workshop. This part of the program is always enjoyed by participants and is successful. Good group facilitation is important, as is a well-managed feedback session.

The next part of the program provided local librarians with the opportunity to promote the library and describe some of the services that they offered and to explain. This part of the program was generally not successful partly because it was, and is, difficult to maintain the attention of people who have come to acquire generic skills only to be faced with what appeared to be a soft sell for libraries. The way in which library services support and augment health care is now more subtly introduced in open discussion around such issues as document delivery and the location of fugitive or "gray" literature.

After a break, participants were introduced to the range of print and electronic information sources. This proved to be tedious to do and even more tedious to listen to. At the end, the evaluation provided the opportunity to comment on the workshop as well as to suggest improvement.

A. Postpilot Activity

Following the pilot, modified versions of the workshop were held in each of the four counties that comprise the Anglia and Oxford Region. It had always been intended that the pattern of the workshop should not be seen as immutable, but rather that it should be regarded as a template to be tailored and adapted to the particular needs of the environment. Modifications thus arose as a result of local needs, the character of the expected participants, and the preferences of individual librarians. However, all recognized that good supporting documentation kept up to date was likely to be essential for all workshops. A regional group was formed to maintain and develop the content of workshops, encourage the participation of as many local librarians as possible, and highlight any additional training that might be required for librarians leading these workshops.

The group of people working on the development of these workshops became known as the CASPfew Team. They worked together to produce a comprehensive Workshop Organizer, which was seen as a key educational support tool for anyone who wished to understand and run Finding the Evidence workshops. The expectation was that the organizer would be seen as a flexible template that could then be tailored and adapted to meet local needs. This has indeed proved to be the case in the workshops that have been held subsequently.

For the CASPfew Team there were, however, a number of problems. First, the materials quickly became out of date, and the existing format of paper file and diskette did not provide an effective and efficient mechanism for gathering feedback, developing the teaching material, and disseminating changes back to network members. Second, unlike the critical appraisal workshops, local libraries were already offering user education in information skills, and careful consideration needed to be given to how the program would integrate with existing work.

The questions that needed to be addressed could be summarized as the following:

How to meet demand for more workshops, both regional and local

How to make the most of resources and materials developed centrally in order to maintain quality and reduce duplication of effort

How to promote and support implementation and ownership of local programs

How to provide training in appropriate skills for librarians to support workshop delivery

How to provide feedback on local experiences and expertise into further development

How to evaluate the impact of training programs on end users

How to serve the needs of users unable to attend workshop events

It was clear that a strategic approach to further development and implementation was required that would aim to:

Further develop centralized resources at a regional level using a CASPfew Web site to maximize access and reduce duplication of effort

Provide training and support in new teaching, learning, and facilitation skills

Monitor the quality of the materials used in training programs

Carry out impact evaluation of training programs and methods

Enable local librarians to offer cross-organizational and multidisciplinary training and share subject and training expertise

Thus the task was to balance centralized development and the maintenance of quality while at the same time empowering library staff and encouraging local ownership. It was also sensible to exploit the potential of the HCLU Web site and ensure that the electronic network complemented the existing human network of contacts and expertise, thereby developing a two-tier approach—the human and electronic network.

The following elements were seen to be important in any strategic planning

A regional CASPfew team

Local CASPfew teams

CASPfew Web site

Training the Trainers Programme

Distance Learning Initiatives

B. Regional CASPfew Team

The Regional CASPfew Team was responsible for centralized developments that would benefit all and reduce duplication of effort. This included developing regional strategies, updating materials, developing toolkits and web resources, organizing training, undertaking impact evaluations, and liaising with other health professionals at a regional level.

C. Local CASPfew Teams

Local strategies, the delivery of local workshops, liaison with local CASP teams, sharing expertise and training opportunities, and feedback into regional development were seen to be the task of local CASPfew teams that are in an ideal position to establish alliances with other health professionals in order to make sure that information skills training is incorporated in the local multidisciplinary training agenda.

D. CASPfew Web Site

At the center of the strategy is the development of the CASPfew Web pages. These are designed to provide background and contact information on CASPfew and enable the development and dissemination of high-quality workshop and teaching materials to local teams. The CASPfew Toolkit contains hints and tips on workshop planning; teaching materials including scenarios, activities, and handouts; sample forms and questionnaires; and slide presentations. The materials can be viewed via a browser or downloaded for local adaptation and use. In this way the quality, relevance, and effectiveness of materials can be monitored while encouraging use, feedback, and further development. We have found that once local teams have been established, they gain in confidence and skills, and both teams and individuals have the potential to gain encouragement and recognition from sharing their work. In addition, the health libraries network as a whole is strengthened and benefits from the promotion of a collaborative, resource-sharing culture.

XIII. Training the Trainers

In order to deliver high-quality end-user training, librarians need to be provided with high-quality professional development. Although the Librarian of the 21st Century Project provided a foundation for developing new roles and skills, such as in teaching and learning, facilitation skills, new technology, marketing, and change management, it was recognized that librarians from within the region may require additional training in the management of workshops. It was also recognized that librarians from outside the region who wished to hold similar workshops might require training. A Training the Trainers Workshop was therefore developed and marketed to other regions in the United Kingdom, together with the Workshop Organizer.

The Training the Trainers workshop looks at the skills and planning involved in organizing successful Finding the Evidence events. Topics covered include the background and structure of CASPfew, workshop planning and content, teaching methods and evaluation, and using the CASPfew Toolkit. The workshops are highly interactive and use group work, scenarios, and demonstrations to help people organize events in their local settings.

XIV. Beyond the Workshop— Distance Learning

More recently, it has become clear that there is now an increasing need to develop our teaching materials beyond the workshop. Limited accessibility and the increase in demand for the skills required in an evidence-based culture have required CASP and CASPfew to investigate alternative training methods. Although the face-to-face and group work aspects of the CASP model are hard to replicate, the inherent difficulties in relying on workshop models to train large numbers of health professionals in finding, appraising, and acting on evidence are obvious. A decision was therefore taken to convert the teaching materials into a distance learning format, which could both meet a wide variety of needs and take advantage of developments in technology. This will increase accessibility and extend support networks to those working in all areas of the health service, particularly those in primary and community care. Distance learning, by allowing learners to learn at their own pace, time, and level, can provide flexible training in appraisal and information skills to meet a wide range of learning styles and organizational requirements. Two projects have been completed that have translated the workshop content both into a series of printed books and into a CD-ROM for use by distance learners (CASP and HCLU, 1999). Close collaboration continues between the Centre for Evidence-Based Medicine and the Centre for Evidence-Based Mental Health, both in Oxford, to investigate the development of a Web-based version of these teaching materials.

XV. Discussion and Conclusion

The Librarian of the 21st Century Project has been important for three reasons. We have shown librarians *how* to enhance and improve their skills, not merely exhorted them to do so. We have also provided a cohort of librarians with the same package of experience and with the training that we feel to be essential to support evidence-based patient care. It would be difficult to overestimate the importance of shared learning by a cohort of practitioners who are in regular contact with each other. The experience affects not only the way in which they carry out their own jobs, but also the quality of library provision to the ultimate benefit of all health professionals. Finally, from the viewpoint of an individual librarian, we have provided a package of learning events whose content has wider applicability and significance than for health care alone.

The Librarian of the 21st Century Project and the Libraries and Librarian Development Programme have also had impact beyond the boundaries of the Anglia and Oxford Region. In other NHS regions where a coordinating regional library unit such as HCLU existed, similar programs were, and are now being, developed. In other regions where there are no regional library units, progress has been slower and more uneven. Elsewhere in the United Kingdom, there are other foci of development. Most notably, in Sheffield, Andrew Booth (Hicks, Booth, and Sawers, 1998) at the Sheffield School of Health and Related Research (ScHARR) (Booth, 1996), inspired by the McMaster work and by work being done in Oxford, developed a series of training workshops for librarians.

Our experience has shown the value of coordinated library networks and the importance of providing librarians with enhanced skills and awareness so that they are able to play an active role within an evidence-based framework. The existing human network within the Oxford region has been enhanced by the development of an electronic network that complements this pool of expertise and supports the work of local staff. HCLU continues to work at a regional and local level in order to help librarians play a high-profile, proactive role as mediators, educators, and facilitators, helping their users to find the evidence.

The combination of changes in health care, information technology, and wide area networking have combined to present an unprecedented challenge to the role and value of libraries and librarians. Health care professionals will be able to access more and more high-quality information without having to visit libraries or tailor their needs to the opening hours of local health care libraries. In other sectors, these winds of change may not yet be so forceful or so apparent as in health care. However, there is little doubt that within the next few years these same issues will become increasingly important for all who work in libraries and information provision. This has already begun to happen in education, where school librarians are now aware that the traditional custodial role is no longer tenable and that the library must make an active contribution to teaching and learning (Rogers, 1994). Similar trends can also be seen in colleges of further education (Streatfield and Markless, 1997). The report, *New Library: The People's Network*, by the Library and Information Commission (LIC) in the United Kingdom (LIC, 1998) on the development of the public library service, emphasizes that if access to knowledge, imagination, and learning is to be provided for all, then a training strategy must be developed for the 27,000 employees in the public library sector.

It is generally true that if libraries and librarians are not to be increasingly marginalized, we must recognize that an investment in continuing professional development is one of the most important weapons we have if we wish to continue to be taken seriously by other professional groups and by those who use our libraries.

References

Barry, C. A. (1997). Information skills for an electronic world: training doctoral research students. *Journal of Information Science* **23,** 225–238.

Booth, A. (1996). In search of the evidence: Informing effective practice. *Journal of Clinical Effectiveness* **1,** 25–29.

Bradley, J. (1996). The changing face of health information and health information work: A conceptual framework. *Bulletin of the Medical Library Association* **84,** 1–10.

British Library Research and Development Department (1992). Report of a seminar on health care information in the UK; 1 July 1992 at the Kings Fund Centre London, chaired by Baroness Cumberledge. The British Library, London.

British Library Research and Development Department (1994). Report of a seminar on managing the knowledge base of healthcare; 22 October 1993 at the Kings Fund Centre London, chaired by Baroness Cumberledge. The British Library, London.

Corrall, S. (1996). Defining professional competence: Skills and prospects for the information profession. *Vision 2020: Training for the New Millennium.* Paper presented at the Circle of State Librarians Annual Study Day (unpaged).

Corrall, C., and Lester, R. (1996). Professors and professionals: On changing boundaries. In: *Critical Appraisal Skills Programme and Health Care Libraries Unit* (1999) *Evidence-Based Health Care, an Open Learning Resource for Practitioners* (5 vols. and offprints). Oxford: CASP and HCLU.

Critical Appraisal Skills Programme and Health Care Libraries Unit (1999) *The Evidence-Based Health Care Workbook Including the Evidence-Based Health Care CD-ROM.* CASP and HCLU, Oxford.

Evidence Based Medicine Working Group (1992). Evidence-based medicine: A new approach to teaching the practice of medicine. *JAMA* **268**(17), 2420–2425.

Gordon, T. (1974). *Teacher Effectiveness Training.* McKay, New York.

Guyatt, G. H. (1991). Evidence-based medicine. *ACP Journal Club* March/April A-16.

Haines, M. (1995). The Cumberlege seminars in England. *Health Informatics* **1,** 3–9.

Hicks, A., Booth, A., and Sawers, C. (1998). Becoming ADEPT: Delivering distance learning on evidence-based medicine for librarians. *Health Libraries Review* **15**(3), 175–184.

Johnson, F. E. (ed.) (1998). Symposium: NLM planning grants for the education and training of health sciences librarians. *Bulletin of the Medical Library Association* **84**(4), 513–568.

Klein, M. S., Ross, F. V., Adams, D. L., and Gilbert, C. M. (1994). Effect of on-line literature searching on length of stay and patient care costs. *Academic Medicine* **69,** 489–95.

Langlands, A. (1994). A clear future for the NHS. Speech given at IHSM Conference on 10 June 1994 reported in *Network Special,* 10 June, 1994.

Library and Information Commission (1998) *New Library: The People's Network.* Library and Information Commission, London.

Marshall, J. G. (1992). The impact of hospital library on clinical decision making: the Rochester study. *Bulletin of the Medical Library Association* **80**(2): 169–78.

Marshall, J. G. (1997). Creating a vision for the 21st century: The way ahead for library and information professionals. On the Edge. Proceedings of the 7th Asian Pacific Specials, Health and Law Librarians' Conference, Perth, 1997. Australian Library and Information Association, Perth.

Medical Library Association. (1992). Platform for change. MLA, Chicago.

Milne, R., and Chambers, L. (1993). How to read a review article critically. *Health Libraries Review* **10,** 39.

Palmer, J. (1996). Where is the evidence? Teaching health professionals how to find the evidence. In: *Health Information Management: What Strategies?* Paper presented at the 5th European

Conference of Medical and Health Libraries, Coimbra; 1996: Ed. Bakker S, Dordrecht: Kluwer 1996: 299–301.

Palmer, J. (1997). Skills for a virtual future. *Bibliotheca Medica Canadiana* **19**(2), 62–65.

Palmer, J., and Streatfield, D. (1995). Good diagnosis for the twenty-first century. *Library Association Record* **97**, 153–154.

Peto, R. (1987). Why do we need systematic overviews of randomized trials? *Statistics in Medicine* **6**, 233–240.

Price, D. J. de Solla (1963). *Little Science, Big Science*. Columbia University Press, New York.

Rogers, R. (1994). *Teaching Information Skills: A Review of Research and Its Impact on Education*. British Library Research/Bowker Saur, London.

Smith, L. C. (1996). Interdisciplinary multiinstitutional alliances in support of educational programs for health sciences librarians. *Bulletin of the Medical Library Association* **84**, 560–567.

Streatfield, D. R., and Markless, S. (1997). *The Effective College Library*. Developing FE, FEDA Report vol. 1 (8). British Library Research and Innovation Report 21. FEDA, Bristol.

Urquhart, C. J., and Hepworth, J. B. (1995a). *The Value of Information Services to Clinicians: A Toolkit for Measurement*. Open Learning Unit, Department of Information and Library Studies, University of Wales, Aberystwyth.

Urquhart, C., and Hepworth, J. (1995b). The value of information supplied to clinicians by health libraries: Devising an outcomes-based assessment of the contribution of libraries to clinical decision-making. *Health Libraries Review* **12**(3), 201–213.

Increasing Diversity
Programs and Internships in ARL Libraries

Teri Switzer
Colorado State University
Fort Collins, Colorado 80523-1019

William Gentz
University of Pittsburgh
Pittsburgh, Pennsylvania 15260

I. Introduction

Educational outreach to ethnic populations is an important aspect of creating a pluralistic society, and in order to ensure the training of this workforce, active recruitment to educational opportunities and professions must occur. As the agendas of human rights and affirmative action strive to increase minority recruitment and retention in academia, the academic research library has found itself vying for its share of the diversity pie and coming up short. Even though diversity has been discussed and affirmed, the facts show that the library and information science discipline has not come close to making progress in increasing the minority representation in libraries.

After reviewing the literature and the data, it is apparent that recruitment of minorities to library and information science has to be a partnership among the library schools, the professional associations, and library practitioners. As an important component in the library practicum category, academic libraries have an important role in the recruitment process. However, their role is not only one of recruitment to the library and information science profession, it is also one of recruitment to academic libraries. This chapter provides a look at the presence of ethnic minorities (Native Americans, Asian Americans, African Americans, and Latinos) in the library and information science profession in the United States, and then focuses on the use of internships and/or residency programs in Association of Research Libraries (ARL) members as a recruitment tool to both the profession and to academic libraries. For ease of usage, the terms "minority" and "minorities" are used.

169

II. The Multicultural Population

A. A Population Shift

For several years, the American workplace has been positioning itself for the changes that will be occurring. Demographers predict that by the year 2000, one-third of the workforce will consist of citizens from several different cultural backgrounds. In fact, United States Bureau of Census officials predict that by the year 2020, the United States population will increase by 25%. Although this may not seem significant, one only need review the data to see the impact. The Asian populace will increase 156%, Latinos will increase 104%, Native Americans will increase 43%, and African Americans will increase by 41%. A large percentage of these increases will be a result of immigration; however, legislative efforts, such as California's Proposition 187, have the potential of creating a distinct negative impact. Nonetheless, as Alire (1996, p. 129) asserts, "people of color will no longer be in the minority." It is anticipated that this population shift will open up opportunities for minorities to become more recognized as positive additions to their communities and their professions.

B. Minorities in Higher Education

Compared to the Caucasian population, minorities have long been associated with lower economic prosperity and social status, thus stressing the importance of higher education. In addition, more minorities are recognizing the need for additional skills in order to be competitive in today's labor market.

Even though civil rights cases in the 1940s and 1950s opened up educational opportunities for minorities, the real impetus to broaden higher education channels started with the Civil Rights Act of 1964, which states, "No person in the United States shall, on ground of race, color, or national origin . . . be subjected to discrimination under any program receiving federal financial assistance." Since then, strategies to increase minority student recruitment and retention have been employed by most colleges and universities. Enrollment trends for minorities have not been constant during the past few years, but there has been a steady increase in minority enrollments (Carter and Wilson, 1996). For several years, colleges and universities relied on the 1978 Supreme Court ruling in *The Regents of the University of California vs. Bakke* (438 U.S. 265 (1978). This case held that the fostering of a diverse student body, where using race as a "plus factor" in admissions, is constitutionally allowed. It was a turning point for colleges and universities.

With the assistance of court cases like *Bakke*, the number of minorities enrolled in colleges has slowly increased to the point that there are now approximately 3.5 million African American, Native American, Asian American, and Latino students enrolled in United States colleges (Statistical Abstract, 1997). An analysis of degrees earned by ethnic minorities shows that between 1985 and 1993, the number of associate degrees earned by minorities increased 37.1%, bachelor degrees earned increased 59.3%, and master's degrees increased 53.2%.

Although there have been improvements in increasing the presence of minorities on our college and university campuses, it is imperative that this progress continues. Race sensitive admissions policies have helped increase the representation of ethnic minorities on college campuses and promote interracial interactions. To illustrate this, Bok and Bowen (1998) conducted an in-depth study of 45,184 people who were accepted into 28 selective colleges during the years 1976 and 1989. An analysis of their data shows that graduation rates of minorities (primarily African American, Asian American, and Latino) equal those of Caucasian students. They conclude that, "academically selective colleges and universities have been highly successful in using race-sensitive admissions policies to advance educational goals important to them and societal goals that are important to everyone else."

Challenges to race-sensitive initiatives are not new to academic institutions. In 1995, the University of Maryland–College Park suffered a setback when an all-black scholarship program was deemed unconstitutional. However, prior to the Maryland case the most celebrated of the affirmative action cases in recent years, *Hopwood v. Texas* (78 F3d 932 (5th Circ. 1996)), *cert denied*, 116 S. Ct. 2581 (1996), acknowledged that race could not be a consideration for admitting students. *Hopwood* argued reverse discrimination and its ruling provided the impetus for other universities and colleges to question their own affirmative action programs. The threats cases such as these, and more recently cases like *Piscataway Township Board of Education v. Taxman* (91 F.3rd 1547 (3rd Circ. 1996, *cert dismissed* 118 S. Ct. 595 (1997)) and *Gratz and Hamacher v. Regents of the University of Michigan* (filed December 3, 1997), pose to increasing diversity are undeniable. In fact, in *Piscataway*, it was argued that the end of affirmative action is a formula for the destruction of the great public universities. Even though affirmative action is under attack, these cases have not completely invalidated *Bakke*, nor have they tainted statements such as that of Justice Powell, who argues "the benefits of integrated education accrue to all students, and affirmative action to increase diversity is appropriate" (p. 312).

However, as college campuses address their minority graduation rates, some states find that they are being confronted with legislation designed to curtail the proactive minority recruiting efforts that have been implemented. The California Civil Rights Initiative, Proposition 209, is an example of such legislation. During late 1997, the Supreme Court rejected a challenge to this amendment, stating that Proposition 209 was, indeed, constitutional, and state and local agencies, including public institutions of higher education, could not use race or gender as a preference in admissions practices.

The presence of legislative initiatives and court cases is bringing challenges to colleges and universities. Discrimination litigation is quickly becoming a trend. Institutions of higher education are being forced to implement other measures that fall within the letter of the law while continuing to create an inviting environment for minority students. Some institutions are revising their recruitment and scholarship wording, using "diversity" in lieu of "minority." Still others are partnering with specific ethnic minority organizations in order to direct scholarships, grants, internships, and residency programs to ethnic minority groups. At least one other academic institution has dropped the minority and diversity designation completely from its advertising and program titles. It is finding that scholarship activities must address the population as a whole, and is now requiring applicants to write an essay in which they share their personal philosophy and efforts towards increasing diversity. Thus, the focus is on those individuals who *value* diversity, even though they may not be from an ethnic minority group. Educators recognize that creating a more pluralistic and welcoming educational experience is vital to the nation. Students of all races can only benefit from multiculturalism. Diversity should be an institutional priority and infused in recruitment as well as teaching and research endeavors.

C. Minorities in Library Science

Although there have been improvements in recruiting and retaining minority students to colleges and universities, the impact on the library science profession has been minimal. Affirmative action is relatively new to library schools. In fact, prior to the 1970s, many library schools were segregated (Williams, 1987). Data collected by the Association for Library and Information Science Education (ALISE) for 1992–1993 through 1996–1997 shows that minority (not including international) graduation rates have increased by 10% since 1994 from 400 MLS graduates in 1993 to 444 MLS graduates in 1997. Caucasian graduation rates have increased by 5.4%, yet still comprise 89.9% of the total MLS graduates in any given year. Native American graduation rates have remained fairly constant, except for 1994–1995 when the number of graduates decreased 75%. In fact, 1994–1995 was not a promising year for any group with the exception of Latino/Hispanic graduates who increased 118% and Caucasian graduates who increased 54%. This is notable because the total number of minority MLS graduates decreased 8.4%. Even though the number of ethnic minorities who have graduated with a MLS has increased since 1992–1993 and the number of Caucasian graduates has remained fairly constant, the recruitment of ethnic minorities continues to be a challenge.

To put this into perspective, however, one must compare the total number of minority librarians to the United States minority population. The United States minority (Native Americans, African Americans, Asian Americans, and Latino/Hispanic) population increased from 25% to 27% of the total population between the years 1993 and 1997. During the same period, the number of MLS minority graduates has increased from 9.6% to 11%, which is slightly less than the increase in total population. In all respects, however, the MLS graduation rates are not in parity with their corresponding populations. In addition, if one considers the minority population projections, the discrepancy becomes more apparent. There definitely is room to expand, and the library and information science field is being enlisted to become proactive and recruit from this growing population.

III. Recruitment to the Library and Information Science Profession

With the number of library and information science graduates remaining fairly constant and the number of ethnic minorities receiving degrees increasing (albeit a small number), there is concern that some library schools may not have the incentive to actively recruit to the profession because they see their total enrollment as being steady. It is apparent that in order to more fully reflect today's pluralistic society, the library and information science profession is obligated to actively and successfully recruit more ethnic minorities to the profession. Direct involvement is paramount to achieving increased diversity. The active recruitment of minorities requires commitment and cooperation among library schools, library associations, and libraries as employers in order to
- establish dialog and influence the curricular direction of the program
- encourage and support diversity initiatives
- commit the human resources needed to achieve the diversity goal (Jennings, 1993b)

A. The Role of Graduate Programs

Graduate programs in library and information science have been under scrutiny. The closing of a few recognized programs has opened an opportunity for other graduate programs to examine their courses and consider the infusion of multiculturalism into their curriculum.

Progress in the recruitment of underrepresented groups to academic and research libraries has been slowly accomplished. Many ask, "Whose responsibility is it?" The libraries defer to the library schools and the library schools defer to the professional associations. Library schools tend to examine their role as educators and not as employers.

Welburn (1994) suggests that there are three important considerations that library and information science programs should integrate into their programs, and they are as follows:

1. The need for rethinking the curriculum at large.
2. The trifold concept of the linkage between the multicultural contexts of information, its users, and information providers.
3. The distinction between diversity as a workplace issue and diversity as a service issue.

Library school recruitment efforts have been meager, but there have been positive developments from the schools as Welburn's recommendations are accepted. Programs similar to those at the University of Denver, SUNY–Buffalo, and the University of Pittsburgh have either initiated or expanded proactive strategies to attract minorities. In fact, Pratt, San Jose, Clark Atlanta, Hawaii, Queens, Rutgers, Illinois, North Carolina Central, North Texas, and Wayne State lead the institutions with ALA-accredited master's degree programs in minority graduation rate (ALISE, 1998). These 10 graduate programs accounted for 46% of the total number of minorities receiving master's degrees in 1996–1997 (ALISE, 1998). Predictably, Clark Atlanta topped the list of graduate programs, with 25 African American graduates and Hawaii was well represented with 25 Asian Pacific graduates. North Carolina Central graduated 2 Asian Pacific students and 14 African American students. Illinois and Wayne State showed a well-rounded representation with Illinois' graduating class including 6 Asian Pacific, 7 African American, and 4 Latino graduates, and Wayne State graduating 4 Asian Pacific, 11 African American, and 2 Latino students. Pratt and Queens, who had minority graduating classes of 29 and 23, respectively, surpassed all of the graduate programs. The most notable achievement, however, is granted to San Jose and its graduating class of 12 Native Americans, 6 Asian Pacific Islanders, 4 African Americans, and 6 Latinos.

Some graduate programs have implemented mentoring programs that pair students with minority professionals in the hopes of establishing a realistic link with the working world. Others have made curricular changes where specific courses have been developed that prepare librarians to service the emerging communities. Examples include courses in urban librarianship, services to ethnic communities, and ethnic awareness/race relations (Knowles and Jolivet, 1991).

B. The Role of Associations

The second facet of the partnership role in increasing diversity in library and information science involves professional associations. Since the late 1980s, there have been several diversity-related initiatives endorsed by various professional library associations. The importance of minorities in libraries has been recognized and addressed by the American Library Association (ALA) in its policy manual. The manual notes that "librarianship recruits a racially and ethnically diverse group of high caliber persons" and "libraries are proactive agencies which meet the challenges of social, economic, and environmental change." In addition, Policy 60 states in part:

> The American Library Association promotes equal access to information of all persons and recognizes the urgent need to respond to the increasing racial and ethnic diversity among Americans. African-Americans, Hispanic Americans, Asian American, Native Americans, and other minorities have critical and increasing needs for information and library access. . . . Therefore, the role played by libraries to enable minorities to participate fully in a democratic society is crucial. . . . Concrete programs of recruitment, training, development, and upward mobility are needed in order to increase and retain minority personnel within librarianship.

Keeping these words in mind, ALA has taken an aggressive stand. Its most recent recruitment tool is the ALA Spectrum initiative. Starting in Fall 1998, this program provides 50 scholarships of $5000 each annually to ethnic minorities who are pursuing library and information science as a career. Spectrum's purpose is to "address the specific issues of underrepresentation of critically needed ethnic librarians within the profession and to serve as a model for ways to bring attention to other diversity issues in the future."

Along these lines, ARL started its proactive diversity measures in 1990 when they appointed their first diversity officer, Kriza Jennings. In 1994, Association for Research Libraries/Office of Library Management Services (ARL/OLMS) created a special 2-year partnership program with libraries, library schools, associations, consortia, networks, and state libraries. This program focused on the collaboration and promotion of library and information science as a career and provided the impetus needed to further develop their diversity commitment.

More recently, supplied with a Department of Education grant, ARL established a Leadership and Career Development Program (LCDP) that is operated by the ARL Diversity Program in collaboration with the OLMS. The first year of the program was quite successful and stressed the importance and value of continuing education for ethnic minority librarians and prepares them for top leadership positions in academic and research libraries. In turn, the LCD graduates serve as mentors to ALA's Spectrum Initiative scholars.

Ethnic professional library associations have a visible and powerful role in recruitment and retention to the library and information science profession. The most active ethnic associations are REFORMA, ALA Black Caucus, Chinese American Library Association, American Indian Library Association, and the Asian-Pacific Librarians Association. Even though there are now several ethnic library associations, there was a time when they had to overcome obstacles in order to warrant their existence. The few minorities in library science were members of ALA, but they believed that they did not belong. The association did not represent them well and, in turn, created an environment that did not encourage their active participation (Echavarria and Wertheimer, 1997). The 1970s brought a wave of activism, and ethnic associations were formally organized. Several of these associations are affiliated with ALA and actively participate in the ALA Office to Literacy and Outreach Services, but it has taken determination and hard work to make this a reality.

Ethnic library associations have established their own proactive agendas and actively recruit to the profession. For example, the Chinese American Librarians Association (CALA) established a scholarship award to enrolled library science students who are of Chinese heritage. This initiative encourages the development of leadership in Chinese American librarianship. Another scholarship initiative encourages service involvement and furnishes monetary support to a student of Chinese heritage to attend an annual ALA meeting.

Recruitment efforts have also been a focus of divisions and state library associations. One of the more recognized division commitments has come out of the Association of College and Research Libraries (ACRL) Task Force on Recruitment of Underrepresented Minorities. The task force identified that the three causes of low recruitment and retention rates of minority academic librarians are a lack of institutional commitment to change and accountability, personal and institutional racism, and barriers to advancement and retention (Beaudin, 1990). In addition, the ACRL Strategic Plan reinforces its commitment to diversity and stresses the need to "support recruitment efforts to bring into the profession those individuals who will enrich the diversity of the profession" (p. 571).

Another example of a division's pledge to creating a more pluralistic society is the cultural diversity grant started by the Library Administrative and Management Association (LAMA). The grant's goals are to create and disseminate resources that will assist library administrators in developing a vision and commitment to diversity, promote the advancement of people of color in the field of library administration, and create partnerships between LAMA and national organizations representing minority interests.

An excellent example of a successful state initiative is the Diversity ToolKit, a product of the Colorado Council for Library Development's Library Services to Ethnic Minority's Committee. This kit has been very popular in promoting librarianship to ethnic minorities. Similarly, the Ohio Library Council created an exciting 10-minute video designed to interest teenagers in librarianship as a career. *Me? A Librarian?* dispels common myths about libraries, discusses the benefits of becoming a librarian, outlines the necessary skills needed to be a successful librarian, and details advancement opportunities. It is an excellent recruitment tool for teens of all racial backgrounds.

C. The Role of Academic Libraries

Part of the recruitment of minorities to the profession clearly focuses on the findings of the ACRL Task Force on Recruitment of Underrepresented Minorities. As illustrated in the task force report, minority librarians tend to be seen as ill prepared and lacking the necessary skills even for entry-level professional positions. This may stem from the fact that the white middle class, who represent the majority of librarians, work in a culture that they are familiar with. Minorities, however, come into the profession without these same attitudes and experiences. Many do not do the same things as their white counterparts, and they often see things differently (St. Lifer and Nelson, 1997). Minorities also seem to have fewer opportunities to get involved and become aware of the work opportunities available (St. Lifer and Nelson, 1997).

Nonetheless, this small pool of librarians tends to shy away from academic librarianship. Instead, they gravitate to public and school librarianship (Jennings, 1993a). Some minority librarians select the public library arena because public libraries actively recruit minorities, and minorities seem to want to contribute to his or her community. Others find the atmosphere of academic libraries unwelcoming (Winston, 1998). In some situations, the prospect of becoming a faculty member directly out of graduate school is frightening, and many minorities are unfamiliar with the opportunities in academic libraries for advancement, continuing education, and professional development. In addition, the "publish or perish" requirement, most notably associated with academic librarianship, seems to contribute to the hesitancy of pursuing a career in an academic library. Jennings (1993a) noted that this is an experience to which minorities have not been exposed, and therefore are concerned with the ramifications.

In all respects, the opportunities to teach, train, and develop programs exist in academic libraries, just as they do in public libraries, but the latter does a better job marketing its employment opportunities (Jennings, 1993a). Until recently, some academic libraries hired only the experienced librarian, thus closing the door on the younger, less-experienced minority librarian. Practices like this foster an attitude that is less appealing to minorities, and put up an invisible barrier to receiving an appointment and being confident of success.

For too long, many libraries only vocally expressed concern about attracting minorities into academic librarianship. The primary focus of their complaints was at the library schools. Boissé and Dowell (1987) maintain that some library directors have complained that new MLS graduates are not prepared to translate the theory of graduate school into practical day-to-day operations. As a partial remedy to this plight, many library schools have added internships to the list of requirements for receiving a MLS. Academic libraries such as the University of Delaware, the University of Pittsburgh, University of Illinois, and the State University of New York (SUNY) system have realized this trend and have implemented postdegree programs. These programs give minorities the experience they need to become more prepared to apply for positions in libraries, and they not only provide diversity to their staff but also provide work experience to potential and/or newly degreed librarians. Other research libraries are initiating their own internship and residency programs as funding becomes more available either from home institutions or from federal grants. It has become apparent that academic research libraries must take the issue into their own hands and respond to the needs of both the minority librarian and the academic library.

IV. Survey of Association of Research Libraries Internship/Residency Programs

A. Association of Research Libraries (ARL)

The ARL is a prestigious group of 121 academic and research libraries in the United States and Canada. For many librarians, pursuing one's career in an ARL library is an accomplishment. However, ARL libraries have a tendency to be very selective in their hiring process, making it difficult for inexperienced, new MLS graduates to receive an appointment. This type of selection criteria, therefore, limits the breadth of qualified candidates.

As a remedy to this, many ARL members have implemented internships and/or residency programs. For purposes of this study, the following definitions are used: Internship: Preprofessional work experience taking place during graduate course work or after course work but preceding the degree; and Residency: Postdegree work experience designed as an entry-level program for recent ALA-accredited MLS graduates (ALISE, 1992).

B. Methodology

In order to assess the current (1998) status of internships and/or residency programs implemented in ARL libraries, a 13-question survey was sent to the ARL membership in July 1998. The survey sought information regarding program specifics, number of participants, types of appointments, recruitment strategy, retention of participants within librarianship, and evaluation techniques. It also asked for an assessment of the program's impact on minority representation within the institution and profession, as well as whether the program had been challenged to any degree. Return rate of the survey was very good, considering it was sent out in the middle of the summer when many administrators take annual leave. Seventy-eight (64.4%) of the surveys were returned. Twenty-three percent of the respondents (15% of the total membership) either presently have or have had an internship and/or fellowship program.

C. Program Characteristics

Of the 18 ARL institutions that responded that they had a minority internship or residency program, 12 indicated the program was for post-MLS graduates (residency). Only 6 indicated that their program was an internship for MLS students, or a combination of both pre-MLS internship and post-MLS residency. The length of time such programs had been in existence ranged from a few months to 14 years. Several of the respondents indicated that their programs were not strictly intended as minority programs; however, the responses indicated that a substantial number of minority candidates had been participants of the programs.

The structure of the programs possesses many commonalities. The internship programs generally consisted of providing a tuition scholarship for the candidate to pursue the MLS while working within the library for a stipend; this is typical of the "GSA" model. The intern's assignments are generally rotational with the intent of providing exposure to a wide variety of library functions. These are ordinarily listed as public services, technical services, and collection development. One new program awards a partial internship to a current staff member to focus on assessing the diversity climate within the library system in exchange for tuition remission, travel funding, and a salary increase. Of the six internship responses, four indicated that the program was associated or "worked closely" with a local library school. The availability of a library school (or lack thereof) may explain the higher proportion of post-MLS residency programs versus pre-MLS internships.

Many of the responses that listed having a post-MLS residency program provided insufficient detail to compare the structure of the programs; however, most indicated the residencies were of 1–2 years duration and all included a salary comparable to that of entry-level librarians at the institution. Based on information gathered from residency announcements found in the professional literature as well as those received in mailings, the assignments are generally a reflection of the needs of the particular institution combined with the particular interests of the resident. One of the survey responses indicated that their program had a special focus on training for science and technology. Half of the incumbent's assigned time included taking coursework focused in networked information retrieval and science–technology resources whereas the other half of the time was spent gaining practical experience in science–technology librarianship. Another respondent indicated that their resident was appointed with the specific goal of developing a more comprehensive minority residency program within the library system.

The majority of the responses indicated that the internship or residency does not automatically lead to a permanent appointment at their institution; only four indicated that it did. Of these, two indicated that this appointment was at full faculty status (tenure-track) and two with professional/academic librarian status. Many of the respondents indicated that even though such an appointment was not guaranteed, the incumbents were encouraged to apply for vacancies within the institution and interpreted retention of the incumbents as an indicator of the program's success. Five of the respondents indicated that their institution had hired at least one of their interns/residents into permanent positions either through a national search or an alternative hiring process.

The survey asked respondents to indicate the number of previous interns/residents who had secured permanent appointments in librarianship, and within academic librarianship in particular. The numbers cited were impressive and indicate the success of these programs in providing entry into the profession. Of a total 117 interns/residents, 104 (88%) had secured permanent appointments within librarianship. Based on the survey data provided, 75 (72%) of these appointments were in academic librarianship. The numbers may actually be low, however, because some of the surveys left this question blank or only partially completed. This may indicate little follow-up with incumbents once they have completed the internship/residency, an area that needs further attention in order to fully evaluate the long-term success of such programs.

Methods for evaluating the success of the intern/resident varied, but the majority were dependent on some form of written assessment (several programs were too new to have actually reached this stage). These evaluations are frequently gathered on an annual basis, although a few institutions reported more frequent assessment (e.g., quarterly). The most common sources for submitting these reports are supervisors, program coordinators, and mentors. The success of interns is also determined by satisfactory academic progress and completion of the MLS program. In assessing the success of the internship/residency program itself, the majority of respondents indicated that feedback from the participants and successful completion of the program were prime indicators. Other factors included successful placement of the incumbent (either during or on completion of the program), feedback from supervisors or others who have worked with the program, level of staff interest in working with the interns/residents, number of applications received to the program, quality of the candidates attracted, quality of the projects and assignments proposed by staff, and recognition by the university community and/or the library profession as gauged by reputation or modeling of the program by other institutions. Two areas that were not addressed but that may provide significant information for assessing a program's success would be (1) follow-up with the incumbent after he/she has been in a permanent appointment for a period of time, and (2) follow-up with the institution that employed the incumbent on a permanent basis. Both methods of follow-up could provide valuable feedback regarding the types and level of experience gained during the internship/residency in preparing the incumbent for professional performance.

The survey also asked respondents to indicate whether they believed their program was an effective tool for increasing minority representation within their library system as well as within the profession. Twelve responses indicated that it was an effective tool for both their library system and the profession, whereas two responded it was not effective in their library system. Again, several of the programs were too new to address this question, but other comments (e.g., "not as much as was hoped," "to a degree") indicated a sense of ambiguity on this issue. One reason cited was the lack of suitable permanent positions available at the institution at the time the incumbents completed the program, and thus there was little impact within their library system on a permanent basis. Although the majority of the respondents believed that an internship/residency program is an effective tool for increasing minority representation within their system, it is clear that this can only be one part in the overall effort and other methods must also be employed.

The authors also wished to find out what impact the current challenges to affirmative action had on minority internship/residency programs. Of the responses gathered, only three indicated that their program had been challenged to any degree; however, one respondent commented, "But I expect it each year I recruit." Two of the programs that have been challenged responded by dropping the word "minority" from the title of the program and the postings, using the word "diversity" in its place. One commented that they were not allowed to advertise for minorities specifically (although that was the intent of the program), and had difficulty in forming a strong pool of candidates. Another respondent underlined the importance of working closely with the institution's affirmative action office and within the guidelines established by that institution. Because it can only be assumed that further challenges to affirmative action programs will occur, it is likely that more institutions hosting minority programs will be faced with difficult decisions in the near future.

V. Program Considerations

A. Institutional Concerns

In reviewing the survey responses as well as the professional literature, a number of considerations surfaced regarding the impact of such programs as well as the content. A few of the respondents indicated that programs initiated at their respective institutions had failed, and valuable lessons were learned. Reasons cited include the following:

1. Loss of institutional funding
2. Inadequate planning of the program
3. Insufficient support within the system
4. Lack of applicants

The first reason, loss of institutional funding for the program, is a very real concern for any program supported through "soft money" designated by institutional administrators. Although such funding is often the springboard for initiation of a minority internship/residency, the fact that it is allocated on an annual basis leaves it continuously open to revocation. Proper long-term planning is difficult in such an environment, and may leave little room for recruitment postings to provide a substantial pool of applicants. Often such last minute funding creates an environment in which the program is implemented "on-the-fly," and both the program and incumbent can suffer as a result. One solution to this dilemma is for the library to create a permanent budget line for the program, often utilizing a position that has become vacant. Such a solution requires strong support from the library administration as well as the affected units in order to avoid any sense of resentment.

The second reason cited, inadequate planning of the program, can have a devastating impact on the recruitment of candidates as well as the newly arrived intern/resident. A program that is not thought out in advance quickly becomes apparent and only heightens the apprehension commonly felt by the incumbent, who is often already dealing with a sense of bewilderment and isolation. Conversely, knowing that the program has been well planned can do much to alleviate not only the uncertainty of the incumbent, but the staff as well. It is critical to the success of the program that short- and long-term goals are identified, and assignments (as well as those responsible for oversight) are supportive to the success of both the incumbent and the program. Those institutions considering implementation of such a program are advised to consult the available literature; for example, *SpecKit #188*, "Internship, Residency, and Fellowship Programs in ARL Libraries" and Julie Brewer's article, "Implementing Post-Master's Residency Programs" (Brewer, 1998).

The third reason, insufficient support within the system, is often closely linked with inadequate planning but may also be reflective of the institution's culture. It is vital that the purpose and importance of the program be communicated clearly to the staff and that the environment be as supportive and welcoming as possible. The program coordinators and administration should evaluate the "readiness" of the culture when first implementing such a program, and not expect that a minority internship/residency program be the sole initiative for addressing diversity issues. Staff should be involved in the planning of assignments for the intern/resident to encourage an understanding of their critical role in the success of the program as well as in the professional development of the incumbent. By providing program goals and guidelines to the staff at the outset of the program, a foundation is created on which the staff are able to plan assignments more effectively as well as have a sense of "personal ownership" for the success of the program. Such involvement can also prevent resentment by the staff, who otherwise might feel that the intern/resident was "dumped" on them without any input on their part. It is interesting to note that in reflecting on their own experiences, many interns/residents credit supportive supervisors and colleagues as the main source for their success as well as for their interest in particular aspects of librarianship (Neely and Abif, 1996). Informal mentoring of this kind is likewise rewarding for staff and should be promoted as yet another positive outcome of internship/residency programs.

The fourth reason cited, lack of applicants to a program, can be a result of many factors. Although it may seem obvious, it is important to make the program known to as broad a pool as possible to ensure a satisfactory number of candidates. Announcements should be posted in widely read professional journals as well as the newsletters of minority-based associations. Online sites have become an ever more effective source for wide and rapid dissemination. Announcements should also be sent to library schools, library system deans/ directors, and personnel administrators. The power of networking should not be underestimated, and often the best recruiters are former interns/ residents because their encouragement to potential candidates carries far more weight than the most carefully worded announcement. Timing of postings is also important, and should allow sufficient opportunity for interested applicants to comfortably plan further steps in the process. This is particularly important if the candidates must apply for acceptance into a library school (internships) or relocate to the area. For those institutions located in areas perceived as unwelcoming or lacking in community support for minorities, it is especially critical that the institution provide information on resources available for providing the incumbent with a sense of social support.

B. Intern/Resident Concerns

At this point in time there is not a substantial amount of literature that evaluates internship/residency programs from the participants' viewpoint. As stated earlier, this is an area that requires more attention in order to make such programs as effective as possible. What can be gleaned, however, points to several areas that anyone involved in developing or coordinating a minority internship/residency program should take into consideration.

First of all, it is important that the intern/resident be treated as a professional within the institution as reflected by salary, project assignments, and professional development opportunities. One of the primary goals for most programs includes exposure to a wide variety of library functions, and this is most often accomplished through a "rotational" schedule involving varying timeframes within the library departments. Although this is of great value to the incumbent, care should be taken that such assignments allow sufficient time to gain adequate experience within the area. The danger here lies in overwhelming the incumbent by "schedule frenzy," which only allows enough time in each area for superficial exposure. Not only does this limit any substantial professional development, it hinders the development of collegial relationships and informal mentoring opportunities. Although this is not meant to undervalue the importance of broad exposure to library functions, program coordinators should be aware of the challenge that rotational schedules present to the intern/resident and be alert to providing support during this time. As one successful former intern, Jon Cawthorne, noted, "The first year of a two-year internship can be both exhausting and interesting. It was exhausting because of a nomadic schedule that kept me moving from department to department. To be honest, it was a challenge to digest all the information I was given in the first year" (Neely and Abif, 1996, p. 53). The nature of the assignments should also reflect professional-level expectations rather than a "student–worker" mentality; it should be assumed by the incumbent and the staff that the intern/resident will be a productive contributor to the organization. Reporting on a survey of former residents, Brewer (1997, p. 534) notes that valuable experiences included "working on critical projects that contributed to the library mission, being included as members of a team, conducting training sessions for staff, presenting results of professional work to peers, and having opinions and feedback solicited. A number of respondents said they would have liked to have been included on committees." It is also important that interns/residents be given opportunities for professional development equal to that given other professionals within the system. Release time and funding should be given for attending conferences or workshops, and the incumbents encouraged to develop a professional network of their own. Given the temporary nature of intern/resident appointments, such opportunities for networking are often critical for finding permanent placement at the end of the program. At the very least, they provide venues for social and professional support systems that aid in the retention of minority librarians within the profession.

Program coordinators and other staff working with the incumbent should also be aware of the unique environment that a minority internship/residency creates. Minority interns/residents are painfully aware of their own status within a "designated" position, and are often reminded of this status when even well-intentioned actions create a sense of being "on display." As Beavers notes on her own internship experience, "On the one hand, there was a real sense of welcoming and celebration. People made me feel that they had been looking forward to my arrival and they were eager to work with me in the future. On the other hand, I felt that I was under a microscope" (DeBeau-Melting and Beavers, 1994, p. 233). Alire (1997) speaks eloquently on the issue of isolation, and points out that the need for familial support often plays a major role for many minority students in choosing (and successfully completing) a program. Understanding coordinators and mentors can provide support directly by listening to such concerns as well as indirectly by assisting the incumbent in developing a social support system, often through initiating contact with former (and current) interns/residents who are able to relate from their own experience.

VI. Importance of Minority Internship/ Residency Programs

Minority internship and residency programs are important tools for recruiting to the profession for a number of reasons. First of all, they provide an incentive for promising minority students who may not otherwise consider librarianship as a career choice due to lack of exposure to the field, lack of educational funds, or limited prospective employment upon completion of the graduate program. Brewer (1997) points out that such programs were often the defining factor for participants who selected research and academic librarianship as their career. Internship or residency programs can open the door for marketing academic librarianship as a desirable and rewarding career, which Wright (1991) points out as a vital ingredient for recruiting minority candidates. The experiences gained during an internship/residency do more than just prepare the incumbent with the requisite technical skills; they can open doors to a world that may be very different from that which is familiar while doing so in a structured, supportive environment. In reflecting on her own experience as a resident, Beavers (DeBeau-Melting and Beavers, 1994) notes that it allowed her to be privy to many more levels of the library system and university community than would have been possible if hired through more "traditional" channels.

The financial support that internship/residencies supply is also an important factor for successful recruitment of minority candidates. Businesses (and other academic disciplines) long ago recognized the need for providing financial support in recruiting a diverse workforce, and have had much more success as a result. This is especially critical for research and academic libraries to realize if they hope to compete in such an environment. For too long libraries (and library schools) have taken the stance that there are not enough minorities interested in the profession, but Josey (1991) argues that this simply is not true. He contends that there are plenty interested in the field, but lack of financial resources prevents them from entering graduate programs. Scholarships, financial aid, and minority internships and residencies can help provide the necessary support, if even on a limited scale.

The benefits of minority internships and residencies are not limited solely to the incumbent; they can also have a significant impact on the organization hosting the program as well. The relationships that develop among those working with the participants promote not only an awareness but hopefully an appreciation of cultures and life-experiences different than one's own as well. This interaction can extend beyond broadening the individual's own assumptions and begin to have an effect on how library services are provided as well as collection development policies (DeBeau-Melting and Beavers, 1994). The internship/residency program can provide opportunities for dialog that may not have existed otherwise. In a time when many institutions are wrestling with successful implementation of diversity awareness programs, the minority internship or residency is certainly one viable element of any multidimensional program.

VII. Conclusion

Our society still is not immune from racism and discrimination. The 1960s were a turning point, and each year since then there has been more acceptance of minorities as capable and viable members of the workforce. Libraries are a microcosm of today's society and it is imperative that they reflect today's society—a multicultural society. Recruitment and retention of minorities to the library and information science profession and, in particular, the academic profession must continue to be a priority for academic libraries.

Although recruitment of minorities should be a multifaceted approach using initiatives from library schools, professional associations, and library practitioners, academic libraries have a duty to address recruitment and retention of minorities. Because ARL libraries are noted to be the top research libraries in the United States and Canada, their recruitment efforts should not only reflect their commitment to diversity, but also show a depth of commitment that is proactive and values the continuing education and training of librarians.

Strategies such as internships and residency programs are a step toward actively addressing the underrepresentation of ethnic minorities in the library and information science profession. Minority recruitment is a challenge that is ongoing and is vital to the future of the services provided by academic libraries to their constituents.

References

ALA Bylaws and Policies. Gopher://ala1.ala.org:70/00/alagophviii/policy.hb.

Alire, C. (1997). It takes a family to graduate a minority library professional. *American Libraries* **28**(10), 41.

Alire, C. (1996). Recruitment and retention of librarians of color. In *Creating the Future: Essays on Librarianship* (S. G. Reed, ed.), pp. 126–143. McFarland & Company, Jefferson, NC.

ALISE (1992). *Guidelines for Practices and Principles in the Design, Operation, and Evaluation of Post-Master's Residency Programs.* Association for Library and Information Science Education, Washington, DC.

ALISE (1994–1998). *Library and Information Science Education Statistical Report.* Association for Library and Information Science Education, Washington, DC.

Association of Research Libraries, Office of Management Services (1992). *Internship, Residency, and Fellowship Programs in ARL Libraries* (SPEC Kit #188). Association of Research Libraries, Washington, DC.

Beaudin, J. (1990). Recruiting the underrepresented to academic libraries. *College and Research Libraries News* **51,** 1016–1024.

Boissé, J. A., and Dowell, C. V. (1987). Increasing minority librarians in academic research libraries. *Library Journal* **112,** 52–54.

Bok, D., and Bowen, W. G. (1998). *The Shape of the River: Long-Term Consequences of Considering Race in College and University Admissions.* Princeton University Press, Princeton, NJ.

Brewer, J. (1997). Post-master's residency programs: Enhancing the development of new professionals and minority recruitment in academic and research libraries. *College and Research Libraries* **58,** 528–537.

Brewer, J. (1998). Implementing post-master's residency programs. In *Leading Ideas* **4,** pp. 2–7. Association of Research Libraries, Washington, DC.

Carter, D., and Wilson, R. (1996). *Minorities in Higher Education.* American Council on Education, Washington, DC.

Cawthorne, J. E. and Weil, T. B. (1996). Internships/residencies: Exploring the possibilities for the future. In *In Our Own Voices: The Changing Face of Librarianship* (T. K. Neely and K. K. Abif, eds.), pp. 45–71. Scarecrow Press, Lanham, MD.

DeBeau-Melting, L., and Beavers, K. M. (1994). Positioning for change: The diversity internship as a good beginning. In *Diversity and Multiculturalism in Libraries* (K. Hill, ed.), pp. 227–242. JAI Press, Greenwich, CT.

Echavarria, T., and Wertheimer, A. B. (1997). Surveying the role of ethnic American library associations. *Library Trends* **46,** 373–391.

Jennings, K. (1993a). Minority recruitment: Assuring diversity in the work place. *ARL: A Bimonthly Newsletter of Research Library Issues and Actions*, **166,** 11–12.

Jennings, K. (1993b). Recruiting new populations to the library profession. *Journal of Library Administration* **19,** 175–191.

Josey, E. J. (1991). The role of the black library and information professional in the information society: Myths and realities. In *Educating Black Librarians* (B. F. Speller, Jr. ed.), pp. 51–59. McFarland & Co., Jefferson, NC.

Katyal, N. K. (1995). Why affirmative action in higher education is safe in courts. *Journal of Blacks in Higher Education*, **9**, 83.

Knowles, E. C., and Jolivet, L. (1991). Recruiting the underrepresented: Collaborative efforts between library educators and library practitioners. *Library Administration and Management*, **5**, 189–193.

Neely, T. K., and Abif, K. K. (eds.). (1996). *In Our Own Voices: The Changing Face of Librarianship*. Scarecrow Press, Lanham, MD.

Spectrum Initiative Mission (1998). http://www.ala.org/spectrum/mission.html.

U.S. Bureau of the Census (1994). *Current Populations Reports: Population Projections for States, by Ages, Sex, Race, and Hispanic Origin: 1993 to 2030*. Government Printing Office, Washington, DC.

St. Lifer, E., and Nelson, C. (1997). Unequal opportunities: Race does matter. *Library Journal*, **122**, 42–46.

U.S. Bureau of the Census (1997). *Statistical Abstract of the United States*. Government Printing Office, Washington, DC.

Wellburn, W. C. (1994). Do we really need cultural diversity in the library and information science curriculum? *Journal of Education for Library and Information Science* **35**, 328–330.

Williams, H. E. (1987). Experiences of blacks in predominately white library schools, 1962–1974. In *Activism in American Librarianship* (M. L. Bundy and F. J. Stielow, eds.), pp. 153–161. Greenwood Press, NY.

Winston, M. (1998). The role of recruitment in achieving goals related to diversity. *College and Research Libraries*, **59**, 240–247.

Wright, J. C. (1991). Recruitment and retention of minorities in academic libraries: A plan of action for the 1990s. In *Educating Black Librarians* (B. F. Speller, Jr., ed.), pp. 51–59. McFarland & Co., Jefferson, NC.

What Is Women's Information?

The History and Future of a Longstanding Tradition in Librarianship

Marije Wilmink and Marlise Mensink*
International Information Centre and Archives for the Women's
Movement (IIAV)
Amsterdam, The Netherlands

I. Women's Information in Context

Women's information is a subject that is often approached with confusion
and biased assumptions. In an era where global institutions have gender at
the top of their agenda, however, it becomes crucial to understand what
women's information is and offers. The Fourth United Nations World Conference on Women, held in Beijing in September 1995, identified the lack
of women-specific information as a major concern, and established that gender
statistics and data must be used for effective policy decisions. In the Platform
for Action, which contains the resolutions of the conference and was signed
by all participating governments, there was agreement to support, consult,
and provide women specific information. In order to develop and monitor
policies, governments and communities need to have information on the
position of women available (United Nations, 1995).

The idea that knowledge and information should be shared is obviously
not new. Indeed, the sharing of information has been considered such an
important task that for centuries, this task has been professionalized. Currently, we have every conceivable type of library or archive or documentation
center. They are organized by content (social libraries, medical libraries,
law libraries), by level (grassroots or academic), or by size (national library,
municipal library). There is, however, a sort of information service that
surpasses the different kinds just mentioned. Women's information and the
services that deal with it go beyond these categories because women's informa-

* *Although both authors are connected to the IIAV (Wilmink as editor of Mapping the World and*
Lover—Magazine on Feminism, Culture and Science *and Mensink as staff member for International*
Relations), the views expressed in this article are theirs and not necessarily those of the IIAV.

tion can be found everywhere and at every level. For many information services, however, and for many customers, women's information is almost invisible.

So what exactly is women's information? Does it consist of information about the position of women? Not exclusively. Is it information meant for women? Well, not exactly. Does women's information refer to information produced by women? No, not entirely. Women's information includes all three of these definitions. The term is used for information by, for, and about women that is relevant and crucial for those involved and interested in the position of women in society, in both public and private life. It envelops a wide spectrum of material from past to present, including cultural, political, and educational data.

The collection of this sort of information has gone through several new developments. One of the essentials is the growing communication, information exchange, and cooperation between institutions dealing with women's information worldwide. The field is evolving in the direction of globalization, not in the least because of the new possibilities for exchange of information facilitated by technological developments.

However, before addressing these developments, we want to look back a little. Although the title of this series, *Advances in Librarianship*, suggests a focus on progress and innovation, we would like to point out that women's information itself is not a new development. On the contrary, it has its own history, going back to the beginning of the twentieth century and even further. Women have collected, indexed, and disseminated information for at least a hundred years. Yet it is only during the twentieth century that centers have been set up for the specific purpose of collecting and documenting what has come to be known as women's information. The International Information Centre and Archives for the Women's Movement (IIAV) in the Netherlands, which we are both connected to, offers a fine example, as it is one of the most important institutes worldwide which collects and preserves women's information.

II. The Dutch National Women's Library and Archives: IIAV

At present, the IIAV is the national information service in the Netherlands on the position of women and women's studies, and the Dutch focal point for international exchange of information on the women's movement. This means that the IIAV is a main source, intermediary, and supplier of information and documentation for everyone involved with and interested in the position of women. Books, periodicals, photographs, "new media" products, statistics, addresses, and archives, both current or historical, national or international—the IIAV has it or knows where to find it.

The collection is divided into several departments, including a scientific library, an information and documentation center, an archives department, a picture archive, and a periodicals department. The major users are scholars and students, politicians, policy makers, journalists, educators and others with a professional interest.

A. Development of the Institute

Although we will never know for sure, it seems the IIAV has lived up to the expectations of its founders. The Institute was founded in 1935 under the name International Archive of the Women's Movement (IAV). It was a private initiative of three women: Johanna Naber, Rosa Manus, and Willemijn Posthumus-van der Goot. Johanna Naber was a well-known historian who published several historical studies on women and the women's movement. Rosa Manus was an advocate of women's suffrage, who had quite a voluminous personal library and also inherited the books and personal papers of Aletta Jacobs (the first woman medical doctor in the Netherlands and long-time leader of the Dutch suffrage movement). On May 20, 1930, Rosa Manus wrote to Clara Hyde, the secretary of Carrie Chapman Catt: "Dr. Jacobs' books have come to me now, and I am organizing a real feministic library which I hope, will prove useful to the feminists" (Douze and Mevis, 1998, p. 1). Willemijn Posthumus-van der Goot was the first Dutch woman with a doctorate in economics and chairperson of a committee concerned with women and work.

These three women, although representing different backgrounds and generations, joined forces to create a place where the letters, notes, books, and archives of the women from the women's liberation movement were kept. All were convinced of the need to collect documents and papers and the need to facilitate research. They believed it was necessary to gather and preserve the cultural heritage of women—as a way to pass on knowledge and information from one generation to the next—and that scientific insight into the women's movement should be acquired (IIAV, 1991).

The initiative was not unique. In other countries women undertook similar enterprises. The only other initiative aimed at an international level was the World Center for Women's Archives, which was founded in 1936 in the United States, but failed to become a permanent institute. Among others, Rosika Schwimmer and the famous historian Mary Beard participated in this initiative (IIAV, 1991). On a national level, however, several women's archives were established in the first half of the twentieth century. Still existing today are the Fawcett Library in London, Bibliothèque Marguerite Durand in Paris, Biblioteca Popular Francesca Bonnemaison in Barcelona, Sophia Smith College in Northampton Massachusetts, and the Schlesinger Library on the History of Women in Boston.

The IAV started with a collection consisting of several personal and organizational archives and of the books and papers belonging to the legacy of Aletta Jacobs, donated by Rosa Manus. The material covered issues such as women's labor, education, suffrage, peace, morality, and legislation. It is in these early years that some of the most valuable documents were acquired. The Aletta Jacobs Papers, for example, include the correspondence of this feminist leader with several other internationally famous feminist activists from the beginning of this century. These papers contain dozens of letters from Carrie Chapman Catt, the well-known American women suffrage activist, concerning the preparation of the world propaganda tour for women's suffrage that Jacobs and Catt undertook in 1911–1912. The journey took them all the way to China. Another example is the archive of the oldest women's society in the Netherlands called "Arbeid Adelt" (Labor Is Ennobling). It promoted the economic independence of women—for example, by selling the needlework of impoverished ladies. Another treasure is the archive of the Nationale Tentoonstelling van Vrouwenarbeid. This exhibition of women's labor was held at the end of the nineteenth century in The Hague. One of the reasons to have this exhibition was to celebrate the inauguration of Wilhelmina (who was the first queen the Netherlands had known following a long line of kings). Women of all backgrounds worked together to give an overview of the work of women in the Netherlands and in the Dutch colonies at the end of the nineteenth century. Apart from collecting documents and books, the IAV published several yearbooks containing scientific studies on the past and present of the national and international women's movements.

The flourishing beginning of the IAV ended abruptly when, in 1940, the collection was stolen by the Nazis. All the books and archives, and even the curtains and furniture, were taken away and shipped off to Germany. A mere 4 of the 40 boxes that were seized were returned after the Second World War, in 1947, containing only books. It was not until 1992 that the remaining material was tracked down in Russia and was put on microfiche, in which form it is now available to visitors to the IIAV again. So far, considerable efforts to have the original archives returned to their rightful owner have been frustrated by laws and new laws, and mostly overwhelmingly bureaucracy (Douze and Mevis, 1998).

After the end of World War II, a process of rebuilding the collection started. The pre-war collection consisted of 4500 books, 150 periodicals, and 5 linear meters of archives. In 1956, the IAV had managed to rebuild a collection of 120 periodicals, 5000 books, and 22 meters of archival material.

Nevertheless, in the period that followed the IAV could best be described as a sleeping archive, with a relatively small collection, a small group of visitors, and only a part-time librarian. It was the social turmoil that started at the end of the 1960s that brought new life to the institute, causing an enormous increase in the number of (new) visitors, a growing hunger for information on the history of the women's movement, and an urgent need to document and record the new wave of feminism.

As the ideas of the second feminist wave spread through society, women's emancipation became one of the major postwar developments and therefore a key issue in Dutch governmental policy on many levels. The IAV was one of several organizations that received government funding from 1981, as the government considered a good information service to be an essential part of the emancipation process (Rijsbosch, 1990). In addition, the IAV was seen as the caretaker of part of the Dutch cultural heritage.

With government money, more books could be bought and more staff could be paid. The IAV's collection grew rapidly, filling with archives of second-wave feminist initiatives such as magazines, publishers, women's schools, and conferences. In 1977, the IAV received the first archive of a black women's organization, the National Association of Single Arab Women. The number of publications—books as well as periodicals, articles, theses, dissertations, and papers—on feminist issues such as child care, incest, economic independence, and equal treatment also expanded quickly (Douze, 1990).

Not only the IAV blossomed. Several other women's documentation centers and libraries were established in the Netherlands in the 1970s and 1980s. It became clear that there are a lot of differences between women—and therefore a lot of different information needs. Dutch lesbian women, for example, criticized the IAV for the lack of material on lesbian women. That resulted in the establishment of several lesbian archives. On similar grounds, black and migrant women also started their own documentation service and library called Flamboyant. The professionalizing of the women's movement brought with it a further range of specialized information services, on law or on trafficking in women for example.

In 1988, a fusion between the IAV, the Information and Documentation Centre for the Women's Movement, and the periodical *Lover*—a magazine on feminism, culture, and science—resulted in the establishment of the International Information Centre and Archives for the Women's Movement, or IIAV.

B. The Current Collection Policy Evolves

The IIAV collection currently consists of 63,500 Dutch and foreign books (including gray literature), 600 periodicals, 425 linear meters of back issues of women's magazines, thematic dossiers, pamphlets, newspaper cuttings, 5000 biographical dossiers, 371 archives of women's organizations and individual women with a total length of 625 linear meters, egodocuments from 155 different people (consisting of diaries, correspondence, and other autobiographical and personal documents), and 15,000 posters, photographs, and postcards. Its collection is internationally oriented and can be accessed via the Internet. In 1994, the IIAV moved to a large former Catholic Church that was renovated to fit the requirements for a library, as the former housing definitely was becoming too small for the expanding collection.

The history of the IIAV illustrates that the answer to the question what is women's information, is changing from time to time. The IAV in the 1930s collected other sorts of information than does the modern-day IIAV. A nice illustration is the discussion about collecting information resources on the traditional life of women, such as cookbooks, dime novels, and traditional women's magazines. Ideas on this have changed over time (Douze and Mevis, 1998). In the beginning, cookbooks were collected as resources on the life of women; in the early 1970s, they were sold because the IAV decided to collect academic books or books on the women's movement only. In the late 1970s, with larger budgets, the cookbooks were bought back. Now, the IIAV has stopped collecting this kind of information because it does not concern "the specific position of women," according to the most recent collection policy. Could the cookbooks in the context of the 1930s and 1950s be considered "information for women"? In the context of the 1990s, that is no longer so. It is not the material, but the definition of the field to which it belongs that is the variable.

A similar thing has happened with fiction. The IIAV once collected all new Dutch books by female novelists, but recently limited the novel collection policy to "feminist fiction." This decision was backed by the fact that the work of female novelists has been available in all mainstream libraries in the Netherlands since 1980.

Similarly, the decision was made regarding the degree to which the IIAV collects specialist information. If there is another thematic women's information center available in Dutch society (on women and law, women and health, or lesbianism, for example), the IIAV collects in a limited way. It can be said that it is the network of women's information centers that covers the "nation's women" in the Netherlands.

The enormous growth in the publication of books and journals during the past decades has forced the IIAV to select more strictly. It is no longer possible to collect all information that is interesting both for and about women. Because of this, the collection policy is limited to information on the specific position of women in society. A special focus is awarded to women's studies and information on black, migrant, and refugee women, as the Netherlands has become a multicultural society, which the collection on the nation's women should reflect (IIAV, 1996).

III. The World of Women's Information

The IIAV is a fine example of a Western, highly professionalized women's library and archive, with its roots in the women's movement of the early twentieth century. There are others like the IIAV, especially in Europe and North America. The oldest women's library of the world is probably the Spanish Biblioteca Popular Francesca Bonnemaison in Barcelona (1909), which is not a direct result of the feminist movement but of the ideals of charity worker Bonnemaison, who wanted a public library promoting culture and education among women (Romeny, 1998). In countries like France, Turkey, Denmark, the United Kingdom, and the USA, there are institutions that on a general level could be compared with the IIAV. However, the world of women's information has more than one face. Women's information services differ greatly in resources, funding, technical level, and scope. The estimated number of women's information services around the world approaches 2000, and their activities are as diverse as their geography. Some show a highly academic character, whereas others have a more grassroots profile. Some services are highly specialized, or may extend beyond providing information alone—training or research for example—and therefore aim at different target groups. Some centers are institutionalized stable organizations like the IIAV, with a professional staff and structural funding, whereas others depend on volunteers and have much more unstable financial resources. When visualizing it on a scale, you could say that at one end there are services consisting of a volunteer who is collecting and distributing information via, for example, fax machine on a regular basis, whereas at the other end of the scale there are specialized libraries on women and gender, fully integrated into national library networks.

As for regional diversity, one could say that the most stable and professionalized women's information centers acting on a national level are to be found in the Western industrialized parts of the world. Outside these regions, women's information services are often a result of grassroots initiatives that started with a focus on a particular subject—health, for example. For these kinds of organizations, the dissemination of information probably came up in the slipstream of other activities like education, research, or relief work, and developed from a derivative into a full-blown issue in itself. At the moment, this process is quite visible in Central and Eastern Europe, for instance. The disintegration of communist regimes and the establishment of new democracies form the background for an evolving interest in women's information. Since the late 1980s, women have begun searching for ways to improve their own position in society. After being kept without information for years, they have begun to initiate research to develop information on all aspects of their lives, often with the intention of contributing to the democratization process. The information produced is used to lobby for reforms in laws on abortion and on sexual violence against women (Cummings, 1999). Many women's centers operate in the field of democracy or reproductive rights, and consider collecting and offering information a support activity, not a goal in itself.

It is also in the form information services take that one can see geographic differences. The developments within information and communication technology, for example, have had profound implications in this context. It is no longer strictly necessary to establish a center—which requires funds for housing, furniture, and building a collection—in order to be able to collect and disseminate information. Apart from the necessary workforce, a computer offering access to the Internet can be means enough to start an information service. In Asia and the Pacific, where the women's movement must cope with isolation by distance and water, the impact of new information and communication technologies is substantial. In Africa too, the dissemination of information via media such as radio and the Internet proves to be very effective. Although there is still a lack of infrastructure, African women's groups have succeeded in obtaining better access to worldwide information networks. The Nordic countries in Europe have also begun to set up a Nordic Virtual Women's Library.

A. Initiatives for Cooperation

Although the world of women's information is characterized by great diversity and variable contexts, there are collective goals: give women a voice; empower women and strengthen their position through information; and keep women's history alive by making its sources available. Since the late 1980s, more and more initiatives have been taken to cooperate on a regional and global level. The resulting developments show an increase in strategic networking, organization, and exchange of knowledge within the profession.

The first international initiatives for cooperation were taken in the late 1980s. From the "outside," the first initiative was taken by the United Nations Division for the Advancement of Women. In 1988, it organized the "Seminar on Information Systems for the Advancement of Women for National Machineries," held in Vienna, Austria. It brought together 15 experts from governmental women's information services and 51 observers from member states. Their aim was to elaborate on the implementation of the resolution of the UN Nairobi World Conference in 1985, concerning the use of information that should be important for decision making and the supply of that information through the design of effective systems for documentation, information collection, storage, and retrieval (Mathiason, 1988). The participants resolved to communicate, meet regularly, and develop these services together. The proposed follow-up, however, never took place.

From within the field, the Philippines-based women's information service ISIS/WICCE organized an international conference on documentation and communication concerning women and development held in Geneva in 1989 (Kramer, 1991). Approximately 20 representatives from documentation centers in the developing countries or from centers focused on "women and development" came together, establishing a supportive network.

In 1991, the Women's Library and Information Center in Istanbul, Turkey, celebrated its first year of existence by inviting "mentor" organizations from five countries to come to Turkey and discuss the future of women's information services and the possibilities of exchange programs and cooperation at the First International Symposium of Women's Libraries. The IIAV was one of the participants. Among the many decisions made at the symposium was the decision to continue meeting, and widen the range of information services participating (Women's Library and Information Center Foundation, 1991). The US-based Schlesinger Library on the History of Women offered to host the next meeting. The meeting Schlesinger organized was called "Women, Information, and the Future: Collecting and Sharing Resources Worldwide," and took place in Boston in 1994. The idea behind the conference was that women's information networks should be encouraged to foster cooperation and ease communication across national boundaries and geographic divides. "Such information networks promote the ability to think creatively and to work collaboratively and will be essential if women are to take their rightful place in the world of tomorrow" (Steiner, 1995, p. xiv). The conference hosted more than 200 information specialists from more than 40 countries. The themes discussed in more than 100 paper presentations were grassroots organizing, institution building, women's studies in established libraries, archival collecting and archival administration, introduction to information technology and advanced information technology, and oral history. The Information Statement drawn up at the closing of the conference demanded, among other things, that women's access to information and the means of dissemination be prioritized as a matter of public policy.

It was the IIAV that offered to organize the next conference, as the need was clearly stated for exchanging experience and strategies regularly.

The meeting scheduled by the IIAV was preceded by the Fourth United Nations World Conference on Women in Beijing in 1995. During the NGO Forum in Huairou—the so-called shadow-conference of the Fourth UN World Conference—several workshops on information services were organized. Information specialists of some 30 organizations came together. Topics discussed were once again, cooperation between women's information centers on a regional and international level and the use of the Internet for research and dissemination of relevant information for women. The participants in the workshop entitled "The Document and Its Passage," which lasted 1 full day, discussed their experiences in producing, compiling, organizing, and disseminating information for and about women. They varied from grassroots efforts as well as established institutions, from achievements to empower illiterate women through information for identifying an improved conceptual foundation for monitoring human rights through the Internet (Vazquez, 1995).

The product of the official Beijing conference, the Platform for Action, which was ratified by representatives of the governments present, stated the need to generate "disseminate gender disaggregated data and information for planning and evaluation" (United Nations, 1995, H.3).

Beijing gave new input and context for the third world conference. When the IIAV started preparing for the Know How Conference on the World of Women's Information, one of the questions was how the United Nations and the governments of the world were getting along in developing the intentions formulated in Beijing, and how the women's information services were meeting the challenge to collect and provide the necessary information. The growing recognition of the importance of information to support policy-making as well as advocacy was the founding principle.

B. The Know How Conference, 1998

The Know How Conference on the World of Women's Information took place in Amsterdam, the Netherlands, during August 1998. The conference aimed to improve the accessibility and visibility of women's information and provide a broad public insight into the range of services that the term *women's information* represents. To ensure a truly global effort, the conference was committed to creating a forum where ideas and experiences from the south, north, west, and east were equally represented (Pugh, 1998).

It was a milestone meeting in the development of women's information, attended by 300 women's information specialists from 83 countries, representing all regions of the world as well as governments, UN organizations, international women's networks, national and local women's information services, lesbian archives, and indigenous women's organizations.

The fundraising efforts had been so successful that the organization was able to invite more than 80 colleagues from around the world to participate in the event. This success was a clear indication that among many others, the Dutch embassies abroad and the Dutch development agencies like

Novib, Hivos, Bilance, Ecco, and Mama Cash considered the conference important.

The conference was convened with the purpose of establishing global and local networks among workers in women's information centers, archives, and services throughout the world. In particular, it reaffirmed the Fourth World Conference on Women's Platform for Action—namely, to integrate and disseminate gender disaggregated data and information for planning and evaluation and cooperate with women's information services as partners by generating and disseminating gender-specific information for policy, planning, and evaluation. The Know How Conference resolved that all women's information services should commit themselves to ensuring that a gender perspective is reflected in all government, NGO, media, education, research policies, and programs. It argued that "information is a human right and therefore a women's right" and decried the "growing distance between the information possessed by the 'haves' and that of the 'have-nots,'" encouraging women's centers, archives, and documentation centers in the Western world to use their resources to narrow this gap (IIAV, 1998). This conference itself underlined again the importance of women's information, an importance that had already received international recognition when it was included in the Platform for Action and was a big step forward in the enhancement of a worldwide network as well as regional networks for women's information services.

The establishment of networks of this kind enables international cooperation, which leads to substantial progression within the field. There are already several examples of regional and international projects that show the need and the advantages of further cooperation. We present two of these examples here: the development of a European Women's Thesaurus and the establishment of Mapping the World, a database providing access to women's information services all over the world.

IV. European Women's Thesaurus

Currently in Europe, there is a great diversity of women's libraries, documentation centers, and archives. Italy has a national network of women's libraries (called Lilith), as has Spain and the Netherlands. The Dutch network is called Lovi. The women's libraries and documentation centers of the German-speaking countries have organized themselves in a network called i.d.a. All these libraries have designed or adopted their own systems in regard to indexing the materials, books, reports, and newspaper clippings of their collections. The German-speaking countries have built their own women's thesaurus called ThesaurA, as have the Spanish- and the Italian-speaking countries.

Many of the public catalogs of these information services are now available on the Internet. However, if you would like to search a German catalog, you would have to know the German term in order to be able to find the exact information you are looking for. A standardized European indexing system would make it possible to start building common European databases immediately. In the future, if more collections were indexed using the same thesaurus, integrated searches in several catalogs of these collections would be possible. A researcher in any country initiating a search on a certain subject would find answers in, for example, Italy, Denmark, Belgium, and Norway. Therefore the IIAV decided to apply for funding from the European Community in order to develop a basic European Women's Thesaurus (EWT).

In March 1992, the IIAV had presented the Dutch Women's Thesaurus, a standardized list of semantically and generically related terms with detailed instructions for use. After a process of 7 years, with extensive research, a feasibility study and literature studies, the Dutch and Flemish women's libraries had their own nonsexist indexing system with more than 2200 related terms. The development of a national women's thesaurus was considered crucial, as it could be seen as a reflection of developments within the Dutch women's movement and within women's studies, and of the complexity and subtlety of women's lives and work. Even though this thesaurus was constructed as a professional tool for students, researchers, and librarians to describe and locate women's information, the Dutch Women's Thesaurus also proved to be a resource on hand for mainstream libraries that enabled them to incorporate new perceptions on women's issues in their own indexing systems (Mensink, 1998). Good experiences in the use of the Dutch thesaurus fueled the objective to have a standardized EWT. A proposal was written for the Equal Opportunities Unit of the European Commission, in the context of an action program for Equal Opportunities between women and men. The partners in this transnational project were, apart from the IIAV, the Nordic Institute for Women's Studies and Gender Research (NIKK), the Danish National Centre for Information on Women and Gender (KVINFO), the Documentation Centre for Equal Opportunities and Women's Studies (RoSA), and the Women's Documentation Centre and Library of Bologna. The project group was completed by the consultancy of two European networks: Women's International Studies Europe (WISE) and Women's Information Network Europe (WINE).

The project started in August 1997. The first step in the process was the translation of the Dutch Women's Thesaurus into English. After the translation was finished, a group of women's studies experts (selected by WISE) carefully checked the translation to see if all terms were translated correctly and truly reflected the developments within women's studies. After their comments and suggestions and also those of the project group, the IIAV started compiling a first draft version of the EWT.

To develop a thesaurus means to start a continuous process of updating and maintenance. As said before, a thesaurus is the reflection of the use of language in a specific field—in this regard, the women's movement and women's studies. The production of a EWT was meant to produce a concrete start, but at the same time to secure continuation of a process. Furthermore, the project group thought it very important that the EWT would be a product that could be widely applicable. Therefore, concept versions were continuously presented to a broad spectrum of experts for comments and new ideas.

In May 1998, the project group invited representatives of the national focal points for women's information from all the member states within the European Union. The meeting in Brussels, hosted by the Flemish women's library and documentation center called RoSa, proved to be a great success as the development of the EWT was strongly supported. Most representatives saw opportunities to start using the EWT, either as a new indexing system or beside their existing systems.

The commitment to the continuation of the process is shown by the desire of this group of experts to get together again to discuss possible follow-up projects in more detail. After the production of the first EWT, a series of projects should be set up to implement the use of the EWT in the several women's libraries and documentation centers around Europe. In November 1998 in Barcelona, at a meeting hosted by Bonnemaison Library, definite steps were taken to ensure the continuous development of the EWT.

V. Mapping the World

Another example of an international project is the building of Mapping the World, an inventory of women's information services available throughout the world. It comprises a database and website providing information on a wide range of women's information services and detailed information on where to find specific information pertaining to the position of women and girls everywhere in the world. The database on women's information services is made available and supported by the IIAV website on the Internet (http://www.iiav.nl/mapping-the-world). For those who do not have access to Internet, a paper version of the database was included in a book on worldwide women's information services (Cummings *et al.*, 1999). The idea for something like Mapping the World had circled around for some time before it was put into practice by the team working on the Know How Conference. As they were organizing this conference, a wealth of information and data came their way. The idea to make the network that was building up visible to all resulted in the Mapping the World project. This project was cofunded by the IIAV and the Unit for the Promotion of the Status of Women and Gender Equality of the United Nations Educational, Scientific and Cultural Organization (UNESCO). The types of women's information services included in the inventory comprise international, national, and local women's information services, women's documentation and research centers connected to universities, gender information sections of governmental and nongovernmental organizations, and research centers in which, among other data, women's information is collected. Where the development of women's information is still in its early stages—for example, in newly democratic countries or countries in which war has destabilized development—focal points for women's information were selected. This means that radio stations, magazines, or women's centers specializing in specific subjects can be included, when they may be one of the few places in a country where information on women can be obtained.

The database can be searched by country and region as well as by subject, sort of material, and type of information service. It includes details of the collections, the availability of material, the systems of indexing, the history of the service, and activities and services offered. The website also offers 10 text profiles of women's information services operating in the different regions of the world. These profiles include not only regular women's information centers, but also women's art documentation centers, virtual documentation centers, communication networks, and lesbian archives.

On a long-term basis, Mapping the World aims to form an ongoing database and website, providing access to women's information centers in all countries and all significant communities, such as indigenous communities and migrant communities. The website means to facilitate communication between governments and civil societies, women's organizations, researchers, journalists, and librarians on gender-specific issues.

VI. Conclusion

A. Cooperation as a Way of Life

Women's information services are increasingly involved in facilitating research and education, mostly still in the field of women's studies. These services can help to build the curriculum by making information available, such as historical photographs, to be used in textbooks. The IIAV has had several researchers who have done extensive work in the archives and produced voluminous dissertations about their findings. How could anyone ever write about the 50 years of history in consults for housewives in women's magazines if somewhere some librarian had not decided that is was important to keep these "trivial" magazines? Women's historians have learned to subversively use traditional sources, such as church records, for example. Also, however, women's historians have learned to use nontraditional sources for indicators of societal changes. Egodocuments form a good example of this. Within the field of women's information, these have been discovered as a valuable source of information (IIAV, 1991). Women do not leave many traces in the official depositories of archives, as they spend more time in the private sphere than in public life—in Western culture, that is. People interested in women's history therefore searched for alternative sources that would illustrate the history of daily life, as opposed to traditional history dominated by wars, kings, and other exceptional events and people. They turned toward another kind of document, such as oral history (spoken information, collected through interviews with women) and so-called egodocuments (letters, diaries, note-books).

Attention to these new kinds of sources has not been restricted to the world of women's information, however. Just as the women's movement has changed general views on society, women's information has changed the view on what information is useful, relevant, and worth collecting. It is an added value that women's information services have preserved these nontraditional kinds of sources and have also underlined the need to continue doing this.

For women's information services, it is also important not to wait for users' needs to grow, but to actively promote the availability of information and, by doing so, create a need. The developments in new technologies make this an easier task. An example of this is facilitating teachers and students in distance education and lifelong learning in the field of women's studies, two approaches that are very often combined. The Internet more frequently offers this education. Women's information services could link to that by including services for students to do integrated searches in the different public catalogs available on the Internet. A future scenario could be that students have access to several digitized picture archives in the different women's libraries, and by doing so can compare posters or pamphlets of the different waves of feminism. These developments are moving fast. Another result of the Beijing Women's Conference in 1995 was the inclusion of the promotion of adult education for women in the Platform for Action. UNESCO and the European Union, among others, have given money to the Gender and Education Office of the Council for Adult Education (based in Uruguay) to start organizing regional meetings to discuss these developments. For women's information services, it can be considered a true achievement and recognition that they are invited to participate in these meetings.

In Europe a network was launched called AIOFE (pronounced "Eve") of academic institutions in women's studies. One of the projects within this network, called "Athena," is planning to use the newly developed EWT as a subject of research on methodology.

B. How Political or Mainstream Is Women's Information?

It is clear that if libraries, documentation centers, and archives worldwide have made a decision to build collections consisting of women's information, they want to speed the realization of equal opportunities between men and women. In that sense, women's information services have made and continue to make political choices. The way this information is used in politics however, depends on the users of the information that is provided.

The International Federation of Library Associations (IFLA) has a Round Table on Women's Issues that started as a round table concerned with the position of women as librarians. Very often within IFLA it was proclaimed that the majority of people employed in libraries are women, implying that equal opportunities had been achieved in their field. However, as elsewhere, in this profession women have also been confronted with the glass ceiling. There are not as many managers in libraries as there are information specialists, and most managers are men. Therefore, the Round Table on Women's Issues of IFLA rightfully started their activities addressing these issues. Currently they start to take the specific information needs of women into consideration as well (Hildenbrand and Biblo, 1998). For this they can make use of the expertise and experiences women's information services have gained in their profession.

C. Is it Clear?

The intention by the end of this article was to have given some clarity about what can be understood by the term *women's information*. Information is produced everywhere and by everybody. Women's information is produced by everyone as well, sometimes without even being fully aware of this. International governmental institutions like the European Union, the United Nations, or UNESCO produce information on an hourly basis that can be considered women's information. It is of the utmost importance that this newly produced information is available for those who can benefit from it. The reality, however, is that much information does not reach the audience it is produced for. Women's information services around the world have the knowledge, the expertise, and the experience to help facilitate this process. It is, therefore, a promising development that the global network of cooperating women's information services are finally taking shape. The growth of the Dutch National Women's Library and Archives and its extensive collection form but one example of developments in women's information resources. Initiatives such as the Know How Conference, the European Women's Thesaurus, and the Mapping the World project sit happily among international cooperative efforts to improve the provision, visibility, and accessibility of women's information. For women and librarians, this is a true advance in librarianship!

References

Cummings, S. (1999). Introduction. In *Women's Information Services and Networks: A Global Sourcebook* (S. Cummings, H. van Dam, and M. Valk, eds.). KIT Uitgeverij, Amsterdam.

Douze, M. (1990). Vrouweninformatie: Wat, waar en hoe. *Bibliotheek & Samenleving* **10**, 363–367.

Douze, M., and Mevis, A. (1998). *Documenting a Nation's Women: Obstacles and Opportunities* (unpublished paper). IIAV, Amsterdam.

Hildenbrand, S., and Biblo, M. (1998). International library women: Identifying problems, seeking solutions. In *Libraries: Global Reach—Local Touch* (K. de la Peña McCook, B. J. Ford, and K. Lippincott, eds.), pp. 187–194. American Library Association, Chicago.

IIAV (1991). *Overzicht van de Archieven in het Internationaal Informatiecentrum en Archief voor de Vrouwenbeweging*. IIAV, Amsterdam.

IIAV (1996). *Policy 2001*. IIAV, Amsterdam.

IIAV (1998). *Declaration of the Know How Conference on the World of Women's Information, Amsterdam 22–26 August 1998*. http://www.iiav.nl/knowhow/decl.html.

Jungschleger, I. (1985). *De vergeelde blauwkous*. IIAV, Amsterdam.

Kramer, M., and Larsen, J. (1991). *Resources for Providing Information and Documentation in the Field of Equal Treatment for Men and Women in the European Community*. IIAV/KVINFO, Amsterdam/Copenhagen.

Mathiason, J. (1988). *Seminar for Information Systems for the Advancement of Women for National Machineries* (unpublished paper). Centre for Social Development and Humanitarian Affairs, Vienna.

Mensink, M. (1998). *European Women's Thesaurus: Report of the Making of a Non-Sexist Indexing System*. IIAV, Amsterdam.

Pugh, L. (1998). *Evaluation of the Know How Conference on the World of Women's Information. Amsterdam 22–26 August 1998*. IIAV, Amsterdam.

Rijsbosch, E. (1990). Feminisme, zo'n neutraal onderwerp als aardappelteelt: Het overheidsbeleid ten aanzien van vrouwenemancipatie. *Bibliotheek & Samenleving* **10**, 369–373.

Romeny, R. (1998). *Francesca Bonnemaison: A public library to promote culture and education among women*. http://www.iiav.nl/mapping-the-world/focspa.html

Steiner Moseley, E. (1995). *Women, Information, and the Future: Collecting and Sharing Resources Worldwide*. Highsmith Press, Fort Atkinson.

United Nations (1995). *Platform for Action*. Fourth World Conference on Women, Beijing.

Vazquez, L. (1995). Reports of the NGO Forum workshops on Women's Information Services. *International Newsletter on Women's Information Services* **1**, 1–2.

Women's Library and Information Center Foundation (1991). *Women's Memory: Proceedings of the International Symposium of Women's Libraries*. Kadin Eserleri Kütüphanesi ve Bilgi Merkezi Vakfi, Istanbul.

World Bank (1998). *What Is Knowledge Management? A Background Paper for the World Development Report of the World Bank*. World Bank, Washington, DC.

Lifelong Learning and the University for Industry

The Challenge for Libraries in the United Kingdom

Andrew McDonald
Director of Information Services
University of Sunderland
United Kingdom

I. Introduction

Improving learning opportunities for people throughout their lives, and encouraging people of all ages into learning as often as they want, are likely to be the most dramatic developments in education over the next few years. The new government in the United Kingdom sees widening access and lifelong learning as playing a crucial part in achieving "social inclusion" and prosperity for the nation. It is actively planning the learning "revolution" that is needed to achieve a new learning society, and one of the most radical developments will be the creation of the University for Industry (UfI). This will be an entirely new organization that sets out to make learning part of everyday life for individuals and companies by linking learners with the learning opportunities they require.

Although lifelong learning and the UfI are now well-known pieces of educational and even political jargon in the United Kingdom, it is important to understand the full extent of the planned learning revolution and the significant culture change that is required within the whole world of learning and its libraries. It is also important to consider how libraries themselves might assist in facilitating the necessary culture change, and how the network of libraries can be developed to deliver the new services required for supporting community-wide, lifelong learning in the new "Learning Age."

II. Lifelong Learning

A. Lifelong Learning Climbs the Political Agenda

Making lifelong learning a reality has been an important goal in Europe and beyond for some time. There have been numbers of reports from the OECD,

UNESCO and other international organisations, and reports from the European Commission (EC) culminated in the designation of 1996 as the European Year of Lifelong Learning. As Edith Cresson, EC Commissioner for Education, Training and Youth, remarked, the need is for all citizens to be encouraged and empowered to take on more responsibility for planning and carrying through their own personal and professional development on a lifelong basis.

The influential Jacques Delors (1966) offered a wonderful vision of lifelong learning:

> There is a need to rethink and broaden the notion of lifelong education. Not only must it adapt to changes in the nature of work, but it must also constitute a continuous process of forming whole human beings—their knowledge and aptitudes, as well as the critical faculty and ability to act. It should enable people to develop awareness of themselves and their environment and encourage them to play their social role at work and in the community. (p. 21)

In the United Kingdom, lifelong learning can be traced back through the activities of the Workers' Educational Association, the extramural work of universities, and even to the foundation of the Mechanics' Institutes in industrial towns in the early nineteenth century (Brophy, 1999b). In more recent years, the former Conservative Government's consultative paper on lifetime learning, published in 1995, focused on continuing education and training and on the updating of skills beyond the initial education phase in schools, colleges, and universities. The paper looked toward the role of employers and government in developing the culture of lifetime learning, and it stressed the importance of "a highly motivated, flexible and well-qualified workforce to the UK's international competitiveness" (p. 7).

A related initiative is the Royal Society of Arts *Campaign for Learning* (RSA, 1996), which emphasized the current "messiness" of learning and the need for each individual to be encouraged to find their own learning style and model (Brophy, 1999b).

However, lifelong learning has only really become a major concern of governments since 1996, when the UK Government, along with others such as the governments of Portugal and Finland, published significant policy papers on the topic. A European conference on lifelong learning (*The Learning Age: Towards a Europe of Knowledge*) discussed a number of issues at the very heart of the Labour Government's policy in the UK—lifelong learning, employability, social inclusion, and active citizenship. Lifelong learning has now reached the top of the political agenda in the United Kingdom through a series of policy papers and reports published since the new Labour Government took office in May 1997. These include the Dearing (1997), Kennedy (1997), and Fryer (1997) reports; the *National Grid for Learning* proposals (DfEE, 1997); the Library and Information Commission's Report, *New Li-*

brary: The People's Network (LIC, 1997); and the government's consultative
paper, *The Learning Age* (DfEE, 1988b).

B. The Vision for a Learning Society

The consultative paper, *The Learning Age: A Renaissance for a New Britain*
(DfEE, 1998b), sets out the UK Government's vision for the learning society
and an ambitious practical agenda to achieve it. Baroness Blackstone, the UK
Minister of State, Department for Education and Employment, so eloquently
gave the government's rationale for investing in learning during an international conference (Blackstone, 1999):

> Learning is the key to the future well-being of this country. It is essential to a strong
> economy and an inclusive society. It is the heart of the Government's programme. Our
> aim is to create a fairer, more prosperous society. We wish to empower all people to lead
> a fulfilling life. Learning does just that.
>
> The development of skills can give people confidence and hope. They can help people
> overcome the barriers to work, and so open up the route out of poverty. Skilled and
> confident people gives businesses the edge that they need to be successful in this ever more
> competitive world.
>
> It is a virtuous circle. In economic terms, skilled people contribute to the success of
> businesses and thereby to their own prosperity. And in social terms, skilled people are able
> to make a greater contribution to society—to feel that they have a stake in it—and society
> itself is thus made all the stronger. (p. 6)

A similarly passionate case was made in the UK Government's consultative paper itself (DfEE, 1998b, p. 7): "As well as securing our economic
future, learning has a wider contribution. It helps make ours a civilised society,
develops the spiritual side of our lives and promotes active citizenship. Learning enables people to play a full part in their community. It strengthens the
family, the neighbourhood and consequently the nation."

The key principles on which the government wishes to build the Learning
Age are investing in learning to benefit everyone; lifting barriers to learning;
putting people first; sharing responsibility with employers, employees, and
the community; achieving world-class standards and value for money; and
working together in partnerships. It believes that lifelong learning is the
key to prosperity for individuals, businesses, and the nation. The practical
proposals set out in the consultative paper include overcoming the barriers
to learning through, for example, the launch of the UfI; supporting investment
in learning through Individual Learning Accounts; facilitating learning in the
workplace; and working with further, higher, and adult education to deliver
the learning society. The rationale is to address the collective interests of the
economy and community through what might be called a "managed market
model" (McNair, 1998). Individuals and firms will choose what learning to
buy, but there will be underpinning support from the state through guidance,

brokering, and quality frameworks, which will ensure that the broader public interest is preserved.

C. What Is Lifelong Learning?

In his valuable research concerned with the development of academic library services in the United Kingdom in the context of lifelong learning, Brophy (1998) adopts a useful definition of lifelong learning: "Lifelong learning is a deliberate progression throughout the life of an individual, where the initial acquisition of knowledge and skills is reviewed and upgraded continuously, to meet challenges set by an ever changing society" (p 5). By using this definition, Brophy seeks to draw attention to a number of salient features of lifelong learning, namely that:

It relies on a *deliberate* decision by an individual to pursue learning—although we all learn from life all the time—the term "lifelong learning" implies that there is a decision to pursue learning in order to acquire new knowledge and skills.

It continues *throughout* life, so that a series of learning activities are undertaken, and it is never supposed that learning is complete or that new learning cannot be undertaken.

There is a process of *review* so that the experience of earlier learning occasions is subjected to careful consideration, with gaps and new opportunities identified.

A process of *updating* is undertaken, so that skills and knowledge acquired earlier in life are brought up to date and made current in the light of developments in knowledge and changes in society.

The updating of knowledge and skills is seen as a *continuous* activity, such that they are not allowed to become seriously out of date or irrelevant to current concerns and practices.

Individuals are open to the *challenges* to their knowledge and skills that are presented by changes in their own lives and in society, and they use learning opportunities to respond to those challenges.

It is accepted that *society* is in a constant state of change, and lifelong learning is one of the main agencies through which individuals can respond to and cope with that change. Conversely, it is accepted that society itself needs individuals to learn new skills and knowledge if it is to remain viable and prosper in an increasingly competitive world.

In other words, lifelong learning is about learning throughout the whole of life, and it is not restricted to the postschool to postretirement period that is the primary and important focus of the UK Government's consultative paper (DfEE, 1998b). It is for all people, not just the elite, and it is about people entering and re-entering learning at relevant points in their lives as parents, citizens, and at work.

D. The National Skills Challenge

The scale of the task of creating a learning society should not be underestimated. Although UK universities are recognized as setting world-class standards, as a nation, we have demonstrable weaknesses in our performance in basic and intermediate skills. The stark facts are as worrying as they are astonishing (Fryer, 1999).

Thousands of people are literally "turned-off" learning at every stage of the system, and this is a national tragedy in view of the established importance of motivation in successful learning. It has been estimated that within the United Kingdom's population of some 60 million, more than 40% of 18-year-olds are not involved in any training or education, and that 7 million adults have no formal qualifications at all. Even more surprising is that more than one in five of all adults have poor literacy and numeracy skills. This puts the United Kingdom ninth in a recent international survey of 12 industrial countries in Europe (DfEE, 1998b).

Our traditional education system seems to have widened the learning divide between social classes since the late 1980s. The unskilled now have a two-thirds chance of being wholly unqualified, and a less than 1% chance of having a degree. At the start of the 1990s, the figures were 60% and 3%, respectively. By the end of the 1990s, the professional classes have a less than 3% chance of being wholly unqualified and a two-thirds chance of getting a degree. In 1990, the figures were 7% and 30%, respectively.

The skills needs and earning potential in employment have changed. Today, 70% of jobs need cerebral skills, but only 30% need manual skills. At the end of the 1940s the reverse was true. People without qualifications currently earn 20% less than the average wage, and 25% less than those with Advanced Levels (academic examinations mostly taken by 18-year-olds), and 50% less than graduates.

As George Bernard Shaw (1960, p. 15) said, poverty is "the greatest of our evils and the worst of our crimes." Poverty is not only the lack of material wealth, it is also the lack of opportunity and the lack of hope, and it is a waste of human potential that the nation cannot afford (Blackstone, 1999). The creation of a learning society and the investment in a new learning culture are crucial to remedying these serious historical defects. The UK government recognizes that education, knowledge, and skills are the key to success and prosperity in the new age.

E. A Culture of Lifelong Learning for All

Fryer (1999) suggests that creating a culture of lifelong learning for *all* is the single largest challenge to reaching the Learning Age. It requires a rethinking of the way in which learning is embedded in society, and of how it can be delivered in the home and workplace as much as in formal educational institutions and training centers. Learning should become something that is "normal" for everyone, and it should be integrated and relevant to people's lives and work. It is important to overcome people's fear and anxiety of learning that, for so many, is associated with their first taste of formal education. People should have the choice about where, when, and how they learn, and their learning should be relevant to their personal, family, community, and work projects.

The culture must embrace pre-16-year old persons because this is when individuals form many of their attitudes, aspirations, and values in relation to learning and life. Our existing education system places too great an emphasis on nongeneric skills and seems to provide a demotivating experience for many who never return to learning. Indeed, it is estimated that as many as one in three adults in the United Kingdom take no formal education or training after leaving school. Hillman (1996) reminds us that lifelong learning must start at school with a broad and solid foundation, followed by recurrent and progressive periods of learning. The post-55-year-old persons are also an important group. There are more than 14 million people who are older than 55 in the United Kingdom, and it has been estimated that this number will grow by 50% by 2010.

Fryer (1997) identified various groups who were "excluded" from learning, including unskilled and unemployed people; part-time and temporary workers; those living in isolated locations; some ethnic and linguistic minority groups; older adults; some women, particularly lone parents; and disaffected young adults. The proportion of low-skilled and low-knowledge employment in the economy is declining, and there is a very real risk of generating an underclass who will effectively be excluded from employment and all the social and economic benefits that it brings. There are great dangers in excluding people from lifelong learning on grounds of morality, economic efficiency, and political stability (McNair, 1998).

F. Some Other Considerations

Society faces all sorts of other significant challenges that will make it increasingly important for people to have the opportunity to update and renew their skills, knowledge, and learning.

The nature of work will change as a result of globalization, the increased mobility of people and industries, and the knowledge-based economy. Patterns of employment will change as people make several career changes in the course of their working lives and with the predicted decline in permanent, full-time work.

Many regard new technology as the key to opening up learning opportunities. There is great potential for creating an accessible, user-friendly learning infrastructure and for exploiting interactive media, digital television, and other new forms of technology for learning. Puttnam (1999), for example, points to the convergence of moving image and print, and the convergence between entertainment and education ("edutainment"). The importance of motivation and the creative use of new technology for active and creative learning should not be overlooked (Edmunds, 1999).

There is considerable interest in many parts of the world in developing learning or intelligent communities of various types—learning towns, learning cities, learning states, and even learning islands—in which the emphasis is often on social and economic regeneration as much as lifelong learning. A key factor in their success has been the existence of an overarching policy that embraces all aspects of the learning environment and gives the necessary political commitment and financial incentive to bring the diverse elements involved into a cohesive working partnership. Whereas a great deal is reported about the physical, economic, social, and support infrastructure required (DfEE, 1999a), it is sometimes the case that the important role of libraries in learning communities is overlooked. In some learning cities, such as Sunderland and Utrecht, libraries are leading the way in forging cross-sectoral partnerships and opening up the world of learning to their local communities. Indeed, as society and its institutions change, the social and cultural role of libraries, as places where people of all types like to come together and interact and learn, should not be underestimated (Revill, 1999).

III. The University for Industry

A. Development of the Concept

The University for Industry (UfI) is a simple but challenging concept, particularly for those who are closely involved with the traditional, elite educational system. This new organization was first proposed as long ago as 1991 by the now UK Chancellor of the Exchequer, Gordon Brown MP, whose vision was to create a national learning network, based on public and private partnership, that he believed would be of central importance to Britain's economic and social future. The concept and framework for development for this radical new organization were fleshed out by Hillman (1996) of the Institute for Public Policy Research in a book entitled *The University for Industry: Creating a National Learning Network*. The UfI is central to the proposals set out in the UK Government's consultative paper, *The Learning Age* (DfEE, 1998b):

> [W]e propose to make it easier for individuals to learn and firms to meet their skills needs by creating the University for Industry. . . . It will provide a fast and responsive service

in meeting the skill and business needs of employers, employees and of the self-employed, using leading-edge technology to make learning available at work, in learning centres, in the community, and at home. (DfEE, 1998c, p. 9)

The Department for Education and Employment (DfEE et al., 1998) then published ambitious targets in the *University for Industry Pathfinder Prospectus.* "By 2002, we expect that 2.5 million people or businesses a year will be using the UfI's range of services and over 600,000 a year will be pursuing programmes of learning organised through UfI" (p. 6). There has been substantial investment in the UfI by the government. £15 million was announced for 1998–1999 to get the new organization started, and a further £40 million for 1999–2000, together with £16 million from the Further Education Funding Council and £6 million for Learning Direct. The Corporate Plan for 1999–2002 will cover the commissioning of ICT systems and learning materials, working with pilot projects, franchising learning centers, setting up promotional campaigns, and establishing the headquarters in Sheffield. This radical new organization will be launched in 2000 and is expected to have a huge impact for the learning society in the country.

B. What Is the University for Industry?

The UfI is at the heart of the Government's vision for a learning society and it will be the "lever for starting the cultural shift to make lifelong learning a reality" (Blackstone, 1999, p. 7). Its strategic objective is to stimulate national demand for lifelong learning among businesses and individuals and so enhance skills for employability and competitiveness in particular. It aims to open up access to high-quality learning opportunities to everyone, and encourage new learners to take up learning (DfEE *et al.*, 1998).

The UfI will be the "hub" of a new national learning network, linking or connecting learners with learning opportunities in new ways so as to meet the skills needs of both individuals and companies. It will operate as a broker in the learning market, providing access to information, advice, and guidance on education and training opportunities. Using state-of-the-art information and communications technology to market, provide, and manage learning, it will help people identify the learning they need and access that learning how, when, and where they want—at work, at home, and in learning centers throughout the country.

The UfI will be an entirely new kind of organization, and it is important to be clear that, despite its current name, it is neither a university nor a service exclusively for industry. It will be a way of brokering learning opportunities and will not itself be a teaching institution or a direct provider of courses. It will promote learning in general and not just to industry, although one core objective will be improving the skills of the nation's workforce and stimulating learning at work.

Libraries have always been at the heart of the universities they serve, but UfI is not a traditional university, and it is interesting to speculate as to the role of libraries in supporting this learning innovation (see Section IV.B.4).

C. Learning Aims and Priorities

The learning aims of the UfI are access, flexibility, relevance, quality, and cost-effectiveness. In its first years, it will focus on promoting basic skills (literacy and numeracy), information and communication technologies, and small- to medium-size businesses. Certain key sectors of the economy have been identified: automotive components, multimedia industry, environmental technology and services, and distributive and retail trades. The UfI will be important for reaching the government's target of doubling the number of adults who are helped to improve their basic literacy and numeracy skills to 500,000 a year by 2002. Small- to medium-size businesses are an important target sector because it is estimated that 30% of the British workforce now work in companies that employ 20 or less staff, and lifelong learning and skills development are as important as they are difficult for these companies.

D. Partnerships

Successful partnerships are absolutely crucial for building the UfI and the learning community. The UfI requires the specialist expertise of a wide range of public and private partners, and this goes much further than the course providers themselves. Significant partners will include: further and higher education; business; employers; trade unions; Training and Enterprise Councils; Chambers of Commerce; publishers; broadcasters; local authorities; Regional Development Agencies; and the private, public, and voluntary sectors. Indeed, the UfI is a very interesting example of where the interests and perspectives of multiple stakeholders can be applied to a common goal of lifelong learning.

E. The Learning Model

The UfI learning model has a number of important components: promotion and marketing; comprehensive information; learning materials; learning centers and home learning; learning support; membership services and facilities; and learning routes for people.

The UfI will make use of mainstream marketing techniques and publicity campaigns to promote itself, and there are plans for a high-profile launch. The marketing power of broadcasting will be exploited because experience has confirmed that television is a very powerful way of creating demand for learning. The BBC's campaign, *Computers Don't Bite*, generated an astonishing

89,000 calls in just over a week. In its publicity, considerable attention will be given to the development and management of the UfI "brand" or "badge."

Comprehensive information, particularly about courses and learning opportunities, will be made available in a variety of ways. There will be a telephone helpline, a comprehensive database, a Website, a client management system, and a public service. A major part of the vision is Learning Direct, a national telephone helpline, which provides information and advice about learning and career opportunities in the United Kingdom. The free phone number has been widely publicized on television and radio, and received a staggering 240,000 calls in just the first 4 months after its launch, illustrating a real hunger for learning.

The UfI will also analyze trends in the demand for learning in order to identify and inform providers about unmet needs, and commission new programs and materials where gaps exist.

Effective learning materials are very important. New materials will be commissioned and existing materials enhanced and endorsed, and they will emphasize certain key learning principles and criteria. Learning materials will be in a variety of media, with an emphasis on ICT, and mechanisms for feedback will be fully integrated.

A nationwide network of learning centers will be established in a variety of locations to suit people's lifestyles, including the workplace and the community, in places such as libraries and shopping centers. These will be in formal or informal settings, and the centers may be linked consortia or satellites of broader provision. Lifelong learning in the workplace will be stimulated through company learning centers with strong links to the UfI, and they will be established with the help of businesses, employees, and their trade unions.

Learning support is critical to the success of the UfI. Support will include induction, mentoring, specialist tutorials, and chat groups. UfI membership services will be offered to both individuals and corporate organizations as a way of encouraging commitment to learning and loyalty to the UfI, and as a way of communicating information and establishing learning networks. A variety of membership packages and discounts are planned, and regional services and support will be established.

The UfI will also provide a quality assurance framework across the whole range of its provision, so that users can be confident of the quality of what is being offered. It will work through existing quality systems and will establish certain criteria or standards for learning materials and learning delivery. There will be an emphasis on staff development, and a virtual center of excellence in open, distance, and distributed learning is planned.

F. The UfI Pilot Project

The University of Sunderland and the Institute for Public Policy Research have together coordinated a pilot project in the North East of England designed to test the UfI model (Milner, 1998) (Thorne and Milner, 1998). Launched in 1997 by Baroness Blackstone, the UK Minister of State, Department for Education and Employment, it has successfully encouraged more than 8000 registrations for courses and "tasters" in just 15 months in the North East alone, which is traditionally an area of low participation in post-compulsory education.

The pilot model is really quite simple—it acts as a customer-focused, impartial broker that connects individuals and companies to the learning programs they require from various providers—it does not provide courses itself. There are four key elements: innovative marketing; a call center with a direct booking service; a specially designed Internet system with details of thousands of courses and "tasters" (www.ufi.org.uk); and 85 UfI learning centers.

Essentially, the UfI pilot project is a one-stop shop for education and training—a gateway to existing lifelong learning opportunities available in North East England. It is a "hub" at the center of the regional learning network that connects learners with courses, and markets and manages learning. By calling a single free phone number, people have easy access to information, advice, and enrollment for a whole range of courses and tasters. It operates 12 hours a day, 6 days a week. Staff at the call center, and individuals with access to the Internet, can search the database for suitable courses from more than 2000 available from a number of providers. The process is very simple: callers are initially asked for their learning requirements and postal codes—two pieces of very valuable marketing information.

Current providers include the University of Sunderland, local further education colleges, the Open University, the National Extension College, the BBC, commercial training providers, and local companies. The 15 free taster courses that emphasize key skills for work have been most popular, especially those concerned with IT. They can all be studied immediately at home by means of open learning workbooks. Many lifelong learners want to start learning immediately and they are sometimes frustrated by the way in which traditional educational institutions timetable courses rigidly into terms and semesters. Providers take responsibility for the information about their courses on the Internet system, and for the content, cost, and delivery of the courses on offer. Initially, the pilot project focused on skills for work—IT and the Internet, communication, finance, and the business environment.

The courses can be studied in a variety of ways, and about a third of enrollments are for learning at home or work. Eighty-five UfI learning centers have been established in the region in places convenient for learners. They are based in companies, stores, shopping malls, health centers, churches, Internet cafés, factories, and, not least, in libraries. One is based in Sunderland Football Club's Stadium of Light, where people are taking the "Football Fan's Guide to the Internet" taster course in IT. It is reassuring to note that public libraries have turned out to be among the most popular learning centers with these new lifelong learners.

Marketing is key to stimulating demand for learning, and many of the direct marketing techniques of the commercial world have been used success-fully, including telemarketing, advertising on television and radio, leaflets through household doors, poster campaigns on buses, and family learning events. Publicity has all been professionally designed and bears strong mes-sages, such as "Learn more, earn more," "A no-nonsense approach to improv-ing your skills," "Courses to help you get a job or to get a better one," and "Learn where it suits you and where it fits in with your daily life." The publicity is designed to encourage people to call the free phone number, and experience has shown that people will comfortably discuss their learning requirements with call center staff who follow up on all initial telephone enquiries and with all enrolled learners so as to ensure the UfI is the natural choice when people require new or further learning. One surprising statistic is that "cold" telephone calling has achieved a staggering 22% success rate in enrollment. The UfI "brand name" has been readily accepted in the learning marketplace.

The call center can monitor demand and identify gaps in the provision of courses, in the mode of delivery and in availability in particular geographic areas. The UfI can respond to customer demand by commissioning new courses from providers. The single Internet-based system for marketing and managing information about all aspects of the UfI is a very powerful tool.

Engaging companies has not been easy, but the pilot project has worked with a number of companies in the region to ensure their employees have access to learning opportunities provided by the UfI as well as integrating with their training provision and plans. For example, one electronics company in Northumberland has opened up its training room to all employees, their friends and family, and the parents and staff of the local school, and they all have access to the tasters and other courses available through the UfI.

The pilot project was based on a strong, strategic collaboration between a wide range of regional and national partners, including companies, Training and Enterprise Councils, local authorities, the media, colleges, universities, volunteer organizations, sponsors, publishers, and software companies. The project has clearly shown the fundamental importance of partnership in pro-viding lifelong learning and, in particular, the value of public–private partner-ship and of organizations providing substantial support in kind. Indeed, it shows that there can be a sensible balance between competition and collaboration, even between course providers, so long as the partners understand their roles and see the benefits. The UfI is by no means solely dependent on courses provided by further and higher education: companies, trade unions, and other bodies can and will deliver learning in this way. Although much content already exists, the trend will be for more tailored and personalized learning. Initially, funding was based on major sponsorship from Sunderland City Training and Enterprise Council, Sunderland City Council, and the NatWest Bank, and experimentation is continuing with European Social Funding.

The pilot project demonstrated two particularly successful features of this innovative approach to learning. First, a customer-focused system with direct marketing can and has uncovered a huge unmet demand for learning. Second, that learners liked the taster courses, which are quite unlike traditional courses. They are free, short, focused, and flexible; and they can be studied at home, straight away without tutoring or assessment. Some learners progress from these taster courses to other courses.

Other key benefits have been its accessibility to everyone; the relevance to people's lifestyles; the single, simple, and cohesive service provided in the region; the free phone helpline; and the choice of a variety of courses from a range of providers. The University of Sunderland/Institute for Public Policy Research pilot project has been the first test of the UfI concept. It demonstrated that there is great unsatisfied demand for learning, and that given the opportunity and the necessary encouragement, people are ready and happy to take responsibility for their learning; indeed, they even take delight in their learning. Clearly, the UfI has huge potential for making a real difference for lifelong learning when it is established nationally.

IV. Libraries and Lifelong Learning

A. The Role of Libraries

There is a growing recognition in political circles of the unique contribution of libraries to lifelong learning, and this received a welcome endorsement in the Fryer Report (1997), *Learning for the Twenty-First Century:*

> In promoting lifelong learning, and widening access, full use should be made of the major community resource which is invested in libraries, museums and study centres. They already have an excellent track record in providing learners of all ages and from a variety of backgrounds with a rich and diverse range of materials, opportunities, information, facilities and staff support. They need to be seen more widely as part of a mosaic of both local and national provision, offering additional arenas through which the culture of lifelong learning for all can be fostered and sustained. They too need to be connected to the proposed

National Grid for Learning and their staff should be supported in developing further the skills and aptitudes which will be necessary to carry through the new strategy. (p. 61)

Fryer (1997) went on to point out the great value of libraries in the learning culture as major sources of information, understanding, knowledge, creativity, culture, heritage, and leisure. They provide access for both individuals and communities. He stressed the importance of strategic partnerships and networks of libraries, and he recommended that the contribution of libraries to lifelong learning should be recognized through additional funding, staff training, and IT provision.

The Library and Information Commission's Report, *New Library: The People's Network* (LIC, 1997), highlighted the valuable contribution that libraries make to realizing the vision of the learning society.

Tomorrow's new library will be a key agent in enabling people of all ages to prosper in the information society—helping them acquire new skills for employment, use information creatively, and improve the quality of their lives. Libraries will play a central role in the University for Industry, in lifelong learning projects, and in support of any individual who undertakes self-development. (introduction)

The report reminded us that the public library service in the United Kingdom is one of the most widely used information and learning resources, and is also one of the most respected public services. Around 400 million visits are made to public libraries every year, with 10 million users making a visit at least once a fortnight, and almost 60% of adults are library members.

The UK government has published its exciting plans for the Public Library IT Network in its encouraging response to *New Library* (DCMS, 1998).

We intend it to play a central role in delivering the Government's wider objectives for the role of information technology in society. As such, the development of the library network is an integral part of the vision of the "Our Information Age" launched by the Prime Minister in April which provides the framework for ensuring that we seize the opportunities provided by new technology. (Blackstone, 1999, pp. 11–12)

It is clear that the successful implementation of the Public Libraries IT Network depends on partnership involving the private sector, local government, and library users (Blackstone, 1999, p. 12).

Government can establish the strategic framework and set the directions and pace of this process, but it cannot by itself deliver the network. To do that, we must rely on the determination, dedication and motivation we know exists within the sector. I know my colleagues in the Department for Culture, Media and Sport have been impressed by the expertise and enthusiasm already developing for the network. I am sure that it will ensure libraries continue to be a strong and vibrant link in the chain of lifelong learning.

Baroness Blackstone (1999, p. 10) has reassured the library community that she does "not underestimate the contribution libraries are already making to lifelong learning and the potential contribution they are uniquely placed to make in the future." Interestingly, she refers to the importance of partnerships between different types of libraries for supporting community-wide lifelong learning and commented: "The City of Sunderland is pioneering library initiatives, being the first city to open its college, university and public libraries to all learners in the city" (p. 10). She went on to say that the government regards public libraries as key contributors to some of its most important policy objectives:

> In addition to underpinning education by providing essential support for children, students and lifelong learners, they enhance public access to the world's store of knowledge and information, they combat social exclusion by helping to bridge the gap between those who can afford access to information and those who cannot, and, increasingly, they have a role to play in the modernisation and delivery of public services. Our plans for the development of the library sector are intended to enable libraries to play an even more significant role in all these key objectives. (p. 11)

The National Adult Learning Survey 1997 (DfEE, 1998a) was the first extensive survey of learning and nonlearning that has been carried out, and it highlighted the important role that libraries play in providing information, particularly information to those people classed as "nonlearners." Through initiatives such as the National Year of Reading, libraries demonstrated their experience, ingenuity, and creativity in combining traditional and electronic services. Blackstone (1999) confirms that blending new means of delivery with core values of customer service and the promotion of literacy is central to the government's vision of the development of a Public Libraries IT Network and as part of the *National Grid for Learning*. Campaigns such as the Library Association's Adult Learners' Week are invaluable in generating demand for learning.

The Library Association (1998), in its response to the government's consultative paper, also pointed out that libraries of all types and in all sectors are a strategic national and regional resource for lifelong learning. Libraries already make a huge contribution to the provision of basic and employment-related skills, and public libraries in particular have a fine track record of reaching groups with low participation.

B. Library Services for Lifelong Learners

There are a number of welcome developments taking place in the provision of new services with lifelong learners in mind.

1. Academic Libraries

Students who are studying on franchised courses run by the University of Central Lancashire, but who are dispersed throughout North West England, may now use the services of the Virtual Academic Library of the North West (VALNOW), which was launched in 1997 (Brophy, 1999a). VALNOW represents a serious attempt to provide a working model for the academic library operating in a distributed environment that seeks to serve the needs of students whose learning is increasingly "lifelong." Nontraditional higher education students require these library and information services if they are to be enabled to make the most of their educational opportunities. Services include access to centrally mounted datasets on CD-ROM, for which additional licence fees were paid by the university; access to national data services, to which they are entitled as registered university students; access to the university's online catalog, coupled with an additional facility to enable remote users to order items that were "in library"; the delivery of books to the college sites; and a subject enquiries service by videoconference link for students starting work on dissertations.

A number of future developments are being considered. A catalog "clump" consisting of the university library's catalog together with those of the college libraries, local public libraries, and other resources could be created. Library materials could be delivered to homes, but on-campus students may feel disadvantaged themselves by denial of such attractive services. Directory services may be a possibility, including sophisticated authentication of users operating in multiple environments. VALNOW would provide a useful testbed for the use of multifunctional smartcards operating across sectors. There is also research into the application of the hybrid library concept (traditional and electronic library) for groups of remote learners as part of the UK higher education electronic Libraries Programme.

Sheffield Hallam University offers a Distance Learning Support Service with a range of services to off-campus distance learners (Bye, 1998). As well as sending out books and journal articles in the mail to students in the United Kingdom, the service also offers extended book loans for up to 3 weeks, a book renewal service by telephone, mediated literature searches, information enquiries, and an interlibrary loan service. Assistance is given to learners in accessing their local academic libraries, including the payment of subscription fees in certain circumstances. Distance learners can access the library's online catalog with its self-service renewals and reservations service by telnet or modem, and can also access several databases through the Internet. Learners can communicate with the service by mail, telephone, fax, or e-mail, and increasing use is being made of First Class conferencing software.

Bye (1998) stresses the need for a flexible and responsive service for distance learners that exploits a mixture of both electronic and "extended" traditional services. User education should concentrate as much as possible on generic information skills rather than institution-specific knowledge. He reminds us that distance learners have varied working conditions, and that they may be difficult to contact and are often under enormous time pressures.

The University of Sunderland provides similar special services for its distance learners, and these are well used, particularly by overseas masters students who are undertaking project work as part of their studies. Services include a document delivery service by mail and fax, mail loans in the United Kingdom, access to a number of Internet-based information and retrieval services, literature searching, and an enquiry service by telephone, fax, or through a dedicated Web page. Renewals and reservations can be made either directly or by using the self-service facilities on the online catalog. Assistance is given to learners in gaining access to their local libraries. As part of the library's commitment to quality, distance learners are surveyed annually about their awareness and experience of these services, and they are asked for their recommendations for development.

Although perhaps not motivated primarily by the needs of lifelong learners, two cooperative initiatives, the Consortium of Academic Libraries in Manchester (CALIM) and the London-based "M25" Group, offer an important strand of development for nontraditional learners and, particularly, learners based at a distance from their "home" institution.

The Open University is launching new electronic services, including the Resources for Open University Teachers and Students (ROUTES) system, which is building up a database of learning support materials available online. Electronic library facilities will play an important role in the University of the Highlands and Islands Project, which aims to develop a new university offering students in the remoter areas of Scotland the opportunity to undertake a growing number of higher education courses on a full- or part-time basis that can be attended at a specific college or at a remote location.

2. Public Libraries

There are a number of encouraging developments in the public library sector as well.

For example, Birmingham has established itself as a Learning City. Its strategic commitment has four overarching themes—social inclusion and equality, ICT and lifelong learning, information advice and guidance, and marketing lifelong learning. Birmingham libraries are committed to supporting lifelong learning from "cradle to grave" through a variety of services and initiatives. There is bookstart, early learning with leisure, family literacy, and homework clubs. Provision is made for specific learning needs, marketing lifelong learning, and open and flexible learning. Current projects include core skills development, targeting small- to medium-size enterprises through a UfI project, working with the BBC, and developing local learning partnerships.

A number of projects in Birmingham involve collaborative working with other libraries and organizations and are externally funded and supported (Dolan, 1999). "Futures Together" is a British Library–funded research project looking at networking in relation to unique and special collections (from literary archives to contemporary resources) across different library sectors, with a view to improving access to and information about them for users. "Stories on the Web" is also a British Library–funded project that will introduce children to the Internet through creative literature and reading, and involves Leeds and Bristol libraries, authors, and publishers. "Training the Future" is a partnership with Shropshire Libraries to explore the training needs of library staff and the new roles anticipated in the networked environment. "ASSIST" is the city's Web site development for which the library is the lead service, and is negotiating partnerships with diverse contributors, including city council departments and organizations in the private and voluntary sectors.

Dolan (1999) predicts that external and partnership funding will become increasingly important, and he suggests that this creates new expectations of library managers and requires new skills and approaches if we are to be successful and innovative. He goes on to point out the need to replace competitive policies in the world of learning with communication, collaboration, and convergent strategies.

3. Cross-Sectoral Library Initiatives

A unique example of cross-sectoral library collaboration to promote lifelong learning is the Libraries Access Sunderland Scheme (LASH; McDonald, 1999). Under LASH, anyone who lives, works, or studies in Sunderland has free access to all the libraries in the city. This includes the 21 public libraries, the four learning centers in the city college, and the four libraries in the university (the three partner organizations). Learners can study at any of the 3000 reader places in these libraries spread around the city, and they can make use of the collections and services provided there. All the users need is a current membership card for the public library or one of the academic libraries, and they are simply asked to respect the regulations of the library they are using and study in a responsible way with consideration for the needs of other learners.

The scheme was launched in 1997 and has a number of benefits:

It opens up the world of learning to people of all ages in the city
Learners can use the whole range of public and academic libraries in the city
People have somewhere to study and learn with free access to books, IT,
    and services

Learners can use the nearest or most convenient library, and this may be
    particularly attractive to part-time and disadvantaged students
The public are encouraged to use academic libraries and may get their first
    taste of life on campus
Registered staff and students of the city college and university have reciprocal
    access rights for the first time
The academic institutions are reminded of the value of the public library
Sharing resources means that everyone can benefit from the investment in
    libraries in the city
Learners in the community are encouraged to step on the *ladder of learning*
    and to develop their interests without unnecessary institutional barriers

None of the three libraries have been overwhelmed by new users, and
the new lifelong learners have not presented any major difficulties. Although
the scheme has not been formally evaluated, anecdotal evidence suggests that
women returning to learning are now making greater use of the university's
libraries. The costs have been minimal and have simply been shared equally
between the partners.

Other collaborative achievements include joint staff training and development, sharing online catalogs, delivering several thousand full-text electronic
journals through a unique city-wide license, supporting the UfI and other
learning initiatives, and undertaking research projects. There are a number
of planned developments. As well as further joint staff training and electronic
information initiatives, a city-wide document delivery service and a common
library card or smart card are being considered. It is also planned to involve
school libraries, electronic village halls, the UfI learning centers, and libraries
in the surrounding areas in the North East of England.

Another example of a cross-sectoral library initiative that sets out to
develop services to meet the many and varied requirements of lifelong learners
is Access to Libraries for Learning in Northamptonshire (ALLIN; Martin,
1998). This bilateral agreement between Nene University College Northampton and Northamptonshire Libraries and Information Services is designed
to foster and support learning and research throughout Northamptonshire.
It aims to consolidate and extend collaborative activity, promote access, and
provide a framework for future cooperative development. Since its launch in
1997, there have been three main strands of activity: promoting access through
publicity, cooperative projects (including a pilot interlibrary loan scheme,
coordinated dyslexia support, and a staff development exchange scheme), and
encouraging broader participation in ALLIN through the UfI.

The "People Flows" research project has investigated the extent of the
"cross-use" of libraries in the public, college, and university sectors, focusing
on the areas of Sheffield and Birmingham/Solihull (Nankivell, 1998). Interest-

ingly, they found numbers of library users who were engaged in study but who were not full-time students (18% in the public library, 53% in the university library, and 62% in the college library). About 16% of public library users were in full-time education. A whole range of people were making use of the academic libraries, including those in full- and part-time work, those looking for work, and retired persons.

4. Libraries and the University for Industry

Libraries have played an important part in the UfI pilot project in the North East of England (McDonald, 1998, 1999). All the libraries in the city of Sunderland have been designated as UfI learning centers along with the centers created in other places convenient for learners, and this was made possible quickly through LASH (described in Section IV.B.3). In fact, the public library has proved to be the most popular learning center outside the formal educational institutions. The new lifelong learners have appreciated the accessibility and opening hours of the libraries, and have welcomed the use of study facilities, access to information and IT and, not least, the support of trained professional staff. Libraries have proved to be good locations for advertising the UfI and other lifelong learning and career opportunities, and they have the potential to be places where learners can enroll for courses too. Their established role in promoting literacy, learning, and IT literacy has also been a useful contribution.

It is ironic, but by no means surprising, that the traditional public library service should emerge as centrally important to a radical lifelong learning initiative such as the UfI. This simply emphasizes the tremendous contribution that public libraries have always made to supporting community-wide, lifelong learning. Rather like the UfI, libraries are customer-focused services in which people find it conducive to study in what is an unthreatening and supportive learning environment. Indeed, the network of libraries in our communities could emerge as the "active heart" of the UfI. There is great potential for exploiting both public libraries and the learning environments of colleges and universities, as places where lifelong learners can study and access learning materials and as local gateways to the global network of electronic information. Library and information professionals will also have an increasingly valuable role as learning facilitators and mentors for the new lifelong learners.

5. European Development Projects

The European Commission is funding a number of projects designed to improve access to networked library services for supporting learning and training across Europe (Pigott, 1999). As a result, national authorities are beginning to recognize their importance for supporting lifelong learning. Libraries in a number of countries are now providing a range of sophisticated Internet-based services. These include children's library services, music services, and access to electronic journals. Encouraging progress has been made in developing models for distributed services, single-card access to resources, and Web support for public libraries.

A number of projects have directly addressed the problem of supporting distance learners through libraries:

BIBDEL   Libraries without walls: the delivery of library services to distant users (a toolkit of techniques was developed as a practical and cost-effective guide to learners throughout Europe)

EDUCATE   End-user courses in information access through communications technology (courseware in electrical engineering, physics, and other subjects, with attention given to the training of librarians in the distance learning environment)

HYPERLIB   Hypertext interfaces to library information systems (recognizes the importance of the World Wide Web in providing remote access to libraries)

MURIEL   Multimedia education system for librarians introducing remote interactive processing of electronic documents (support for education and training for librarianship in the networked environment)

PLAIL   Public libraries and adult learners (access to distance learning through public libraries and training of librarians)

Having enhanced awareness of the problems involved, a number of current projects are tackling the needs of distance learners of all types:

ELVIL   The European legislative virtual library (a Web-based resource on European law and politics, including an educational aid for students, teachers, and librarians)

CHILIAS   Children in libraries: improving multimedia virtual library access and information skills (training children to make good use of Web-based resources)

VERITY   Virtual and electronic sources for information skills training (guiding teenagers in finding and managing information held in libraries and on electronic networks)

DERAL   Distance education in rural areas via libraries (involvement of public libraries in distance learning services, especially for those living in rural areas)

DEDICATE   Distance education information courses through networks
                  (developing distance education courses in information lit-
                  eracy for academic libraries in Eastern-European coun-
                  tries)
LIBERATOR   Libraries in European regions—access to telematics and
                  other resources (access to a wide variety of information
                  resources to large regional public library networks)

The forthcoming Fifth Framework Programme for Research and Development will provide specific support for "creating a user-friendly information
society" (Pigott, 1999, p. 95). One of the goals is to develop widely accessible
services based on multimedia content: libraries, museums, galleries, archives,
and other public institutions will have an important role to play in providing
mediated access to these rapidly evolving resources. It is anticipated that the
integration of print and digital information will ultimately allow users to
benefit from a whole range of seamlessly integrated services. Over the next
few years, new economic models will be required for managing access to
vastly expanded and widely distributed stores of digital information. The
long-term goal is ensuring continuity of access for future generations. The
commission recognizes the role of both academic and public libraries in
providing access to knowledge and learning for all the citizens of Europe,
and is working toward making this vision a technically achievable goal.

C. The Library Problems of Lifelong Learners

Although there are some excellent initiatives in all library sectors, there is
relatively little coordinated effort, and what might be called "nontraditional"
learners are very often left to negotiate a bewildering array of library facilities
(Brophy, 1999b).

   In the academic sector, much is known about the problems faced by part-
time students, for whom restrictions in opening hours, the lack of professional
support out of normal hours, and the lack of access to information skills
training are all key concerns. The library is often an important social center
for part-time students. Some interesting research (Unwin, 1998) also investigated the experiences of franchise students and distance learners.

   Unwin (1998) reveals that distance learners experience a whole raft of
"obstacles" in using libraries. They often have very restricted access to local
university libraries. There is a lack of clarity as to their rights in particular
libraries, and they often come to rely on the sometimes limited resources of
the public library. Indeed, there seems to be a worrying "air of illegitimacy
as students see themselves as operating outside the normal expectations of
academic and student life" (p. 205).

The-all-too familiar dilemma is of autonomous learners without direct access to the library services of their host institution, but who, in many ways, have an even greater need for effective library support than the traditional, on-campus learner. The dilemma is aggravated by the lack of communication between course providers, library managers, and the learners themselves. Course providers show a disturbing lack of concern about how student learning should be organized in relation to library use, and they rarely include librarians in their course planning. Indeed, the role of the library, especially the public library, is often poorly understood.

The research shows that many academic libraries have not developed services to meet the needs of distance learners, not least because of a genuine fear among many library managers that the well-stocked libraries could become overwhelmed. Although there seems to be a willingness among some university libraries to develop more effective services for distance learners, the research concluded that the arrangements currently made often seem to be somewhat *ad hoc*, unsatisfactory, and poorly advertised.

V. The Challenge for Libraries

A. Public Libraries

The influential and impressive *New Library* (LIC, 1997) report sets out a number of challenges for the complete transformation of public libraries in the UK:

> *For government*—to take a lead in developing and delivering an integrated national information policy with a strong emphasis on a central role for libraries.
> *For the technology and communication industries*—to seize the opportunity for provision and management of network infrastructure, services and content for libraries.
> *For libraries and library authorities*—to embrace the concept of the new library and to provide a new and dynamic interface between people, technology and information.
> *For educators*—to ensure that the benefits that can be delivered by information and communications technologies are available both to those in schools and formal education and to independent lifelong learners. (pp. 101–102)

The government's response (DCMS, 1998) confirmed its commitment to the Public Library IT Network, and that it sees the public library service as a key platform for the delivery of its strategic policy objectives of economic prosperity built on social inclusion and a caring community of self-supporting and self-confident people (Dolan, 1999). Lifelong learning, and more particularly lifelong learning related to employment, has emerged as an overarching theme.

Dolan (1999) reminds us that an essential part of the New Library concept is the retraining of public library staff at all levels to deliver new services in new ways through a UK-wide network with agreed standards for quality, service, and accessibility. A significant issue is the capacity of public library staff to undertake new or more diverse roles, not only in creating a library resource that will be a focal point for community access and learning, but also in adopting the role of active supporters and facilitators, almost teachers, for people who may not otherwise have access to new learning resources. There is a real need for public librarians to become more aware of the courses undertaken by the new lifelong learners, and especially of the nature, learning outcomes, and support materials involved. In the new Learning Age, the role of public librarians will increasingly become one of actively supporting learning as much as providing information and advice to their users.

B. Academic Libraries

Brophy's (1998) major study on the impact of lifelong learning on academic libraries concluded with 23 recommendations directed at funding councils, institutions, librarians, and the professional associations, and these ranged from:

> There should be continued encouragement at the highest level for cooperative approaches to comprehensive library provision suitable for supporting lifelong learners. In particular, given the likelihood of courses of any one institution being followed by students across the UK and any one student following modules from more than one institution, there is a need to go beyond regional arrangements and consider the issue again from a national perspective. (p. 62)

to

> Institutions should ensure that when they offer courses designed to appeal to lifelong learners, and especially where those courses will not be delivered primarily on-campus, there is a clear statement of the learning resource, including library support, which will be available and a commitment to its delivery. Work is needed to develop understanding of the costs and benefits of library support in these contexts. (p. 63)

The report (Brophy, 1998, pp. iv–v) also drew 13 conclusions that clearly indicate that the new lifelong learning agenda will have a profound effect on higher education libraries, and that academic libraries will have to make strenuous efforts to achieve a culture change within which the needs of life-long learners are given some sort of equality with those of its traditional students.

1. Higher education libraries must commit themselves to develop, pub-licize, and deliver a *basic set of library services designed for lifelong learners*. As Dearing (1997) found, it is the basic "bread and butter" services, such as access to books and study space, that learners themselves

regard as the highest priority. Redesigning service delivery to account for the needs of lifelong learners is therefore a very high priority.

2. However, libraries need to refocus their services on *content* rather than form, and ask themselves how the required content can be delivered to the lifelong learner. Here they can provide leadership in how information sources can be presented within the structures of learning that teaching staff devise.

3. The *hybrid library* concept has much to offer the lifelong learner through its emphasis on a managed mix of traditional and electronic services. Current projects on hybrid libraries and catalog clumps should be encouraged to take on board the needs of lifelong learners.

4. *Convergence* (bringing together library, computing, and other learning support services) should be seen as a positive step for the lifelong learner because it provides a single point of contact for academic support services and ensures that a single policy is pursued in their interests.

5. The future of library support for higher education lifelong learners will best be secured through *multiagency provision*, by which is meant a planned and managed cooperative alliance of providers (university, further education, public libraries, and others). However, because courses will be marketed nationally and internationally, it will not be adequate to rely only on regional cooperation.

6. A key issue will be the extent of *integration of library services into learning*. As new learning environments are designed and established, the role of the library will change—what is being introduced is an entirely new kind of environment where the student can easily, and within the same interface, access information ("library") and expertise ("tutor") while discussing ideas with fellow students ("seminar") and use a self-diagnostic tool.

7. Libraries will continue to play their sometimes unrecognized role as *social centers*. They are places where people can meet, study in groups as well as individually, and find supportive experts. For the off-campus lifelong learner, this role might be found in the public or college library, but will only be satisfactory where it is planned, resourced, and managed with lifelong learners in mind.

8. *Information quality* will be a matter of increasing importance because electronic services are often not subject to the level of quality control exercised over printed and other traditional publications. Libraries have an important role to play in quality assurance, and again, lifelong learners will need this support, especially where their study is unmediated and off-campus.

9. *Electronic resources* offer new and exciting opportunities for supporting lifelong learners with the information they need. However, we lack, as a library community, good models of the electronic library in its worldwide networked setting. We also, as a profession, lack the depth of knowledge that is needed to design and create the electronic services of the future.

10. *Information skills* pose a particular problem for the lifelong learner, who is typically short of time and may be remote from the physical library with its expert advisers. Where, as Dearing (1997) recommended, skills work is embedded in the curriculum, librarians will have to redouble their efforts to ensure that information skills are adequately covered and assessed.

11. For the nontraditional lifelong learner, the provision of good *help desk services* may make the difference between success and failure. However, these services must be designed as part of the overall learning environment, so that academic staff are involved in and take account of their design and function, and the help desk is not the last, desperate port of call.

12. If lifelong learning is to be a reality, universities must think in terms of developing *lifelong relationships* with their clientele. Libraries, through their "external" and other membership arrangements, could be in the vanguard of this movement.

13. Finally, the rate of change is so rapid, and the agenda to be addressed so vast, that academic libraries must have *dynamic management* if they are to serve the needs of lifelong learners.

C. The Network of Libraries

The UfI, the *National Grid for Learning*, and the *People's Network* are all major initiatives designed to open up learning by exploiting new technology. Libraries are well placed to make sure that a learning infrastructure is developed that is accessible to everyone (Bulpitt, 1998). He points out that:

> Academic libraries have considerable expertise in helping students to exploit information resources, and the network of public libraries offers a ready-made base for people to gain access to learning materials. But, of course, learning is about more than working with materials—even in electronic form. Students need guidance, support, encouragement and motivation. The challenge for public libraries, will be to provide an environment which brings all these elements together for new learners.
>
> For university librarians, the challenge will be to support programmes of study which are delivered in new ways, and at times, which meet students' needs rather than the convenience of institutions. (p. 3)

Confirming Fryer's recommendations for the way forward, Bulpitt (1998, p. 3) goes on to suggest that "Perhaps the real challenge is for all libraries to work together and share skills to support lifelong learning and achieve an inclusive society for all."

The Library Association (Shepherd, 1998) urges that libraries should be engaged from the onset in the development of national, regional, and local partnerships for learning, and that this should be across institutional, corporate, and sectoral boundaries. A key challenge for the learning society is to develop the "public architecture for learning" demanded by Fryer (1997), and the Library Association suggests that investment in the network of libraries will yield a high return, but that there should be secured funding that encourages cooperation and coordination between institutions and across sectors. It usefully draws attention to the importance of both informal, non-structured, life-experience learning and formal, accredited learning, and the need for quality assurance mechanisms and qualification structures that fully recognize the whole breadth of learning achievement. Information and knowledge skills should be explicit elements in key skills programs. The Library Association also gave a timely reminder of the significant threat posed by copyright compliance and licensing restrictions to wider access to learning materials in the digital environment.

VI. Concluding Remarks

The UK Government set out its exciting vision for the new Learning Age and a clear commitment to lifelong learning as a key element of moving toward a more prosperous and "inclusive" society. It has embarked on a whole range of initiatives designed to achieve the necessary culture change and realize this vision. The UfI is perhaps the most radical of these, focusing particularly on one of the nation's weakest areas—key skills for employability and competitiveness. The government established challenging targets for the number of people to be encouraged back into learning. The UfI pilot project in the North East and other lifelong learning experiments have clearly demonstrated the tremendous demand for learning throughout society. The new Learning Age, with its emphasis on wider access and lifelong learning, will be very different. Demand for learning will be led more by the changing needs of customers, empowered with their individual learning accounts, than by the traditional interests of established learning providers.

The network of libraries already makes a considerable contribution to supporting community-wide, lifelong learning, but the significant challenge is how the library community can respond to these dramatic changes and enhance its contribution. Ways must be found of supporting this new learning, which will not only be delivered in traditional educational institutions, but will also, increasingly, be delivered in the home, the workplace, the community, and learning centers. Services must be developed with learners, the new lifelong learners, at the center, rather than libraries and their parent institutions, and this will require exploiting the full potential of both traditional approaches and electronic networks. Libraries must collaborate with each other across traditional sectors and develop partnerships with other bodies in order to deliver an accessible network of learning opportunities to people when, where, and how they need it. We need "joined-up" thinking in the planning and delivery of library services. The culture change required in the library and information world may be just as dramatic as that predicted for the broader world of learning.

There are several barriers to achieving greater collaboration and partnership working in the library world: the funding, politics, and culture of the various sectors; institutional competitiveness; and inequalities in funding. Indeed, some librarians receive little encouragement to develop strategic partnerships and certainly do not receive any additional resources in order to promote new cross-sectoral initiatives. They often refer to poor vision and direction at the institutional level. However, in some cases it may be the attitudes of the librarians themselves that are the barriers to change. Developing partnerships need not be a costly exercise, and the allocation of library resources is always a matter of priorities. What is clear is that the lifelong learner in any city can face a bewildering range of libraries and some formidable barriers to gaining access to the library services necessary to support their learning. There is considerable investment in developing digital databases and networks, but it would be a tragedy if learners were denied access to this information, either because it is locked up in selected academic libraries, or because of restrictive copyright legislation or prohibitive licensing costs, or because of a simple lack of investment in IT and staff training in libraries.

As the *Declaration from the Library and Information Community* published by The Library Association *et al.* (1998, p. 2) put it:

> The Library and Information Community in the UK will break down barriers and create the new alliances necessary to realise the vision of a Learning Society and attain the objectives of the National Grid for Learning and the People's Network. We believe the challenge ahead must be addressed by a global response—a response that embraces all sectors of the library and information world. We are committed to working with government, local government and all other stakeholders to achieve this end.

If libraries fail to grasp the nettle and deliver the learning support required in the new Learning Age, there are many other organizations that are well-placed to do so—broadcasting and software companies, to name but two. One can only speculate where resources may be invested or redirected in the Learning Age, but higher education should not underestimate the importance of further education, and neither sector should underestimate the importance of schools and public libraries. However, no one should underestimate the tremendous potential of innovations such as the UfI for delivering the UK Government's agenda for lifelong learning.

It is reassuring that the government and other official bodies in the United Kingdom have recognized the huge contribution of libraries to lifelong learning, but it is crucial that libraries are fully integrated with government planning for the Learning Age (Evans, 1999). Libraries must also make sure that their particular role in distributing and supporting learning is taken into account by those planning learning cities and intelligent communities.

There is a tremendous future for libraries in the Information Age. Indeed, the new Learning Age could lead to the rediscovery of the fundamental value of libraries for lifelong learning. The various libraries in any community form an accessible, trusted network of "social" places where all learners can study, access information of all types, use IT, and benefit from the support of trained information professionals. Libraries are also the hub for distributing networked electronic or virtual services beyond their walls. More important, they provide access to electronic information for the "have-nots." The experience of the UfI pilot project in the North East of England confirms the central importance of libraries in supporting innovation in the delivery of learning. Libraries are well placed in the new Learning Age because, like the UfI, they set out to provide helpful and responsive services that are focused on the needs of customers.

The UK Government's consultative paper (DfEE, 1988) described the new Learning Age as a "renaissance for a new Britain," but it could equally witness a remarkable renaissance in the nation's library and information services. The network of libraries is used by millions of people a year and, given the necessary investment and encouragement, this tremendous contribution to community-wide, lifelong learning could be further enhanced and developed. Libraries are a good example of the *ladder of learning* that can be extended into our communities. Indeed, the simple message proclaimed on the promotion bookmark for the Libraries Access Sunderland Scheme remains a very important one: "Libraries for lifelong learning—all you need is a library card."

References

Blackstone, T. (1999). The learning age. In *Libraries in the Learning Community: Building Strategic Partnerships.* Proceedings of an international conference, University of Sunderland, 22–23 June, 1998. (A. C. McDonald, V. Edwards, and J. Stafford, eds.), pp. 5–12. University of Sunderland Press, Sunderland.

Brophy, P., Craven, J., and Fisher, S. M. (1998). *The Development of UK Academic Library Services in the Context of Lifelong Learning.* Library Information Technology Centre, London.

Brophy, P. (1999a). The VALNOW service: Reaching the distance learner. In *Libraries in the Learning Community: Building Strategic Partnerships.* Proceedings of an international conference,

University of Sunderland, 22–23 June, 1998. (A. C. McDonald, V. Edwards and J. Stafford, eds.), pp. 103–108. University of Sunderland Press, Sunderland.

Brophy, P. (1999b). Strategic partnerships for lifelong learning: How libraries must change. In *Libraries in the Learning Community: Building Strategic Partnerships.* Proceedings of an international conference, University of Sunderland, 22–23 June, 1998. (A. C. McDonald, V. Edwards, and J. Stafford, eds.), pp. 151–160. University of Sunderland Press, Sunderland.

Burgess, R. (1999). Library partnerships for lifelong learning: Research findings. In *Libraries in the Learning Community: Building Strategic Partnerships.* Proceedings of an international conference, University of Sunderland, 22–23 June, 1998. (A. C. McDonald, V. Edwards, and J. Stafford, eds.), pp. 117–123. University of Sunderland Press, Sunderland.

Bulpitt, G. (1998). The challenge of lifelong learning. *Relay* **46**, 3. (The Journal of the University College and Research Group of The Library Association.)

Bye, D. J. (1998). Information service provision for distance learners: The case of Sheffield Hallam University. *Relay* **46**, 11–12. (The Journal of the University College and Research Group of The Library Association.)

Dearing, R. (1997). *Higher Education in the Learning Society.* The Report of the National Committee of Inquiry into Higher Education. Chairman, Sir Ron Dearing. The Stationery Office, London.

Department for Culture, Media and Sport (DCMS) (1998). *New Library: The People's Network: The Government's Response.* DCMS, London.

Department of Education and Employment *et al* (DfEE) (1995). *Lifetime Learning: A Consultation Document.* DfEE, London.

Department for Education and Employment (DfEE) (1997). *Connecting to the Learning Society: National Grid for Learning.* The Government's consultation paper. The Stationery Office, London.

Department for Education and Employment (DfEE) (1998a). *National Adult Learning Survey 1997.* The Stationery Office, London. (Research Briefs, Research Report No. 19.)

Department for Education and Employment (DfEE) (1998b). *The Learning Age: A Renaissance for a New Britain.* The Stationery Office, London. (Cmd 3790.)

Department of Education and Employment (DEE) (1998c). *The Learning Age: A Renaissance for a New Britain.* HMSO, London (consultative leaflet).

Department for Education and Employment *et al.* (DfEE *et al.*) (1998). *University for Industry: Engaging People in Learning for Life.* Pathfinder Prospectus. DfEE, London.

Department for Education and Employment (DfEE) (1999a). *Learning Towns and Cities.* (http://www.lifelong learning.co.uk/learningcities/front.htm)

Department for Education and Employment (DfEE) (1999b). *UK Lifelong Learning.* (http://www.lifelong learning.co.uk)

Department of Trade and Industry (DTI) (1998). *Our Information Age.* HMSO, London.

Delors, J. (1996). *Learning: The Treasure Within.* Report to UNESCO of the International Commission on Education for the Twenty-first Century. UNESCO, Paris.

Dolan, J. (1999). Towards the lifelong library: Experiences from Birmingham. In *Libraries in the Learning Community: Building Strategic Partnerships.* Proceedings of an international conference, University of Sunderland, 22–23 June, 1998. (A. C. McDonald, V. Edwards, and J. Stafford, eds.), pp. 59–64. University of Sunderland Press, Sunderland.

Edmunds, E. (1999). The library: Access and individual creativity. In *Libraries in the Learning Community: Building Strategic Partnerships.* Proceedings of an international conference, University of Sunderland, 22–23 June, 1998. (A. C. McDonald, V. Edwards, and J. Stafford, eds.), pp. 125–130. University of Sunderland Press, Sunderland.

Evans, X. (1999). Libraries and learning. In *Libraries in the Learning Community: Building Strategic Partnerships.* Proceedings of an international conference, University of Sunderland, 22–23

June, 1998. (A. C. McDonald, V. Edwards, and J. Stafford, eds.), pp. 13–16. University of Sunderland Press, Sunderland.

Fryer, R. H. (1997). *Learning for the Twenty-First Century*. First report of the National Advisory Group for Continuing Education and Lifelong Learning. HMSO, London.

Fryer, R. (1999). Towards the learning age. In *Libraries in the Learning Community: Building Strategic Partnerships*. Proceedings of an international conference, University of Sunderland, 22–23 June, 1998. (A. C. McDonald, V. Edwards, and J. Stafford, eds.), pp. 25–29. University of Sunderland Press, Sunderland.

Hillman, J. (1996). *The University for Industry: Creating a National Learning Network*. Institute for Public Policy Research, London.

Johnstone, D. J. (1998). Lifelong learning for all. *OECD Observer* **214.**

Kennedy, H. (1997) *Learning Works: Widening Participation in Further Education*. Further Education Funding Council, Coventry.

Library and Information Commission (LIC) (1997). *New Library: The People's Network*. Library and Information Commission, London.

Martin, A. (1998). ALLIN: Cooperation in Northamptonshire. *Relay* **46,** 10. (The Journal of the University College and Research Group of The Library Association.)

McDonald, A. C. (1998). University for Industry—a renaissance for libraries? *Relay* **46,** 9. (The Journal of the University College and Research Group of The Library Association.)

McDonald, A. C. (1999). LASHed in Sunderland: A partnership for learning in the city. In *Libraries in the Learning Community: Building Strategic Partnerships*. Proceedings of an international conference, University of Sunderland, 22–23 June, 1998. (A. C. McDonald, V. Edwards, and J. Stafford, eds.), pp. 45–57. University of Sunderland Press, Sunderland.

McNair, S. (1988). Lifelong learning: a radical agenda? *Relay* **46,** 5–7. (The Journal of the University College and Research Group of The Library Association.)

Milner, H. (1998). The broker and the catalyst. *Adults Learning* **9**(5), 15.

Nankivell, C. (1998). Cross-use of libraries and the lifelong learner. *Relay* **46,** 12. (The Journal of the University College and Research Group of The Library Association.)

Pigott, I. (1999). Networked learning through libraries of Europe: From vision to reality. In *Libraries in the Learning Community: Building Strategic Partnerships*. Proceedings of an international conference, University of Sunderland, 22–23 June, 1998. (A. C. McDonald, V. Edwards, and J. Stafford, eds.), pp. 89–95. University of Sunderland Press, Sunderland.

Puttnam, D. (1999). The learning challenge for the nation. In *Libraries in the Learning Community: Building Strategic Partnerships*. Proceedings of an international conference, University of Sunderland, 22–23 June, 1998. (A. C. McDonald, V. Edwards, and J. Stafford, eds.), pp. 17–23. University of Sunderland Press, Sunderland.

Revill, L. (1999). Creating a setting for the learning city. In *Libraries in the Learning Community: Building Strategic Partnerships*. Proceedings of an international conference, University of Sunderland, 22–23 June, 1998. (A. C. McDonald, V. Edwards, and J. Stafford, eds.), pp. 137–142. University of Sunderland Press, Sunderland.

Royal Society of Arts (RSA) (1996). *For Life: A Vision for Learning in the Twenty-First Century*. Royal Society of Arts, London. (Campaign for Learning.)

Shaw, G. B. (1960). *Major Barbara*. Penguin Books, Harmondsworth (originally published in 1907).

Shepherd, R. (1998). The learning age—responding on behalf of the profession. *Relay* **46,** 4. (The Journal of the University College and Research Group of The Library Association.)

The Library Association (1998). *The Learning Age: A Renaissance for a New Britain—the Response of The Library Association*. Information Services, The Library Association, London.

The Library Association *et al.* (1998). *A Declaration from the Library and Information Community*. The Library Association, London.

Thorne, M., and Milner, H. (1998). The University for Industry pilot project. In *The Virtual Campus: Trends for Higher Education and Training*. IFIP TC3/WG3.3 & WG3.6 Joint Working Conference, 27–29 November, Madrid, Spain. (F. Verdejo and G. Davies, eds.) pp. 50–57. Chapman & Hall, London.

Unwin, L., Stephens, K., and Bolton, N. (1998). *The Role of the Library in Distance Learning: A Study of Postgraduate Students, Course Providers and Librarians in the UK*. Bowker-Saur, London.

The Role of Libraries in Providing Curricular Support and Curricular Integration for Distance Learning Courses

Margaret M. Jobe
International Documents Librarian
University of Colorado at Boulder

Deborah S. Grealy
Non-Traditional Programs Librarian
University of Denver

I. Introduction

The goal of distance teaching and learning programs is to provide a balanced education to students to whom the traditional classroom is inaccessible, enabling them to pursue lifelong learning independent of the constraints of time and place. Central to this vision are the concepts of self-paced study and asynchronous learning. Information literacy and information self-sufficiency are equally important because they provide the infrastructure on which critical thinking is based. To facilitate the development of critical and evaluative skills in students, librarians have developed bibliographic and library instruction programs that enhance the ability of learners to gain access to, use, and evaluate information from a variety of sources and that support learning and assist in problem solving, thus leading to the generation of new knowledge (Sayed and de Jager, 1997, as cited by Behrens, 1998).

According to the Association of College and Research Libraries (ACRL), the role of bibliographic instruction is "not only to provide students with the specific skills needed to complete assignments, but to prepare individuals to make effective life-long use of information, information sources, and information systems" (ACRL, 1987, p. 257).

According to the model statement objectives, students should understand:

1. How experts identify and define information
2. How information sources are structured

3. How information resources are intellectually accessed by users
4. How information resources are physically organized and accessed.

Academic bibliographic instruction helps resident students achieve "information literacy"—the ability to locate, evaluate, and incorporate information into a cognitive process that, in turn, develops new knowledge and understanding. For generations, libraries have provided a physical space for research, reflection, and social interaction. In addition, libraries have developed services and collections designed to meet the needs of residential students. Libraries must rethink and retool services and collections to meet the needs of distance education. Students enrolled in distance education programs are challenging libraries to provide the electronic equivalent of physical space and the services that space provides.

Academic libraries are dynamic institutions—meeting new challenges throughout their history. Although many of the services they traditionally offer are based on the concept of place, academic (and other) libraries are rapidly metamorphosing into the digital library of the future. Just as libraries adapted in the past, they must change in the present and future to continue as viable organizations within the academy. These changes require careful analysis of the needs of both students enrolled in distance education and students on the traditional campus. The changing needs of the electronic library should drive institutional changes to the benefit of both groups. In their collective history, libraries have continually proved to be highly adaptable and responsive to changing needs. Initially, for example, academic libraries brought organization to the world of knowledge with the creation of indexes, catalogs, and classification schemes. Once organization systems were in place, libraries focused on meeting the needs of readers and increasing library use. McElderry (1977) observes that libraries have always been responsive to the needs of users. Early on they began to analyze reader patterns. Using data on use gathered by many researchers, libraries altered both physical plant and policies to increase readership. These alterations included open stacks; flexible building designs; quiet, lighted study areas; liberalized circulation policies; and other practices designed to promote library use. Libraries have evolved from places where materials are housed to active partners in student education. They have incorporated new technologies into their missions and physical facilities. Now they must use these analytic skills to implement a new future that transcends the traditional boundaries of place. The digital library of the future will be a collection of services available to users anywhere at anytime. Supporting distance education demands that some changes must occur now.

Although distance education is widely considered to be an area with strong growth potential, academic institutions must overcome significant challenges to provide sufficient research support to students enrolled in such programs. These challenges include: identifying needs, forging collaborative partnerships with teaching faculty, and obtaining the institutional support necessary to launch new programs and services. In a survey of institutions of higher education, the National Center for Education Statistics (1997) found that a majority of institutions that did not plan to offer distance education courses cited lack of access to library resources as a barrier to starting or expanding programs. Although the study was published in 1997, it reports data collected in 1995. Many of these reluctant institutions may have chosen to offer distance education programs by this time. If history predicts the future, academic libraries will resolve these problems. Libraries have always been responsive to change—developing new services and practices in response to need. The core values of libraries—equity of access and freedom to use materials—will remain core values in the digital library.

II. Bibliographic Instruction and Curricular Support in a Traditional Campus Environment

A. Collection Development and Faculty Liaison

In the last years of the nineteenth century, many colleges and universities lacked centralized libraries. Library collections were housed in departmental libraries containing materials selected by teaching faculty. When academic disciplines were compartmentalized and the publishing output was smaller, teaching faculty devoted a small part of their time to selecting materials. That practice probably served the overall institutional needs. However, academic disciplines became more interdependent, publishing output increased, and demands on faculty time changed. Departmental libraries were very inefficient, with multiple units processing orders and preparing materials for use. They also resulted in significant duplication of titles in scattered collections. In addition, researchers needed to use multiple card and book catalogs to find materials. To remedy this situation, major universities began to build centralized libraries that coordinated the acquisition, processing, cataloging, and shelving of materials. As the centralized library emerged, the role of the librarian also changed. A history of collection development practices in American academic libraries (Edelman and Tatum, 1977) traces a shift in collection development from a faculty selection model to one in which a centralized library system provides coordinated collection development by librarian selectors. Williams and Lunde (1997) also attribute the shift from faculty to librarian selection to additional factors, including fundamental changes in educational practice, proliferation of resources, expanding budgets in the 1970s, and the development of approval purchase plans.

Although there has been a shift to librarian selection of materials, it is not a universal practice. Writing on collection development, Sandler (1984) found a spectrum of institutional policies ranging from faculty selection to librarian selection, with many institutions falling somewhere in the middle by combining selection by librarians in active collaboration with teaching faculty. With responsibility for the budget, even libraries with active selection by faculty have a strong role in collection development.

The emergence of library/faculty liaison programs can be attributed, in part, to the need of libraries to maintain control over the materials budget and involve teaching faculty in the selection of materials. A survey of member libraries by the Association of Research Libraries (ARL, 1992) found that 47% of the responding libraries employed librarians with some level of responsibility for faculty liaison. Libraries have stressed the importance of building strong relationships with faculty (Sandler, 1984; Drummond, Mosby, and Monroe, 1991). Some institutions have found the liaison relationship so critical to their respective missions that they have developed formal guidelines for effective liaison (Wu *et al.*, 1994; Davis and Cook, 1996). Although guidelines may differ in the specifics, they all call for active communication between librarians and teaching faculty, and involvement of teaching faculty in materials selection. In the electronic environment, this is both more important and more complicated. The issues include materials costs, stability of electronic media, duplication of materials, and license negotiations. Development of the electronic resources required to support delivery of distance education requires active collaboration with the faculty who design and deliver the programs.

B. Bibliographic Instruction

Librarians have always played an important role in education. Although the role of libraries and librarians in education has long been recognized, formal programs in bibliographic instruction (BI) are a comparatively recent phenomenon. Early academic libraries sometimes appointed a "professor of books," whose responsibilities included training students and faculty in the use of the library. Early BI made strong use of the physicality of the library— handling the card catalog, turning the pages of the indexes and encyclopedias, using microform readers, and retrieving materials from the stacks. Emphasis was on use of specific indexes and encyclopedias, use of the card catalog, note taking, organization of notes, and other activities with a strong connection to physical objects. Students were learning how to use the library—not how to locate, analyze, and incorporate information to produce new knowledge.

As materials proliferated, librarians experienced an increased demand for training in the use of catalogs and indexes. Thoughtful commentators also urged American colleges and universities to incorporate original research and scholarship into the undergraduate curriculum. In a seminal report on undergraduate education sponsored by the Carnegie Foundation for the Advancement of Teaching, Boyer (1988, p. 165) observed that "Students should be given bibliographic instruction and be encouraged to spend at least as much time in the library—using its wide range of resources—as they spend in class." Although the demand was present, it was not until the 1970s that BI librarians established their own section in the ACRL and published guidelines on bibliographic instruction (ACRL, 1977). Despite a slow start, by 1991 the membership of the BI section made it the largest section within ACRL, and BI librarians had a journal devoted exclusively to bibliographic instruction, *Research Strategies* (Farber, 1991).

With the maturing of BI as a discipline, BI librarians developed two models of instruction: course-integrated instruction and formal courses in bibliographic methods. A 1995 survey of library instruction practices (Shirato and Badics, 1997) found that 30% of the responding libraries offered a credit course in library use. Although some institutions offer stand-alone courses in library research, many librarians (Farber, 1991; Isbell, 1995) argue for course-integrated (embedded in course sequences of a particular major) instruction. Others (Seiden, 1997) use both the course-integrated model and stand-alone courses. In the course-integrated model, librarians work collaboratively with teaching faculty to instruct students in bibliographic resources closely related to the course subject matter and objectives. This course-integrated instruction may provide an overview of appropriate resources, more in-depth presentations on research methods at time of need, or an integration of BI throughout the course. Isbell (1995) describes a writing course taught by both a professor of English and a librarian who share equally in the course content, presentation, and grading. He attributes the successful collaborative effort to strong and effective liaison relationships between the librarian subject specialists and academic departments on campus. These liaison relationships have contributed to an enhanced role for librarians on campus. Although Isbell attributes positive outcomes to this collaboration, few libraries have the staff to participate in academic instruction to this extent. Most course-integrated instruction involves the librarian for specific assignments or projects. Although most libraries are constrained by the size of the professional staff, many would agree with Lipow (1991) when she argues that librarians must also instruct faculty in bibliographic methods: to teach new concepts and skills, empower faculty as information seekers, promote library liaison to students through faculty, and promote the changing role of the library. This will become more critical as more courses are developed by faculty for distance delivery. Viable and vibrant distance education requires close integration of course materials and opportunities for discovery in the electronic library, just as Boyer (1988) recommended use of the physical library to complete the educational process.

With the emergence of BI as a discipline within librarianship, practitioners adopted instructional models based on theories of learning and cognition. Approached from the viewpoint of learning theory, the needs of the user become paramount. Kuhlthau (1993, p. 4) describes a shift in emphasis to a model of library services that recognizes that the "personal meaning that the user seeks from the information becomes as critical a consideration for library and information services as the content represented in texts." BI has evolved from teaching space-based information (using the physical collections) to teaching brain-based information (understanding the multiple relationships between information systems and meaning). It has adopted a larger goal of teaching information literacy. Warmkassel and McCade (1997, p. 80) state that the information-literate individual can "sift through the enormous amount of information available, effectively using appropriate sources to solve problems and make decisions in all areas of their lives." In the Web-based environment, the problem intensified as more resources become available. Tate and Alexander (1996) outline criteria librarians can use to instruct students in evaluating the quality of information found on the Web. These criteria include accuracy, authority, objectivity, currency, and coverage.

Although BI literature is currently focused on learning theory, learning styles, and other topics, many librarians have no formal training in methods of BI let alone theory. Even though BI is recognized as an important component of library service, many librarians are ill-prepared to provide this important service. Sullivan (1997) found that 57.5% of library schools offered separate courses in library instruction, 15.2% included library instruction in a larger course, and 27.3% of library schools did not offer any formal education in library instruction.

As teaching faculty develop courses designed for distance delivery, librarians must integrate learning theory into BI designed for remote users. Although many librarians learn on the job, library education is beginning to include courses in Web content and design. In addition, by partnering with teaching faculty in the design of instructional materials, librarians will develop a new understanding of the practical applications of educational theory.

C. Services and Support

1. Reference Support

In addition to providing instruction in the use of the collections and research methods, libraries have provided direct assistance to patrons with reference services. In his history of services to readers, McElderry (1977) notes the comparatively slow development of reference services. Early practitioners of the emerging profession of librarianship concentrated on technical aspects of managing collections, such as cataloging materials, arranging materials by subject matter, and developing indexes and bibliographies. Although these technical services created access to the contents of the collection, they also created a need for instruction and assistance in the use of these tools. Reference service, as a recognized function of academic libraries, emerged in the first quarter of the twentieth century. Coughlin and Gertzog (1992, p. 296) observe that the need for a person to "answer questions" was referred to at the turn of the twentieth century. Although the need was recognized early on, by 1936 only 12% of liberal arts colleges sampled had a reference position. By the 1940s, most libraries had reference librarians. Although reference is a widely accepted service, philosophies of service vary between libraries, ranging from individual instruction in the use of catalogs, indexes, and other tools of reference to the direct supply of information. This direct supply might take the form of bibliographic searches performed by librarians, answering questions, providing appropriate resources, and evaluating the information sources. Currently, many libraries offer three varieties of reference service: at the reference desk in a face-to-face interaction; via telephone; and, increasingly, through e-mail.

2. Direct Provision of Services

a. Interlibrary Loan and Document Delivery. Interlibrary loan (ILL) services are a natural outgrowth of the reference process. Reference services often provide the user with instruction in the use of bibliographic tools, bibliographic verification, and database searches. Because no one library is likely to own all of the material cited in a bibliographic database or index, the need to obtain materials follows closely on the heels of the reference process that identified them. ILL uses many of the same databases and indexes (used by reference to assist the patron) to verify bibliographic citations before submitting requests for loans or copies. Many ILL departments report directly to the reference department because of the close affiliation of these two services (Bibliographic File, Bopp, 1995). Electronic bibliographic utilities such as Online Computer Library Center (OCLC) and Research Libraries Group (RLG) have increased access to bibliographic citations and improved the speed of ILL services with electronic transmission of requests. Although in the past many academic libraries restricted ILL to faculty and graduate students, ILL is now open to all primary users (faculty, students, and staff) in most academic institutions. The National Interlibrary Loan Code [Reference and Adult Services Division (RASD), 1993] states that "interlibrary loan is essential to the vitality of libraries of all types and sizes and is a means by which a wider range of materials can be made available to users." The development of electronic transmission methods (fax, digital transmission via the Internet) and resource-sharing agreements between libraries have overcome two significant barriers to widespread use of ILL: speed of delivery and cost of materials.

Access to bibliographic citations has also spurred the need to develop alternative methods of materials delivery. The term *document delivery* refers to the direct provision of materials to patrons in one of two ways: the patron submits a request for materials held by the library, which then supplies the original or photocopies from its collections directly to the patron; or the patron submits a request for materials not owned by the library and the library then purchases a copy of the material for the patron from the publisher, a vendor, or an information broker. ILL lending and borrowing relies on cooperation between libraries. Document delivery usually bypasses the "cooperative" part of the equation to speed the supply of information. Many libraries use a combination of traditional ILL and document delivery to obtain the materials needed by their patrons. Rapid and efficient ILL and document delivery services are critical to both on-campus and distance education programs.

b. Database Searching.   As noted earlier, librarians once concentrated their energies on cataloging materials and developing indexes and bibliographies. With the development of computer-based applications, indexes and bibliographies have matured into complex and comprehensive databases that also provide wide varieties of other information. Electronic databases have proliferated at an astonishing rate. Faced with a bewildering variety of databases available via modem, the Internet, or on CD-ROM, many users are ill-equipped to conduct comprehensive research on a topic. Databases frequently overlap in their coverage and vary widely in the power and complexity of their search syntaxes. In this environment, selection of appropriate databases, searching using complex commands, and evaluation of search results became the province of the librarian, either a generalist comfortable with search strategies or a specialist with both knowledge of search strategies and of a specific academic discipline. Successful librarian-conducted searches require close collaboration between the librarian and user. The librarian must conduct a careful search interview with the patron to determine the type and amount of information needed, time constraints, and other factors that could influence the search strategy. In a face-to-face situation, the librarian can use visual cues to help interpret the needs of the patron. In the distance education environment, librarians must develop alternative strategies to conduct a successful reference interaction.

In the 1970s, 1980s, and early 1990s, database searching remained largely within the province of the librarian. The fee structure of most databases was based on the length of time spent using the database and the number of citations retrieved. To reduce the cost for each search, a user would need to spend time preparing for the search. The preparation involved reviewing the scope of the database and indexing structure, consulting thesauri and other tools to locate relevant terms, and crafting a search strategy before initiating a connection.

With the introduction of CD-ROMs in the early 1990s, many vendors began offering databases in this format. This technology enabled database producers to create menu-driven (rather than command-driven) versions of their products. Users could sit down at a workstation and access a local version of a database. Without the time constraints associated with the on-line version, users had the luxury of conducting more leisurely searches. Libraries began offering end-user searching to their patrons. Because users were usually not well trained on searching databases, outcomes were frequently imprecise. However, even imprecise searches created additional demands on library services. A search of almost any bibliographic database retrieves a great number of citations for material not owned by the local library. This increased access created additional pressures on the ILL and document delivery services of the library. In addition, many library users (undergraduate and graduate students alike) may have been seduced by the lure of the on-line database—bypassing altogether materials held locally. Although access to information (through bibliographic citations) rather than ownership (local holdings) is the model adopted by most libraries, few are equipped to handle a glut of ILL and document delivery requests generated by ill-constructed searches. To remedy this situation, many reference librarians became instructors in search techniques rather than expert database searchers themselves.

III. Bibliographic Instruction and Curriculum Support in a Changing Environment

A. Changing Environment

The rapid growth of the Internet is having profound effects on the services that libraries provide their clients. Most library catalogs are now available on-line with remote access via modem or the Internet. In addition to providing information about local collections, many of these catalogs are now information malls that offer locally mounted databases, connections to other library catalogs, and connections to bibliographic and full-text databases. Many students believe that everything is available online. Although libraries can now license electronic versions of traditional library resources such as encyclopedias, bibliographic indexes, and full-text versions of popular and scholarly periodicals, electronic products only complement the physical collections of libraries. These Internet-accessible databases may duplicate print and CD-ROM versions of indexes and other materials housed in the library. However, the Internet has helped create increasing demands for "virtual libraries." Libraries now face tough choices. Few can afford to purchase a title in all of the available formats: archival (print), local electronic (CD-ROM), and remote (Internet) versions. Maintaining collections in multiple formats also places multiple demands on the library staff. In the traditional library, technical and public services handle the physical material, cataloging, processing, shelving, and circulating. In the electronic library, multiplicity of formats increases the demand for BI and other reference services. Many struggle to balance these competing demands.

Because the library is still viewed as a place rather than as a collection of services (traditional materials, electronic materials, and the reference and instruction services needed by users of both formats), many institutions are and will be challenged by the changes needed to implement the virtual library. Lewis (1997) observes that the transition to the electronic library will dramatically alter the public services provided by libraries—although at this point it is impossible to predict the nature of the changes. Lewis makes it clear, however, that the electronic library must be oriented to the needs of the user, rather than those of the library, and that serving user needs will require reorganization within the library. Satisfying the needs of the student enrolled in a distance education program will provide a valuable laboratory in which to explore some of the institutional changes necessary to make a successful transition to an electronic future.

1. Market Driven

In the not-too-distant past, libraries analyzed their budgets for acquisition of materials and chose material that supported the curriculum and research needs of the institution. Collection building involved a careful balancing of research priorities, analysis of collection strengths and weaknesses, and availability of funds. Although no library could purchase all of the material it wanted or needed, purchase decisions involved rational choices. In the emerging electronic information market, collection development is somewhat analogous to shopping for a new car in a showroom. The library may know what it wants and needs in terms of features, but it may be forced to purchase "options" that are bundled into an information package. These decisions are based on the availability of products, rather than on need for these products. A library might have to buy a suite of information products that do not meet a stated research need to gain access to one needed product. Vendors seem to be laboring under the illusion that information products are weighed (and priced) by the pound.

A case in point is Medline, the bibliographic database of the National Library of Medicine (NLM). Until recently, libraries contracted for access to the database with information services such as Dialog, FirstSearch, Ovid, or NLM. However, as the number of Internet medical sites offering free access to Medline grew steadily, NLM reevaluated its policy and began to offer free access to the database. Now that Medline is free or inexpensive, it is now bundled into products from many vendors—each with its own syntax and screen design. Regardless of whether a library needs or requires multiple search interfaces for Medline, it probably accepts multiple access methods (and the training needs that follow) as the price of obtaining access to the information it needs and wants. Medline is not unique—databases are routinely added to and dropped from information products. Thus, a library decision to provide access to a service is contingent on fluid market factors. Personal experience suggests that it may be difficult to make collection development decisions in this rapidly changing electronic marketplace and support these decisions with appropriate bibliographic instruction and reference services to the users. Personal experience also suggests instructing users on the distinction between a database and a vendor can be challenging. Both on-campus and remote users need intervention and instruction that enables them to use the most appropriate version of a database.

2. New Users, New Expectations

Higher education in the United States is changing. As the demographics of the population shift, colleges and universities are exploring ways to attract different types of students. A study by the National Center for Education Statistics (1997) found that most institutions offering distance education were targeting their offerings to two groups: professionals seeking recertification and workers seeking retraining or updating of skills. A smaller group of institutions targeted individuals with disabilities, military personnel, Native Americans, and non-English-speaking populations. The needs of these students are much different than those of undergraduate and graduate students housed on or near a campus with easy access to library and computing services. In addition to this new pool of users, the traditional users of library services have new expectations. Writing in 1992 (eons ago in the current environment), Campbell (p. 32) observed that "our users are gradually changing. They want information quickly, and they want it delivered to them." He also notes that they want it electronically.

In addition to rising expectations, there are also rising misconceptions. Although faculty members may be well versed in the research methods appropriate to the traditional library, their students may not be. These same faculty members may not be familiar with the research methods needed for the electronic library or the Internet. The proliferation of Internet resources and their glamorous portrayal in the media have led many students to conclude that the Internet is the library. The fascination with the machine has blurred the distinction between access to scholarly information in electronic format and access to electronic information of dubious origin and worth.

Although assumptions about electronic access are often erroneous, White (1997) argues that most libraries and university administrations have not grappled adequately with the costs the virtual library entails. In his view, universities must understand that information technology is an essential component of education, it is expensive, and the costs might be better controlled if the information technology budget is in the hands of the library. Just as libraries wrested control of materials purchasing and cataloging from departmental libraries, they need to wrest control of the information technology infrastructure and budget from academic and technical departments.

3. Technology Driven

In his analysis of the future of electronic libraries, Buckland (1992, p. 44) observes that "There is a steady growth of documents in electronic form, and access will necessarily have to be provided for them." That is the issue. Libraries must, as a matter of course, provide access to electronic publications—thus shifting from a place to a service. However, some libraries may lack the necessary human and technological resources to fully develop the electronic library. In today's technology-driven environment, many libraries are exploring strategic alliances with campus computing departments. Thoughtful commentators (Ferguson and Bunge, 1997; Dougherty and McClure, 1997) stress that libraries need to develop closer connections with computing services to implement the electronic library of the near future.

B. Changing Needs

In 1988, Boyer argued that librarians needed to "extend learning resources on campus and be a leader in linking campus libraries to knowledge networks far beyond the campus" (p. 166). In 1998, many libraries have begun to implement his vision, providing seamless links from the electronic catalog to catalogs of other libraries, bibliographic and full-text databases, and global bibliographic utilities. Although the infrastructure is partially in place to support this vision, the users remain bewildered and confused by the array of information choices. Ferguson and Bunge (1997) discuss the need to develop a holistic, user-centered method of delivering reference and information services in an era when the digital library is gradually replacing the paper library. In their analysis of the future of reference services for the digital library, Ferguson and Bunge (1997, p. 263) observe that reference services "help them [the users] realize their own goals, rather than forcing them to use information sources on the library's terms." Hirshon (1996, p. 15) predicts that in the library of the future, "customer service clearly will remain as the primary objective and driver for change, but information technology remains the major enabler of that change."

C. Changing Role

As the library shifts from being a place to being a collection of services, librarians have pondered the future of their profession and their roles in the information age. Campbell (1992) thinks that reference and bibliographic instruction should be scrapped. For Campbell, reference is an activity suited to the paper collection of the past. To use reference services, the user had come to reference. It is a "building-centered, old style 'make them come to us' model." Campbell advocates new duties: knowledge cartography, consumer analysis, and access engineering. As knowledge cartographers, librarians would be versed in the types of information sources available and chart the "virtual information universe." Librarians should also begin to evaluate how consumers need information and tailor information sources to those needs. Finally, Campbell advocates that librarians become access engineers—skilled at bringing the information to the consumer, not the consumer to the information. This entails rethinking relationships between library departments and services to meet the needs of the end user.

Gapen (1993) also envisions a different role for librarians in the virtual library. In the "library as place" model, the librarian applies rules (classification, and subject headings); provides BI, subject expertise and searching skills, and technical knowledge of information systems; and warehouses material. Gapen calls the virtual library "mind-to-mind" contact. For knowledge and learning to occur in this environment, the librarian designs information management systems; educates, researches, and solves problems and synthesizes the results; and navigates the full range of information services with the needs of the user always in mind. According to Gapen, this is a logical extension of the "control revolution" proposed by James R. Benninger in *The Control Revolution: Technological and Economic Origins of the Information Society* (1986)—a time in the history of the information age when libraries created tools and programs to categorize and make accessible the output of human knowledge. However, the success of the virtual library hinges on the abilities of libraries and librarians to understand and facilitate the interaction of the user (remote or local) with information.

Kuhlthau (1993) advocates a process approach to reference and instruction. In response to user needs, the librarian assumes the role of mediator in the information-seeking process. Kuhlthau identifies five levels of service. In level one, the librarian/library is the organizer of the material. In level two, the librarian is the locator, a function similar to ready reference. In level three, the librarian is an identifier, helping the user identify an appropriate group of tools for an information need. At level four, the librarian is an advisor, making recommendations on the appropriate materials and sequence of their use. At level five, the librarian becomes a counselor. The user and the librarian enter into a dialog, with the librarian following the process to its conclusion.

For libraries and students alike, distance education will test these ideas. Can libraries respond effectively to the needs of students for whom the "library as place" concept is irrelevant? Can they provide sophisticated instruction that provides information from the user's point of view? And can they provide meaningful electronic collections and services that provide the student with the materials needed to create new knowledge—not merely to parrot phrases stated on Web pages?

IV. Bibliographic Instruction and Curricular Support in a Distance Education Environment

A. Prerequisites

1. Faculty Liaison/Communication

Virtual library support for distance learning and for nontraditional student populations is currently a growth area in academic libraries. An ACRL task-force, convened in 1988, prepared a revision of the *ACRL Guidelines for Extended Campus Library Services*, which were approved at the 1990 ALA Annual Conference. The revised guidelines were "designed to outline direction, support a process, stress overall coordination, and to support the educational objectives of the extended campus program" (ACRL, 1990). These guidelines define the extended campus community as all individuals and agencies directly involved with academic programs that are offered away from the main campus of the institution and its students, faculty, administrators, and support personnel. This definition includes faculty and staff involved in distance teaching and learning initiatives as we have come to know them. Also stated is that the parent institution's support addresses the information needs of its extended programs, and that this support should be equitable with that provided for members of the on-campus community.

The implications of the ACRL guidelines for libraries involved in distance programs are profound. In his article on the Internet college, Chepesiuk (1999, pp. 52–53) estimates that "two-thirds of all institutions of higher learning and more than five million students of all ages and backgrounds are involved in some form of distance learning," and that about 60% of American public universities plan to offer increasing numbers of courses through distance programs. If these ACRL guidelines are to be followed, the growth of such programs calls for a corollary increase in support to the libraries that are charged with maintaining them in terms of infrastructure, information resources, technology, and staff. Unfortunately, adequate levels of support are not always available.

In a paper presented at Korea National Open University, Dr. A. W. Bates stated, "Just as important as the physical infrastructure are the people required to make the physical infrastructure work" (1997, para. 67). According to Bates, the human support side is not always adequately funded. The most consistent complaint from universities involved in technology applications for education are insufficient levels of support, and this is certainly true in libraries. "Developing the necessary resources . . . takes time, energy, and most importantly, people, who often have to be diverted from other work activities" (Chepesiuk, 1998, p. 55).

Although such activities may be labor intensive, they are completely necessary. Goodson (1996) asserts that any time an institution provides for-credit courses at an off-site location, it is obligated to provide adequate learning resources and services to support the courses, programs, and degrees offered. This is wholly in keeping with the ACRL Guidelines. Schneider (1998, p. 90) discusses equal access to the supplemental resources that are "essential for a quality educational experience" for off-campus and distance students.

According to Mary Beth Susman, President of Colorado Electronic Community College (CECC) (Susman, quoted in Chepesiuk, 1998, p. 54), one of the biggest challenges to the integration of the library into distance learning programs is "the novice distance learning faculty who feel reluctant to assign library research because they think it may not be accessible to far-flung students." The prerequisites for library curricular support and BI for distance education are the same as those required in a more traditional setting. Collaborative curriculum development between academic departments and infrastructure service units ensures that limited resources are allocated wisely and cost-effectively and that students receive the guidance necessary to develop the critical thinking skills that are essential for lifelong learning. Because few librarians are formally trained in either instructional design or in learning theory, instruction librarians need to work with the teaching faculty, becoming completely familiar with the subject areas covered. They should also have a thorough knowledge of the library resources that support course work and research in those areas. Libraries can build on existing liaison relationships to develop these competencies.

Cooperation and networking are essential to program development in distance education. Communication and collaboration through a faculty liaison network is one way to involve the library in planning for distance course development. Initial involvement with the faculty who design distance courses ensures that librarians can proactively allocate resources and staff so that collections and services adequately support distance ventures. Unfortunately, "getting faculty to understand the role of the college and university library in on-line education is just one of many challenges that have to be met before this system of education can be truly viable" (Chepesiuk, 1988, p. 55).

2. Collection Development and Maintenance

One model for resource provision in distance education programs is traditionally used for extended campus programs. It involves making borrowing and use agreements with remote local or regional libraries to support off-campus student information needs (Colbert, 1995). Walling (1996) describes a similar model used by remote programs at the College of Library and Information Science (CLIS), University of South Carolina. Its faculty and students identify potentially valuable resources and make arrangements for students to use various local and regional collections. According to Walling, although students must often travel to major libraries to complete some assignments, they do so willingly and uncomplainingly. There is also strong support for the students in many libraries in the states involved. If problems arise (if students are seen as a drain on local resources), an immediate resolution is sought. A side benefit for CLIS students is that they can see a variety of library systems in operation and can compare what they are learning in class to the real world. Students also rely on interlibrary loan, fax, and the Internet to obtain materials.

In distance teaching and learning, collection provision involves much more than the location and selection of appropriate research materials. Faulhaber (1996, p. 854) claims that distance learning requires digital library support and is not possible without "electronic surrogates for traditional paper-based class handouts or course readers." According to Holowachuk (1997, para. 7), the success of the distance learner depends on library service. She identifies three critical areas of need: the need for materials and facilities, the need for information services, and the need for user services. In addition, librarians must evaluate, select, manage, and use information technologies designed to provide remote access to library resources. To accomplish this, the librarians' traditional network must be expanded to include administrators, technical experts, and database vendors (Burke, 1990). Collaboration is particularly important in this arena because few librarians have experience and training in the technology used to create interactive learning environments.

Interactions with remote students also require effective communication networks. Mail, telephone, fax, and e-mail have become standards in offering off-campus library support for distance education, whether the transactions involve traditional ILL, document delivery, mediated searching, or ftp-based interactions. Adequate levels of institutional support are needed for units participating in distance teaching and learning initiatives. If adequate staffing and funding for support and service is not available, students might experience delays and frustration, and possibly even alienation.

Web page development can provide excellent support to distance teaching and learning initiatives. In the electronic environment, collection development and bibliographic instruction tend to merge. Providing a tutorial for instruction on how to use licensed resources and providing mediated links to carefully selected databases (both licensed and free access) tend to fall into both realms. According to Ardis (1998), teaching opportunities will continue to change as more and more information is delivered directly to users' desktops, and the obvious mechanism for delivering customized tutorials and training to users is the same one used to provide desktop delivery—the Internet. Internet- or Web-based tutorials contain specific "how-to-use" instruction, and can be integrated with advice on how to select an appropriate tool or database. This information can be delivered virtually around the clock in a neutral, consistent manner that is available repeatedly to any user who needs it. Ardis points out, however, that although such tools and tutorials are potentially valuable learning tools, they cannot increase learning potential, which depends on the learner's self-regulation. Nor can they teach something people do not want to learn. Rather, they should be seen "as a fusion of [the librarian's] skill with the will or motivation of our users" (Ardis, 1998, p. 18).

Although Ardis explains that Internet-based tutorials should be legible, visible, and recognizable, she does not really address the question of who is responsible for developing and maintaining such Web pages. This critical question has important staffing implications for academic libraries. As noted earlier, library staff members who participate in remote service provision are all too often diverted from other work activities.

Institutions actively involved in distance program provision may be adequately funded if sustainability can be demonstrated to be of cost benefit to the institution. Start-up funds are not always readily available and some institutions rely on grant support to develop pilot projects to launch distance user support programs (Grealy, 1998). Pilot projects provide valuable information needed by libraries to design services for distance education. In fairness, according to Goodson (1996), costs involved in serving off-campus students should be borne by the college or university that collects tuition from these students, in keeping with the ACRL Guidelines.

Out-of-date and inadequate materials in a traditional library setting can frustrate students and slow their progress, as can cumbersome, overly bureaucratic service policies. In a distance setting, however, broken Web links, outdated resources, and inadequate infrastructure support prohibit access to materials, inhibiting a student's ability to complete coursework. For this reason, librarians must carefully monitor and select external sites. Web pages must be maintained and licensed databases must be routinely evaluated to ensure that they continue to meet the curricular needs of the students. Timely and effective instructional guides, tutorials, and pathfinders must also be made available. Above all, materials should be accessible and usable in the shortest time frame possible to ensure that the extended campus community has the same level of access to needed information as students on campus (ACRL, 1990).

Many students currently enrolled in distance education courses are non-traditional or adult learners, and adults tend to share real-life constraints on time and energy. Coulson (1998, pp. 14–15) summarizes accepted techniques for assisting the adult user in a training environment. She outlines strategies like "make the learner comfortable . . . explain the benefits . . . make every mistake count . . . capitalize on learning styles . . . [and] close the loop." Burge (1996, p. 846), going even further, states that a librarian "who has studied adult learning processes and principles will be able to act more appropriately when approached by a learner suffering from the inevitable pain of significant learning or coping with unhelpful home conditions."

Tools that simplify information retrieval and research enhance the learning experience of distance students. Useful tools include remotely accessible Web-based library catalogs and electronic indexing and abstracting tools. In a Web-based catalog, it is possible that all of these tools can be superficially similar in appearance. Students become readily familiar with dialog boxes, pull-down menus, and advanced search options. They also become adept at e-mail and full-text/full-content retrieval when institutions support these options. The semblance of screen uniformity makes basic information retrieval transparent for the user (Grealy, 1998). In this way, a student can ask for periodical articles to be delivered to the desktop anywhere without having to know command languages or complicated search protocols. When more sophisticated intervention is required in the search process, an on-call reference librarian can mediate the search electronically and transmit the results to the requester. Although electronic subscriptions cannot (and should not) replace a library's traditional periodical holdings, readily available digital formats are of inestimable value to students who have limited time available to spend in the library. Many libraries are beginning to experiment with digital scanning technologies that provide full-text access to electronic reserves, special library collections, archives, and non-copyrighted materials.

Use and cost studies currently underway will offer a better picture of attendant costs and benefits involved in Web-based distance learning support service (Schiller, 1998).

Support for distance teaching and learning may require a librarian to learn technologies such as interactive and cable television, microwave relay, satellites, fiber optics, and computers in order to deliver training and BI to students at remote locations (Burke, 1990). Close partnerships with campus computing departments will facilitate this access to technology. The Internet is also a widely available and effective delivery mechanism for training and BI (Kruse, 1997). Training in generic information technology literacy rather than application-specific knowledge and skills allows students to use the apparently seamless interface of Web-based library search engines quite effectively (Anderson, 1998). By eliminating the need to learn specific command structures, students can concentrate on information content. Search strategies and information retrieval are executed electronically in an environment that, if not transparent, is at least largely intuitive. Site licensing, scripted access, proxy servers, and limiting access to specified Internet Protocol (IP) addresses allow libraries to provide access to licensed commercial products without students having to worry about passwords, firewalls, or other restrictions.

B. Bibliographic Instruction for Electronic Resources:

1. Creating Interactive, Instructional Courseware for Nonresident Students

"The Internet is changing both the way people access information and the way librarians assist patrons with information access" (Hansen and Lombardo, 1997, p. 68). New paradigms for organizational collaboration are being made possible through technology, and librarians are being asked to provide instruction to an increasingly diverse clientele. According to Hansen and Lombardo, the demand for computer-aided instruction now occurs "in the reference area, in the electronic classroom, and beyond."

An effective strategy for assisting the remote user is to mount a series of interactive tutorials and pathfinders on the library's home page. Simple "point and click" tutorials provide basic information on library and information retrieval protocols such as controlled vocabulary, keyword searching, Boolean logic, truncation, and word proximity searching. Instructions on basic database navigation protocols can be mounted in a similar way, and can be linked to vendor support pages as well. An additional level of support and guidance can be supplied by linking to discipline-specific pathfinders containing annotations, locations, and hypertext links where appropriate (Grealy, in press). More sophisticated, interactive tutorials may also be made available by using CGI-bin and Java scripts, along with multimedia and other

Web enhancements. Care should be taken, however, to ensure that lower-level access to the same information is available to students with less technological capability. Interfaces that permit text-based browsers such as Lynx and other nongraphical options facilitate access to information without contributing to technological chauvinism.

Although many librarians possess skills in creating content and in formatting that content, these two components can easily be separated and delegated to different units in the library. As Web authoring and course management software become more widely available, libraries may be able to reintegrate these two functions.

As in traditional BI settings, librarians may partner with teaching faculty when an information component is integral and knowledge of specific resources is essential to course completion (Isbell, 1995). Integration of library research into distance education courses is most easily accomplished when libraries and academic departments have strong liaison relationships. In traditional academic settings, librarians also participate in teaching infomatics courses or research methods and strategies in more formal classroom settings. In some cases, discrete for-credit courses in information retrieval and research methods are designed and taught by librarians. These are also eminently suitable for Web-based delivery (Hinchliffe, 1998).

2. Remote Interaction with Students

Academic librarians routinely struggle with the problem of how to train users effectively and help them approach the research process critically. In today's environment, increasing numbers of students are nonresidential, and more library materials are electronically licensed rather than physically owned. Instruction on demand and at point of use is needed. BI also becomes increasingly important as distance teaching and learning programs grow in number and scope. Institutions like the Open University, the University of Phoenix, and the Western Governor's University are establishing on-line libraries to support their curricula. Although the suite of available resources may be impressive, often missing are the instructional and service components that are taken for granted in most academic settings. Here, the strategic question of virtual library support becomes critical.

Moss (1997) found that of 66 ARL libraries that provide remote reference services, 30 do so by e-mail, 31 by Web forms, and 4 by both means. Moss also states that most libraries restricted these remote reference services to brief, factual answers. She concludes that librarians must learn question negotiation and feedback when visual cues are absent. One-on-one reference and research assistance can also be difficult to mediate when there is no clearly defined physical collection and no controlled learning environment. Telephone, e-mail and fax can be utilized effectively to support distance course delivery. Equipment and software incompatibility issues need to be resolved up front, preferably before a course is launched. Requiring standard hardware and software configurations for all student and faculty computers is one way of limiting potential problems. Bulletin boards and chat rooms are effective ways to mediate classroom information queries. Although these techniques have been used in distance course delivery, privacy and confidentiality implications may prohibit their full implementation in libraries and must be more closely examined.

As noted before, in an electronic setting, communicators are deprived of nonverbal cues and overtones. Without body language, expression, and intonation it is more difficult for the librarian to mediate an information query. In a virtual setting, the reference interview may be reduced to a simple transaction or exchange of data. Librarians providing electronic support to remote students must make special efforts to personalize and incorporate human elements into their interaction and delivery, and follow-up and feedback become absolutely essential (Sarkodie-Mensah, 1997). In the near future, affordable digital cameras and the use of CU-See-Me technologies may facilitate the reference interview.

3. Reference Support

Remote access to electronic library materials is not a new concept, but the process of training remote users to exploit technological access to these resources effectively is. Library resources are no longer confined within a physical structure; nor are they accessible at any one location. No longer a construct of place, the virtual library has truly become a collection of services. Information is available electronically through networks and consortial licensing agreements 24 hours a day. Although conducting library research no longer depends on the physical presence of library faculty and staff, students and faculty still need to know how to access, evaluate, and use materials effectively. Instruction in the use of library resources is traditionally the province of the library's reference desk or is available individually by appointment. In a virtual environment, research is conducted remotely, often at times when reference support is not available. Instruction librarians should provide guidance to remote users to enable them to use and evaluate information resources asynchronously at point-of-use. Currently, the Internet is a highly effective medium for the continuous delivery of self-paced, user-centered BI.

Skillful mediation of electronic reference questions does support student learning activities. It alleviates anxiety and saves valuable time for remote students. Electronic reference lends itself exceptionally well to the referral process. Not only can the reference librarian refer a student to a resident authority, but in many cases can actually expedite the contact by forwarding the inquiry or providing the user with live links to authoritative Web sites. A further level of support can be provided through direct contact with reference librarians and other library faculty members. E-mail reference, telephone reference, and scheduled appointments provide personal contact and specific problem mediation. Ironically, once seen as a replacement for live reference providers, technological innovation has made human intervention more necessary than ever. The proliferation of resources in a variety of formats has led to higher volumes of reference and information interactions, and has resulted in longer transaction times at the reference desk (Tenopir, 1998). A wider range of choices for users gives rise to more "questions about database content, database selection, and system use," along with questions about equipment and connectivity (Summey, 1997, p. 108).

Electronic reference service is routinely provided in some institutions. In others, its implementation is hotly debated. Staffing an electronic reference desk can constitute a drain on traditional institutional resources if extra support is not provided, and unless this service is seen to be of cost benefit to the institution, it may not be deemed a priority. Unfortunately, as both Bates (1997) and Chepesiuk (1998) point out, funding for infrastructure and technological support and staffing is not always increased as institutions move into new realms of service and delivery. Pilot projects and grants can provide opportunities for start-up projects. After services are in place and of demonstrated benefit, ongoing support may be made available.

4. Direct Provision of Services and Support

College and university libraries generally reflect the larger teaching missions of their parent institutions and, for this reason, academic librarians are charged with helping library users become information self-sufficient rather than with providing full-service information retrieval and document delivery. This pattern is beginning to change, however, as market-driven entities like the University of Phoenix offer competitive, value-added information services to adult students. "These trends will continue, and because more services will be fee-based, user satisfaction and flexibility of service delivery will become increasingly important. We will need to become more 'client focused,' and prepared to tailor services to various classes of users" (Cavanagh, 1997, para. 6). Distance education forces libraries to concentrate on the needs of the individual users. The consumer-driven distance education market reflects the emerging consensus that the needs of the users are more important than those of the library.

ILL is sometimes perceived as a bureaucratic, even cumbersome unit. It can, however, be dynamic and proactive in a distance environment, an active partner in the education of distance students, supporting their studies and propelling the library into a whole new realm of possibilities. In a Web-based environment, libraries can integrate ILL and document delivery request systems with bibliographic indexes, thus removing the artificial barriers between the user and needed information. Innovative and cooperative current awareness services, selective dissemination of information, and document delivery can put a library on the proverbial cutting edge of user support and instruction. In a user-driven environment, full-text and full-content retrieval of information, supported by Internet-based tutorials and responsive reference service, bridges the distance between the student and the institutional library.

C. Conclusion: Future Role of Libraries in Curricular Support

1. Librarians Creating Information Infrastructure

Technology is the key to providing library services and resources to the nontraditional student. Despite initial levels of student technostress, information technology provides remote availability of electronic library resources. When coupled with appropriate training and support, it contributes significantly to student success and satisfaction. Relevant materials are readily accessible without time and travel constraints.

In some cases libraries are beginning to develop their own digital collections. Activities initiated by the Coalition for Networked Information, the National Science Foundation, the Library of Congress, the American Library Association, and a number of other individual libraries and librarians are leading to a greater understanding of the virtual library. In 1995, Cornell's Mann Library formed a taskforce to develop a plan to ensure the high-quality delivery of digital information (Payette in Koltay, Trelease, and Davis, 1996). In addition, digitization projects have been launched at Carnegie–Mellon University, the University of California at Berkeley, the University of Michigan, the University of Illinois at Urbana–Champaign, the University of California at Santa Barbara, and Stanford University (Lange and Winkler, 1997).

Electronic resources also bridge the gap between residential and distance learners and ensure that each receives the same level of service. Electronic access to licensed information products, Web-based training in research and retrieval methods, and electronic reference and referral services are all viable means of providing equal access to information to all members of the university community. Developing programs to ensure that all students benefit by services of similar quality and cost is at the heart of nontraditional and off-campus library service provision (Clark, 1998).

The contribution of the information professional is not always clearly recognized in all quarters. Vendors are taking on roles that librarians are ideally equipped to fill. For example, Cambridge Scientific Abstracts has created a mediated "RouteNet" to publicly accessible Internet sites. Similarly, Northern Light has integrated Web searching with searching a full-text collection of materials originally published in print format. The distinction between the source and the mode of delivery is blurred, and the difference is largely unclear to the end user.

Members of the teaching faculty may design or outsource the design of Web-based courses without considering whether existing information resources are adequate to support them. Librarians need to be proactive in promoting their knowledge and experience, and in negotiating for leave time and funding so that they can be more actively involved in planning and implementing distance learning programs in which the information infrastructure is adequate and intact. In this role, the knowledge base of librarians can be more fully integrated into the learning process in a forward-looking and positive way.

In our rapidly changing information-driven environment, even curriculum is a moving target. Market forces, rather than tradition or policy, determine the directions in which academic institutions are moving. Libraries (long perceived as bureaucratic and procedural by nature and inclination) should actively develop and promote their human capital. In their collective history, academic libraries have changed and adapted. They need to continue their rich tradition of supporting and promoting the learning process in any environment to remain active partners in the electronic academy.

2. Summary of Challenges and Opportunities

a. Institutional Challenges. By aggressively partnering with teaching faculty and actively expanding opportunities for collaboration, librarians can begin to make valuable contributions. Students are taking longer and longer to complete college, and increasing numbers are attending part time. In addition, the competition driving a knowledge-based workforce is creating "heightened expectations for continuous professional learning" (Chepesiuk, p. 54). Participation in planning and implementing distance teaching and learning initiatives allows librarians to put the resources, training, and services needed to support remote instruction in place before the students need them, and assures them of an active role in students' learning process. David Lipsky, Dean of Cornell's School of Industrial and Labor Relations from 1988 to 1997, says that he also sees a role for librarians in implementing and refining the communications technology, and adds, "I'd rather have the librarians than the technologists take the lead in virtual education. The librarians know the content, and it should be the content that dictates the technology, not the other way around" (Lipsky, quoted in Chepesiuk, p. 53).

b. Selection of Electronic Resources. Proactive selection policies in which librarians select the most cost-effective combinations of digital resources can help institutions avoid the vendor-driven "deal-of-the-week" syndrome. Few professionals allow themselves to be pressured into purchasing traditional library materials that are redundant or of marginal benefit. None would buy a new car with an inadequate engine or parts that were "under construction." Yet in the electronic environment, librarians too often make time-pressured decisions about subscribing to package deals based on short-term availability and cost. Crisis-driven decision making works against long-term planning and collection building; adherence to a carefully developed electronic collection development policy can alleviate this problem.

In the rapidly expanding Internet environment, sources must be evaluated in terms of currency, scope, objectivity, authority, stability, accuracy, and stability, just as they were in the past. Library decisions should not be pressured or vendor-driven. Today's market is an information buyer's market, and librarians need to be cannier in negotiating and customizing their own "package deals" with vendors and consortia. By refusing to be seduced by expansive possibilities of increased access to a growing array of format and vendor options, information professionals more effectively plan for the implementation and sustainability of the systems and resources that support and drive teaching and learning initiatives on- and off-campus.

c. Reference Support. Traditional domains of library support and service remain as necessary in the virtual environment as they were in more physical surroundings. Reference support is just as important in an electronic environment as it is in a more traditional setting, and perhaps more so. An effective reference interview is critical, whether it takes place face-to-face or is electronically mediated without benefit of nonverbal communication cues. Follow-up and feedback are still essential to maintaining personal contact and providing opportunities for collaborative learning. Kuhlthau's (1993) process approach to reference and instruction still holds true in the electronic environment. The five levels of service in which the librarian serves sequentially as organizer, locator, identifier, advisor, and counselor remain valid, even as students have less contact with traditional library support structures. They exist within a new context, however, where market forces and technology combine with new expectations and teaching paradigms to create collections and services that ensure that the traditional needs of students are met in the nontraditional teaching and learning environment.

References

Anderson, R. H., and Bikson, T. K. (1998). *Focus on Generic Skills for Information Technology Literacy* (Report RAND/P-8018). Rand Corporation, Santa Monica, California.

Ardis, S. B. (1998). Creating Internet-based tutorials. *Information Outlook* 2(10), 17–20.

Association of College and Research Libraries (ACRL) (1977). Guidelines for bibliographic instruction in academic libraries. *C & RL News* **38**, 92.

Association of College and Research Libraries (ACRL) (1990). ACRL guidelines for extended campus library services. *C & RL News* **51**, 353–355.

Association of College and Research Libraries (ACRL) (1987). Model statement of objectives for academic bibliographic instruction: Draft revision. *C&RL News* **48**, 256–261.

Association of Research Libraries (ARL) (1992). *Liaison Services in ARL Libraries* (ARL SPEC Kit Number 189). ARL, Washington, DC.

Bates, A. W. (1997). Restructuring the university for technological change. In *What Kind of University?* Carnegie Foundation for the Advancement of Teaching, University of British Columbia. Available: http://bates.cstudies.ubs.ca/carnegie.html.

Behrens, S. J. (1998). Developing a curriculum for an information literacy course for off-campus students: A case study at the University of South Africa. In *The Eighth Off-Campus Library Services Conference Proceedings* (P. S. Thomas and M. Jones, eds.), pp. 25–45. Central Michigan University, Mont Pleasant, Michigan.

Benninger, J. R. (1986). *The Control Revolution: Technological and Economic Origins of the Information Society.* Harvard University Press, Cambridge, Massachusetts.

Bopp, R. E (1995). History and varieties of reference services. In *Reference and Information Services: An Introduction* (R. E. Bopp and L. C. Smith, eds.), pp. 3–35. Libraries Unlimited, Englewood, Colorado.

Boyer, E. L. (1988). *College: The Undergraduate Experience.* Harper and Row, New York.

Buckland, M. (1992). *Redesigning Library Services: A Manifesto.* American Library Association, Chicago.

Burge, E. J. (1996). Inside-out thinking about distance teaching: Making sense of reflective practice. *Journal of the American Society for Information Science* **47**, 843–848.

Burke, M. A. (1990). *Distance Education and the Changing Role of the Library Media Specialist.* Syracuse University, Syracuse, New York. (ERIC Document Reproduction Service No. ED 321 775.)

Campbell, J. D. (1992). Shaking the conceptual foundations of reference: A perspective. *Reference Services Review* **20**(4), 29–35.

Cavanagh, T. (1997). Library services for off campus students: At the crossroads? *Journal of Library Services for Distance Education.* [online serial] **1**(1). Available: http://www.westga.edu/library/jlsde/vol1/1/.

Chepesiuk, R. (1998). Internet college: The virtual classroom challenge. *American Libraries* **29**(3), 52–55.

Clark, J., and Store, R. (1998). Flexible learning and the library: The challenge. *Journal of Library Services for Distance Education.* [online serial] **1**(2). Available: http://www.westga.edu/library/jlsde/vol1/2/.

Colbert, G. (1995). Extended campus programs and four year institutions. *Colorado Libraries* **21**, 12–14.

Coughlin, C. M., and Gertzog, A. (1992). *Lyle's Administration of the College Library* (5th ed.). Scarecrow Press, Metuchen, New Jersey and London.

Coulson, M. (1998). Great expectations: Reach to teach. *Information Outlook* 2(9), 13–15.

Davis, M. A., and Cook, M. K. (1996). Implementing a library liaison program: Personnel, budget and training. *Collection Management* **20**, 157–65.

Dougherty, R. M., and McClure, L. (1997). Repositioning campus information units for the era of digital libraries. In *Restructuring Academic Libraries: Organizational Development in the*

Wake of Technological Change (C. Schwartz, ed.), pp. 67–80. (ACRL Publications in Librarianship no. 49) American Library Association, Chicago.

Drummond, R. C., Mosby, A. P., and Munroe, M. H. (1991). A joint venture: Collaboration in collection building. *Collection Management* **14,** 59–72.

Edelman, H., and Tatum, G. M. (1977). The development of collections in American university libraries. In *Libraries for Teaching, Libraries for Research* (R. D. Johnson, ed.), pp. 34–57. (ACRL Publications in Librarianship no. 39) American Library Association, Chicago.

Farber, E. I. (1991). Teachers as learners—the application of BI. In *Working with Faculty in the New Electronic Library: Papers and Session Materials Presented at the Nineteenth National LOEX Library Instruction Conference* (L. Shirato, ed.), pp. 1–5. Pierian Press, Ann Arbor, Michigan.

Faulhaber, C. B. (1996). Distance learning and digital libraries: Two sides of a single coin. *Journal of the American Society for Information Science* **47,** 854–856.

Ferguson, C. D., and Bunge, C. A. (1997). The shape of services to come: Values-based reference service for the largely-digital library. *College and Research Libraries* **58,** 252–65.

Gapen, D. K. (1993). The virtual library: Knowledge, society, and the librarian. In *The Virtual Library: Visions and Realities* (L. Saunders, ed.), pp. 1–4. Meckler, Westport, Connecticut.

Goodson, C. (1996). Continuing challenge for libraries: Meeting the needs of distance education students. *MC Journal: The Journal of Academic Media Librarianship* [online serial] **4**(1). Available: http://wigs.buffalo.edu/publications/mcjrnl/v4n1/goodson.html.

Grealy, D. S. (1998). Web-based learning: Electronic library resources and instruction. In *Distance Learning '98: Proceedings of the 14th Annual Conference on Distance Teaching and Learning* (C. Olgren and S. Saeger, eds.), pp. 133–37. University of Wisconsin, Madison, Wisconsin.

Grealy, D. S. (in press). Technological mediation: Reference and the non-traditional student. *The Reference Librarian.*

Hansen, C., and Lombardo, N. (1997). Toward the virtual university: Collaborative development of a Web-based course. *Research Strategies* **15,** 68–97.

Hinchliffe, L. J., and Treat, T. (1998). Teaching information literacy skills in online courses. In *Distance Learning '98: Proceedings of the 14th Annual Conference on Distance Teaching and Learning.* (C. Olgren and S. Saeger, eds.), pp. 517–20. University of Wisconsin, Madison, Wisconsin.

Hirshon, A. (1996). Running with the red queen: Breaking new habits to survive in the virtual world. *Advances in Librarianship* (I. Godden, ed.) Vol. 20, pp. 1–26. Academic Press, San Diego, California.

Holowachuk, D. (1997). *The Role of Librarians in Distance Education.* Available: http://www.slis.ualberta.ca/598/darlene/distance.htm.

Isbell, D. (1995). Teaching writing and research as inseparable: A faculty–librarian teaching team. *RSR: Reference Services Review* **23**(4), 51–62.

Kruse, K. (1997). The promise and the perils of Web-based training. In *Competition Connection Collaboration: Proceedings of the 13th Conference on Distance Teaching and Learning,* pp. 165–167. University of Wisconsin, Madison, Wisconsin.

Kuhlthau, C. C. (1993). *Seeking Meaning: A Process Approach to Library and Information Services.* Ablex Publishing, Norwood, New Jersey.

Lange, H. R., and Winkler, B. J. (1997). Taming the Internet: Metadata, a work in progress. *Advances in Librarianship* (I. Godden, ed.) Vol. 21, pp. 47–72. Academic Press, San Diego, California.

Lewis, D. W. (1997). Change and transition in public services. In *Restructuring Academic Libraries: Organizational Development in the Wake of Technological Change* (C. Schwartz, ed.), pp. 31–53. (ACRL Publications in Librarianship no. 49) American Library Association, Chicago.

Lipow, A. G. (1991). Outreach to faculty: Why and how. In *Working with Faculty in the New Electronic Library: Papers and Session Materials Presented at the Nineteenth National LOEX Library Instruction Conference* (L. Shirato, ed.), pp. 7–24. Pierian Press, Ann Arbor, Michigan.

McElderry, S. (1977). Readers and resources: Public services in academic and research libraries, 1876–1976. In *Libraries for Teaching, Libraries for Research* (R. D. Johnson, ed.), pp. 58–70. (ACRL Publications in Librarianship no. 39) American Library Association, Chicago.

Moss, M. M. (1997). Reference services for remote users. *Katharine Sharp Review* [online serial] **5.** Available: http://edfu.lis.uiuc.dedu/review/5/moss.html.

National Center for Education Statistics (1997). *Distance Education in Higher Education Institutions.* Available: http://nces.ed.gov/pubs98/distance/index.html.

Reference and Adult Services Division (RASD) (1993). The national interlibrary loan code for the United States, 1993. *RQ* **33,** 477–79.

Payette, S. D. (1996) Sidebar 5: Moving towards optimal: planning for delivery of full text at Mann. (Sidebar accompanies Koltay, Z., Trelease, B., and Davis, P. M. Technologies for learning: Instructional support at Cornell's Albert R. Mann library, 83–98.) *Library Hi Tech* **14**(4), 94–95.

Sandler, M. S. (1984). Organizing effective faculty participation in collection development. *Collection Management* **6,** 63–73.

Sarkodie-Mensah, K. (1997). The human side of reference in an era of technology: The reference librarian. In *Philosophies of Reference Service* (C. H. Mabry, ed.), pp. 131–138. Haworth Press, Inc., New York.

Schiller, N., and Cunningham, N. (1998). Delivering course materials to distance learners over the World Wide Web: Statistical data summary. *Journal of Library Services for Distance Education* [online serial] **1**(1). Available: http://www.westga.edu/library/jlsde/vol1/1/.

Schneider, K. G. (1998). Net-based continuing education: What it takes. *American Libraries* **29,** 90.

Seiden, P. (1997). Restructuring liberal arts college libraries: Seven organizational strategies. In *Restructuring Academic Libraries: Organizational Development in the Wake of Technological Change* (C. A. Schwartz, ed.), pp. 213–230. (ACRL Publications in Librarianship no. 49) American Library Association, Chicago.

Shirato, L., and Badics, J. (1997). Library instruction in the 1990s: A comparison with trends in two earlier LOEX surveys. *Research Strategies* **15,** 223–237.

Sullivan, B. S. (1997). Education for library instruction, a 1996 survey. *Research Strategies* **15,** 271–77.

Summey, T. P. (1997). Techno reference: Impact of electronic reference resources on traditional reference services. In *Philosophies of Reference Service* (C. H. Mabry, ed.), pp. 103–11. Haworth Press, Inc., New York.

Tate, M., and Alexander, J. (1996). Teaching critical evaluation skills for World Wide Web resources. *Computers in Libraries* **16** (November/December), 49–52, 54–55.

Tenopir, C., and Ennis, L. (1998) The impact of digital reference on librarians and library users. *Online* [online serial] **22**(6). Available: http://www.onlineinc.com/onlinemag/OL1998/tenopir11.html.

Walling, L. L. (1996). Going the distance: Equal education, off campus or on. *Library Journal* **121,** 59–63.

Warmkessel, M. M., and McCade, J. M. (1997). Integrating information literacy into the curriculum. *Research Strategies* **15,** 80–88.

White, H. S. (1997). Dangerous misconceptions about organizational development of virtual libraries. In *Restructuring Academic Libraries: Organizational Development in the Wake of Techno-*

logical Change (C. A. Schwartz, ed.), pp. 54–66. (ACRL Publications in Librarianship no. 49) American Library Association, Chicago.

Williams, S. R., and Lunde, D. (1997). Preservation and collection development in academic libraries of the United States: Joint history and future prospects: A review article. *Advances in Librarianship* **21,** 73–89.

Wu, C., Bowman, M., Gardner, J., Sewell, R. G., and Wilson, M. C. (1994). Effective liaison relationships in an academic library. *C & RL News* **55,** 254, 303.

Deconstructing the Indexing Process

Jens-Erik Mai
Royal School of Library and Information Science
Birketinget 6, 2300 Copenhagen S, Denmark

I. Introduction

The representation of knowledge contained in documents is one of the central and unique areas of study within library and information science. One might therefore be surprised to learn how little there is actually known about this area. It is common in the indexing and classification field to demand a set of rules or a prescription for *how* to index. When this demand arises, it is usually based on the assumption that it is possible to explain the intellectual operations that take place in the subject indexing process.

Shaw and Fouchereaux (1993) report on an investigation that the Research Committee of the American Society for Information Science undertook a few years ago. They identified a number of areas within information science which need more research, one of these areas is, "What are the cognitive processes involved in indexing and classification?" Milstead (1994) likewise discusses the need for more research in indexing and notes that "perhaps the most important need for research is one that has never been directly addressed . . . we have no idea of the mental processes involved when an indexer decides what a piece of information is 'about.'" More recently, Vickery (1997) investigated presuppositions in information science. He notes that if the indexing process is carried out by humans, as opposed to automatically, it "requires that [the indexer] establishes a *meaning* for the message, so that the choice of the 'most significant' elements may be made." Hutchins (1978) nicely sums up the situation:

> The literature of indexing and classification contains remarkably little discussion of the processes of indexing and classifying. We find a great deal about the construction of index languages and classification systems, about the principles of classification, about the correct formulation of index entries . . . and about the evaluation of indexes and information systems. But we find very little about how indexers and classifiers decide what the subject of a document is, how they decide what it is "about." (p. 172)

Statements like these can often be found in the indexing literature. This chapter takes up the challenge and makes a further investigation into the problems of determining the subject content of a document. This is done through literature review. By critically examining previous understandings, a new understanding of indexing will emerge. It is not claimed that what is presented is the full answer to the fundamental question of how the subject content of a document is determined. What is presented here is the foundation for understanding the problems related to the task of determinig the subject content.

Retrieval of documents relies heavily on the quality of their representation. If the documents are represented poorly or inadequately, the quality of the searching will likewise be poor. This reminds one of the trivial but all too true phrase "garbage in, garbage out." The chief task for a theory of indexing and classification is to explain the problems related to representation and suggest improvements for practice.

By reviewing significant literature surrounding the indexing process this chapter explains some of the problems related to the representation of knowledge and, more specifically, deconstructs the subject-indexing process to explore what indexing is really about. This results in a call to redirect research in the field from striving at making general prescriptions of how to index and explaining the exact actions any indexer should take during the process for the optimal result, to a more holistic and operational approach. It is here suggested that research on indexing should be concerned with the broader questions of what indexing is.

The basic assumption underpinning the present study is that the main problems of the representation of documents is concerned with meaning and language. Similar assumptions have been taken by others; Fairthorne (1969), for instance, noted that "special topics can be treated as isolated topics only at the risk of sterility; therefore some acquaintance with the general problems of language and meaning is essential." Blair (1990), in the introduction to his book on language problems in information retrieval, notes that understanding of language is important. "The central task of information retrieval research is to understand how documents should be represented for effective retrieval. This is primarily a problem of language and meaning. Any theory of document representation . . . must be based on a clear theory of language and meaning" (p. vii–viii). In this respect, this paper argues that the subject-indexing process consists of a number of steps. These steps should be viewed as *interpretations* and not as rules of the mind. The object here, therefore, is to match this reality by taking an *interpretive approach* (Cornelius, 1996). What is needed is an understanding of the uncertainty and interpretative nature of the subject-indexing process in order to be able to properly teach and study indexing.

Benediktsson (1989) has noted the interpretative nature of the indexing process and the need for guidelines that recognize the significance of interpretation. "[A]ny sort of bibliographical description . . . can be considered as descriptive. When it comes to interpretation, the question is: Ought not the description follow a method or standard as any canon which makes interpretation possible?" (p. 218). Before the literature is reviewed, a larger framework of problems related to the topic of this study is introduced. The understanding of how phenomena are perceived is the basic assumption underpinning an interpretative approach to indexing theory.

II. To See and Interpret

Sometimes it happens that two people see the same thing, but claim to see two different things. Why is that? Why is it that when two people see the same document, they cannot agree on the subject matter of the document? These basic, unanswered questions are at the core of the present review; questions that have puzzled psychologists and philosophers for centuries. This chapter does not, however, claim to answer these questions.

The problem of why people claim to see different things is often explained by illustrations. One example is the Necker cube (Fig. 1). Hanson (1958) notes about the Necker cube that it can be seen as representation of many kinds of things. "Do we all see the same thing? Some will see a perspex cube viewed from below. Others will see it from above. Still others will see it as a kind of polygonally-cut gem . . . It may be seen as a block of ice, an aquarium, a wire frame for a kite—or any of a number of other things" (p. 8). Wittgenstein (1958) also discussed the Necker cube. He argued that such an illustration could appear several places in a book and each time be understood differently. "In the relevant text something different is in question every time: here a glass cube, there an inverted open box, there a wire frame of that shape, there three boards forming a solid angle. Each time the text supplies the interpretation of the illustration" (p. 193). It seems that the context in which the illustration is found determines the meaning of the illustration. Even so, Wittgenstein argues that the context does not limit our interpretation.

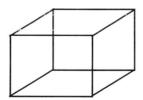

Fig. 1 The Necker cube.

"But we can also *see* the illustration now as one thing now as another. So we interpret it, and *see* it as we *interpret* it" (p. 193). The cube remains the same, but the interpretation of the cube changes. The cube itself does not change, and yet we see it differently. The basic question is how these differences can be accounted for. Although Wittgenstein is tempted to figure out what is actually going on inside his brain as he sees the illustration, he argues that the only way we can learn about the different ways in which the illustration can be seen is by the different descriptions of it. He rejects a mental investigation and relies on what is said and done. The reason for this is that he finds that what is important is what is done. "Do I really see something different each time, or do I only interpret what I see in a different way? I am inclined to say the former. But why?—To interpret is to think, to do something; seeing is a state" (p. 212). Other views must be acknowledged or recognized before a particular view can be argued for. The same holds for the indexing of documents; the indexer must be aware of what he or she picks as the subject entry, among the many subjects contained in the document, before the indexer is able to defend the view the indexer has chosen to index the document from. Indexing is not about seeing a document's text, but about interpreting its content and potentials.

Merrell (1995) likewise discusses this. He states that "people see, not retinas; cameras and eyeballs are blind." The process of seeing the cube entails two distinct operations, namely that of retinal stimulation and that of interpretation. That of retinal stimulation is an immediate feeling, and that of interpretation is a mediated intellectualization, "a synthesis of feeling and the effect . . . of something 'out there' on the sensory organs" (p. 47).

Merely seeing a document does not ensure that the subject matter of the document is "seen." This involves an interpretation of the document. The interpretation of a document involves the context in which the document is interpreted.

If the discussions and assumptions mentioned here are correct and valid, would it then ever be possible to represent the subject matter of documents? If any interpretation is as good and valid as any other, how would it ever be possible to claim that the subject matter of a document is this or that? The argument here is that this is possible, if the different kinds of interpretations involved in the subject-indexing process are known and understood, and the subject-indexing process is well described.

III. The Subject-Indexing Process

Various scholars have noted how little is actually known about the subject-indexing process. Farrow (1991) remarked after a thorough investigation of the problem that "there is in any case a need for more research into the indexing process itself, if only because the validity of the analogies and parallels contained in the model is untested. It is surely remarkable that so little is really known about so basic a professional activity" (p. 164).

After Austin (1974) presented the theoretical and technical history of the PRECIS system, he simply stated that in a typical sequence of operations the indexer first examines the "document, and mentally formulates a title-like phrase which summarizes its subject content" (p. 49). Moss (1975) wonders why Austin uses only two lines on this matter, and more than forty pages on the rest of the indexing process. Moss points out that "it is apparent that the first—very much taken-for-granted—step is the crucial and vital one in any indexing and classification" (p. 116). Swift (1975) noticed that "Mr. Moss . . . touches on a major blind spot in thinking about indexing, at least for the social sciences. He draws attention to the glossing over . . . of what is involved in the first stage of indexing" (p. 117).

Jones (1976) later sums up the Austin–Moss–Swift discussion, and states that there have been "few attempts to . . . to establish the nature of the indexing *process*. Most studies claiming to be about indexing are, in fact, about indexes" (p. 118). Jones (1983) later supports this conclusion by an investigation into the nature of research into the subject indexing process. He found that "the relationship between text and index is rarely examined" (p. 1); more often, such research is concerned with the technical aspects of indexing and indexing languages.

A. How to Find the Subject of a Document

Manuals on classification and indexing are generally rather uninformative about how to identify the subject of a document. They merely recommend the indexer to examine tables of contents, scan chapter headings, and examine forewords and introductions.

The introduction to the *Dewey Decimal Classification* (DDC; 1996) gives guidelines for the determination of the subject matter of a work. In sum, these guidelines state that the indexer should investigate; (1) the title; (2) the table of contents and/or chapter headings; (3) the preface, the introduction, the foreword, and the book jacket and/or accompanying material; (4) the text itself; (5) bibliographical references and index entries; (6) cataloging copy from centralized cataloging services and the cataloging-in-publication data; and (7) outside sources such as reviews, reference works, and subject experts.

The DDC system's guide to determining the subject of a work merely points the catalogers to obvious places where the subject of a document could be found and states that the subject analysis might already have been done. Little is said, however, about the intellectual processes involved in the determination of subjects and of how the various pieces of information could be used in the determination of subjects.

The ISO standard (1985) on determining the subject of documents is similarly vague. It merely states that special attention should be paid to certain sources of information, many of which are similar to those found in the DDC's directions.

1. the title
2. the abstract, if provided
3. the list of contents
4. the introduction, the opening chapters and paragraphs, and the conclusion
5. illustrations, diagrams and tables and their captions
6. words or groups of words that are underlined or printed in an unusual typeface. (p. 581)

After the indexer has examined these parts of the document, the ISO instruction states that the indexer should identify the essential concepts that make up the subject of the document. This is done by consulting a checklist on which a number of questions are enumerated, such as the following:

1. Does the document deal with the object affected by the activity?
2. Does the subject contain an active concept (for example, an action, an operation, a process, etc.)?
3. Is the object affected by the activity identified?
4. Does the document deal with the agent of this action?
5. Does it refer to particular means for accomplishing the action (for example, special instruments, techniques, or methods)?
6. Were these factors considered in the context of a particular location environment?
7. Are any dependent or independent variables identified?
8. Was the subject considered from a special viewpoint not normally associated with that field of study (for example, a sociological study of religion)? (p. 581)

These two sets of guidelines, DDC and ISO, do not state anything about *how* the examination of the sources should be done or explicitly what the indexer or classifier should look for. They merely state the potential sources for finding the subject.

Many practitioners follow and use such guidelines, and they constitute the most common way to determine the subject of a document. However, it is quite obvious that these guidelines are vague and that they do not specifically state how to determine the actual subject of a document. Wilson (1968) notes that such manuals often refer to the subject of works, but they "are curiously uninformative about how one goes about identifying the subject of a writing" (p. 73). Lancaster (1998) argues the ISO standard hardly can be considered a true standard, because "a true standard should be exact . . . and enforceable" (p. 147). Considering that the intention of the ISO standard is to "promote standard practice," the chance of error is great.

Furthermore, neither of these standard guidelines provide help for the cataloger or indexer who wants to determine the subject content based on an analysis of the users' needs or potential needs. These guidelines approach the subject-indexing process as a bottom-up process, where the aim is to determine the *subject* of the document, and not the potential uses of the document.

This suggests that it is almost impossible to formulate guidelines on how to determine the subject of a given document. There is, however, nothing new to this conclusion. Bates (1986), for example, has observed that "it is practically impossible to instruct indexers or catalogers [i] how to find subjects when they examine documents. Indeed, we cataloging instructors usually deal with this essential feature of the skill being taught by saying such vague and inadequate things as 'Look for the main topic of the document'" (p. 360). Cooper (1978) noticed that there has been some investigation into the problems of the process. He states that "it can be said that for one reason or another the findings have not been as enlightening as one could wish on the subject of how an indexer actually index [*sic*]" (p. 107). Cooper also notes that some studies of indexing have the character of investigations of how indexers *do* index, and not how they *should* index. He concludes that "the upshot is that there is as yet no concensus [*sic*] among experts about the answers to even some of the most basic questions of what indexers ought to be told to do or of how an indexer's performance should be evaluated" (p. 107).

Wilson (1968) pointed out four possible methods to determine the subject of a document: (1) the purposive method, (2) the figure–ground method, (3) the constantly referred to method, and (4) the appeal to unity method.

1. The Purposive Method.
    The *purposive method* is author oriented in the sense that the indexer seeks to find out what "the writer is trying to describe, report, narrate, prove, show, question, explain" (Wilson, 1968, p. 78). This is the subject of the document. The indexer should look for clues in the document, such as passages where the author writes explicitly what the purpose of the document is, such as: "I will show that . . . " or "It shall be proved that . . . . " The problem with this approach is that many authors do not state their aims openly.

2. The Figure–Ground Method.
    In the *figure–ground method*, the indexer tries to determine certain

aspects of the document that stand out or are most emphasized. This method relies heavily on the indexers' impression of the document, and this impression may vary from person to person.

3. The Constantly Referred to Method.

The constantly referred to method (also known as *automatic indexing*) is the most objective method because the subject is determined by counting frequencies of occurrences of words in the document. It is assumed that if the word "Hobbes" occurs many times in the document, then the subject of the document is Hobbes. The problem is that there is not necessarily any correlation between occurrences of words in a document and its content.

4. The Appeal to Unity Method.

Finally, in the *appeal to unity method*, the indexer tries to determine what makes the document cohesive or what makes the document a whole. The subject is what makes the document complete. Again, this relies heavily on the individual indexer because any two indexers might not agree on the same unity.

It should be noted that Wilson leaves out one major method of indexing that has received much attention lately: namely what could be named the *requirement-oriented method* or *user-oriented method*, which is essentially a variant of the purposive method. In the purposive method, the cataloger or indexer attempts to identify the author's intentions with the document. In the requirement-oriented method, the indexer attempts to identify the users' potential information needs and indexes the document accordingly.

Wilson ends up by saying that any of the methods could be used, and that the use of any of the methods might result in different descriptions of the subject matter of a document. However, none of the methods could be claimed to be better than the others. As Wilson says, "the notion of the subject of a writing is indeterminate" (p. 89).

Wilson follows a tradition within text analysis that typically has stipulated that there are two ideas of interpretation. As Eco (1994) explains, to interpret a text is either to "find out the meaning intended by its original author" or to assume that the text "can be interpreted in infinite ways" independently of the author's intentions (p. 24). If the latter approach is taken, one faces the dilemma of deciding where the meaning of the text then is found. The meaning could be determined by "(i) what the text says by virtue of its textual coherence and of an original underlying signification system or (ii) what the addressees found in it by virtue of their own systems of expectations" (p. 51).

Eco argues that there has been a change in focus from focusing on what the text says by virtue of its textual coherence, to focusing on what the readers find in the text. The first understanding focuses on textual structure and is favored by structuralism, the latter focuses on the pragmatic aspect of reading and is favored by social constructivism.

IV. Document and Subject Analysis

A. Steps Toward Indexing

The representation of a document's subject takes, according to varying scholars, either two steps (Frohmann, 1990; Petersen, 1994), three steps (Farrow, 1991; Miksa, 1983; Taylor, 1994), or four steps (Chu and O'Brien, 1993; Langridge, 1989).

The two-step procedure consists of one step in which the subject matter is determined and another step in which the subject is translated and expressed in the indexing language. The three-step procedure inserts a step in which the subject matter is formulated explicitly or implicitly. In the four-step procedure, the translation of the subject matter into the indexing language consists of two steps. The indexer first translates the subject matter from his or her vocabulary into the vocabulary used in the indexing language. Then the indexer constructs the subject entry in the indexing language in the form of index terms, a class mark, or a subject heading.

For experienced indexers and catalogers, all steps, regardless of how many one supposes to be effective, may take place almost simultaneously. However, it is useful to operate with intermediate steps when analyzing the process. The three-step model is used for analysis here.

The first step, the *document analysis process*, is the analysis of the document for its subject. The second step, the *subject description process*, is the formulation of an indexing phrase or subject description. The third step, the *subject analysis process*, is the translation of the subject description into an indexing language.

The three steps link four elements of the process. The first element is the *document* under examination. The second element is the *subject* of the document. This element is only present in the mind of the indexer in a rather informal way. The third element is a *formal written description of the subject*. The fourth is the *subject entry*, which has been constructed in the indexing language and represents the formal description of the subject.

Miksa (1983) introduced a geometrical diagram to represent the subject indexing process, or "scope matching process," which implies that subsequent stages of the process are based on interpretations of earlier stages (Fig. 2). This model implies that the referents of each stage in the process are the cataloger's or indexer's understanding, and hence that the results of the process are rather indeterminate and dependent on the cataloger and indexer who performs the analysis. "Given the document *S*, its subject may be repre-

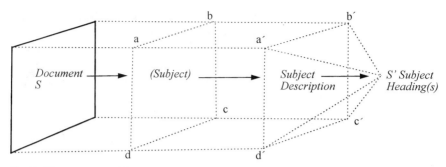

Fig. 2 The scope-matching process.

sented by the arbitrary figure a, b, c, d; the description of the subject by 'a,' 'b,' 'c,' 'd'; and the name of the subject that is useful as a subject heading and that portrays the essential nature of the subject by 'S'" (p. 5). The figure suggests that there is a "certain undefinable substantiality or scope" to the process.

Miksa further discusses what the referent of a subject heading is. He argues that the literature of subject representation tends to answer this question simply by stating that "a subject heading should express or match in some essential way the topical content of a work" (p. 5). He argues that the correspondence between a subject heading and the subject of a document has only a casual correspondence because the subject matter of documents cannot be measured precisely.

The task of a subject cataloger is to move from the document to the subject entry in order to devise a subject name for the subject content of the document. In other words, the task of the subject cataloger is to transform the content of the document into a representation of the document. This process is successful when the subject cataloger has determined a "name or names . . . (which) suggest, represent, fit, match, etc., . . . the supposed substantiality of the topical content" (p. 7).

Miksa's geometrical figure may be modified. The size of each square in Fig. 3 indicates the range of possible referents at each stage. In Miksa's model the three squares are of identical size. In Fig. 3, however, the squares reduce in size during the process. This indicates that the range of possible referents is larger at the beginning of the process than at the end. The idea is that the possible referents are greater for a document than for a subject entry.

B. Novice and Expert Indexers

If the argument that indexing is a set of closely related interpretations is valid, then an investigation of the subject-indexing process most likely reveals

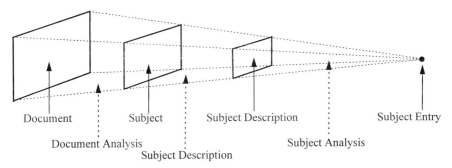

Document   Subject   Subject Description   Subject Entry

Document Analysis   Subject Analysis

Subject Description

Fig. 3 The subject-indexing process.

that novice indexers often break down the indexing process to individual processes and that expert indexers seldom think about indexing as consisting of more steps. Dreyfus and Dreyfus (1986) developed this idea and identified five stages from being a novice to becoming an expert. These stages are introduced here and related to the skills an indexer has at the different stages.

Stage 1: Novice. "The novice learns to recognize various objective facts and features relevant to the skill and acquires rules for determining actions based upon those facts and features" (Dreyfus and Dreyfus, 1986, p. 21). The novice is only able to apply the learned rules in familiar situations. The learned rules are therefore *context-free rules.* The novice applies the learned rules in a particular situation, if the situation matches the learned proto-situation. The novice is not able to accommodate for the given context of the situation. The novice indexer has typically read manuals and guidelines and applies these strictly to every indexing situation. True novice indexers are probably only found in introductory classes in library schools.

Stage 2: Advanced beginner. As the novice becomes familiar with real situations, they advance "through practical experience in concrete situations with meaningful elements, which neither an instructor nor the learner can define in terms of objectively recognizable context-free features" (Dreyfus and Dreyfus, 1986, p. 22). Thus, the advanced beginner uses both context-free rules and "situational" elements in performing a task. The advanced beginner has learned the basic rules and indexed some documents and is able to engage in discussions of the indexing of particular documents in a particular system.

Stage 3: Competence. The competent performer approaches the situation with a plan to organize the situation in mind. The situation is then examined according to the plan, and only those factors that are important to the given plan are given consideration. The competent performer "feels responsible for, and thus emotionally involved in the product of choice" (Dreyfus and Dreyfus, 1986, p. 26). The competent indexer looks for certain information in the document and, from that information, indexes the document.

Stage 4: Proficiency. The proficient performer relies on intuition and not on rules when performing a task. Intuition here means the "sort of ability we all use all the time as we go about our everyday tasks" (Dreyfus and Dreyfus, 1986, p. 29). It is unlikely that the proficient performer is able to explain in detail how she solved the problem. The proficient indexer examines the document at hand without manuals and guidelines in mind. She follows intuition without being able to articulate the exact actions taken. When the proficient performer has decided on a subject entry, she most likely is not able to explain how the result was reached.

Stage 5: Expertise. "An expert generally knows what to do based on mature and practiced understanding" (Dreyfus and Dreyfus, 1986, p. 30). The expert does not see problems in a detached way; she is so much a part of the situation that she does not need to be aware of the situation to handle it. When things work as they normally do, the expert is able to deliberate before acting. However, this deliberation is not based on calculative problem solving, but on critically reflecting on her intuition. As the performer becomes an expert, her performance becomes fluid. The expert is not able to legitimize decisions, but seldom makes wrong decisions. The expert indexer typically has years of experience within the same environment. Unlike the lower-level performers, the expert indexer is able to index the same document using different approaches. In other words, the expert indexer is able to choose to index a document according to an entity-oriented or according to a user-oriented conception (these conceptions are discussed later in the chapter).

The action taken by indexers with different levels of experience might not be exactly the same, but the steps and elements of the subject-indexing process are considered fundamental for any indexing process. Whether this assumption actually is the case is beyond the scope of the present investigation.

Dreyfus and Dreyfus' idea of the development from novice to expert is helpful in explaining the different stages indexers go through.

V. Studies of Indexing

This section reviews and discusses a portion of the literature on the problem of how to determine the subject matter of documents. The aim is to show the range of topics discussed in the field and argue that the higher aim of these studies basically has been to find the best way to index.

First, however, a terminological clarification. The phrase "subject analysis" is used in at least two different ways in the library and information science literature: (1) to denote the area of study concerned with the construction and use of indexing language and classification systems, and (2) to denote analysis of the topical content of a document. The first area has received most attention. It has been reviewed by, for example, Lancaster, Elliker, and Connell (1989), Liston and Howder (1977), Schwartz and Eisenmann (1986), and Travis and Fidel (1982). The concern here is with the latter definition of the phrase—namely, that of determining the subject content of a document. In this tradition of study, *subject analysis* is sometimes used to denote the last step of the process (Chan, Richmond, and Svenonius, 1985) and sometimes to denote the first step (Langridge 1989). Hjørland (1997) notices that other terms have been used; for instance, content analysis, conceptual analysis, information analysis, aboutness analysis, and text analysis.

To clarify the vocabulary in the area, as discussed previously, it is suggested that the phrase "document analysis" is used for the first step in the process and "subject analysis" for the last step (see Fig. 3).

A. Perceptual and Conceptual Indexing

Farrow (1991, 1994, 1995) examined the subject indexing process on the basis of speed-reading studies. Farrow argues that the process could be analyzed as a top-down process, using information that is not contained in the document, but is part of the indexer's world knowledge; or as a bottom-up process, using information that is contained in the document for indexing. Farrow calls the first process (top-down) *conceptual indexing*, and the last process (bottom-up) *perceptual indexing*.

Perceptual indexing takes the form of scanning the text for cues. This might be long words, words that are italicized or underlined, or words in headings or otherwise emphasized. The focus of the scanning could also be areas of the texts such as the introduction, conclusion, or lead sentences, such as: "In this paper, we . . . ," "We will, in this paper, prove that . . . ." The indexer simply picks out words or phrases from the text.

Conceptual indexing, however, relies on the knowledge of the indexer. The indexer's knowledge of the subject matter, as well as the structure of the text itself, influences the quality of indexing. Farrow adds three more factors: indexers' knowledge about (1) the system they are using, (2) the users of the systems, and (3) the background of general world knowledge.

Farrow provides a model for indexing, abstracting, and classification, based on a comprehension model that is simple and highly structured. However, he fails to mention the importance of the knowledge on which the indexing process relies: namely, system knowledge, user knowledge, and world-knowledge. He further argues that this framework of understanding pinpoints the "causes of inadequate or inaccurate indexing" (p. 163).

B. Conceptions of Indexing

Albrechtsen (1992, 1993) argues that there are three general conceptions or viewpoints of subject analysis and indexing (Fig. 4). She argues that these relate to the type of information that constitutes the subject and which method of indexing is being used. The model incorporates three conceptions of subject analysis and indexing: the simplistic conception (subjects as objective entities), the content-oriented conception (implicit subjects), and the requirement-oriented conception (focusing on users' needs).

Albrechtsen has in a very simple but effective way drawn the boundaries for discussing subject analysis and indexing. She provides a very useful framework for investigating and studying the limits and problems in subject analysis and indexing. More specifically, she argues for a pragmatic approach to indexing in which the subject of the document is determined by the use of the document, and not merely by the text in the document.

C. Information Needs and Indexing

Weinberg (1988) discusses why traditional indexing fails to satisfy the needs of researchers. She argues that scholars and researchers are interested in "ideas and theories, and want to know whether specific ideas have previously been expressed in the literature" (p. 3). Traditional indexes do not provide this kind of information, and indexers are not trained to derive this kind of information from the documents. Weinberg concludes that researchers and scholars have to rely on extensive reading and prodigious memory.

Vickery (1968) discusses analysis of information, by which he means "deriving from a document a set of words that serves as a condensed represen-

Conceptions of subject analysis and indexing	Type of subject information	Indexing method
Simplistic conception	Explicit information	Extraction
Content-oriented conception	Implicit information	Assignment
Requirement-oriented conception	Pragmatic information, contextual potentials	Assignment

Fig. 4 Conceptions of subject analysis and indexing.

tation of it" (p. 355). He notes that any text could be used for multiple purposes, depending on the needs of the user. Simultaneously, each of these purposes could represent a point of view from which the subject analysis could be made. He makes the crucial observation that "the subject analysis we make will depend on the users we expect to serve" (pp. 359–360). Vickery holds that any analysis must have the potential users of the documents in mind, and the analysis should be based on the needs of these users.

He notes that there are two types of indexers—namely, those who fully understand or attempt to fully understand the subject content of the document under investigation, and those who do not. The first are capable of expressing the subject content in words other than the authors'. The second merely pick out words that the authors have emphasized, such as title section headings, conclusions, and summary. Vickery notes that very little is known of how it is possible for indexers to achieve such an understanding.

Cooper (1978) developed an indexing method, Gedanken Indexing— thought experiment indexing—that is based on users' probable *utility* of one index term versus another. Cooper argues that the indexer should perform the following task to decide whether to assign a given index term:

1. Predict the relative propositions of future users who will derive negative and positive utilities from their experiences with the card (index term).
2. Predict the average negative utility.
3. Predict similarly the average positive utility.
4. Compute the predicted average utility by adding the results in (2) and (3) weighted by the propositions determined in (1). (p. 114)

The idea is that the indexer should try to picture what a sample of her library users might look for under each of the terms under consideration. The task is to "picture their precise information need" (Cooper, 1978, p. 112).

The method requires that a list of suitable index terms actually be available. The method then assumes that the user population is fixed and well known by the indexer. For indexing in large scale databases in which the user population is not well known this method does not seem feasible.

It is evident that any representation of documents must take the users', or potential users', information needs into account when determining the subject of the document. The problem is that it is difficult, perhaps even impossible, to prescribe how to do this.

D. Summarization vs. Depth Analysis

Taylor (1994) defines subject analysis as that part of cataloging that deals with the conceptual analysis of an item, the translation of the analysis into the conceptual framework of the classification system, and the translating of the conceptual framework into specific classificatory symbols or specific terminology. A conceptual analysis of an item deals with determining what "the intellectual content of an item is 'about' and/or determining what an item 'is' " (p. 101).

Taylor argues that one must have a clear idea of which approach to exhaustivity will be applied. Depth indexing identifies all the main concepts dealt with in the document and recognizes many subtopics and subthemes. Summarization identifies only a dominant, overall subject, and recognizes only concepts embodied in the main theme. Taylor argues that library cataloging has traditionally been concerned only with the summarization level, which is the attempt to identify one overall concept that would encompass the whole document and has been justified by extensive back-of-the-book indexes. The users would retrieve a large class of books based on the summarization of the books in catalogs and pick the relevant ones on the basis of the back-of-the-book indexes.

Taylor defines the difference between *document retrieval* and *information retrieval* as the difference between summarization and in-depth indexing. Summarization allows the user to retrieve documents (document retrieval), after which the user will use the document's (book's) internal subject index to retrieve the relevant information (information retrieval). Taylor's differentiation between information retrieval and document retrieval is less useful. There has been much research and development in document retrieval in which the level of analysis is in-depth analysis, but what is retrieved is still documents and not information. It might be more useful to simply say that information retrieval is the same as document retrieval.

E. Empirical Investigation

Chu and O'Brien (1993) argue that the first step of the subject indexing process has been neglected. The authors therefore set up an investigation of how well indexers perform the first critical step. To emphasize that they were only interested in the first step, they asked experimental participants to condense a text into a single sentence.

The authors asked a total of 104 students from the departments of library and information studies at the University of California at Los Angeles and Loughborough University of Technology to read three short, popular articles and subject analyze the documents. One article selected represented science, one represented social science, and one represented the humanities.

The participants were asked to fill out a questionnaire in which they were asked about the subject of the article and what they would consider the primary and secondary subjects and their relative importance. They were further asked how easy it had been to determine the subject and whether the layout (defined as the bibliographic apparatus, e.g., title, abstract, first and last paragraph, keywords, illustrations, and the physical presentation) of a work had helped the analysis.

The authors concluded that it is possible for novice indexers to determine the main subject of a short text, but added that there seems to be "a serious problem when participants are required to isolate primary and secondary topics" and that "the bibliographical apparatus is a major factor in determining the general subject matter of a text" (Chu and O'Brien, 1993, p. 453).

It does not seem possible to generalize the results of Chu and O'Brien's study to the indexing of longer articles or books. It is inevitable that longer and more complex texts will make it more difficult to determine the subject and the potential uses of the document. It should also be noted that Chu and O'Brien used novice library and information science students as participants, and used popular articles that required very little (or no) specialized knowledge.

F. Mentalism

Frohmann (1990) criticizes what he calls "mentalism in indexing" as it has been promoted by Farradane (1979, 1980), Anderson (1985), and Beghtol (1986). The intention of these studies is to find the rules by which one should index.

Frohmann argues that "there must be some rules guiding the mental activities of indexers, for otherwise it becomes impossible to explain *how* they are able to utter or to write down an indexing phrase for the text. The problem is to discover the precise form of these rules" (p. 84).

The mentalistic-oriented conception of indexing assumes that it is possible to uncover the intellectual processes within the process and that when these rules are uncovered it would be possible to prescribe the best way to index. This assumption is closely connected to the cognitive viewpoint in information science that became popular through the 1980s. This approach was, to a certain degree, based on the cognitive science movement, as it, for instance, was defined by Gardner (1985), who argues that "it is necessary to speak about mental representations and to posit a level of analysis wholly separate from the biological or neurological, on the one hand, and the sociological or cultural, on the other" (p. 6). The idea is that the indexers derive the subjects of documents by invoking mental rules, and thereby automatically generate the mental representation of the subject matter from the mental representation of the documents.

Frohmann argues, in the words of Wittgenstein, that to follow a rule is a practice, technique, or custom, and hence rules are embedded in social life. To understand a rule therefore requires an understanding of the practice.

Rules and practice are of the same kind and cannot be understood separately. He argues that mentalism in indexing research conceals "fruitful directions of inquiry in at least the following five areas" (p. 94):

1. Mentalism focuses on *discovering* the rules of the indexer when focus should be directed toward *constructing* the rules. It is false to believe that tacitly known rules are followed unconsciously.

2. Mentalism favors rule systems that take their ground in the rules of the mind, and thereby conceal other rule systems.

3. Mentalism conceals the text. The text is not regarded independently of the object of study; namely, the mental representations.

4. Mentalism conceals intertextuality by focusing on single-text processing.

5. By focusing on the processes that occur in the mind, mentalism conceals the crucial social context of rules.

Common for much of the literature on indexing is that the authors are searching for an answer to *how* to index. They are driven by the need to find the rules that an indexer must follow to represent knowledge properly. Frohmann challenges this common assumption. He argues that such an approach *conceals* very important aspects of the process.

Frohmann argues that an attempt to find the rules of indexing is bound to fail. There are, in principle, two reasons for this; first, the *application* of rules always take place in a social praxis, and this praxis determines whether the rule is correctly used; and second, the *creation* of rules always take place in a social praxis, and the meaning of the rules are determined by the social praxis. The social praxis, the creation of rules, and the application of rules are closely connected. The mentalistic approach attempts to create context free rules that can be applied in any social context. This is not possible.

VI. Five Conceptions of Indexing

There is a trend in the indexing literature to discuss the advantages and disadvantages of different approaches to indexing. Such discussions have often led to dual conceptions of indexing; Soergel (1985) discusses the difference between entity- and request-oriented indexing; Fidel (1994) discusses the difference between a document- and a user-oriented approach; and, as shown here, Albrechtsen (1992, 1993) discusses the difference between user- and requirement-oriented indexing. These discussions have led to the belief that there are only two approaches or conceptions of indexing, and that these are opposed. A closer look at the conceptions reveal that it is possible to enumerate at least five conceptions. These conceptions are syntheses of understandings discussed in this chapter, but they are furthermore argued to be based in different epistemological positions.

Hjørland (1997) argues that there are four basic epistemological positions that are of interest to knowledge representation. He defines these as (1) empiricism or positivism—the view that knowledge is given *a priori*, that knowledge is modular, that individual sensations are the basis for obtaining knowledge, and that knowledge only can be obtained empirically; (2) rationalism—the view that it is possible to formulate basic principles for obtaining knowledge, that the primary source of knowledge is reason, and that a good analysis will lead to the truth; (3) historicism—the view that the principles for obtaining knowledge develops historically, that it is not possible to define exhaustive and fundamental principles for obtaining knowledge, that knowledge is defined by cultural and historical contexts and not by individual sensations or rationalizing, and that knowledge is not modular; and (4) pragmatism—the view that knowledge develops primarily from praxis, that the future use determines the context for knowledge, and that knowledge is context dependent. In the following discussion, the relationship between different conceptions of indexing and different epistemological positions are brought together.

The five basic conceptions of indexing are therefore defined and argued as follows:

1. The *simplistic conception* of indexing. This conception is similar to Wilson's (1968) constantly referred to method and Albrechtsen's (1992, 1993) "simplistic conception," and focuses solely on automatic extraction and statistical manipulation of words. The idea is that the sum of the words in the document constitutes the subject matter; therefore, this conception of indexing is linked to empiricism.

2. The *document-oriented* conception focuses on the information that is present in the document. This relates to Farrow's (1991, 1994, 1995) definition of perceptual indexing and to Wilson's (1968) figure–ground and purposive methods. In this conception, the indexer investigates specific parts of the document, and the importance of the information is determined by the indexer. The document-oriented conception is closely related to the rationalist position—that by pure reasoning it is possible to objectively determine the subject matter of documents. Such an approach to indexing defines some fundamental principles by which it is possible to determine the subject matter objectively.

3. The *content-oriented* conception attempts to describe the content of the document as fully as possible. This is an objectivist conception that, in the extreme, would claim that there is only one correct analysis

of a given document. As with the historic epistemological position, the content-oriented approach assumes that by a careful investigation into the different interpretations of the document, it is possible to determine the subject of the document. This conception determines the basic subject matter of the origin of the document; that is, the context in which the document is produced. In other words, it is historical and cultural circumstances that determine the subject matter of the documents.

4. The *user-oriented* conception focuses on users. Focus is directed toward the user's general knowledge level or toward the user's work or research domain. The indexer pays special attention to the knowledge level of the users. Users at a public library may require a different kind of indexing than users at a university library, even for the same document. If the indexer works in an organization that serves users with a particular interest or work domain, the indexer should pay special attention to the work domain, and not to the individual users. The user-oriented conception is clearly based on the potential future use of the document, and is therefore based in a pragmatic epistemological position. The analysis of the document is shaped by the potential user group's work in a domain. In such an approach, the subject matter of documents cannot be determined objectively. It changes as the members of the user group changes, as the interests and tasks of the user group changes, and as the domain changes.

5. In the *requirement-oriented* conception, the indexers have knowledge about the users' individual information needs and work tasks. A requirement-oriented conception is only useful in smaller organizations—for example, a consulting firm that employs 15 consultants, in which it is possible for the librarian to know the needs and tasks of each individual. As with the user-oriented conception, the requirement-oriented conception is also based in the pragmatic epistemological position. The requirement-oriented conception is more narrow in focus because it bases the document analysis on specific information needs of specific persons. However, common to both is that they base the analysis on the potential future use of the documents. Indexing done according to the requirement-oriented conception, like the user-oriented conception, changes over time.

The conceptions cannot be seen in isolation. There is probably no indexing unit that bases their indexing solely on one of the conceptions mentioned here. They are related to each other, as on a continuum. An indexing unit will most likely choose a combination of two of the five different conceptions. A consulting firm might choose to combine the user-oriented conception with the requirement-oriented conception to ensure that the indexing is of some lasting value. University and public libraries might choose to combine the user-oriented conception with a content-oriented conception, again to ensure lasting value of the indexing.

The upshot is that it is impossible to claim that an indexing unit is based in only one conception. It is most likely using a combination, and it is impossible to define one conception of indexing that works better than others—it all depends on the particular situation of the indexing unit. Moreover, as is shown here, each conception is closely tied to different epistemological positions.

VII. Relevance Studies

Measuring the performance of an information retrieval (IR) system is a central aspect of information retrieval theory. Relevance is used to measure how well a particular IR system or technique retrieves documents on the basis of a request or information need. The underlying assumption for this chapter is that researchers of the concept of relevance must operate (explicitly or implicitly) with a concept of subject in order to measure how well a system or technique retrieves documents on a particular subject. Thus, if they operate with a particular concept of a subject, that concept might have bearing on the conception of the subject-indexing process.

Cooper (1971) distinguishes between two uses of relevance; namely, relevance as a logical relationship between the topic sought and the document found, and relevance as usefulness for the user. Cooper argues that it seems viable to argue that relevance is a relation between portions of stored information in documents and something called an *information need*. Cooper does not attempt to define what an information need is, but merely states that it is a psychological state that is not directly observable. He further acknowledges that the words stated by the user are *not* the same as the information need. The aim, therefore, is to define relevance as the relationship between the stored information and the user's information need as stated.

Cooper argues that because the utility of documents is relative to different users it is not possible to measure such a concept of relevance. He believes that relevance should be defined as the relation between topics of the stated need and the retrieved documents. Cooper's definition of relevance also requires a clear concept of subject.

Swanson (1977) defines two frameworks for understanding relevance. Within the first framework relevance is understood as something that users create or construct from whatever new knowledge they derive from the document. In this sense, relevance is not something that is present in the document that can be measured or judged. The relevance judgment is solely based on the requester's use of the information in the document. Within the second framework of relevance, "relevant" is defined as "being on the same topic." In this sense, a document is relevant if it is on the same topic as the question that the user enters into the system. The judgment of relevance in this sense can be made by people other than the user. It is important to note that even though a document provided and a stated request are on the same topic, the document might not necessarily fulfill the user's underlying need for information.

Buckland (1983) distinguishes between three uses of the term *relevance*. He defines these as (1) responsiveness: the measurement of the system's ability to retrieve correct data on the basis of the attributes used as the basis for retrieval; (2) pertinence: a narrower use of responsiveness—namely, when the attribute used for retrieval is the subject matter; and (3) beneficially: the degree to which the user of the system can utilize the retrieved data.

Buckland argues that relevance in the third sense, the degree to which the document is beneficial to the user, cannot properly be used to evaluate the performance of retrieval processes as retrieval processes. Relevance should only be used in the narrower definition, in which it is the ability of the system to respond to an inquirer's formulated inquiry.

Buckland argues that measurements of relevance need to leave out the user's subjective and individual information needs because it is not possible to objectively measure the effectiveness of an IR system on the basis of how users utilize data retrieved from the system. However, a measurement of an IR system based on the *pertinent* sense of relevance, in which relevance is measured against the subject of the document, and the query requires a theory of how to derive the subject matter of a document.

Saracevic (1970) clarifies confusing terminology used in literature on relevance. On the basis of earlier definitions of relevance, he develops an algorithm in which he joins these definitions:

Relevance is the ___A___ of ___B___ existing between ___C___ and ___D___ as judged by ___E___ .

where: A represents the gage of measure;
        B represents the aspect of relevance;
        C represents the object upon which relevance is measured;
        D represents the context within which relevance is measured;
        E represents the assessor. (p. 120)

With the appropriate words inserted, many statements could be formulated (Fig. 5). By combining the terms from the five categories, different connotations of a definition of relevance may be given, but the basic problem remains the same: A judgment of relevance is a subjective measurement. Two people with the same information need will not have the same perception of the

Relevance is the	of	between a
a. measure	a. utility	a. document
b. degree	b. matching	b. document representation
c. extent	c. informativeness	c. reference
d. judgment	d. satisfaction	d. textual form
e. estimate	e. appropriateness	e. information provided
f. appraisal	f. usefulness	f. fact
g. relation	g. correspondence	g. article
h. quantity	h. importance	
i. dimension	i. connection	
	j. fit	
	k. similarity	
	l. applicability	
	m. closeness	

and a	as judged by a
a. question	a. requester
b. question representation	b. intermediary
c. research stage	c. expert
d. information need	d. user
e. information used	e. person
f. point of view	f. judge
g. request	g. information specialist
	h. librarian
	i. delegate

Fig. 5 Definition of relevance.

relevance of a document. Saracevic's definition of relevance clearly shows the many variables the notion has and how problematic the concept is.

Green (1995) argues that other relations than topicality might influence the relevance judgment of documents. Green distinguishes between strong and weak relevance. Strong relevance is the relationship between the user's need for information and the documents, whereas weak relevance is the relationship between the topic of the user's request and the topic of the documents. Green states that the ideal system must be one that considers relevance as "the property of a text's being potentially helpful to a user in the resolution of a need" (p. 647).

Thus, the measurement of the system should rely on the system's ability to provide the user with useful information. It is not enough simply to measure the system's ability to retrieve topical relevant information.

Barry (1994) argues that there are two important implications for the evaluation of IR systems. First, there are factors other than topical appropriateness that influence users' judgment of relevance. Second, users are apparently able to recognize and discuss nontopical aspects of documents that influence their judgments. Barry argues that because "users approach information retrieval systems in hopes of finding information that has some *meaning* for them" (p. 151; author's emphasis), retrieval mechanisms based primarily on topical matching may be failing to address the needs that users bring to the systems. Barry, however, advocates that it must be accepted that IR systems can only retrieve documents based on topicality and should thus be evaluated on that basis alone.

Park (1994) argues that topical relevance is context free and is based on fixed assumptions about the relationship between the topic of a document and a search question, ignoring an individual's particular context and state of needs. Measurements of relevance therefore must take into account the users' individual information needs and base the evaluation on these.

The best summary of the problem of defining the concept of relevance is probably given by Rees and Saracevic (1966), who incorporated findings of the early research on relevance measurement into basic characteristics of relevance.

There is a sharp distinction between relevance to a question and relevance to the underlying information need.

Only the user can judge whether a document is relevant (i.e., the relevance judgment is subjective).

Relevance judgments are not constant; they will change over time.

Documents found relevant by one user will not necessarily be found relevant by another user with the same question (i.e., the underlying information need may differ for users with the same question. (p. 229)

VIII. Information Needs, Relevance, and Indexing

The essence of the relevance debate seems to be about what the relevance judgment should be matched against, and therefore which level of information need documents should be represented to satisfy. None of the reviewed authors specifically deals with the subject-indexing process and they only touch on the concept of subject—because their focus is somewhere else. Furthermore, there is a trend in the newer literature to focus solely on the users' utility of the document and not on the relation between representation of the documents and retrieval of the documents.

Nearly every researcher who is concerned with the relevance measurement problem seems to agree that relevance is a relationship between an information need and information contained in documents, and that relevance judgments rely on much more than a match in topicality. The major disagreement is on the degree to which these subjective judgments should be used as the basis for evaluation of IR systems/techniques. In other words, they disagree about the level of the information need the information contained in documents should be measured against.

Taylor (1968) has defined four stages in the development of the information need:

1. The visceral need.
2. The conscious need.
3. The formalized need.
4. The compromised need.

As the information need moves from stage 1 toward stage 4, it becomes expressed in words, narrower, and more measurable. The essential problem in relevance measurements is to agree on which stage the document should be related to. If the first two stages are used, the definition of relevance is based on the degree of usefulness the document has for the user, whereas if one of the later stages are used, the measurement of relevance is based on the degree to which the *topic* of the request and the *topic* of the retrieved documents match. The first type of relevance measurement is usually defined as *user-oriented relevance* and the latter is usually defined as *topical relevance*.

When testing an IR system's ability to retrieve relevant documents, it makes a difference which of the two kinds of needs it is being tested against.

Suppose a researcher is writing a paper on nurses who in the 1840s traveled around in Texas and visited poor farm villages to care for the ill, and that these nurses brought a number of books with them that they sold to wealthier people. The researcher is writing a book about this and wants some more knowledge about this. This is the writer's information need. She comes to the IR system with this need and reformulates it into a number of demands for information, such as "I want literature about farm villages in Texas in the 1840s"; "I want literature about nurses' working conditions in the 1840s"; "I want literature on the reading habits of wealthy people in Texas in the 1840s." The librarian might help her reformulate her information need into these requests for literature. The IR system might be able to retrieve a number of relevant documents that meets each of the researcher's demand for literature, although it does not solve her problem that generated the information need. Was the IR system successful? Depending on whether it is assumed that the IR system should be tested on its ability to retrieve *useful* information for the users (user-oriented relevance), or the IR system's ability to retrieve *topical* relevant information (topical relevance), the answers differ.

Researchers of IR evaluation have focused their concern mainly on defining the kind of information need that the documents should be related to. They assume that as documents are indexed, this side of the problem has been solved. The assumption is that only the user side of the problem is relative, the subject of the document can be objectively defined.

A subject representation of a document has two primary functions: (1) it must represent the subject content of a document, and (2) it should help the users of the system find documents on a particular subject. The challenge is to find a balance between these two functions. As discussed in the previous section on the five conceptions of indexing, this is a balance because indexing should not solely be based on the users' requirements or on the document's text.

If one focuses solely on the representation aspect and ignores future users, one might risk representing documents in a way that would be of no use for the users. An indexer who does not pay much attention to the users might choose to represent subjects of documents that are of no interest to the users, or might use a different vocabulary from the users, or might represent the subject on a level that is too broad or too narrow for the users. However, if the indexer pays too much attention to the users of the system, the indexer might represent documents in such a way that the subject representation of the documents only serves the current users and those current information needs.

In relevance studies, the balance between the two functions is highly important. Evaluation of relevance that tests only the users' ability to find documents that will solve, or be useful for, their particular information needs tends to forget the difficulties and possibilities of subject representation. A study that solely discusses and investigates a group of users' information needs and how they solve these needs by using a particular information retrieval system reveals little about how well the subjects of the documents are represented.

IX. Summary and Conclusion

In the late nineteenth century, Charles A. Cutter (1904) defined a set of universal objects of a catalog. These much cited objects state that one of the central objects of a catalog is to provide access to documents on the basis of their subject matter.

Although efforts have been made to describe the process of indexing, it seems quite obvious that it is poorly documented as well as poorly explained. That there has been no adequate theory to explain the indexing process, nor a recognition that such a theory should focus on what indexing is, at the expense of determining how to index. The existing manuals and guidelines for determining the subject matter of documents are insufficient for their purpose. Attempts to describe actual methods of indexing have likewise been unsuccessful. The indexing process can be deconstructed to show three steps (document analysis process, subject description, and subject analysis process) and four elements (document, subject, subject description, subject entry). A general analysis of these steps and elements indicates that they can be viewed as interpretations. An indexer goes through a number of stages from being a novice indexer to becoming an expert indexer.

Much of the literature on the subject-indexing process is concerned with finding the rules of indexing. The one major goal that has guided research in the field has been to find out what it is that indexers do when they index. The goal of this kind of research has been to be able to prescribe *how* to index. This has been challenged; it has been argued that it will not be possible to find these rules. Even if such rules are found, they will not be of much use. By using Wittgenstein's argumentation, Frohmann shows that a rule has meaning only in a social context.

A common discussion in the indexing literature is to define two distinct conceptions of indexing, one that takes its basis in the document itself, and another that takes as its basis the users' needs or potential needs for information. This paper suggests that these two conceptions should be expanded to five conceptions of indexing, and that in practice, a combination of these should be used.

A central concept in the library and information science field is relevance. This might even be the most important and most central concept of all. Some literature on this concept was reviewed in order to search for conceptions of the subject-indexing process and the concept of subject. It was concluded that most researchers do not explain the concept of subject they use, and none of them discusses the subject-indexing process *per se*. There is also a trend to investigate the users' utility of the documents at the expense of investigations into the relations between representation of the documents and the retrieval of the documents.

Investigations into, studies of, and the teaching of indexing should be taught as and thought of as a number of choices or interpretations rather than an exact skill to be learned. No matter how much time is spent searching for the rules of indexing, they will never be found, and it will never be possible to determine the exact actions an indexer or cataloger should take during the process. The focus should therefore be shifted toward explaining what indexing is.

Indexing is often defined as the process of creating entries in an index. Most of the studies of indexing have been concerned with technical aspects of translating the subject description into the vocabulary of the indexing language—the first step in determining the subject matter has largely been ignored. The reason for this could be that indexing has been approached as an exact skill that can be mastered, such that inter-indexer inconsistency can be eliminated. Instead, indexing must be thought of as a humanist interpretative art.

Studies of indexing must be tied more closely to studies of relevance and evaluation of information retrieval systems and the practice in which the indexing and retrieval is conducted. Indexing cannot be studied separately from the social context and domain in which the indexing is done and the users operate. Studies of evaluation must be tied to the representation process and not solely to the retrieval process. There needs to be a shift from objective scientific methods to hermeneutic qualitative methods, and more holistic and operational approach to research in indexing.

References

Albrechtsen, H. (1992). PRESS: A thesaurus-based information system for software reuse. In *Classification Research for Knowledge Representation and Organization*. Elsevier, New York.

Albrechtsen, H. (1993). Subject analysis and indexing: From automated indexing to domain analysis. *The Indexer* **18**(4), 219–224.

Anderson, J. D. (1985). Indexing systems: Extensions of the mind's organizing power. *Information and Behavior* **1**, 287–323.

Austin, D. (1974). The development of PRECIS: A theoretical and technical history. *Journal of Documentation* **30**(1), 47–102.

Barry, C. L. (1994). User-defined relevance criteria: An exploratory study. *Journal of the American Society for Information Science* **45**(3), 149–159.

Bates, M. (1986). Subject access in online catalogs: A design model. *Journal of the American Society for Information Science* **37**(6), 357–376.

Beghtol, C. (1986). Bibliographic classification theory and text linguistics: Aboutness analysis, intertextuality and the cognitive act of classifying documents. *Journal of Documentation* **42**(2), 84–113.

Benediktsson, D. (1989). Hermeneutics: Dimensions toward LIS thinking. *Library and Information Science Research* **11**, 201–234.

Blair, D. (1990). *Language and Representation in Information Retrieval*. Elsevier Science Publisher, New York.

Buckland, M. (1983). Relatedness, relevance and responsiveness in retrieval systems. *Information Processing and Management* **19**(3), 237–241.

Chan, L. M., Richmond, P. A., and Svenonius, E. (1985). *Theory of Subject Analysis: A Sourcebook*. Libraries Unlimited, Littleton.

Chu, C. M., and O'Brien, A. (1993). Subject analysis: The first critical stages in indexing. *Journal of Information Science* **19**, 439–454.

Cooper, W. S. (1971). A definition of relevance for information retrieval. *Information Storage and Retrieval* **7**(1), 19–37.

Cooper, W. S. (1978). Indexing documents by gedanken experimentation. *Journal of the American Society for Information Science* **29**, 107–119.

Cornelius, I. (1996). *Meaning and Method in Information Studies*. Ablex Publishing, Norwood, New Jersey.

Cutter, C. A. (1904). *Rules for a Dictionary Catalog* (4th ed.). Government Printing Office, Washington, DC.

DDC (1996). *Dewey Decimal Classification and Relative Index*. Forest Press, Albany.

Dreyfus, H. L., and Dreyfus, S. E. (1986). *Mind Over Machine: The Power of Human Intuition and Expertise in the Era of the Computer*. Basil, London.

Eco, U. (1994). *The Limits of Interpretation*. Indiana University Press, Bloomington.

Fairthorne, R. A. (1969). Content analysis, specification, and control. *Annual Review of Information Science and Technology* **4**, 73–109.

Farradane, J. (1980). Knowledge, information and information science. *Journal of Documentation* **2,** 75–80.

Farradane, J. (1979). The nature of information. *Journal of Information Science* **1,** 13–17.

Farrow, J. F. (1995). All in the mind: Concept analysis in indexing. *The Indexer* **19**(4), 243–247.

Farrow, J. F. (1991). A cognitive process model of document indexing. *Journal of Documentation* **47**(2), 149–166.

Farrow, J. F. (1994). Indexing as a cognitive process. *Encyclopedia of Library and Information Science* **53**(16), 155–171.

Fidel, R. (1994). User-centered indexing. *Journal of the American Society for Information Science* **45**(8), 572–576.

Frohmann, B. (1990). Rules of indexing: A critique of mentalism in information retrieval theory. *Journal of Documentation* **46**(2), 81–101.

Gardner, H. (1985). *The Mind's New Science: A History of the Cognitive Revolution.* Basic Books, New York.

Green, R. (1995). Topical relevance relationships. I. Why topic matching fails. *Journal of the American Society for Information Science* **46**(9), 646–653.

Hanson, N. R. (1958). *Patterns of Discovery.* Cambridge University Press, Cambridge.

Hjørland, B. (1997). *Information Seeking and Subject Representation: An Activity–Theoretical Approach to Information Science.* Greenwood Press, Westport, Connecticut.

Hutchins, W. J. (1978). The concept of 'aboutness' in subject indexing. *Aslib Proceedings* **30**(5), 172–181.

ISO (1985). *Documentation—Methods for Examining Documents, Determining Their Subjects and Selecting Indexing Terms.* International Organization for Standardization.

Jones, K. (1983). How do we index? A report of some ASLIB informatics group activities. *Journal of Documentation* **39**(1), 1–23.

Jones, K. (1976). Towards a theory of indexing. *Journal of Documentation* **32**(2), 118–125.

Lancaster, F. W. (1998). *Indexing and Abstracting in Theory and Practice.* University of Illinois, Champaign, Illinois.

Lancaster, F. W., Elliker, C., and Connell, T. H. (1989). Subject analysis. *Annual Review of Information Science and Technology* **24,** 35–84.

Langridge, D. W. (1989). *Subject Analysis: Principles and Procedures.* Bowker-Saur, London.

Liston D. M., Jr., and Howder, M. L. (1977). Subject analysis. *Annual Review of Information Science and Technology* **12,** 81–118.

Merrell, F. (1995). *Semiosis in the Postmodern Age.* Purdue University Press, West Lafayette, Indiana.

Miksa, F. (1983). *The Subject in the Dictionary Catalog from Cutter to the Present.* American Library Association, Chicago.

Milstead, J. L. (1994). Needs for research in indexing. *Journal of the American Society for Information Science* **45**(8), 577–582.

Moss, R. (1975). PRECIS (letter). *Journal of Documentation* **31**(2), 116–117.

Park, T. K. (1994). Toward a theory of user-based relevance: A call for a new paradigm of inquiry. *Journal of the American Society for Information Science* **45**(3), 135–141.

Petersen, T. (1994). Introduction. In *Guide to Indexing and Cataloging with the Arts and Architecture Thesaurus.* Oxford University Press, New York.

Rees, A. M., and Saracevic, T. (1966). The measurability of relevance. *Proceedings of the American Documentation Institute* **3,** 225–234.

Saracevic, T. (1970). The concept of relevance in information science: A historical note. In *Introduction to Information Science.* R. R. Bowker, New York.

Schwartz, C., and Eisenmann, L. M. (1986). Subject analysis. *Annual Review of Information Science and Technology* **21,** 37–61.

Shaw, D., and Fouchereaux, K. (1993). Research needs in information science. *Bulletin of the American Society for Information Science* **19**(3), 25.

Soergel, D. (1985). *Organizing Information: Principles of Data Base and Retrieval Systems.* Academic Press, San Diego.

Swanson, D. R. (1977). Information retrieval as a trial and error process. *Library Quarterly* **47**(2), 128–148.

Swift, D. F. (1975). PRECIS (letter). *Journal of Documentation* **31**(2), 117–118.

Taylor, A. G. (1994). Books and other bibliographic material. In *Guide to Indexing and Cataloging with the Arts and Architecture Thesaurus.* Oxford University Press, New York.

Taylor, R. S. (1968). Question-negotiation and information seeking in libraries. *College and Research Libraries* **29**, 178–194.

Travis, I. L., and Fidel, R. (1982). Subject analysis. *Annual Review of Information Science and Technology* **17**, 123–157.

Vickery, B. (1968). Analysis of information. *Encyclopedia of Library and Information Science* **1**, 355–384.

Vickery, B. (1997). Metatheory and information science. *Journal of Documentation* **53**(5), 457–476.

Weinberg, B. H. (1988). Why indexing fails the researcher. *The Indexer* **16**(1), 3–6.

Wilson, P. (1968). *Two Kinds of Power: An Essay on Bibliographic Control.* University of California Press, Berkeley.

Wittgenstein, L. (1958). *Philosophical Investigations.* Macmillan Publishing, New York.

The United Kingdom Library and Information Commission

Judith Elkin*
Dean of the Faculty of Computing, Information
  and English
University of Central England
Birmingham, B42 2SU, United Kingdom

I. Introduction

The United Kingdom Library and Information Commission (LIC) was established in 1995 as a national source of expertise to government on all issues relating to library and information services. The commission aims to contribute to the improvement of services to users of all types of library and information services through its information, research, and national strategy coordination activities. The commission's ways of working toward its aims include: focusing on cross-sectoral and strategic issues; being proactive in consulting on policy and giving advice; developing and facilitating strategic alliances; and promoting and demonstrating best value.

The commission's vision is that the United Kingdom will play a leading role in the global information economy through providing universal access to the products of the human mind (connectivity), creating a digital library of the United Kingdom's intellectual heritage of culture and innovation (content), and equipping individuals and organizations to play their full role in a learning and information society (competence).

The commission believes that library and information services are operating in a rapidly changing and increasingly sophisticated external environment. It aims to promote their added value to an information society and encourages recognition of this value in economic, education, and social policy development and in recent UK government initiatives such as the National Grid for Learning and the University for Industry. Planning for the Commission's activities in the future takes into account the policy priorities of the UK

---

* *The views expressed in this paper are those of the author, and not necessarily those of the Library and Information Commission in the United Kingdom.*

299

government, the core remit of the commission, and the commission's own vision of library and information services in the twenty-first century.

The priorities identified in the LIC's first 3 years include establishing effective partnerships with a wide range of Library and Information Services (LIS) bodies and establishing the commission as an independent body whose advice is sought by a wide range of government departments and agencies. Particular achievements in the commission's first 3 years include a UK-wide national research strategy for the LIS sector; a UK-wide public library networking strategy; launching the UK National Focal Point for the European Libraries Programme, and establishing a task group on cross-sectoral issues in training LIS professionals.

II. Purpose of the Library and Information Commission

The UK LIC is both a nondepartmental public body and a company limited by guarantee. It was set up in 1995 as a national source of expertise to advise government on all issues relating to library and information services. Its aim is to contribute to the enhancement of the services provided to users by library and information services of all types and in all sectors, on the basis of the financial resources available and in the context of rapid technological change. The commission operates to a Memorandum of Understanding, which identifies the commission's core objectives as:

1. advising government departments
2. coordination of the various sectors of the library and information system
3. international work
4. research
5. development of a national information policy
6. advice to particular government departments on specific issues
7. Library and Information Commission structure

A. Advising Government Departments

The LIC provides a single coherent and efficient source of advice to government on all issues in the field of library and information services where the government requests such advice and draws the government's attention to emerging issues and suggests appropriate responses to them. It provides all advice on the basis of as full a process of consultation within the library and information community as necessary and as time allows.

B. Coordination of the Various Sectors of the LIS System

This is achieved by providing high-quality advice to government and library and information practitioners on how use of resources might best be coordinated to reduce duplication and maximize benefits to users and value for money for funders, by facilitating and improving bilateral cooperation between institutions in different sectors, and by acting as a catalyst for exchanges of information and the dissemination of best practice across the library and information community as a whole. This is achieved by setting up, maintaining, and developing efficient mechanisms for cooperation between the commission and other bodies with a coordinating role in the library and information field in the United Kingdom and by consulting other public- and private-sector bodies whose work affects or is affected by developments in the library and information sector.

C. International Work

Where requested by the government and in accordance with government policy, the LIC is expected to represent the interests of the UK library and information community in discussions on the European Union (EU) and Council of Europe library and information policies and funding programs. In addition, it acts as the national focal point to ensure that UK organizations involved in bids for funding under the European Library Plan or its successors receive a prompt and effective response to requests for advice on the preparation of those bids. It monitors the development of all EU policies that affect library and information services and ensures an efficient flow of information to the government and to and from the library and information community on the implications of these policies. It has developed efficient mechanisms for cooperation between the commission and international library and information bodies, associations and networks, and facilitates useful contacts between these organizations and relevant bodies and individuals in the United Kingdom.

D. Research

The LIC was charged with developing in accordance with government policy and in consultation with all interested parties, a UK-wide research strategy for the library and information field and, through that strategy, to advise on how resources available for research, notably the funds disbursed for this purpose by the British Library, could be directed in such a way as to provide maximum benefit to the public, in particular through the new applications of technology. In addition, the LIC has a role to disburse the commission's own research funds in accordance with the strategy, to facilitate its advancement, and to ensure that appropriate mechanisms are in place for the monitoring and evaluation of the use by other organizations of monies supplied to them by the commission for the purposes of research.

E. Development of a National Information Policy

In collaboration with other relevant bodies including those in Scotland, Wales, and Northern Ireland, the LIC was charged with assessing the feasibility of a national information policy and taking a leading role in advising the government on drawing up detailed proposals for such a national information policy.

F. Advice to Particular Government Departments on Specific Issues

The commission provides independent expert advice as necessary on specific issues referred to it by government departments or other relevant bodies. Such issues remain the responsibility of the relevant departments or bodies, at whose discretion the commission is asked to comment or undertake research work. Examples include advice on the provision of information within the health sector, private sector information provision, the provision by government agencies of information to business, the potential contribution of libraries to information provision for job seekers, and to vocational training and any other area within its competence that departments wish to refer to it.

G. LIC Structure

To meet the previously mentioned objectives, the work of the commission is carried out through its committees and secretariat. The LIC has been a "lean, mean" machine. Its secretariat is small (four people), but its work has been very substantial, working through its commissioners and its two major committees, Research and International. This has required commissioners and committee members to be active. The commission itself has 18 members drawn from a wide field of expertise, from the private and public sector and largely not library and information practitioners. The chairman, Matthew Evans, is also the chair of Faber and Faber Publishing. Committee members are drawn from commissioners and other externals with expertise in the field. In addition, there is a committee on Finance and Administration and a Task Group on Training.

III. Library and Information Commission in Action

The commission works in ways that make best use of its resources and that do not unnecessarily duplicate the work of other national agencies. The commission takes the view that a holistic rather than a sectoral approach is required to ensure the full contribution of the LIS community to society. It therefore focuses on cross-sectoral projects or on projects in which the lessons are transferable. As a national advisory body, the commission focuses its attention on national and, as appropriate, UK-wide strategic issues. The commission may advise on local issues if it can be demonstrated that issues concerned are generalizable. Within the United Kingdom, alliances with national coordinating and professional bodies are important in promoting a UK-wide approach to the Information Society. Liaison with European organizations offers the potential for harmonization of national with European policy developments. Liaison with organizations outside Europe enables the sharing of experiences and understanding of the global context.

The commission reacts to requests from government for advice but is also proactive in bringing issues to the attention of government where there will be an impact on the LIS sector or where the sector can make a valuable contribution to the broader debate on Information Society issues. All advice to government is given on the basis of as wide a process of consultation with the LIS community and the public as possible. Often, the time-frame necessitates focused consultation, which is why partnerships are so important. Similarly, the commission's policy is to disseminate information on its activities as widely as possible through conferences and seminars, information posted on the Internet, and publications. The commission advises government on how to achieve best value in the delivery of LIS to the public. It is particularly interested in promoting best practice in this regard including collaborative activities, use of private-sector funding, and sponsorship. The commission itself attempts to demonstrate best value in its own operations through pooling resources with other agencies to achieve results beyond the capabilities of the individual partners and through efficiency measures.

IV. Vision for 2020

One of the first priorities set by the commissioners was to develop their vision of libraries in the twenty-first century. This vision statement, *2020 Vision* (UK Library and Information Commission, 1997a) reproduced as follows is designed to articulate the LIC's vision of the value of library and information services, to set a context for the LIC's action plan, and to provide a framework to shape a dynamic role for the commission in encouraging government to demonstrate that value in economic, education, and social policy development. A holistic rather than sectoral approach is taken throughout this statement to emphasize the potential value of LIS in society.

A. The Global Economy

The commission believes that the United Kingdom will play a leading role in the dominant global information economy through connectivity: providing universal access to the products of the human mind; content: creating a digital library of the United Kingdom's intellectual heritage of culture and innovation; competences: equipping individuals and organizations to play their full role in a learning and information society.

B. External Environment

The commission recognizes that LIS are operating in a rapidly changing and increasingly sophisticated external environment in which the following apply:

1. technology gives the potential for universal access to information and all information becomes potentially available
2. access to knowledge/information underpins a democratic society
3. information is an international commodity
4. knowledge underpins all successful economic activity
5. industry is increasingly dependent on an informed workplace
6. information must be accessible
7. information must be organized and managed
8. information skills are fundamental coping skills
9. information needs are increasingly complex and may be met from multiple sources
10. the discontinuities between technology and our abilities to deal with it need to be understood and managed
11. the library and information sector is a substantial part of the UK economy

C. Value of LIS

The commission believes in the added value of LIS that perform the following:

1. form a substantial sector of the economy; the United Kingdom's leadership role in the international LIS sector can be translated into a leading role in the global information economy
2. are necessary to the well-being of individuals, communities, and society
3. are the memory of society through collecting and preserving knowledge
4. work with knowledge; add value by evaluating, making accessible, mediating, packaging, and promoting knowledge
5. provide access to: opportunities for literacy and lifelong learning; the knowledge that underpins all successful economic activity; the

information that is central to a democratic society; the information, knowledge, and works of creative imagination that embody healthy social and cultural diversity and understanding; and a socially inclusive cultural and creative environment

6. reach into people's lives in many ways; people use a range of LIS throughout their lives and often use several different "libraries" for different purposes at any one point in their lives

7. empower the individual by providing resources and information for particular user groups, especially children and young people, and facilitating the development of the information skills that are essential for modern-day living

8. embody the value of collective activity; engender a sense of community within places and organizations; and provide a space where people can feel secure within a shared value system

D. The Vision for 2020

Given the impact of LIS values on external factors, the commission's vision for 2020 is as follows:

1. Governments, companies, and individuals will put a top priority on information.

2. The United Kingdom will be an information/knowledge-based society, with the United Kingdom acting as a knowledge powerhouse and a hub of the global information economy.

3. In the global information economy, the United Kingdom will be a world leader in connectivity, standards, content development, management, and mediation skills.

4. Industry and commerce will be more knowledge-intensive learning organizations.

5. There will be an information economy that empowers citizens through a network of information/knowledge centers acting as flagships for access in their community.

6. There will be a digital library collection coordinated nationally/ internationally embracing the world's knowledge and creativity, in which the United Kingdom's heritage of intellectual property will be globally available in digital form.

7. Value-added content and universal connectivity will ensure that every individual will have unfettered access to global information/ knowledge.

8. Individuals will need a range of literacies to enable them to maximize their potential individually and collectively.

V. Achievements of the Library and Information Commission, 1995–1997

Since 1995, the commission has made significant progress in fulfilling its core objectives and in undertaking work that will facilitate its strategic vision of libraries, for example, *2020 Vision*, outlined previously. It has raised its profile with government and has established regular and effective communication channels with all relevant government departments but particularly with the Department of Culture, Media and Sport (DCMS), the Department for Education and Employment (DfEE), and the Department for Trade and Industry (DTI), and the Cabinet Office.

Cooperation and collaboration, particularly cross-sectoral, have underpinned everything the commission does. Since 1995, the commission has cooperated with a variety of UK national coordinating LIS bodies on national strategy development, including the Scottish Library and Information Council, and the Library and Information Councils for Wales and Northern Ireland. It has also cooperated with other professional bodies and libraries such as the Library Association, Coalition on Public Information (COPI), Task Force Pro Libra (TFPL), and on seminars to exchange information that is then used to underpin commission policy.

Under the direction of the International Committee, the UK National Focal Point for the European Libraries Programme of the European Commission was relaunched in 1996. This committee has been involved in advising the EU on issues such as copyright, data protection, the role of libraries in an information society and with the renewal of the UK membership in UNESCO, and with UNESCO information activities.

The Research Committee commissioned a research mapping exercise and a UK-wide consultation exercise to inform the development of the national research strategy. It also commissioned other research and development work to support its early policy-making activities, including a survey of Internet availability in public libraries, a feasibility study on linking public libraries to the Internet, a survey of digitization in local authority libraries and archives, and a cross-sectoral study of library involvement in lifelong learning. These are discussed further in the next section.

VI. Achievements of the Library and Information Commission, 1997–1998

With the restructuring of its Secretariat in place early in the year, 1997–1998 saw the commission fully establishing its identity as the national focus of expertise in LIS. The year saw the launch of the commission's web site (www.lic.gov.uk) and a dramatic increase in output of policy reports.

A. Research Strategy

The key task for the commission's Research Committee, when it was set up in 1996, was to develop a national research strategy. A research mapping exercise and a UK-wide consultation exercise were completed in 1997 and their findings were incorporated into a consultative document that was widely distributed throughout the UK and Europe. The final research strategy document, *Prospects: A Strategy for Action* (UK Library and Information Commission, 1998a), was based on the commission's vision of the value of library and information services in an information society, as expressed in its published statement *2020 Vision* (UK Library and Information Commission, 1997a). It focused on the key themes and the infrastructure issues that should be addressed if this vision is to become a reality. In developing these proposals, the commission was guided by the principle that, for any group in society to maximize its contribution in a changing environment, adaptive strategies are needed to anticipate change; build on core skills and unique abilities; improve collaboration with other players; and use innovative tools and technology.

Research was seen as a key adaptive strategy that combines all these objectives. The library and information sector is already diverse and complex in its structures and relationships. The Research Strategy was based on the belief that adaptation and cultural change in this sector particularly required coordination between existing institutions. More particularly, the strategy sought to provide a framework for improving the effectiveness, impact, and value-for-money of research activity; maintain a national agenda of research issues; encourage intersectoral collaboration and organizational partnership; facilitate access to existing knowledge acquired through research activity in relevant disciplines; ensure that research produces relevant evidence for practice and policy making, without unnecessary duplication of effort; and stimulate and support insight and innovation in the many applications where LIS contribute to society.

The Research Programme has five major themes, derived from the commission's *2020 Vision*. Three core themes—connectivity, content, and competences—relate directly to the commission's perception of what will be required for the United Kingdom to take a leading role in the global information economy. These are, therefore, all areas in which the commission wishes to promote and facilitate initiatives and collaborate with other players within the wider information community. To these are added two fundamental themes—value and impact, and economics—that underpin the program as a whole and relate to the commission's role in articulating the value and impact of LIS and positioning them more prominently in the information society. By making these themes explicit, attention is drawn to the critical importance of libraries and information services to national policies and developments, to decision makers in the information industry as a whole, and ultimately to information users at the point of service delivery.

Together, these form a high-level, coordinating national framework for research requirements and highlight priority areas rather than being prescriptive in each field. The thematic framework offers considerable flexibility to accommodate new issues. Convergence between the themes reflects the all-pervasive nature of the information society agenda. Although it is anticipated that they will provide a long-term framework, the themes and their subordinate issues must be reviewed and refreshed to ensure that they remain valid over time.

B. Public Library Network Strategy

Maybe the greatest achievement to date of the commission is the production of a UK-wide networking strategy for public libraries. This was the result of a request from government to provide advice on how public libraries could respond to the challenge of information and communication technologies (ICT). *New Library: The People's Network* (UK Library and Information Commission, 1997b), the report of the cross-sectoral Public Library Networking Working Party chaired by Matthew Evans, the chair of the commission, was produced in 3 months to critical acclaim from the government and the LIS community.

The report's key messages were that government should establish a Public Library Networking Agency, which would both create the backbone infrastructure and negotiate with library authorities to upgrade their local networks to a common UK standard. It should also procure and/or develop content and services and develop a training strategy for all 27,000 (full-time equivalent) employees in the public library sector.

Produced to a high specification for maximum impact, the report included a verse by the then Poet Laureate Ted Hughes. The report was launched in front of an audience of more than 300 people at the National Film Theatre by the secretary of state for Culture, Media and Sport and the Commission Chairman, and received widespread media coverage. Copies were also sent to local authority chief executives, directors of education and chief librarians, as well as to all Cabinet members, selected members of Parliament, and other key opinion formers in the United Kingdom. There was a highly enthusiastic response from sources such as chief executives of local authorities, the Society of Chief Librarians, and the Scottish, Welsh, and Northern Ireland Offices. In the response to *New Library: The People's Network* (UK Department for

Culture, Media and Sport, 1998a), the secretaries of state for Scotland, Northern Ireland, and Wales joined the secretary of state for Culture, Media and Sport, Chris Smith, in highlighting the fact that libraries contribute to four of this government's most important policy objectives:

> They underpin education providing essential support for school children, students and lifelong learners; they enhance public access to the world's storehouse of knowledge and information; they promote social inclusion, by helping to bridge the gap between those who can afford access to information and those who can't, and, increasingly, they have a role to play in the modernisation and delivery of public services. (UK Department for Culture, Media and Sport, 1998a, p. 1)

The government will:

1. help public libraries across the country to make full use of information technology (IT) to encourage lifelong learning and educational services for everyone. "We will make a substantial contribution to kickstart this initiative and ensure its ongoing success."
2. ensure that £50 million of National Lottery money is made available through the New Opportunities Fund for digitization of educational and learning material, much of it held in public libraries; the material will support the government's proposed National Grid for Learning, to which libraries, schools, and other institutions will be connected
3. ensure that £20 million of lottery money is provided for training all the United Kingdom's 27,000 library staff in IT skills
4. establish a Library and Information Commision committee to act as a focal point for implementing a public library IT network throughout the United Kingdom to provide expert advice, leadership, and coordination; develop a technical specification; and consider how industry can best be challenged to provide network services
5. in England, provide £6 million pump-priming investment by 2001 through the DCMS/Wolfson Public Libraries Challenge Fund to support "Libraries of the Future"

In a government press release, Chris Smith said:

> Public libraries play a vital social, economic and educational role in the daily life of the nation. They are among our best loved public services, used by ten million people every fortnight. The development of IT provides new opportunities for them to deliver better services to more customers to complement their core book services. Making sure that library users have access to ever wider storehouses of knowledge and information through new communications technology is of enormous importance for the future. . . . The Government wholly endorses the objectives for the public libraries IT network set out by the LIC. It will do all it can to create the conditions required to ensure success. Our proposals today will allow libraries to make the "IT shift" necessary for this change to happen. (UK Department for Culture, Media and Sport, 1998b, p. 2)

Public libraries hold the key to ensuring that we don't end up as a divided information society, with some citizens having access to knowledge through their home computer systems, and others left behind. Libraries can help to put the balance right, to make access available to all, and to remove the veil of mystery that hides the value of new technology from too many people at present. . . . The key to success in providing these opportunities lies in creating partnerships between the private sector, local authorities and Government. Our aims and ambitions for the libraries network are challenging and will not be easy. But the prize of a reinvigorated public library service will make the journey worthwhile. (UK Department for Culture, Media and Sport, 1998b, p. 3)

The report of the task groups set up as part of this process are discussed in Section IX.

C. National Information Policy

Many developed nations are rolling out formal information policies, and clearly the United Kingdom cannot afford to lag behind. The Research Committee drew up a draft discussion paper on a National Information Policy for the United Kingdom in 1997 (UK Library and Information Commission, 1997c), setting out the benefits of such a policy for citizenship and democracy, as well as economic and community development, health and welfare, culture and recreation, and the legal and regulatory framework. A National Information Policy was seen as an essential prerequisite for realizing the government's vision for lifelong learning; it will be needed to ensure not only that an appropriate infrastructure is in place to meet future educational needs, but also that learning materials are freely available to those who need them. This draft National Information Policy document was recently reinvigorated, after lying dormant for 18 months, by a high-level seminar organized jointly by the LIC and the British Council. This seminar brought together opinion formers from across government departments and public bodies. At the time of writing, the original paper is being updated and revised, with the purpose of resubmitting it to the government, with renewed emphasis on the timeliness of developing a national information policy, to ensure that the United Kingdom does not lag behind other countries and allow the United Kingdom to continue to compete on the European and global stage.

D. Lifelong Learning

The Research Committee commissioned research from the Centre for Educational Development Appraisal and Research (CEDAR) at Warwick University, on the role of LIS in promoting lifelong learning. The report, *The Role of Libraries in a Learning Society* (UK Library and Information Commission, 1998b) presented five case studies, covering further and higher education as well as the public, health, and commercial library sectors in the United Kingdom. Its recommendations covered key strategies necessary for the wider integration of libraries and learning, including the need to develop library partnerships and networks with other agencies. The report also emphasized the need to extend library providers' key skills in offering accessible and proactive service delivery through access to major training initiatives for library staff. It urged the use of evidence to facilitate integration between libraries and learning, and made clear that implementing library development demanded partnerships between policy makers, practitioners, and users. The report was published by the commission and made available on the Web.

Subsequently and in response to a number of government consultative documents, particulary *Our Information Age* (UK Central Office of Information, 1998) and *The Learning Age* (UK Department for Education and Employment, 1998), the commission has produced *Libraries—Lifeforce for Learning* (UK Library and Information Commission, 1999) for wide circulation.

E. Creating the Digital Collection

The Research Committee also commissioned research to review digitization projects in local authority libraries and archives from Information North. The report, *Virtually New: Creating the Digital Collection* (UK Library and Information Commission, 1998c), identified 62 digitization projects already completed or in progress, plus a further 41 in various stages of planning. Its key recommendation called for the creation of an agency to advise on and coordinate public library digitization, specifying its main functions, other operational roles, and relationship to other bodies. It also stated that the automation and networking of catalogs and finding aids was a priority, and that any significant digitization program would require substantial new, targeted external funding or national investment. Other recommendations related to selection of material for digitization, the special potential of local and regional newspapers, reciprocal access to digitized collections, and copyright issues. *Virtually New* was subsequently published by the commission, made available on the Web, and a summary distributed free of charge to library authorities.

F. Changed Roles—New Skills

New roles for libraries require new skills for information professionals. In May 1997, the commission established a new Training Task Group to lead its activities on postqualification training for library and information professionals, and to ensure that these activities have a cross-sectoral focus. Training lends itself to partnerships with a wide variety of organizations, including private training bodies, academic departments and large corporations, and the core focus of the group's early activity is knowledge management. To date, the group has cohosted a seminar on knowledge management with the leading information consultancy Task Force Pro Libra (TFPL). It has subsequently commissioned a research project to identify the skills required for knowledge management and highlight best practice in teaching information management skills to information workers in knowledge management roles. This contract was awarded to TFPL, who will report in 1999.

G. International Partnerships

Internationally, the commission has continued its role as the United Kingdom National Focal Point for the European Commission Telematics for Libraries Programme. There is to be no separate Libraries Programme under the Fifth Framework Programme of the European Community due to start in 1999, but a broader cultural program focusing on cross-sectoral issues of multimedia content development. The LIC is seeking partnerships with both the Museums and Galleries Commission and the Historic Manuscripts Commission with a view to extending the UK National Focal Point's role and also maximizing opportunities for European funding.

VII. Strategic Planning, 1998–2002

In planning its activities for the years 1998 through 2002, the commission examined its priorities against the background of the new government policy agenda and changes brought about by the impact of social, economic, and technological trends. The areas of change that will have the most impact on the work of the LIC are discussed in the following subsections.

A. Education and Training

The UK government's anticipated approach to lifelong learning is likely to specify an overarching framework covering both compulsory and noncompulsory education. It will position the home, community, and workplace as key places within which learning takes place and where the principles of the framework are applied. The policy focus is likely to be for a revolution in attitudes in order to increase understanding of, and demand for, lifelong learning. Choices will increase for the consumer in terms of learning pathways and qualifications. One government initiative, the University for Industry, is central to this policy, as it will provide the underpinning brokerage services and support infrastructure that will enable workers to identify learning pathways and providers appropriate for their needs. A second initiative, the National Grid for Learning, will provide a network for schools in the United Kingdom and will subsequently be opened up to the wider lifelong learning community, connecting public and national libraries, further and higher education institutions, and the workplace.

B. Economic Regeneration, Regional Development, and Devolution

Successful management of information will continue to be a characteristic of competitive advantage in both the public and private sectors. The national and local support systems for commerce will change as businesses demand new forms of information and information systems. The impact of the decision to enter/or not to enter the European Monetary Union (EMU), the single European monetary system, will also be significant in terms of new information needed by businesses and of the changes to financial systems this will require.

At the regional level in the United Kingdom, it is likely that the move toward more regional accountability and strategic direction, with the development of a Scottish Parliament and Welsh Assembly and Regional Development Agencies, will support regional enterprise initiatives through sponsoring services such as regional information and learning networks. This will require new ways of working to construct cost-effective, collaborative networks between libraries, education and training providers, and business stakeholders. The impact of devolution, political reorganization, and constitutional reform within the United Kingdom will lead to greater regional diversity, the drive for regional and local autonomy, and the creation of devolved structures for social and economic decision making. At the regional and local level, there will be major strategic and implementation demands.

C. Open Government

Changes in society's attitudes to both privacy and freedom of information are also likely to be areas for considerable debate and controversy. Attitudes to the communication rich/communication poor gap; the availability of socially undesirable material; personal privacy; and access to government information will be reflected in legislation and legal judgments. Proposals to open up government, including the Freedom of Information White Paper, will make public organizations more accountable to people and increase the extent to which these bodies involve independent individuals in their management. These trends are likely to increase the range and depth of publicly available information that is needed in order for informed decision making to take place.

D. European and International Policy Developments

The LIC needs to be as aware of policy developments from the EU and the G8 countries (the world's economic leading countries) as it is of the UK government agenda. Issues that are particularly important in this regard include: technical standards and content policies related to international information networks and digital information provision; recent directives on data protection, legal deposit, copyright, and intellectual property rights; information and communication technologies (ICT)–related research programs such as digitization of multimedia content; and policies and programs to enhance the cultural and multimedia sector and to provide access to cultural heritage.

E. Social and Technological Change

The role of the individual within the community may change as social inclusion becomes a higher priority. There is an increasing sector of society that perceives itself as socially excluded, including those who are disadvantaged because of disability, ethnic background, rural isolation, or caring responsibilities. Concerns about the gap between the communication rich and the communication poor is already the subject of public debate. The emergence of new forms of technology and its applications will have a profound impact on society. In part, this will be the result of the application of technologies to work systems and processes, but it will also relate to the social and economic impact of technologies on society (e.g., development of digital information and communications services). The integration of ICT skills into the lives of individuals is critical if the benefits of increased economic prosperity and social cohesion are to be realized by the majority of the citizens.

F. Strategic Objectives, 1998–2001

In line with the previously mentioned goals, the seven strategic objectives for the LIC for 1998/1999–2000/2001 are:

1. To contribute through government to the development of a UK national information policy framework.

The commission has produced for government a policy paper on the need for a national information policy framework. It will take this forward through closer liaison with key government officials, particularly those in the DCMS, DfEE, DTI, and the Cabinet Office, and will inform this work through policy seminars and papers that look at national and international developments in national information policy. The commission sees the library network as an integral part of any proactive national information strategy and itself as the appropriate gateway for the library community to contribute to national information policy.

2. To retain an active leadership role in the implementation of a networked UK public library service.

The commission will take a leading role in the implementation of the public library network monitoring and reporting on progress, benchmarking against European and other international developments, and encouraging cooperation and participation through awards schemes. The commission will advise lottery agencies on funding digitization projects and training for librarians in information communication and technology. It will work closely with local government to maintain momentum and commitment to the network, and coordinate rollout of the network National Grid for Learning and relevant initiatives in higher education. The commission will work with other organizations to promote the importance of information skills training throughout life for the general population and the role of libraries in providing this training.

3. To lead national policy development on the "UK Digital Library."

National policies for digitization must be cross-sectoral, cross-domain, and UK-wide in scope. The commission will take the lead in promoting national coordination of digitization activities based on the recommendations in its report, *Virtually New: Creating the Digital Collection* (UK Library and Information Commission, 1998c). The commission will participate in national and international debate on copyright and intellectual property rights as these apply to digital material and advise government accordingly. It will advise funding bodies such as the lottery agencies on criteria for selecting and prioritizing collections for digitization and work with appropriate bodies in the LIS community on promoting nationally recognized digitization standards.

4. To ensure that library and information services are central to the government's plans for a learning society.

The role of LIS in supporting learning throughout life has already been recognized in government papers. The commission anticipates that when the government's plans for education are rolled out, LIS will be center stage. The commission will develop closer relationships with government departments responsible for the National Grid for Learning and the University for Industry, as well as relevant agencies such as the Teacher Training Agency and the British Educational Communication and Technology Agency. The commission will seek joint planning opportunities with key players in the higher and further education sectors such as the Joint Information Systems Committee of the Higher Education Funding Councils.

5. To develop the role of LIS in fostering social inclusion.

LIS have a pivotal role in fostering social inclusion as they provide the information infrastructure that enables disadvantaged citizens to make informed choices about their lives, exercise their democratic rights and responsibilities, and interact with other members of the community. The commission will encourage strategic alliances between LIS and other community organizations in order to strengthen the role of libraries as hubs in their communities and to overcome the barriers between information rich and information poor.

6. To demonstrate the contribution of LIS to regional and economic development.

The commission will consider how to promote LIS in supporting economic activity at local and regional levels and, in particular, how they can assist small and medium enterprises in partnership with Training and Enterprise Councils, Chambers of Commerce, and other business information providers. The role of LIS in economic regeneration initiatives and in relation to the proposed Regional Development Agencies (RDAs) will be explored and promoted to government and to RDAs themselves.

7. To promote the importance of all LIS to opinion formers outside and within government.

The commission will develop strategies to mobilize opinion formers in society who can influence the future development of public LIS, including the 58% of the population who are library users. Successful initiatives such as the "Friends of the New York Public Library" scheme will be examined as models. The value and positive impact of LIS is beginning to be recognized in areas of government policy such as education and health. The commission will promote a positive attitude to all types of LIS throughout government. It will target government departments with evidence of the value and impact of all types of LIS.

VIII. Changing Context

In Autumn 1998, the DCMS published a consultative document, the *Comprehensive Spending Review: A New Approach to Investment in Culture* (CSR; UK Department for Culture, Media and Sport, 1998c). The CSR was undertaken to inform public expenditure decisions for the current Parliament. The principal conclusion was that all the areas for which DCMS was responsible were important, and that continuing public subsidy for sport, tourism, and the cultural sectors was justified by the impact that they have on the lives of individuals and the well-being of the nation. The starting point for the review was to establish new objectives, linking the department to the government's overall policy agenda. At its simplest, the future direction of the department lies in four central themes: the promotion of access for the many, not just the few; the pursuit of excellence and innovation; the nurturing of educational opportunity; and the fostering of the creative industries.

As far as the libraries sector was concerned, the CSR recognized that the sector was fragmented and that a coordinated approach to current problems was sometimes difficult to achieve. It was seen that the work of the British Library, LIC, and the sector as a whole relates in a relatively unsystematic way to other cultural institutions and activities, particularly in the museums sector.

Their respective roles needed to be more clearly defined to allow the British Library to focus on delivering essential core services and the LIC to fulfill its leadership responsibilities across the sector as a whole. This meant helping the LIC to develop a size and status commensurate with its leadership and advisory roles, and refocusing the British Library on those issues that more clearly reflected the government's objectives for the sector.

Among the key proposals relating to the LIC, the CSR proposed:

1. to enhance the role of the LIC by giving it responsibility for undertaking those functions relating to library research currently undertaken by the British Library
2. to consider the case for providing the LIC with the resources necessary for it to lead and coordinate the development of the public libraries IT network
3. in the medium term, to create a new body, merging the LIC with the Museums and Galleries Commission in order to create a single powerful Museums and Libraries Council, promoting greater coordination between national, regional, and local institutions
4. to develop better linkages between libraries and the world of education
5. to encourage greater links between the Royal Commission on Historical Manuscripts (RCHM) and the LIC and to consider it as a candidate for direct funding from the Museums and Libraries Council in the longer term
6. to consider how the LIC can best be enabled to lead and coordinate the development of the public libraries IT network

At the time of writing, the national research of the British Library, the British Library Research and Information Centre (BLRIC), will transfer to the LIC on April 1, 1999, creating a much stronger and more cohesive research base. A design group has been formed to look at the possibility of creating a new and more streamlined body to replace the LIC and the Museums and Galleries Commission, with the aim of bringing this to fruition in Spring 2000. There is considerable concern from the library and information community that the strengths of the LIC, which has been so successful in focusing on library and information matters (albeit cross-sectorally), will be diluted by being absorbed into this new body.

IX. Building the New Library Network

The LIC published *New Library: The People's Network* (UK Library and Information Commission, 1997b), setting out a strategy for a radical transformation in the character and importance of UK public libraries. It proposed that public libraries should be connected to a national digital network, giving libraries a fundamentally new role as managers of electronic content and gateways to a vast wealth of online information. The government's response (UK Department for Culture, Media and Sport, 1998a) was to ask the commission to produce firm proposals to translate its vision into reality.

The commission set up three task groups to look at the network infrastructure, content, and training. These groups met and reported in a very tight timescale. The individual reports were combined into the overall report, *Building the New Library Network* (UK Library and Information Commission, 1998d). It was divided into three sections containing details and costed implementation proposals for each of the three strands of the program, which are discussed in the following subsections.

A. Network

The report proposes to develop a New Library Network, which will initially be based on the Internet but that is capable of evolving into a dedicated broadband network if required. It suggests that local authorities should purchase kitemarked managed services based around a core-user specification that will vary according to local need. This is compatible with the process being developed by the UK education departments for the National Grid for Learning.

B. Content

The report puts forward a framework for defining, creating, and managing the resources available on the network. Libraries will offer access to educational and cultural material and take on an important new role as creators and developers of new digital content.

C. Training

The report sets out a rapid-action program to equip the nation's librarians with new skills to handle information and communication technology, access databases and online information, and take on new roles as guides and instructors.

As the introduction to the report states:

> Central to our report has been the recognition that libraries must play a critical role in realising this government's ambitious plans for lifelong learning. By connecting to the National Grid for Learning, libraries will become a vital extension of mainstream online educational programmes. Easy access to a high performance network will, in addition, encourage adults to use libraries for self-directed and informal learning and for reskilling, and will encourage a rapid acceleration in the amount of instructional material made available online.

As museums, galleries and other important national collections make their treasures available in digital form, the New Library Network will give easy access to more and more of our cultural heritage. As the government's plans for remotely delivered public services reach fruition and all kinds of official information—including legislation and regulations— are made available in easily searchable electronic databases, libraries will become not just a gateway but a key interface between the individual and government at various levels. Furthermore, by seizing the opportunity to become managers and organisers of much local information, libraries will have the opportunity to carve out new roles as information hubs for their own local communities.

By supporting the government's strategy to reposition the UK to meet the challenges of the global information society, the New Library Network will rejuvenate the public library service for the next century. It will add value to the service's traditional role and build on its reputation as a local access point to the world of information and learning. It will also underpin social inclusion in the community and the wider economic prosperity of our society.

The Commission's programme is a clear route map to achieve nothing less than a revolutionary change in the nature and importance of our libraries. . . . It is our collective view that the recommendations set out here must be approached with imagination and resolution and be taken to their collective conclusion—implementation for the greater benefit of our citizens and the modernisation of our country in the information age. (UK Library and Information Commission, 1998d, p. 2)

Fine words, but clearly considerable investment is required to implement this vision. The group looking at the network infrastructure conducted a comprehensive analysis of the likely costs of the network and how these might be met. This took into account the scope for developing the network through public–private partnership (PPP) and identified other sources of funding that might be available. For the network to develop in its fullest form (which would mean an average of 10 terminals in every library, linked to a regional network and a broadband national spine), the capital costs of establishing the initial physical infrastructure was estimated at £48 million. The annual revenue cost associated with the network was estimated—on current prices—at £160 million. Taking existing resources and readily identifiable funding opportunities such as PPP into account, and based on a number of assumptions that are set out in the main body of the report, the group identified a funding gap of around £5000 million over the first 8 years of the network.

At the time of writing, it is still unclear exactly how this funding will be found, although it is expected to be via national lottery funding, or the exact timescale for the rollout of the program, originally planned for an April 1999 start.

X. Summary

The LIC has been in existence since 1995. During that time, it has had considerable impact in terms of advising government, in particular over the establishment of a public library network, and in highlighting the role of libraries and information services in all responses to government consultative documents. The commission has recognized the opportunities and the challenges presented to the LIS sector by new political, societal, and technological trends, particularly access to lifelong learning resources and services and to the nation's cultural achievements and heritage. Linkages between schools, colleges, and higher education institutions and the wider learning community will continue to be a significant part of future developments, as well as the development of mechanisms to improve cooperation and collaboration across library and information sectors through partnerships at local, regional, national, and international levels. The commission will champion initiatives to recognize and market the pivotal role of public libraries in fostering social cohesion and prioritize the implementation of *New Library: The People's Network* and the significance of libraries of all kinds in underpinning the potential of initiatives such as the National Grid for Learning, the New Opportunities Fund, and the University for Industry.

The commission will continue to develop partnerships within the LIS sector to ensure that professionals have the necessary skills and continuous development to manage in new contexts and apply new approaches; ensure LIS research programs address the areas of greatest need in the changing political, economic, social, and technological environments and that research results are effectively disseminated to improve LIS impact in these environments and ensure that key information and communication technology issues and developments are identified and their implications for LIS understood.

XI. Conclusions

In the 4 years of its existence, the LIC has, to my mind, proved its worth. It is the first time there has been a body in the United Kingdom with a remit to cover *all* areas of the library and information community, rather than purely public or academic libraries. I believe that its greatest achievement has been in combining the considerable strengths by bringing together the public, academic, health, government, private, industrial, and commercial library and information sectors and demonstrating their role to government at many different levels. All of the commission's strategy documents, particularly *2020 Vision, Libraries—The Lifeforce for Learning* and *Prospects*, have taken a deliberate cross-sectoral approach, because many of the roles and values of LIS apply equally to large academic, government, public, or industrial libraries as to small school, mobile, or workplace libraries.

In addition, the commission has been sufficiently high profile and politically astute to allow it to be heard in political circles to demonstrate a clear agenda for the role of LIS in the information and knowledge society of the future. Lifelong learning, social inclusion, widening access, and open government are key parts of the government's agenda, and LIS has been shown to be part of the underpinning required for delivery of this agenda, coupled with knowledge management as the key to survival and success of the individual, the community, and the nation.

I believe this has benefitted all librarians working in any sector because the commission has helped to put libraries on everyone's agenda in a way that individual sectors working alone and indeed the professional bodies had not previously achieved.

The commission secretariat has been "lean and mean." This, I believe, too, has contributed to its success. It has had to work through its commissioners and committee members and deliberately has competitively contracted out the research projects and work on developing the public library networking strategy and research strategy. Bringing in the BLRIC from April 1, 1999, will add strengths to this core but will still require much of the strategic work of the commission to be contracted out and may be refocussed. The proposed merger with the Museums and Galleries Commission, a much larger and more bureaucratic body, will pose considerable problems of combining a small, highly focused organization with an apparently large and unwieldy one. Concerns in the LIS profession are currently focused around this process and the potential loss of focus and cross-sectoral strengths of the existing commission.

The commission and its commissioners would be sorry to lose the undoubted progress made since 1995 because there is a strong belief that LIS remain vital to the individual, the nation, and the global community as we head toward the twenty-first century.

References

UK Central Office of Information (1998). *Our Information Age: The Government's Vision*. London: Central Office of Information.

UK Department of Education and Employment (1998). *The Learning Age: A Renaissance for a New Britain*. London: The Stationery Office.

UK Department for Culture, Media and Sport (1998a). *New Library: The People's Network, the Government's Response*. CM 3887. London: Department for Culture, Media and Sport.

UK Department for Culture, Media and Sport (1998b). *DCMS 79/98: Chris Smith Underlines Government Commitment to Public Libraries IT Network*. London: Department for Culture, Media and Sport press statement, 16 April 1998.

The Department for Culture, Media and Sport (1998c). *The Comprehensive Spending Review: A New Approach to Investment in Culture*. London: Department for Culture, Media and Sport.

UK Library and Information Commission (1997a). *2020 Vision*. London: Library and Information Commission.

UK Library and Information Commission (1997b). *New Library: The People's Network*. London: Library and Information Commission.

UK Library and Information Commission (1997c). *Towards a National Information Policy for the UK: A Discussion Paper*. London: Library and Information Commission.

UK Library and Information Commission (1998a). *Prospects: A Strategy for Action*. London: Library and Information Commission.

UK Library and Information Commission (1998b). *The Role of Libraries in a Learning Society*. London: Library and Information Commission.

UK Library and Information Commission (1998c). *Virtually New: Creating the Digital Collection*. London: Library and Information Commission.

UK Library and Information Commission (1998d). *Building the New Library Network: A Report to Government*. London: Library and Information Commission, October 1998.

UK Library and Information Commission (1999). *Libraries—the Lifeforce for Learning*. London: Library and Information Commission.

All publications are on the Library and Information Commission's website: http://www.lic.gov.uk.

Index

Academic librarian. *See also* Librarian
 as access engineers, 251
 advanced subject degrees, 102–103, 108
 education of, 98–102
 electronic reference service, 259–260
 faculty acceptance of, 77–79, 106–107
  acquisition of IT skills, 83–84, 87–88
  course management, 80–81
  information technology support
    planning, 82–83
  quality assessment, 81–82
 generic skills and, 73–75
 higher education and, 72–79
 image of, 93–112
 as information professional, 65
 invisibility, 96
 as knowledge cartographers, 251
 lifelong learning and, 68–69
 minorities, 169–187
  recruitment, 176
 professionalism, 94, 103–111
  and advanced subject degrees, 108
  and change, 104, 109–110
  and research, 106–108
  and self-promotion, 108–109
  and service, 104–105
  supportive organizational climate, 111
  and technical competency, 105–106
 research skills, 98–102
 role of, 63–91
  distance learning, 251–252
  learning support, 77–88
  problem-solving, 78
  research assessment, 85
  research collection, 85
  research support, 84–85
  research training, 84–85
 scholarship, 98–102

 self-perception of, 94–96
 self-promotion of, 94–96, 108–109
 as service provider, 101, 104–105
 status of, 69–72, 93–112
  as faculty, 97–98
  as webmaster, 86–87
Academic libraries. *See also* Academic media
    center; Digital libraries; Libraries;
    Virtual libraries
 distance learning challenges, 241
 diversity and, 169–187
 evolution of, 240–241
  centralized libraries, 241
  departmental libraries, 241
  faculty/librarian collection development,
    241–242
  faculty/librarian liaison programs,
    242–243
  reference service, 244–245
 hybrid library concept, 222, 231
 information gateways, 86–87
 lifelong learning, 221–223
 minorities and, 169–187
  recruitment of, 169, 177–178
Academic media center. *See also* Academic
    libraries
 collaborative relationships and, 43
 digital media and, 42–46
 distance learning and, 43, 45
 funding, 44–46
  charge-back system, 45
  fee-for-service, 45
  mission statement, 44–45
  new initiatives, 44–46
  nontraditional study and, 42
Access to Libraries for learning in
    Northampton, 225
African Americans. *See* Minorities

323

ISBN 0-12-024623-6